The CUISINES of SPAIN

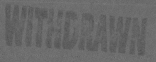

THE CUISINES OF
SPAIN

Exploring Regional Home Cooking

Teresa Barrenechea

Food photography by Christopher Hirsheimer
Location photography by Jeffrey Koehler

TEN SPEED PRESS
Berkeley | Toronto

🔟

Ten Speed Press
Box 7123
Berkeley, California 94707
www.tenspeed.com

Distributed in Australia by Simon & Schuster Australia,
in Canada by Ten Speed Press Canada, in New Zealand by
Southern Publishers Group, in South Africa by Real Books,
and in the United Kingdom and Europe by Airlift Book
Company.

Design by Nancy Austin
Styling by Wesley Martin
Map design by Fineline Maps, Oakland, California

Photography by Christopher Hirsheimer: pages 57, 75, 81,
95, 98, 106, 109, 114, 134, 141, 146, 159, 174, 189, 200, 205,
218, 223, 226, 242, 243, 253, 257, 260, 262, 266, 275, 278, 287,
307, 311

Photography by Aaron Wehner: pages 16, 52, 103 (bottom),
105 (far right), 119, 153 (bottom), 154 (far left), 217, 220, 236,
246, 269 (far right), 296, 301, 305, 321

All other photography by Jeffrey Koehler

Library of Congress Cataloging-in-Publication Data

Barrenechea, Teresa, 1956–
   The cuisines of Spain : exploring regional home cooking /
Teresa Barrenechea ; food photography by Christopher
Hirsheimer ; location photography by Jeffrey Koehler.
      p. cm.
   Includes bibliographical references and index.
   ISBN-13: 978-1-58008-515-1
   ISBN-10: 1-58008-515-6
   1. Cookery, Spanish. I. Title.
   TX723.5.S7B374 2005
   641.5946--dc22

                                        2005020225

Printed in China
First printing, 2005

1 2 3 4 5 6 7 8 9 10 — 10 09 08 07 06 05

RIGHT: *Summer peaches, Catalonia*

PAGE II, CLOCKWISE FROM UPPER LEFT: *Grapes in Priorat,
Catalonia; an old windmill outside El Cotillo, Fuerteventura
(Canary Islands) in late afternoon among barren earth and lava
boulders; the day's catch of sea snails in L'Escala on the Costa
Brava, Catalonia; a fish-cleaning table in Corralejo, Fuerteventura*

PAGE VI: *Fresh Fuerteventura goat cheese*

PAGE VII: *El Cotillo, Fuerteventura*

To all the men and women who work the fields,

fish the seas, and tend the herds,

enabling the rest of us to enjoy the gifts nature provides.

And to my family.

:: CONTENTS ::

:: ACKNOWLEDGMENTS ::

I have been blessed with such a supportive family and with such generous, enthusiastic friends, and without them, this book would have never come to be. Many friends that helped me in my work, whether by sharing recipes, knowledge, or their company across the table, appear in the pages that follow. To those named and unnamed, you are my greatest treasure.

My deepest gratitude to:

Elise and Arnold Goodman, for being much more than my literary agents.

Kirsty Melville, for her belief in me and in this project.

Aaron Wehner, for being the best editor anyone could wish for, and for his additional contribution of beautiful location photography. Aaron, without your insight, tenacity, and caring, I couldn't have done it.

Marchelle Brain, Sharon Silva (whose reading of my mind was a great comfort), Karen Levy, and Ken DellaPenta, for their editorial contributions.

Linda Ziedrich, for her help in the early stages of the project.

Nancy Austin, for her wonderful design that touched my heart; no Spaniard could have done it better.

Bart Wright, for his map of Spain.

Christopher Hirsheimer, for bringing the regional dishes of Spain alive through her outstanding food photography.

Wesley Martin and Fina Cortés, for their inspired assistance at the photo shoot.

Jeff Koehler, for his incredible eye for the beautiful scenery and people of Spain, and for the good times we had while traveling together.

Ana de Diego, my beloved niece, for helping me during the initial stages of the project.

Pat Eskin, Bonnie Foncillas, Penny Thornton, Meme Rubio, Paz Saras, Tony Sayegh, for their precious time.

Gerry Dawes, for his enduring passion for Spain and the insight he has shared with me over the years.

Bruce Shaw, for publishing my first book on Basque cooking.

Carlos Pérez-Desoy, Marisa Escribano, Elvira Sala Pons, Emma Reverter, for their help with the Catalonian recipes.

Tina Read, Miguel Sard, Maria Vicens, and Tina Sard, for being my *cicerones* in the Balearic Islands.

Iñigo Barrenechea, my brother, for introducing me to many of the wonders of the Canary Islands.

Gracia Muñoz Bayo, Juan and Paqui Parra, Maria Antonia Marin de Alfonso, for their help with Andalusian recipes.

Paz Ivison, for her always generous and intelligent contributions.

Santiago Botas, for imparting his vast knowledge of olive oil.

Maribel Cabeza, for sharing her best Cantabrian recipes.

Antonio Linares, for his wisdom, and for sharing his expertise on Extremadura.

Pilar Vico, from the Spanish Tourist Board in New York, for assisting me in my travels.

José Guerra, from Commercial Office of Spain in New York, for his enthusiastic help.

Micky Camarillo, Alfredo Mejía, Narciso Camarillo, Alfredito Vaquero, for keeping the stove at my restaurant burning while I was writing and traveling.

Raynold, my husband and long-time companion, for his incredible patience, and for the countless hours he spent reading the many manuscript drafts, improving my English and making sure I did not leave anything out.

Maria, Teresa, Alejandro, and Lucas, my children, for having cheerfully endured the times I was away, and for always keeping my spirits up.

Two dear friends who were very important to me and this book, and who would have been so happy to see it finished, were Jose Luis Iturrieta and Jean-Louis Palladin; they are both very deep in my heart.

A blooming almond tree in Tarragona, Catalonia

:: INTRODUCTION ::

WHETHER YOU TRAVEL to Valencia on the Mediterranean, to Galicia on the Atlantic, or to Castile in the heartland, a trip to Spain is a culinary pleasure. Choose at random a fancy restaurant, a humble tavern, or a roadside bar anywhere in the country and you will be surprised by the quality of the food. You'll be truly fortunate, though, if you are invited to dine in a private house. In the following pages, we will sneak into home kitchens across Spain to see what's on the stove, because everybody eats well in my country.

When speaking of Spanish food, I refer to the cuisines, rather than the cuisine, of Spain because diversity—rooted in history and preserved by geography—is an integral part of the culinary culture. More than five hundred years ago, before the marriage of Fernando of Aragón and Isabel of Castile and the unification of their respective kingdoms established the territory of Spain as we know it today, a string of independent kingdoms was spread across the Iberian Peninsula. The discrete cultures took great pride in their distinctiveness, maintaining unique languages and dialects, social customs, and culinary traditions. Indeed, in many instances regional cuisines themselves were—and continue to be—diverse; the favorite Sunday dish in one village was typically a different dish in a village just a few miles away.

Even today, the varied terrain of the peninsula helps sustain regional differences. The third largest country in

Europe, Spain is also the third most mountainous (after Switzerland and Austria), and it includes two archipelagos. There are snowy peaks in the Pyrenees and Sierra Nevada a short distance from beaches and deserts in Almería; green pastures for cattle in Galicia and throughout the north; orange groves in Levante; wetlands with rice plantations around the Ebro delta; thousands of miles of coastline on the Mediterranean and the Atlantic; a central plateau, where Madrid reigns as the highest capital in Europe; and vast stretches planted with grapes, olives, and almonds nearly everywhere. A diverse climate also contributes to regional differences. In the winter, when temperatures in the interior are often below freezing, the islands, the coast, and the south enjoy relatively mild weather. Summers are typically scorching hot and dry on the central plateau and cooler along the northern and southern coasts.

Some characteristics, however, transcend the regional distinctions. For example, all Spaniards, no matter their culinary tradition, consider quality to be of paramount importance. Because we are blessed with extraordinary products from the sea and the land, we have come to expect the finest ingredients, and we are demanding when stocking our pantry and refrigerator. We press more olive oil than any other country in the world, and our oils have magnificent flavor. Our wines rank among the best produced anywhere; our fishing fleets navigate every ocean on earth; the fresh produce from our various microclimates is outstanding; our unique hams are food for the gods; and our exceptional canning industry supplies us with seasonal products year-round.

We Spaniards have also been spoiled by our devoted mothers, who take family nourishment seriously. No shortcuts are allowed; every dish is artfully prepared with loving care and according to nearly sacred culinary rules that have been passed down through generations. Watch an average Spanish housewife buying in the market: she will make sure the lettuce leaves are green and crisp; select the most gorgeous seasonal vegetables from the region (*del pais*, as we say); and ask the butcher for this or that cut from a superb selection of veal, beef, lamb, or pork. And she does all this because she is knowledgeable, because she cares, and because taste is of primary importance to her and her family.

In Spain, as elsewhere, culinary trends and products travel faster today. Efficient transportation, television cooking shows, culinary magazines, and, of course, cookbooks from other regions and countries allow individuals access to food products, information about cooking techniques, kitchen tools and equipment, and recipes from far away. But even though you may be served gazpacho in a home or restaurant in the Basque Country, the dish remains singularly Andalusian. The same is true for paella, which, although cooked all over Spain, is indisputably the flagship of the Valencian kitchen. Once I

tasted a fantastic *bacalao al pil-pil* in Madrid, but you are more likely to have the best one in the Basque Country, its place of origin.

⠒⠒   ⠒⠒   ⠒⠒

The recipes in this book can be combined in countless ways to create the delicious meals served in homes throughout Spain. Beyond strong regional traditions, Spaniards have a shared culinary heritage: many dishes belong everywhere, and are cooked and enjoyed with the same passion nationwide. But, when a dish has a distinct origin, even if it is now common to all of Spain, I indicate its provenance next to the recipe title. I want you to be able to assemble with ease a Catalan, Basque, or Andalusian meal should you decide to delight a guest from Spain or elsewhere with the dishes of a particular region.

The recipe chapters are ordered according to the sequence in which I suggest you serve the dishes. But what I have often classified as a first course could certainly be served as a main course; conversely, certain main courses can, in small portions, be served as tapas. A book of this kind—and I will use a wonderful analogy from my dear friend, famed gastronomist Ismael Diaz Yubero—should not try to teach a painter to mix his colors; it should instead provide the information necessary to take up a palette and get started. It is in this spirit that I offer you my recipes.

Orange trees growing beside Sevilla's La Giralda, the minaret of what was originally the city's great mosque

CHAPTER I

From Iberia to España

A Glimpse into Spain's Past and Its Regions

FOR THOUSANDS OF YEARS, the Iberian Peninsula has been the object of desire for many civilizations, all of which have left a permanent imprint on its culture and countryside. The earliest settlers of Spain include the Iberians, the Celts, and prehistoric groups who may be the ancestors of the present-day Basques. But let me start with the Phoenicians, whose traces are still highly visible more than three thousand years later. To cite just a trio of examples of their legacy, they established two major European trading cities in the south, Málaga and Cádiz, still vital today, and they introduced the olive tree, which blankets much of our contemporary landscape. Six hundred years later, the Phoenicians were followed by the Greeks, who ruled Spain, or Iberia as they called it, until their defeat by the Romans.

New rulers, new name: our land became known as Hispania and remained under Roman rule for almost five centuries. In addition to bringing their language, the Romans built roads, bridges, and aqueducts; introduced wheat and the systematic cultivation of the olive; taught us to preserve foods in salt; and established wine making. With the decline of the Roman Empire, Spain became a feudal system of small kingdoms under the control of the Visigoths and Vandals, Germanic tribes who migrated south to expand their territories. During their violent and bloody reign, livestock farming was developed.

Heading north from Africa, armies of Arabs and Berbers, whom the western Europeans called Moors, crossed the Strait of Gibraltar into Spain in 711 AD, where they remained for almost eight hundred years. Spain's vast south—called Vandalus in the time of the Vandals, and changed to Andalus because the Arabic alphabet lacks an equivalent to the letter V—became a Muslim stronghold. Not only did the Moors bring cultural advances in scholarship, science, architecture, and other disciplines, but they also reintroduced the works of the ancient Greeks, which had been lost to Europeans. Fascinated with water, they developed irrigation systems and planted citrus and almond trees in eastern and southern Spain and on the Balearic Islands. They also introduced such everyday staples as rice, sugarcane, figs, apples, pomegranates, mint, cilantro, saffron, cumin, and cinnamon.

A good-sized Jewish population was already resident at the time of the Muslim invasion, having begun emigrating to Hispania primarily during the reign of Hadrian (117–138 AD). The Jews enjoyed recognition for their industrious character and intelligence, but when they suffered the first anti-Semitic legislation in Spain under the Visigoth rule of King Sisebut, they quickly turned their support to the Moors. The Jews already in Hispania and those arriving from Africa with the Moors played an important role in administration, letters, and science. Jewish and Moorish cultures flourished in Spain: their

Zaragoza, Aragón, was a Moorish city for four hundred years, and the influences linger in the architecture.

wise men, including doctors, mathematicians, architects, scientists, and philosophers, greatly enriched the contemporary society.

For centuries, Christians, Jews, and Muslims lived together harmoniously on the Iberian Peninsula, which should serve as an example for the tolerance and compatible coexistence needed today. However, that harmony would end with the expulsion of the Jews in 1492, and the establishment of the Inquisition soon after, an atrocious period forever incised into Spanish history. Pacts made with the Moors of Granada, the last Muslim kingdom in Spain, were broken at the same time, and the Moors were forced to leave or to convert to Christianity. Many basic culinary preferences seen today in some areas, such as the choice of lard over olive oil and pork over lamb, are echoes of the persecution of Jews and Muslims during this time.

Moorish arches in Zaragoza, Aragón

These vile actions were initiated during the reign of King Fernando and Queen Isabel, whose marriage in 1469 led to the unification of the peninsula's two largest kingdoms, Aragón and Castile, in 1479, a union that helped define today's Spain. The Catholic Kings, as they were known, sought not only to unite their kingdoms, but also to reconquer lands still under Muslim rule, as their treatment of the Moors of Granada illustrates. With the kingdoms united, the monarchs were able to turn their attention to the larger adventures that lay ahead in the Age of Exploration. It was under their rule that *la Pinta*, *la Niña*, and *la Santa María* set sail with Christopher Columbus at the helm.

While Spain's national treasury was undeniably enriched with New World gold and silver, its culinary stores were equally enriched with the introduction of crops then unknown to the Old World—crops that would eventually change the cooking habits not only of Spain but of the whole of Europe. What would it have

been like to cook without potatoes, peppers, corn, tomatoes, or—just imagine—chocolate? The Spaniards, in turn, introduced many Old World crops and livestock to the New World, including wheat, barley, sugarcane, wine, bananas, citrus fruits, cows, sheep, pigs, and chickens.

These were golden times for Spain. It was the center of Europe, serving as the gateway to the newly conquered lands in the Americas. The grandson of the Catholic Kings, Carlos I, ruled the sprawling Habsburg empire and became Holy Roman Emperor Charles V. With the seat of the Habsburgs now in Spain, food traditions traveled back and forth all over Europe, affecting the eating habits of the entire continent. In the mid-eighteenth century, the Habsburgs gave way to the Bourbons, who introduced French styles to the Spanish court and upper classes. Naturally, this had its influence on the culinary habits as well, just as the long Spanish rule of Naples and Sicily can still be seen today in many Sicilian dishes. But the French-Spanish exchange went both ways: it has been said that the biggest loot taken during the French rule of Spain was the collection of recipes belonging to the Hieronymite monks in Alcántara. (As is often the case with neighbors, we are in constant rivalry with the French.)

In modern times, Spain's rich and diverse heritage was threatened by the Spanish Civil War (1936–39) and its aftermath, the dictatorial rule of Francisco Franco. In addition to the repression of regional autonomy that followed the National Movement victory, postwar Spain was plagued by an economic depression that lasted into the 1950s. Even people who were well-off were deprived of legal access to such everyday goods as coffee, sugar, and tobacco, and black markets flourished to satisfy the demand. People (usually women) living near the borders even left the country to buy products unavailable at home: in southern Andalusia, they crossed to Tangiers or Ceuta in Africa, and in the north, to France. During this period of scarcity, Spanish cooking became more austere. The dishes based on fresh and stale bread or dried beans popular today, such as various soups and stews, were often the sole means of sustenance during that time of shortages.

After nearly forty years of dictatorship, when Franco died in 1975, Spain moved toward democracy and the nation underwent decentralization. In 1979, the former fifty-six provinces, previously ruled with an iron fist from Madrid, were grouped into seventeen autonomous communities, each with its own parliamentary government. Some of them were made up of many provinces, others of just one. For example, the largest of them, Andalusia, included seven original provinces, whereas Murcia, Madrid, Asturias, Cantabria, and La Rioja were each formed from a single former province.

Once Franco's repressive government was removed, Spain began its race to catch up with more developed countries on the continent. Communities across the country began to reaffirm their cultural and regional distinctions and traditions, sparking a cultural renaissance in Spain that continues today.

During the 1960s and 1970s in France, a group of chefs led by Paul Bocuse, the Troisgros brothers, and Michel Guérard, among others, started the nouvelle cuisine movement, which emphasized fresh, clean flavors in cooking. Their innovations inspired new Spanish chefs emerging from the period of austerity. Luis Irízar, regarded as the father of Basque *nueva cocina*, joined the stream in the early 1970s, and many others soon followed, among them Juan Mari Arzak. Still on top of the wave today, Arzak, along with his Basque countryman Martin Berasategui and two Catalan chefs, Ferran Adrià and Santi Santamaría, has been awarded three stars in the Michelin Guide, and he continues to awaken and inspire new generations of chefs. In fact, the race to excellence has been joined by so many talented chefs from every corner of the country that today Spain can proudly claim that its top restaurants are among the best in the world.

::   ::   ::

Spain is composed of a spectacular variety of landscapes, from high sierra to miles of coastline to river valleys rich in fruit orchards, vegetable gardens, olive groves, and oak forests. Rather than looking at the regions strictly according to their present political and administrative boundaries, I find it more appropriate in some cases to group them by the shared climate, geography, and natural resources that have shaped and continue to shape their cuisines. For example, although Asturias and Cantabria are separate autonomous communities, I have put them together because the fish of their shorelines and rivers, their meat and dairy industries, their crops and foods, and their recipes have much in common. So, in this manner, following bean stews rather than political boundaries, let us begin our journey though the culinary regions of Spain.

Andalusia

Bordered by the Atlantic and the Mediterranean in the south, Portugal in the west, Extremadura and Castile in the north, and Murcia in the east, Andalusia is Spain's largest autonomous community. It comprises seven provinces with diverse landscapes: there are *dehesas*, or large extensions of oak woods and meadows, where the brave bull and the *pata negra* (the famed *ibérico* pig) live; the Sierra Nevada, a mountain range with snow-covered peaks in the winter only an hour away from the beaches of Málaga; the Sierra de Grazalema, which records the

country's highest annual rainfall, just a few miles from summer resorts with hardly any rain; and everywhere oceans of olive trees.

In 756, under Abd ar-Rahman I, Córdoba was established as an emirate aligned with, but independent from, Damascus, which until then had been the center of power of the Islamic world. The Moorish occupation of Andalusia lasted for nearly eight hundred years and left a legacy still visible today. Not only can you see vestiges of those remarkable times in the beautiful palaces and mosques and in the central patios and fountain courtyards in many country homes, but you are also constantly reminded of Arabic influences at the table, even if you only hear the names of local dishes: *alfajores, alboronia, alcachofa, almendra, albóndiga,* and *berenjena,* among others. Whether you are eating at home or dining out, sugar-dusted deep-fried churros, *ajo blanco* (almond gazpacho), fried fish, pastries such as *pestiños* (fried twisted dough brushed with honey), *cabello de*

ABOVE: *Morning view from author's home outside Ronda, Andalusia* LEFT: *A black-footed pig on a farm outside Ronda*

ángel (pumpkin preserve), and any number of sweets and savories seasoned with cumin, saffron, or anise reveal the strong Arabic presence in the culinary customs of the region.

The fascination that this region provoked in the many civilizations that conquered it is still present. Andalusia attracts tourists from around the world, and although today they don't come to conquer, many can't resist settling here for good. Its extensive repertory of traditional foods, a product of its varied physiognomy and rich mix of cultural influences, is one reason why. In its fertile river valleys, of which the Guadalquivir ("big river" in Arabic) is the largest, dishes like the original gazpacho, *ajo blanco*, were invented. An abundance of almonds must have been the inspiration for this delightful cold soup, which combines the nuts with bread, garlic, olive oil, vinegar, and water. (The better-known tomato gazpacho appeared

much later, after the discovery of the Americas and the slow acceptance of the New World tomato.) These same valleys supply a wealth of vegetables, including artichokes and *alcauciles* (wild artichokes), eggplants, endives, *cidra* (a fibrous pumpkin), green beans, fava beans, potatoes, and tomatoes. Most of these vegetables, with the exception of those introduced from the Americas, were first cultivated here by the Moors. Strawberries, or *fresas*, came from the New World and are extensively produced in areas of Huelva and Almería, the region's westernmost and easternmost provinces, respectively; together they constitute the largest supplier of strawberries for the rest of Europe. Along the coast, warm-weather fruits, such as kiwifruits, pineapples, avocados, and mangoes, have found a perfect habitat.

Along Andalusia's northeastern border, the Sierra Morena, the mountain chain that separates the region from the plains of La Mancha, is covered in holm oaks and maquis of laurel, broom, and thyme. A hunter's paradise, the rugged land sustains a cuisine of fowl and game dishes, such as *carne de monte*, venison stew, and *perdiz escabechada*, partridge cooked in vinegar and wine.

Andalusia's olive trees, which flourish on the rolling hills that lie between the mountains and the flatlands, are responsible for some of the best olive oils in the world and account for 75 percent of the country's total production. Not surprisingly, this sizable, top-quality olive oil manufactory falls under the country's rigorous Denominación de Origen (DO) program, a system of quality control that stipulates a product's origin, production method, specific attributes, and other standards. Andalusia is home to eight different DOs for olive oil, including Priego de Córdoba and Baena in Córdoba Province; Sierra de Cazorla, Sierra de Segura, and Sierra Mágina in Jaén Province; Montes de Granada and Poniente de Granada in the province of the same name; and finally, Sierra de Cádiz in Cádiz and Sevilla provinces—a number no other region can match. Made from many olive varieties, these oils offer an ample spectrum of flavors, and when you drive along the roads that border the olive groves and olive mills, the air is filled with the intense aroma of the oil. *Almazara*, Spanish for "olive mill," is derived from the Arabic *al-ma'sara*, which means "press," another reminder of the centuries of Moorish influence in this part of Spain. Even the Spanish word for oil, *aceite*, which refers to any kind of edible oil, whether from olives, almonds, peanuts, soy, or otherwise, is derived from the Arabic *a-zeit*, which means "juice of olive," reflecting the exclusive use of olives for their oil.

The oak woodlands of western Andalusia offer the perfect habitat for the *pata negra* (literally "black hoof," the *ibérico* pig), which is made into the unique cured ham of Spain known as *jamón ibérico*. The Sierra de Huelva produces some of the best in the country. The *pata negra* also is the source of other delightful cured meats, such as *lomo embuchado* (also known as *caña de lomo*), which is made from the loin and rubbed with *pimentón*, salt, and garlic and then air cured, and *morcón*, a large, air-cured sausage made from lean pork cuts chopped and mixed with fat and seasoned with *pimentón*. The latter is also a specialty of neighboring Extremadura.

Every bar in Andalusia (and most bars in the rest of Spain) offers platters of cold cuts that include these or other similar cured meats. They make a perfect tapa and are often served as a first course. At the other end of the region, in the eastern mountain ranges of Granada, *jamón de Trevélez*, another excellent ham, is produced. It is cured for at least fourteen months at altitudes over four thousand feet, and because the pig used in the production of this magnificent ham is a white-coated Landrace, Duroc-Jersey, or Large White, and not the dark-coated *pata negra*, the ham is known as *jamón serrano*, rather than *jamón ibérico*.

The Mediterranean bathes the coast of Andalusia to the sun-bleached town of Tarifa, the most southern point on the European continent. Further west, the waters belong to the Atlantic. Exceptional local fish and shellfish are available in markets and restaurants. Little fish, including anchovies, *chopitos*, and *chanquetes*, are deep-fried, following the Arabic custom. Indeed, Andalusian cooks are masters of deep-frying, and they cook larger fish, such as marinated *cazón* (a member of the shark family), in the same way. These waters are also fished for *urta*, a special local red-skinned fish that is usually baked; *carabineros*, deep red jumbo prawns of exquisite and intense flavor; *gamba blanca*, the white shrimp of Huelva, and *langostinos*, prawns from Sanlúcar de Barrameda, both of which are primarily grilled; and *atún* (tuna), which has been caught in this strait since Roman times.

The unique *mojama*, a dry-cured tuna loin, is produced and celebrated in the fishing villages of Cádiz and Huelva. The only additives in this air-dried delicacy are salt, the sun, and a coastal breeze, exactly as Romans and Moors cured tuna centuries ago. Once the flesh is aged and firm and has turned a deep brownish red, the *mojama* is cut crosswise into paper-thin slices and served alone or on a slice of bread drizzled with olive oil. The fishing village of Barbate in Cádiz produces one of the best versions of this traditional preparation.

Andalusian cheeses are made primarily from the milk of sheep and goats, with the only cow's milk cheese produced in the northwestern corner, near the border with Extremadura. Queso Rey from Ronda, a beautiful and

Tiles inside the Alcázar, Sevilla, Andalusia

ancient city surrounded by several mountain ranges, is one of the region's best cheeses. Sheep and goat herding is widespread around Ronda, and the cheeses produced there vary from fresh to medium cured. The same is true for the other cheeses in the region, with the exception of Pedroches cheese from Córdoba, which is medium cured to cured.

Finally, Andalusia is celebrated for its sweet wines from Montilla, Moriles, and Málaga; the world famous sherries from Jerez de la Frontera and Sanlúcar; and the wines from Condado de Huelva, each with their respective DO. But there are also promising new wines being produced in areas such as Ronda, where a group of progressive winemakers are practicing biologic viticulture. The high daytime temperatures combined with considerable overnight drops typical of high altitudes, and plenty of sunshine especially toward harvesttime, make this area ideal for vineyards.

La Ribera del Ebro: Aragón, La Rioja, and Navarra

If the Nile is Egypt's gift from heaven, the Ebro is heaven's gift to La Rioja, Navarra, and Aragón. The Ebro—its name is derived from the Latin *Iberus*—is the longest and one of the most important rivers on the Iberian Peninsula. Descending from its spring in the Cantabrian Mountains, the Ebro first crosses La Rioja, where it receives the tributary Río Oja, which lends its name to the region. Then it enters Navarra and shares its waters with both regions, serving as their border until it reaches Castejón, where it turns into a true Navarran river for about a hundred miles. Thanks to its tributaries, the Ebro doubles its water volume in this area where, as the popular saying goes, "Ega, Arga, y Aragón hacen al Ebro varón" ("The Ega, Arga, and Aragón rivers make the Ebro a man"). Be it male or female, the Ebro enters Aragón as a considerable waterway. It then travels another two hundred miles before crossing the border into Catalonia with almost the same volume of water it will have when it joins the Mediterranean Sea.

La Ribera del Ebro—the Ebro River valley—is a magnificent, fertile vegetable garden and fruit orchard, supplying the ingredients that constitute the pillars of the local cuisines. Artichokes and white asparagus from Navarra; cauliflower from La Rioja; snow peas from Aragón; and cardoon, borage, leeks, lentils, and Swiss chard, among others, common to all, are everyday ingredients for home cooks and restaurant chefs across the region. Peppers are used extensively in all three areas: *a la riojana*, which usually indicates the addition of peppers to any given dish, is almost identical to the *chilindrones* preparation in Navarra and Aragón. The renowned Pimientos del Piquillo de Lodosa are grown in Navarra, their quality guaranteed by DO guidelines. But peppers don't understand borders or laws, and those growing on the other side of the Ebro in La Rioja are also superb, even if slightly larger and lesser known outside the area. Sometimes *piquillo* peppers are stuffed, other times they are simply sautéed with olive oil and garlic, but no matter how they are prepared, they are excellent.

ABOVE: *The Ebro River flowing past the Basílica de Nuestra Señora del Pilar, Zaragoza, Aragón* RIGHT: *Looking down a pedestrian street to the Basílica de Nuestra Señora del Pilar*

However, La Ribera del Ebro isn't the only important common influence on the region's culinary traditions. La Rioja and Navarra border the Basque Country, which supplies both with excellent fish from the Bay of Biscay, so it is no surprise to find considerable Basque influence in their cooking, and vice versa. Aragón and Navarra border the Pyrenees, and the mountains, rich in game and freshwater fish, have shaped their cuisines in similar ways. *Trucha* (trout) and *cangrejo de río* (crayfish) are often prepared in the same manner in both areas, the crayfish served in a spicy sauce, with or without tomato (the better known crayfish are from La Rioja), the trout wrapped in cured ham and baked. Throughout the mountainous areas, you'll find *migas*, or bread crumbs, cooked for breakfast. Residents in all three areas enjoy both roasted or stewed lamb (the lamb from La Rioja is usually the smallest), especially *chuletitas al sarmiento*, baby lamb chops cooked over a fire of vine cuttings, and a simple dessert of *peras al vino tinto de Rioja*, peaches cooked in wine.

El Camino de Santiago, or the Pilgrim's Trail to Santiago, figures prominently in the common history of the region. Among its mandatory stops where it crosses the Pyrenees are Jaca in Aragón, Leyre and Pamplona in Navarra, and Logroño in La Rioja. A main itinerary for countless pilgrims, the region flourished in the Middle Ages due to the constant influx of cultures. Today, it still has a cosmopolitan feel and remains the primary route for travelers crossing from the Mediterranean to the Atlantic.

Although these areas share many similarities, each also has its local specialties. Chorizos from La Rioja are an essential part of the ubiquitous *patatas a la riojana*, a potato and chorizo stew. The delicate *jamón serrano* from Teruel, Aragón's southernmost province, made from common white-coated pigs (usually Landrace or Duroc-Jersey), is memorable, as is the magnificent olive oil produced close by, between the provinces of Teruel and Zaragoza.

Navarra's contribution to the regional cheese platter is considerable, including Roncal, which is made from the milk of two sheep breeds, Lacha and Rasa, and Idiazábal, a firm, creamy white sheep's milk cheese ripened in mountain caves (though most of the production of the latter takes place in the neighboring Basque Country). Camerano is a delicious fresh goat's milk cheese from southern La Rioja. The cheeses of Aragón are mainly fresh and made from goat's or sheep's milk, or a combination, with the exception of Calanda and Tronchón, which can be medium cured or cured and have an intense flavor and firm texture. Cow's milk cheeses are restricted primarily to the Pyrenean province of Huesca, where Benasque and Ansó-Hecho are made, the latter a mix of cow's milk and sheep's milk.

Locals regularly enjoy their cheeses with wine, so it is fortuitous that wine is also one of the strengths of the

region. La Rioja is home to some of the country's oldest wineries and continues to be one of Spain's leading wine-producing areas. The wine region known as Rioja doesn't quite coincide with the administrative one; rather, it is divided into three sectors: Rioja Alavesa, which, as its name indicates, stretches into the Basque province of Álava; Rioja Alta, on the north bank of the Ebro; and Rioja Baja, on the southern shore. Navarra produces great red and white wines, too, and the region's rosés are considered among the best in the world. It is also the source of *pacharán* (*patxarán* in Basque), a delicious anise liqueur unique to the area made of *endrinas* (sloe berries). Aragón has recently made great strides in the production of high-quality wines. Most noteworthy is the newer but excellent wine from the Somontano DO, grown in an enclave at the foothills of the Pyrenees.

Grazing sheep in the foothills of the Picos de Europa, Asturias

Asturias and Cantabria

Neighboring Asturias and Cantabria share the center of the Cantabrian Mountains, which extend from the western end of the Pyrenees, along the coast of the Bay of Biscay, and down to Portugal. Together they form the middle of so-called Green Spain, which includes Galicia to the west and the Basque Country to the east. The Cantabrian Mountains, crowned by the stunning limestone Picos de Europa in Asturias, harbor a number of protected indigenous species, including many birds, among them the large, dark-plumed *urogallo*, or mountain rooster; wild goats; and bears. The region is ribboned with rivers descending from the mountains, fishing villages, and good pastureland. Here, the meadows shimmer bright green, sandy beaches alternate with rocky coastline, and fishing boats bring in some of the country's best seafood from the Bay of Biscay. Despite its incredible beauty, this area is still largely rural and does not see many tourists.

This cave in Covadonga, Asturias, is the site of the first battle, c. 718, of the Christian Reconquista to regain Spain back from the Moors. The reconquest was completed nearly eight hundred years later.

Asturias and Cantabria are well known for their seafood. *Percebes* (gooseneck barnacles), *mejillones* (mussels), *almejas* (clams), *caracolillos* (snails), and *navajas* (razor clams) are among the delicious mollusks found in these cold waters. Prices range from astronomical for gooseneck barnacles to modest for snails. Crustaceans are equally fresh and varied: *langosta* (spiny lobster), *bogavante* (lobster), *cigala* (langoustine, not to be confused with *langostino*, which is a prawn), and *nécora* (hard-shell crab, known as *andarica* in Asturias). *Erizos de mar* (sea urchins) are eaten raw directly from of the shell with a little lemon or broiled with a creamy sauce. Although becoming more scarce, *angulas* (baby eels) are still caught at the mouths of local rivers. Sautéed with olive oil, a little garlic, and a pinch of hot pepper, they are one of the region's great delicacies.

Fresh *anchoas* (anchovies) and *sardinas* (sardines) are abundant here and of exceptional quality. That bounty is what drew a group of Italian anchovy merchants to Laredo and Santoña toward the end of the nineteenth century. They launched a canning industry, which soon flourished, and today it turns out some of the finest canned anchovies and *ventresca de bonito o atún* (belly of two types of tuna) in the world. A common summertime sight is fresh sardines grilling in the open air in the fishing villages or on the beach.

In both Asturias and Cantabria, *salmón* (salmon) and *lubina* (bass, also known as *perca*) are often poached or baked with *sidra* (cider). Monkfish, which Asturians call *pixín*, is cooked in sauces or rubbed with *pimentón*—the flavorful smoked Spanish paprika—and steamed, giving it the appearance of lobster tails. *Rodaballo* (turbot) is grilled to enhance its natural taste, and tuna is prepared in many different ways. *Atún en rollito* (or *en rollo*), a dish unique to Asturias, features rolls of shredded tuna mixed with dry-cured ham and cooked in an onion and carrot sauce.

Of course, the specialties of the area extend far beyond

mignon with Cabrales, the area's celebrated blue-veined cheese, or with another local cheese is a common dinner-plate pairing.

Asturias is one of Spain's principal cheese-producing regions, turning out more than twenty-five types. The most famous are Cabrales and Afuega'l Pitu, to which *pimentón* is sometimes added. Because most of the cheeses are crafted by small family operations, Cantabrians produce fewer, though no less excellent, varieties than their Asturian neighbors. Exceptional cheeses of the area include two made from cow's milk, the blue Picos de Europa and the creamy Queso de Cantabria, and two mixed-milk cheeses, the blue Picón and the delightful smoked Ahumado de Aliva.

LEFT: *Pouring cider in a* sidrería *in Cangas de Onís, Asturias*
BELOW: *Mosaic on the wall of a* sidrería *in Cangas de Onís*

seafood. Further inland, legumes of the best quality are grown, most notably *fabes asturianes*, the Asturian white beans of remarkable tenderness and size. The signature dish of Asturias is *fabada asturiana*, a stew of these beans with smoked chorizo and *morcilla* (blood sausage). In another dish unique to the area, *fabes con almejas*, the beans are combined with clams. The chickpeas grown in Liébana, at the skirt of the majestic Picos de Europa, are of extraordinary quality and are acclaimed across the country. Cantabrians combine these small local legumes with cabbage, meats, and sausages for their famed *cocido lebaniego*, while they use white beans for their similar *cocido montañes*, which marries them with pork ribs, sausages, cabbage, turnips, and potatoes.

The region's temperate maritime climate and regular and abundant rainfall creates verdant pastureland ideal for raising cattle. Both Cantabria and Asturias are known for their excellent meat and dairy products. Sirloin or filet

Cantabria is also known for its *sobaos* (sponge cakes) and *quesadas* (cheese cake), which are commercially produced and sold across Spain. The "official" Asturian dessert is *arroz con leche*, a luscious creamy rice pudding, often with a crisp caramelized sugar topping. Rice is not commonly used in the region except for this dessert and sometimes when cooked with clams in Cantabria.

The local climate is not ideal for wine making, but it is perfectly suited for apple orchards, so the area makes up for any lack of noteworthy wines with its excellent cider production (page 219). *Sidra natural*, or "natural cider," made without the addition of carbonic bubbles, is drunk by nearly everyone, and there are many *chigres*, or "cider bars," which serve this drink almost exclusively. It is also used in cooking, adding a special regional flavor to many of the area's dishes. The few grapes grown here are used to produce Orujo, a spirit made from pomace. The best comes from Potes in Cantabria.

Balearic Islands

The Balearic archipelago, which lies off the eastern coast of the Iberian Peninsula in the Mediterranean Sea, is composed of two eastern main islands, Majorca and Minorca, and the smaller Cabrera, and two smaller western islands, Ibiza and Formentera, together known as the Pitiusas. The presence of *talayots*, stone structures that date to the third millennium BC, are evidence that this wildly beautiful archipelago has been inhabited since ancient times.

The islands' strategic location attracted conquerors throughout the centuries, from the Carthaginians, Romans, and Vandals to the Byzantines and Moors. In the thirteenth century, the crown of Aragón took control of the archipelago. Catalonia, part of the kingdom at that time, exercised considerable influence over the Balearics, and even today a dialect of Catalan is still spoken on the islands.

Driving out of Palma, Majorca's capital, you will enter a landscape cluttered with windmills. Water is scarce, but olive trees are abundant and some are believed to be more than a thousand years old. The Tramuntana mountain range, which runs from the northeast toward the south-

west of the island, stops the mostly northern winds of the same name. It is not a compact, massive range but one broken by gorges and valleys, creating a shape similar to that of three rolling waves. North of the mountains, the villages are quieter than those in the south, and the coast is lined with rugged cliffs. Deía, a beautiful village on the north shore, is home to many writers and artists. Southern Majorca, less mountainous and with a more temperate climate, has become a major tourist destination.

Smaller and flatter than Majorca, Minorca also has two principal sides: The north is darker, with ground rich in slate and a turbulent sea. The south is mellow, green, and luscious, with lonely, sandy beaches. Cows graze on meadows, and the dairy industry is sizable. Mahón, the capital, a natural port, was important to the British Navy during the eighteenth century. Britain occupied Minorca in 1708, and the Peace of Utrecht legitimized their presence in 1713. With the exception of a short period of French domination, Minorca was essentially under British control until 1782, although the Spanish did not regain full control until 1802. The other islands have remained under Spanish rule since the expulsion of the Moors.

Third in size, Ibiza is closest to the mainland, just a short ride away by ferry. One of Spain's fashionable vacation resorts, it is the gathering place of le beau monde and has an intense nightlife. Formentera—the jewel of the Balearic crown in my opinion—is just a stone's throw away. About three miles long and lined with sandy beaches, it is small and flat and, thanks to strict zoning laws, remains in a glorious state of natural beauty and tranquility.

It would be hard to find a better example of a Mediterranean diet than the cooking from the Balearics. Already during the first century AD, Roman historiographer Pliny praised the excellence of Majorcan olive oil and wines. During the sixteenth century, olive oil production became one of the main income sources for the island, surpassed only by wheat and oats, and most of the farms had their own *almazaras*, or olive oil mills. The main varieties grown today are Empeltre, Arbequina, and Picual, and the oil is protected by the Denominación de Origen Aceite de Mallorca.

Although olive oil is used for most cooking on Majorca, *manteca* (lard), or *saim* in the local dialect, is used to make bread pies, pastries, and especially *ensaimadas*, the famous pastry coils of the Balearics. It is typical to see visitors in the Palma airport carrying the telltale cardboard boxes that conceal these iconic pastries. *Cocas*, or crusty bread pies topped with various ingredients, are also common. Catalan cooks make similar pies, but they are usually square or rectangular in the Balearics and oval in Catalonia. *Cocarrois* and empanadas are savory turnovers filled with vegetables or meats, while *robiols* and *crespels* are sweet. One bread preparation that does feature the celebrated local olive oil is *pa amb oli* (similar to the Catalan *pa amb tomàquet*), which appears on every dinner table. Toasted bread is rubbed with tomato, usually *tomàquets de ramellet* (small, highly aromatic tomatoes), and sprinkled with olive oil—or the reverse, tomatoes are sprinkled with olive oil and rubbed with bread. The experts still don't agree!

Not surprisingly, fish and shellfish are frequent menu items. *Mero* (grouper) cooked *a la mallorquina* (covered with many chopped vegetables and baked), is popular, as are *calamares* (squid) and *raya* (skate). Visitors to Minorca should not miss the chance to try the local spiny lobster, which has a distinctive bluish cast and is usually served in the tomatoey stew known as *caldereta de langosta*. The use of fennel, otherwise rare in the rest of Spain, is typical in these dishes.

The *porc negre*, or "black pig" (not to be confused with the *pata negra* of *jamón ibérico* fame), has lived on the islands for almost seven thousand years. It plays an important role in the life of the locals, many of whom consider it inconceivable to let a day pass without eating *sobrasada*, the islands' signature sausage made from this tasty pork. The humid sea air that makes curing hams in the manner of the mainland impossible helps create the soft texture that distinguishes this intense, semicured, spreadable sausage. It appears in countless ways in everyday cooking, including as a topping for bread and *cocas*, in sauces, and in fillings.

Desserts on the islands rely mainly on almonds. Among them are *gató d'ametlla*, a rich cake made primarily with almonds, sugar, and eggs, and almond ice cream. Ibiza has a delightful dessert called *flaó*, a blend of aniseed, mint, and fresh cheese, and the local apricots, pomegranates, and figs are superb.

The British can be credited with initiating two of Minorca's best-known products, the magnificent Queso de Mahón and the highly praised Xoriguer gin. They encouraged the Minorcans to raise cows and make cheese, and Queso de Mahón, a pure cow's milk cheese available both semicured and cured, is the delicious result. The British established the first gin distillery in Mahón, and today the spirit continues to be made in the traditional fashion, in copper stills (introduced by the Moors) heated by wood fires. The British also figure in the story of mayonnaise, known as *salsa mahonesa*, after the island's capital. The Minorcans insist that is was created by one of their own and sent off to Paris by the French when they took Minorca from the British in the 1750s.

Wines are produced on Majorca and regulated by the Binissalem and Plà i Llevant DOs. The allowed grapes are the native Manto Negro and Callet for red wines and Moll for whites. In both DOs, the use of the native Manto Negro, a large, dark grape that yields a big, bold wine, results in wines ideal for maturing in oak. The local white wines are less distinguished and represent only a small part of overall production. Majorcans also manufacture, in limited amounts, Palo de Mallorca, a celebrated digestive made from cinchona bark, brown sugar, cinnamon, and nutmeg.

Basque Country

Basque Country, called Euskadi in the Basque language, is the easternmost region of Green Spain. Bordering France in the foothills of the western Pyrenees, it runs westward along the Bay of Biscay, with Cantabria to the west and Navarra and La Rioja to the south.

When the Romans arrived, they found people—probably descendants of tribes of the Cro-Magnon era and promptly named the Vascones by the invaders—inhabiting the broad stretch between the western Pyrenees, the Cantabrian Mountains, and the Ebro River. The northern limit, the Bay of Biscay, proved to be more of an opportunity than a limitation, serving as a gateway to the world. After the fall of the Roman Empire, the mostly nomadic Vascones probably united to fight the incursions of Visigoths. Toward the beginning of the seventh century, they were considered a political unit, the duchy of the Vascones, under Frankish suzerainty. In 778, they defeated Charlemagne at Roncesvalles, inspiring the epic *Chanson de Roland* and creating the kingdom of Pamplona, later called Navarre. Portions of that land were subsequently annexed to the Castilian crown, and different kingdoms, battles, and alliances shaped what is now known as the Basque Country.

In this context, it is necessary to clarify two terms. Euskadi, or Basque Country, refers to today's political unit, or the autonomous community within Spain that includes the three provinces of Álava, Guipúzcoa, and Vizcaya. Euskal Herria, also translated as Basque Country, refers to the broader, historical territory, predating the creation of the ancient kingdom of Navarre, which includes today's Euskadi, some areas from the autonomous community of Navarra, and the French Basque provinces on the other side of the Pyrenees.

I come from the Basque Country. When I cross the pass of Orduña in the Cantabrians to descend to my hometown, Bilbao, my heart starts to beat faster. I get carried away by the sight of the green mountains and valleys and the *caseríos* (farmhouses), and by the thought of once again being home with my family and friends. My heart fills with happiness when I anticipate the culinary wonders that my mother, Marichu, will have ready for me.

We Basques live for cooking and eating. I am biased, I know, but I have not found a similar level of passion anywhere I have traveled. I am often asked to describe Basque cuisine, and my standard answer is that it is

Frank Gehry's Guggenheim Museum, a building that revitalized Bilbao and is now its symbol

deeply felt, honors tradition, and respects the natural flavors of the ingredients. These qualities are on display in the significant number of dishes that are distinctively Basque. The international acclaim achieved by the new Basque cuisine movement led by Juan Mari Arzak is only the most recent example of how Basque cookery has influenced the tables of the rest of Spain and beyond.

Basque fishermen have been sailing the northern Atlantic since the eleventh century. While following the whale, which at that time was the most treasured catch, they encountered banks of cod off the coasts of Terranova (Newfoundland) in the Gulf of Saint Lawrence. On nearby islands, some settlements still carry Basque names, and salt cod, or *bacalao*, is a hallmark of Basque cuisine. Some historians believe that Basques landed in America before the arrival of Columbus, but while explorers and discoverers proudly proclaim their findings, fishermen never disclose the source of their catch.

The sea has always provided nourishment for the

Turbot on an outdoor grill in Getaria, Basque Country

Basques. Squid, preferably the small ones called *txipirones*, are cooked in an onion sauce with their ink, to produce *txipirones en su tinta*. The deep black of the sauce initially evokes curiosity and sometimes aversion in the uninitiated, but after the first bite, reservations dissolve in the velvety texture of the squid and sublime taste of the sauce. Though more and more scarce, *merluza* (hake), or *lebatza* in Basque, from the Bay of Biscay knows no paragon (with all due respect to its austral relative from the southern seas). The darker-skinned Basque hake has firm, delicious flesh. Cooks typically panfry the medallions from the upper body and either roast the tail in one piece or cut it crosswise into "steaks" for *merluza en salsa verde*, the classic green sauce preparation.

Marmitako, the potato and tuna stew originally prepared by fishermen on their boats, has become a standard offering in many restaurants. The tuna belly, called *ventresca* (or *ijada* in Basque), is extremely juicy, flakes beautifully, and is the best tuna for salads. It is usually roasted in the oven with just a little garlic and a splash of olive oil. At my family's summerhouse in Mundaka, we preserved the extra tuna in olive oil, and we were always happy during the winter to have done so. The gooseneck barnacles my brothers risked their skins to catch on the nearby rocky shore; baby eels from Aguinaga in neighboring Guipúzcoa Province; the turbot from Getaria; *mojojones* (the Basque name for mussels, as opposed to *mejillones*, as they are known in the rest of the country); and anchovies—all of these and many more bring fond memories of my first tastes as a child of the culinary traditions of my country.

Bacalao, or salt cod, is a staple of the Basque kitchen. Basques are masters of the art of turning a stale and salty fish into something sumptuous, especially when prepared *pil-pil* style, in an emulsion of the cod's gelatin and olive oil. Other cod preparations, such as *a la vizcaína*, *Club Ranero*, and *ajoarriero*, the latter a loan from neighboring Navarra, are also popular.

A la vizcaína, or Biscayne style, describes a dish cooked in *salsa vizcaína*, a dried-pepper sauce. The dried peppers, called *choriceros* because of their importance in the production of chorizo sausages, are harvested at the end of the summer when ripe and hung from the facades of farmhouses to dry. The area surrounding Gernika is famous for these sweet and delicate peppers. Those not destined for drying are harvested while still green, fried with olive oil, and served as an accompaniment to meats and fish, and sometimes alone as a first course. Delicious red beans also come from Gernika, although those from Tolosa are better known. Both are equally tender and buttery and usually cooked with sausages in a stew, supplanting the chickpea stews so popular in other areas of Spain.

All of these dishes are staples of *txokos*, the gastronomic societies of Basque Country. These culinary havens are the dominion of men, as their rules restrict women from joining, though some societies make exceptions and allow us in once a month or sometimes once a year. Their purpose is to give members a place to show off their culinary techniques and creations and to have a good time cooking, eating, and drinking. These tradi-

tional societies have made significant contributions to the annals of Basque cooking, and some dishes that originated in *txokos*, such as *marmitako* made with salmon instead of tuna or various foie gras and duck breast dishes, have become classics.

Equally traditional is barhopping before lunch or dinner, which is essentially a regional sport. Bar counters display numerous *pintxos*, the equivalent to tapas in other areas of the country. Making the rounds consists of popping in and out of several bars, usually the same ones every day, grabbing a *pintxo* and drinking a *txikito* (a small glass of wine) in each one. It is a way to meet friends and acquaintances without arranging a specific date, before heading home for a proper meal.

Cheeses are among the typical *pintxos* found in the region's many bars, with Idiazábal, produced in Navarra as well, the most highly regarded. The sheep's milk cheese holds such importance for the Basques that a contest to judge the best artisanal Idiazábal cheeses is held every September in the town of Ordizia, in Guipúzcoa Province. In September 1999, I was one of twenty jurors at the annual contest. We tried more than seventy different cheeses, and a portion of the winner was auctioned that day for five thousand dollars. I was in heaven trying all of those buttery-textured, strong-flavored, nutty-tasting cheeses.

Rioja Alavesa, one of the three subregions of the La Rioja wine-producing area (page 9), is in the Basque province of Álava, and the wines from there are much lighter and fruitier than the wines from the other two sectors. Txakolí is a distinct wine made from grapes— Ondarribi Beltza for the reds, Ondarribi Zuri for the whites—cultivated in the provinces of Vizcaya and Guipúzcoa (Bizkaiko Txakolina and Getariako Txakolina DOs). Generally young, light, and fresh tasting, it is available everywhere in Basque Country, but especially in coastal areas, where it is a perfect match for seafood. Its effervescence makes it comparable to young whites from Penedès and Rías Baixas. Cider has long been drunk in Basque Country as well, but the wine drinking, perhaps because of the proximity to the Rioja region, is of greater cultural importance.

The Canary Islands

Situated in the Atlantic Ocean seventy miles from the Saharan shore and more than six hundred miles south of continental Spain, the Canaries are a group of islets and seven main islands: Lanzarote, Fuerteventura, Grand Canary, Tenerife, Gomera, La Palma, and Hierro. Much like the islands of Hawaii, the Canaries were formed by volcanic eruptions from the seabed. The highest volcano, at about twelve thousand feet, is Pico de Teide, Spain's tallest peak. Among the islands' main attractions are their many spectacular views: the endless sandy beaches of Fuerteventura; the lunarlike landscapes carved by riverbeds of lava rock on Lanzarote; the lush *barrancos* (deep canyons) on La Palma, Tenerife, and Gomera; and the immense *calderas* (craters) of Las Cañadas on Tenerife.

The climate on the islands is benign, with ever-present trade winds, mild temperatures year-round, and plenty of sunshine. Each island has become a tourist destination for northern Europeans seeking an escape from hard winters to the land of eternal springtime.

The Canary Islands drew transients in the past as well, playing an important role in the Age of Exploration. Christopher Columbus landed in Las Palmas in 1492, on the first leg of the trip that would lead him to the New World, and subsequent expeditions stopped on the islands to replenish supplies. On return trips to Spain, the ships stopped here, and so the islanders were the first to receive and admire the findings from the New World. This explains why many culinary traditions common in the Canaries echo those in the Caribbean and other places in the Americas, such as dishes prepared with bananas, much as they are in Cuba; *sancocho*, a salted fish and potato dish also popular in Puerto Rico; and the use of cilantro, which is rare in the rest of Spain.

Gofio, an ancient food rich in calories and fiber, has long been an important source of nourishment for rural residents of the islands. Sandy-colored toasted flour—

ABOVE: *The small fishing bay of San Ginés in Arrecife, Lanzarote* LEFT: *View from the north end of Lanzarote to Isla Graciosa*

originally made from roasted wheat but now more often from roasted corn, barley, chickpeas, or various roots—is mixed with liquid and added to soups or stews as a thickener at the end of cooking, or it is mixed with water, hand pressed into small balls, and served as a starch accompaniment to main courses. Today, with the abundance of alternative sources of starch, *gofio* is not as widely eaten as in the past.

The islanders are also famous for their *mojos* (sauces or dips), which come in many variations, and while they bear the same name, they are completely different from the *mojos* of Latin America. Canarian *mojos* are made with olive oil, vinegar, garlic, red (dried and crushed) or green peppers, parsley, cilantro, and other ingredients, depending on the dish they are to accompany. They are ubiquitous side dishes for dipping *papas arrugadas* (wrinkled

potatoes), fish, or meats, with red *mojos* usually paired with meats and potatoes and green ones with fish.

The potatoes that we consume today in Europe and in the United States bear little resemblance to those originally carried from South America to the Canaries by the conquistadors. Several of the latter varieties are still grown here today, including the *papa negra*, or "black potato," which is not found elsewhere in Europe. It has almost-black skin and yellow flesh with an intense and delicious flavor. The other crops of the islands are rich in variety but small in production, with the exception of tomatoes and bananas. The plum-shaped Canary tomato, once a vital part of the economy, is still valued for its flavor and aroma. Lettuce, cucumbers, beans, peas, Swiss chard, leeks, spinach, chayote, and many more vegetables are available almost year-round, and *berros* (watercress) is especially popular on the islands, unlike in continental Spain. The small Canary banana, *plátano canario*, is prized for its soft texture and sweet flavor. Bananas were first planted on the islands by the Portuguese, who brought

them from Guinea, and from here they were introduced to the Americas. Many other fruits—oranges, figs, avocados, mangoes, papayas, pineapples, and dates—flourish in the subtropical climate as well.

Surrounded by the relatively cool eastern Atlantic, the coral-free and mostly rocky and sandy fishing grounds offer numerous types of fish, which the islanders cook in just as many ways. *Vieja*, a type of parrot fish, is delicious baked or boiled. *Pargo* and *besugo*, similar to bream and snapper, are grilled and served with *mojos* and *papas arrugadas*. *Cherne* (grouper), which is often salted and used in *sancocho*, is probably the most celebrated fish, although it is quite expensive. More ordinary catch are made into everyday dishes, such as *sardinas en escabeche* (marinated sardines), *caballa con mojo* (mackerel with red *mojo*), and *atún escabechado* (marinated tuna).

The same geography that has made fish a central element of the local table has also defined cheese produc-

ABOVE: *The salinas (salt works) of Cocoteros on the eastern coast of Lanzarote* RIGHT: *Cleaning the day's catch in a tidal pool in Famara, Lanzarote*

tion. Because there is neither room for large cattle herds nor conditions for their grazing, small farmers have plenty of goats and sheep, which require less maintenance and can more easily scale the steep slopes of the green valleys. The result is a healthy production of goat's and sheep's milk cheeses, the most acclaimed of which are the fresh, aged, or smoked goat cheeses of La Palma, such as Queso Palmero. For the same reasons, local meats consist mainly of *cabrito* (baby goat), *cordero* (lamb), and *conejo* (rabbit). The kids and lambs are milk-fed and then slaughtered when they are less than three weeks old.

In the early days, the distinctive terrain of the islands also supported the cultivation of sugarcane, a crop that was taken from the Canaries to the New World near the

beginning of colonization. The Spanish authorities soon realized that sugarcane, and hence rum, production overseas was more cost effective, so they didn't promote the industry in the islands. On Grand Canary and La Palma, sugarcane is still grown and harvested as it has been for centuries, though its production is small. Canarians also produce a local rum, Ron Arehucas, that is delicious, albeit little known outside the islands.

Grapes have fared much better than sugarcane. They were planted on the islands by the Spaniards before the discovery of the Americas. The environment was not perfect, and some adaptation was necessary to marry the vines to the local climate and soil. But the islanders were intent on making viticulture work, so they would able to export wine to the Americas later. For example, Lanzarote, the most volcanic of the islands, has little rain and constant temperatures. To grow vines in these conditions, a special process is required: each vine is nestled in a hole in the lava ash and protected by a semicircular stone wall that shields it from wind erosion. Against all odds, the wines obtained are excellent. The landscape is breathtaking: the black of the lava ash, the reds and browns of the minerals, and the intense green of the vine leaves create a picture of incredible beauty.

Lanzarote is one of eleven DOs in the islands, with Tenerife boasting five of them, and only Fuerteventura without a single one. Although production is small and the wines are mostly consumed locally, the constantly improved quality of some of them has attracted outside attention, primarily from the many visitors who come seeking the sun. The predominant grapes include Güal, Listán Blanco, Malvasía, Marmajuelo, Moscatel, and imported Pedro Ximénez for white wines, and Listán Negro, Tintilla, Negramoll, and Moscatel Negro for reds, as well as an increasing number of such imported grapes as Cabernet Sauvignon, Merlot, Pinot Noir, Syrah, and Tempranillo. The wines made from local grapes are typically fruity, spicy, and mellow in the case of the whites, and intensely colored, fruity, low in tannins, and with light balsamic accents in the case of the reds. The reds, because of low acidity and lack of tannins, are best consumed while they are still young. Some excellent muscatel dessert wines are also bottled on the islands.

The Castiles and Madrid

Castile, or "land of castles," is the largest natural region on Spain's wide central plateau, known as la Meseta Castellana. The plateau nearly coincides with the autonomous communities of Castilla–La Mancha, Castilla y León, and Madrid, making up the country's largest geographic region. Although the Castiles are split administratively, they form a cultural unity, with Madrid at the center.

Old Castile, the area north of Madrid known today as Castilla y León, was the first territory recovered from the Moors during the Middle Ages; more than ten thousand castles and fortresses testify to the long military campaigns that successfully pushed them to the south. The area south of Madrid, today's Castilla–La Mancha, was recovered from the Moors in the mid-thirteenth century; hence, its designation as New Castile. The two Castiles were united soon after, and with the kingdom's power situated here, the area developed into the geographic and political heart of Spain. Until recently, Castilian was designated the country's only official language.

Except for the western border with Portugal, mountain ranges frame the plateau on all sides. To access northern, eastern, or southern Spain, you must first cross mountain passes and only then descend to the coast. The plateau, frequently bleak and arid, has an average altitude of about twenty-five hundred feet and experiences temperatures ranging from bitterly cold in the winter to fiercely hot in the summer. Rain is scarce, and snow is common in the winter only on the mountain peaks where precipitation is higher.

The city of Madrid lies at the very center of Spain. Traditionally, it has been the melting pot for immigrants from other parts of the country (and increasingly from other parts of the world). Originally home to farmers and cattle herders, it remained a sleepy enclave until the mid-sixteenth century, when Philip II designated it the capital of the Habsburg empire. This late recognition explains why ancient buildings and monuments so common elsewhere in the country are absent in the capital. The king could have chosen another city with a richer history and greater wealth, but he saw Madrid's central location as a fitting symbol of a young, unified Spain.

Gran Cafe Zaragoza

The new capital quickly prospered, attracting everyone who wanted to be close to power. The arts flourished, and so did gastronomy. The impetus given to Madrid by the Habsburgs continued under the Bourbons two centuries later. In the mid-eighteenth century, Charles III, a great promoter of the city, initiated a period of major monumental architecture. Now, after almost five hundred years, Madrid remains the political and cultural core of the country.

Because of its role as both capital and melting pot, Madrid has had many influences shaping its cuisine, making it difficult to define a true Madrilenian dish. But if Madrid has a culinary hallmark, it is undoubtedly *cocido madrileño*, a hearty chickpea stew laced with meats and sausages. Every region has its own version of this dish, but the one from Madrid, in my opinion, is the best. Another distinctive local dish is *callos a la madrileña*, tripe in a delicious lightly spiced sauce. Dishes with *riñones* (kidneys), *sesos* (brains), and *mollejas* (sweetbreads) have

always been highly valued not only here but across the country. Even though Madrid is landlocked, and as far from the coasts as one can get in Spain, it is said to have some of the best seafood in the country, with fish arriving daily from every stretch of the Spanish coastline. The magnificent asparagus and strawberries from the nearby vegetable gardens of Aranjuez are also fixtures on the capital's tables. And as in many other parts of Spain, the locals love to eat churros for breakfast.

The traditional cuisine of the Castiles is equally varied, although in the south, where resources are more limited, cooking tends to be more rustic. Roasts of lamb, suckling pig, and baby goat are excellent and common in every corner of the region. In southern Castile, the *galianos* or *gazpachos manchegos*, hearty stews combining bread and fowl, are highly acclaimed, as is *morteruelo* from Cuenca, a pâtélike preparation of hare or rabbit and pork. Partridge and trout are also popular, either cooked or pickled, and each province has a version of *cocido*, the meal-in-a-pot stew. The vegetable stew called *pisto*, which originally consisted of only peppers and tomatoes, has its roots in La Mancha, though it is now cooked all over Spain. The delightful garlic and bread soup, *sopa castellana*, or *sopa de ajo*, is common throughout the Castiles and beyond, and is made with a number of variations, such as the addition of poached eggs or cured ham. In the northwestern province of León, bordering Galicia, empanadas are everyday home-cooked dishes. *Azafrán* (saffron) from La Mancha, *miel* (honey) from La Alcarria, in Guadalajara Province, and *mazapán* (marzipan) from Toledo are reminders of past times when Jewish, Muslim, and Christian cooking and cultures blended, creating the foundation of Spain's culinary repertory.

Specialty foods of the Castiles are appreciated throughout the country. The best *jamónes ibéricos* of Spain are produced in Salamanca, a province northwest of Madrid.

Hanging cured hams from León (though surely raised in the dehesas of Extremadura or Andalusia)

Magnificent sausages, or *embutidos*, including blood sausage from Burgos and chorizo from León, Salamanca, and Zamora, are also much admired. Locally grown legumes, such as *alubias blancas* (white beans) from Segovia and lentils from Zamora, end up in pantries all over the country, and the cheeses made on the plains are magnificent. The sheep's milk cheese Manchego, the best known of them all, was, as its name indicates, originally from La Mancha. (Known to the Moors as al-Manshah, or "dry land," this region was later home to the adventures and misadventures of Cervantes's Don Quixote, and the windmills that punctuate its landscape are reminders of the knight errant.) Other cheeses produced in Castile include the tasty Zamorano from Zamora, north of Madrid; Burgos, a mild and soft cheese that blends sheep's and cow's milk; and the intense blue Valdeón from León, made on the opposite side of the Picos de Europa from where the famed and quite similar Asturian Cabrales is produced.

North of Madrid in Old Castile, magnificent wines are fashioned in Rueda, Ribera del Duero, Toro, Cigales, and Bierzo. In southern Castile, the main wine-growing areas include Valdepeñas, Almansa, La Mancha, Mentrida, and Madrid. Both regions share dryer climate conditions and higher average altitudes than Rioja, for example, which translates into hotter days and colder nights. These extreme variations in temperature result in hearty, full-bodied wines, with Ribera del Duero, Toro, and Cigales producing some of Spain's most acclaimed bottles. Dishes such as suckling pig and lamb go particularly well with these big wines.

Like the winemakers, the residents of the convents and monasteries in the Castiles have played important roles in preserving the country's gastronomic traditions, primarily its confectionary recipes. Saint Teresa of Ávila, in her role as mother superior of her convent, famously reminded the nuns who wanted to skip working in the kitchen in favor of going to the chapel for oration that God also wandered among the pots and pans. In her honor, the Spanish Academy of Gastronomy awards a series of national prizes every year on her saint's day (and mine), October 15. Her legendary sweets, *yemas de Santa Teresa*, are made today the same way as they were centuries ago.

Catalonia

Catalonia is a region of contrasts in both its geography and its culinary traditions. Occupying a triangular area in the northeastern part of the peninsula, it is separated from France by the Pyrenees in the north, and bordered by Aragón in the west, Levante in the south, and the Mediterranean in the east. This autonomous community is composed of four provinces: Barcelona, Gerona, and Tarragona bordering the Mediterranean, and Lérida in the interior.

The Costa Brava, the rocky shoreline of Gerona, the northernmost province, gives way to the sandy beaches of the Costa Dorada, which stretches south to Tarragona. In the south, around the Ebro delta where Catalonia borders Castellón, the northern province of the Levante region, rice plantations dominate the landscape. Olive groves and vineyards are also abundant in the flatlands south of Barcelona, contrasting sharply with the harsh mountainous area in the Pyrenees to the north. Lérida, with Aragón to its west and its three partner provinces to

An old farmhouse in the Catalan countryside

its east, is predominantly agricultural. Unlike other areas of Spain, where large estates are typical, most of this cultivated land is leased or owned by small farmers.

Catalonia was one of the first possessions of the Romans in Spain. Salt Mountain, near the medieval town of Cardona, was used by the Romans as a source of salt for preserving fish, among other foods. An extraordinary geological curiosity, the five-hundred-foot hill of almost pure salt is still mined today. Some of this salt is used in L'Escala, a fishing village in Gerona, to preserve the wonderful local anchovies, which are usually slightly larger than those found in the Basque Country or Cantabria. The preservation includes a pinch of black pepper between the salt layers, giving the fish a characteristic taste.

Catalonia's proximity and longtime links to Italy and France are reflected today in the importance of such dishes as bouillabaisse and *canelones* (cannelloni). In the twelfth century, the high valley in the Pyrenees known in Spain as Cerdaña and in France as Cerdagne was part of Rosellón (Roussillon in France) and belonged to the Aragónese crown. Later it was under the rule of the Majorcan monarchy. In the mid-seventeenth century, Spain ceded most of the area to France, where today

Roussillonaise, a Catalan dialect, is still spoken. (Similarly, another Catalan dialect can still be heard in the Sardinian town of Alghero, where Catalans introduced their language in the fourteenth century.) This web of language and culture has resulted in the Catalan *bullabesa* (*bullir* in Catalan and *bouillir* in French both mean "to boil") and the French bouillabaisse being nearly the same soup, with each a mix of fish and shellfish, parsley, and saffron and served with toasted bread rubbed with garlic.

Foreign culinary traditions became an even greater influence in the late-nineteenth century with the arrival of the industrial revolution in Barcelona. The changing economy attracted business (and other) travelers from abroad, mainly from Italy and France, and prompted a proliferation of hotels and restaurants, all of which hoped to draw the new visitors to their tables. These "fancy" restaurants and hotels, with names like Hotel de Las Cuatro Naciones, Grand Restaurant de France, and Chez Martin, began serving cassoulet and *canelones*, and today *canelones* are so much a part of the local table that they are

traditionally served during the Christmas holiday season.

Catalonia is also known for its bounty of raw ingredients. Magnificent olive oil produced in the southern reaches of Tarragona and Lérida, mainly from Arbequina olives, is a staple in Catalan kitchens. The well-known *alioli*, which marries olive oil, eggs, and garlic in a creamy sauce, is a logical outgrowth of the abundance of olives. Catalan rice, also from the southern area, is cooked throughout the region in many different ways. Along with Valencia and Calasparra in Murcia, Tarragona is a major rice producer under the Delta del Ebro DO, with Bahía as its main variety. Lérida Province, rich in woodlands that climb to the Pyrenees, supplies the region with a magnificent variety of aromatic mushrooms and truffles. At the large, busy Mercado de la Boqueria, in the heart of Barcelona, you will find all these different foods artfully displayed.

Catalans like to combine fowl with fruits, such as *pato con peras* (duck with pears). Their taste for *mar y montaña*, or "sea and mountain," is present in dishes like lobster with chicken or in rice dishes that combine rabbit and seafood, as in the hearty *conejo con sepia*. Seafood casseroles like *suquets* are common in the coastal areas, while fowl is favored inland. Chickens and capons from the Prat DO are a special breed with tasty and tender meat and relatively little fat. The birds have bluish legs and long breasts, and their somewhat large eggs, with reddish shells, are also sold in markets. Vic, a mountain town in the Pyrenees, is known for its *salchichón*, a tasty sausage that resembles French *saucisson*. The distinctiveness of *fuet*, a much thinner cured sausage, and *longanizas* and *butifarras*, specialty sausages unique to Catalonia, can make it difficult to reproduce certain Catalan dishes outside the region.

The cheeses of Catalonia, produced mainly in the Pyrenean provinces of Lérida and Gerona, are intriguing

LEFT: Almond tree in bloom in front of an ancient church in Canet d'Adri, outside Girona, Catalonia BELOW: *Barcelona's Boqueria market*

as well. Queso de L'Alt Urgell y la Cerdanya is a creamy cow's milk cheese with a sweet aroma. Near Olot, the buttery, soft, stark white goat's milk Garrotxa, after a rural district of the same name, is produced. Mató, shaped like an inverted bowl, is a salt-free fresh curd cheese now made from cow's and goat's milk, and in the past from goat's milk. It is popular across Catalonia and is usually served with honey for a simple dessert. Serrat, a sheep's milk cheese sold both semicured and fully cured, also comes from the Pyrenees.

Catalonia's wine landscape is equally diverse. The region's best-known wine is *cava*, one of the world's premier sparkling wines. Ninety-five percent of the *cavas* are produced in Penedès, the area south of Barcelona near the Tarragona border. Their production relies primarily on four grape varieties—Macabeo, Xarel-lo, Parellada, and Subirat—though Chardonnay is also allowed by the regulatory council. In the case of rosé *cavas*, only two red grapes are used, Trepat and Pinot Noir.

The main varieties used in Catalan whites are Xarel-lo, Garnacha Blanca, and, in smaller quantities, Chardonnay, Chenin Blanc, and Gewürztraminer. Reds are predominantly pressed from Garnacha Tinta, Merlot, Tempranillo, Cabernet Sauvignon, Pinot Noir, and Cariñena, combined in varying proportions. The Priorat DO, a relatively small wine area southwest of Barcelona, produces intense, full-bodied reds that are consistently ranked among the best wines in the world. The area harbors the ideal combination of sun, precipitation, and, most notably, a slate-rich soil that imparts deep mineral notes that make Priorat wines taste unlike any others. The predominant grape varieties are Garnacha Blanca, Macabeo, Pedro Ximénez, and Xenin for whites, and Cariñena and Garnacha Negra, along with strategic support from such imports as Cabernet Sauvignon, Merlot, and Syrah, for the reds. Though these much-admired wines complement the local table, the low yields and high labor costs involved in producing them make them expensive for everyday dining.

Extremadura

Bordered by Portugal in the west, Andalusia in the south, and Castile in the east and north, Extremadura—the cradle of many conquistadors—is a land of extremes. *Dehesas*, vast natural prairies that can be blisteringly hot in the summer and bitter cold in the winter, cover most of the area, with the exception of the counties in the north. Stone oaks and *alcornoques* (cork oaks) dot the prairies, creating the perfect habitat for cattle and especially for the *pata negra*, the famed *ibérico* pig. In contrast, the area to the north of the Tagus River is home to fertile valleys with rich pastureland. Freshwater fish and goats and sheep replace pork at the table, and the plentiful wild vegetables—thistles, asparagus, and mushrooms—are cooked with little adornment.

This diverse landscape has, like Spain's other regions, been inhabited by a series of conquerors, all of whom appreciated the varied topography and the wealth of nat-

ABOVE: *Landscape with single oak tree, Extremadura*
LEFT: *Grazing in a* dehesa *in southern Extremadura*

ural resources. The Romans made this part of Hispania, which they called Lusitania, one of their main colonies, as evidenced by the stunning structures still found in Mérida, the contemporary capital.

In the years following the collapse of the Roman Empire and throughout the Reconquista, Extremadura remained a dominant region in the country. Then, in the sixteenth century, the region spawned many of Spain's powerful conquistadors, including Hernán Cortés from Medellín and Francisco Pizarro and Francisco Orellanos from Trujillo. Their exploits abroad introduced not only unprecedented wealth to the kingdom at large and to Extremadura in particular, but also such now common foods as potatoes, corn, and peppers, among others.

Large-scale sheepherding contributed wealth in yet another form to the region, the wool trade. As a result, the status of the herdsmen and their charges was so elevated that rights guaranteeing their free passage on delin-

eated trails, known as Cañadas Reales, were written into Spanish property laws as far back as the thirteenth century. Five of Spain's nine major herding trails either begin or end in Extremadura. Together they total some forty-two hundred miles in the region, a number that underlines the strong influence the herding culture had and continues to have in the area.

But centuries of herding proved damaging to the area as well. Because herdsmen, through their considerable control over the land, essentially dominated the regional economy, they were a primary reason that farming and manufacturing industries did not develop here as they did in other parts of Spain. As a result, a relative austerity and isolation plagued Extremadura during the eighteenth and nineteenth centuries.

The region's *cocina monacal*, or cuisine from the monasteries and convents, remained important through much of this history. In the years after the exploration of the Americas, when few Spaniards were literate, the country's educated monks specialized in writing, transcribing letters, translating manuscripts, and recording customs—

ABOVE: *The tools of a village butcher*
RIGHT: Jamón *factory in Extremadura*

including recipes—of the times. Even today, many monasteries and convents still sell delicious pastries and other sweets to earn money to sustain themselves, and efforts are now under way to revive the favorite dishes of Emperor Charles V, who retired to the monastery at Yuste after ruling much of the Western World for some four decades. In letters to his son Phillip II, he richly describes the delicacies of *la cocina monacal*, most notably those made by the monks in the monastery at Guadalupe. Among them was *técula mécula*, which is included in the desserts chapter.

Residents of the local monasteries and convents were also among the earliest Spaniards to cultivate crops from the New World because they often encountered them first. When Columbus returned from the Americas, he visited the Catholic Kings in Guadalupe, bringing them many gifts, including peppers. The monks there planted them, and gradually other monasteries throughout the area began growing and using them as well. The nearby La Vera valley is now renowned for its *pimentón*, or Spanish paprika, made from these American natives. The county of La Vera, in the northeastern corner of Cáceres Province in Extremadura, comprises the valleys between the Tietar, Alagón, and Arrago rivers. This area is home to about fifty villages, many of which add "de la Vera" to their name, such as Jarandilla de la Vera. Benign temperatures, many hours of sunlight, and extraordinarily fertile soil make this the perfect place to grow peppers.

The cooking of the region is often as austere as some of the local landscape. Cold gazpachos and *salmorejos* are common fare, especially during the hot summer months, and are similar to Andalusian soups. *Ajo blanco*, the white almond gazpacho, is prepared the same way as in neighboring Andalusia. Otherwise rarely used in Spain, except for in the kitchens of the Canaries, cilantro is essential to Extremadura's wonderful Christmas chicken dish, *escabeche de pollo de Navidad*. In the north, above the Tagus River, freshwater fish are caught, especially the *tenca*, a small fish that is typically deep-fried until crunchy. Frog legs are also highly prized, as is lizard, and baby goat is slowly simmered in stews. South of the Tagus River, in the *dehesas*, the meat of choice is pork, above all the famed *jamón ibérico*, and lamb, rather than the goat of the north, is cooked in stews.

Extremadura produces one of the best *ibérico* hams in Spain, Dehesa de Extremadura DO. But it also "assists" other DOs in scoring highly, because many pigs are fattened on acorns on the local *dehesas* and then taken to other regions for slaughtering and curing. In addition to becoming wonderful air-cured hams and *lomos* (loins), the prized pigs provide succulent fresh meat. *Secreto*, or "secret," a special cut from the breast next to the neck, is thinly sliced and simply fried. No seasonings are added, as nothing could improve the taste of the cut; and, indeed, the presence of any other ingredients would awaken the suspicion that the *pata negra* may not have been in excellent condition. Suckling pig, called *cochinito* or *lechoncillo*, is typically cut into small pieces, marinated with garlic, *pimentón*, and wine, and then fried in olive oil until crunchy. Though quite simple, these preparations are difficult to duplicate, since the essential ingredient— fresh Extremaduran *pata negra*—is hard to find outside the region, even within Spain.

Migas (literally "bread crumbs")—of which I have wonderful memories from my stay years ago on an estate in Valencia de Alcántara, near the Portuguese border—is a humble yet delicious dish of bread, oil, vinegar, and garlic, served originally for breakfast but increasingly for lunch. Some cooks add a shot of anise liqueur halfway through the cooking to cheer up the morning hours. In *migas canas*, a milder version, the garlic is removed from the pan before the bread is added, and after the golden crunchy crumbs are fried, they are covered with milk.

Because of the long history and continued importance of sheep farming in the region, the emphasis on sheep's milk cheeses here will come as no surprise. In terms of quality, cheese production in Extremadura is extraordinary. Two of the finest are Torta del Casar and Queso de la Serena, both made exclusively with raw Merino sheep's milk and coagulated with wild thistle rennet. Torta del Casar is so creamy that the top rind is usually cut off horizontally, to prevent the interior from flowing out, and the rich, runny cheese is eaten with a spoon. Yet another delicious local cheese, Queso Ibores, is made from raw goat's milk, and its rind is either rubbed with *pimentón*, yielding a reddish orange finish, or olive oil, which turns it a yellow-ocher.

The cherries grown in the valley along the Jerte River in the northern area of Cáceres Province are yet another extraordinary product of Extremadura. Seven varieties are cultivated, and they are shipped—and cherished— across the country. The association of Valle del Jerte and cherries is automatic in the mind of any Spaniard.

Although Extremadura, like much of Spain, has an ancient wine tradition, its contemporary production has

been regulated only since 1997, and its following outside the region is limited. The Ribera del Guadiana DO controls and protects wines made in an area that includes most of Badajoz Province and the southern part of Cáceres Province. Newer wines are beginning to be more widely recognized and are now being exported successfully, even if only for their exceptional value. The grapes most often used for whites are Cayetana Blanca, Macabeo, and Pardina, while Tempranillo, Graciano, and Garnacha Tinta and some imported Merlot, Monastrell, and Syrah go into the making of reds.

Galicia

Western Spain points to the New World with its prow. But long before its inhabitants dreamed of a land beyond, the Romans aptly named this area—the westernmost point of continental Europe—Cabo Finisterre, or "the end of the world." Part of Green Spain, Galicia seems a world away from the dry south. The climate is mild, and rains are copious.

The arabesques, arched arcades, saffron, cinnamon, gazpachos, and deep-frying of southern Spain are practically nonexistent here because the Moors, with the exception of a few brief incursions, never established themselves in the area. Instead, Celtic settlements and Roman bridges characterize the landscape, and empanadas, boiled fresh hams, scallops, and *pimentón* the cuisine. More than seven hundred miles long, Galicia's coastline is rugged, with fjordlike formations of incredible beauty alternating with sandy beaches. The interior is hilly and covered with woodlands, and where it borders the Castilian *meseta*, or plains, the terrain is mountainous. More than half of Galicia's land is forested, while the rest is split between farms and pastures.

The famous peppers from Padrón, Galicia

Spain's best shellfish comes from Galicia's coast. To me, there is simply no better place on earth to eat seafood than La Piedra, the seafood market in Vigo. At its entrance, you can eat *ostras* (oysters) sold directly by fisherwomen. The area is cluttered with small bars offering the freshest clams, mussels, langoustines, *centollas* (female spider crabs, considered tastier than their male counterparts), and *nécoras* (also delectable—and expensive—crabs). Usually steamed, *berberechos* (cockles) are a delicious local specialty that Italian markets in North America sometimes mislabel *vongole*, though the proper Italian name for this delight is *cuore edule*. Rare in other parts of Spain, *vieiras* (scallops) are abundant and popular in Galicia. In fact, they are so plentiful here that the scallop shell, the symbol of Saint James, remains an icon of the pilgrimage to the saint's tomb in Santiago de Compostela in western Galicia. In the past, returning home with a scallop shell from the journey was regarded as proof of having made the arduous trip.

In Galicia, the quality of the seafood is so good that only minimal intervention in the kitchen is required. Steaming and boiling are popular ways to prepare mussels, clams, and the prized gooseneck barnacles. Galician turbot is spectacular, usually oven baked or roasted with a little *pimentón*. Fresh sardines are mainly grilled, and the smaller ones, *xoubas*, are used for stuffing empanadas. Not limited to the sea, Gallegos also catch *lampreas* (lampreys) in limited quantities from the Miño and Ulloa rivers between December and March, and typically cook them in their own blood mixed simply with olive oil, vinegar, white wine, and garlic.

Pulpo (octopus), another specialty of the area, is usually boiled, cut into small pieces, and served *a la gallega*, that is, sprinkled with *pimentón*, olive oil, and coarse salt. Until refrigeration was widespread, octopuses were salted or air dried. I have heard older friends describe how common it was to see these creatures hanging in the ports and near the beaches, attached with clips to ropes as if they were freshly washed laundry. Fresh octopus tastes much better, my friends say; perhaps this is why the sight has disappeared.

Many dishes beyond the catch of the day are emblematic of Galicia. For example, it is hard to imagine Galician meals without empanadas. The dough is made with wheat flour, sometimes mixed with corn flour, and traditional fillings vary from meats, tuna, cockles, sardines, or scallops to fruits if served for dessert. *Pote* and *caldo gallego* are the Galician versions of the chickpea and other bean soups and stews so beloved across Spain. Here, however, *grelos* (turnip greens) are the green of choice, not just in these dishes but in other soups and stews as well, and *lacón* (boiled ham) is often served with the greens. The local potatoes, called *cachelos* when they are served boiled with their jackets on, are excellent, as are the *pimientos de Padrón*, small green peppers from Padrón, which are usually lightly pierced with a fork and then fried in olive oil. Typically, these peppers are not hot, but when they are, they can bring tears to your eyes. Galicians have the reputation of responding to questions vaguely or even answering with another question. While this may be an unfair generalization, if a Galician serves you *pimientos de Padrón* and you ask whether they are hot, be prepared to hear the characteristic Galician answer, "*unos pican, outros non*" (some are, others aren't).

The pastures in Galicia are green and luscious, perfect for grazing cattle, and Galician beef, like its seafood, is justly famous all over Spain. In fact, until the 1960s, when other areas of the country began to pay more attention to improving cattle rearing, Galicia supplied half of the beef consumed in the country. Two breeds, Rubia Gallega and Morena del Noroeste, predominate. The relatively small, agile animals have traditionally been raised not only for their meat, but also for working in the fields and supplying milk.

Beef is sold according to the age at slaughter: *ternera*, ten months maximum; *añojo*, between ten and eighteen months; and *cebón*, between eighteen and thirty months. My favorite is *cebón*, which is well marbled and full of flavor. The meat from a young animal is usually cut thin and fried briefly. Veal roasts are also popular, as are stews using beef shanks, but the best cut of all is the *chuletón*, equivalent in size to a T-bone, but from a different part of the carcass. It is usually grilled over charcoal, sprinkled with coarse salt, and served with *pimientos de Padrón* and fried potatoes.

The importance of cattle raising in Galicia has meant that cow's milk cheeses play a prominent role on the local table. The best known of them is the soft, semi-cured Tetilla, with a straw-colored rind, mild flavor, and distinctive flattened-cone shape with a pointed tip (*tetilla* means "nipple"). San Simón, also semicured, is lightly smoked over birch, which colors the rind a pale brown. The creamy Arzúa (also known as Queso de Ulloa), similar to Tetilla but aged longer, has a darker rind and deeper flavor.

Galicia's vineyards have been steadily improving in recent decades, gaining more respect at home and beyond. Albariño is the region's primary white wine grape, and the Rías Biaxas DO, on the west coast (*rías* are inlets on the Atlantic), is its most esteemed cultivation area. The grape is said to be a distant relative to Riesling, and its light and pleasing acidity and fruitiness make a convincing case for such a lineage. Galician whites, which marry perfectly with the local seafood, are also highly praised outside Spain. Though traditionally viewed as pleasant but little more, red wines, made from such grapes as Mencía, Garnacha, and Merenzao, are gradually coming into their own.

Historically, Galicians have migrated to every corner of the world, more so than other Spaniards. In Argentina, for instance, all Spaniards are called Gallegos, as if being from Galicia were the only possibility. But even as they move to the far ends of the world, they keep their distinctive traditions alive. Once I joined a group of Galician friends in Argentina preparing *queimada*, the traditional Galician hot drink made from Orujo, which is distilled from grape pomace. I found the experience fascinating. First they combined the Orujo with sugar in a cone-shaped earthenware dish, and then they ignited it with a match, "conjuring" *bruxas* (witches) as they stirred the flaming beverage with a ladle—an ancient tradition they had transplanted to their new home. No matter where they travel, Galicians never lose their deep ties to the customs of their green, misty homeland.

Levante

Levante is the broad term used to describe the eastern region of the country, where the air is filled with the fragrance of orange blossoms. The name comes from the verb *levantar*, "to rise," as though this is where the sun rises in Spain, and the region includes the autonomous communities of Valencia and Murcia. The former is composed of three provinces: Castellón in the north, bordering Catalonia; Valencia in the middle, the home of paella, arguably Spain's most renowned dish; and Alicante in the south, known for its almond plantations. Murcia, which borders Alicante and is closely related to it, is respected throughout Spain for its productive market gardens.

All four areas face the Mediterranean to the east and have mountains at their back. The coastline, especially in the north, is fairly straight, with only a few capes and gulfs, and the beaches are mainly sandy and flat. Toward the south, in Murcia, salt marshes can be found near Cartagena. This area, known as Mar Menor, supplied the salt that the Romans used for, among other things, their celebrated *garum*, an indispensable sauce made by extracting the liquid from fermented sun-dried salted fish—a salty, potent condiment not unlike the fish sauces of Asia. Farther south, where the mountain ranges descend toward the sea, the coast is rugged and steep.

Alicante and Cartagena were founded during the third century BC by the Carthaginians, and Cartagena was soon the busiest port in the Mediterranean. Levante continued to play an important role during the Roman era and through the years of Moorish domination, which ended definitively in 1238, when James I of Aragón completed what Spain's celebrated warrior, El Cid Campeador (born Rodrigo Díaz de Vivar), set out to do a century earlier. Thanks to the Moors, this area and southern Catalonia supply the rest of Spain and beyond with their best rice. The two Denominaciones de Origen of Levante, both of exceptional quality, are Arroz de Valencia and Arroz de Calasparra.

Until the thirteenth century, rice grew around the city of Valencia, which lies on the shores of the Turia River, where it meets the Mediterranean. Then, James I, fearing malaria outbreaks, directed the fields be moved farther away, to a flat marshland area known as Albufera ("lake" in Arabic). The Spaniards employed the same irrigation system for their rice fields that the Moors had used—a system that the Moors had adapted from one first introduced by the Romans. These historic fields, which have spread over the centuries, again almost to the city's edges, remain one of the preeminent rice-growing areas in all of Europe. Calasparra, in the north of Murcia, is Spain's other important rice cultivation region. Although Murcia's production is much smaller, the quality of rice is without equal. Bomba, Senia, and Bahía are the main varieties grown in Valencia, while Bomba and Balilla are the primary types cultivated in Calasparra.

Much of this rice, of course, goes into the making of paella. The origin of the word is difficult to trace. It comes from the Latin *patella*, the term for the large, round dish the Romans used for presenting their gifts to the gods. But apparently the paella pan as we know it today—and what defines a paella from other rice dishes—came many centuries after the name was first used. What we do know, however, is that regardless of the name or the pan, rice preparations have been as important a part of the culinary landscape for the people of the Levante as *cocidos* have been for the people of Castile.

Like the *cocido*, the dish has humble origins. It was created by farmers and agricultural workers who cooked rice in the fields during their midday break. Today it is understood that a paella is a rice dish cooked in a round, shallow metal vessel. The pan, alas, is often wrongly referred to as a *paellera*, while the proper name is paella, and the rice preparation cooked in it is correctly *arroz a la paella*, though Spaniards typically shorten it. Countless other rice preparations exist, including everything from vegetarian rice to luxurious compositions of rice and fish, shellfish, chicken, rabbit, beans, snails, or other ingredients, in myriad combinations, but these are not considered paellas because they are cooked in other types of vessels.

Valencia and Murcia are also known for their extensive citrus orchards. When you drive along the inland roads, it is a joy to see and smell the blossoms—harbingers of oranges, lemons, limes, clementines, grapefruits, and

A Spanish almond tree being pollinated

more—in full splendor. Murcia is renowned, too, for its large patchwork of small market gardens that yield a year-round harvest. Peppers were introduced to the area by the Hieronymite monks from Guadalupe in Extremadura, who, as previously noted, soon planted them in all their monastery gardens, including the one near La Ñora. *Pimentón* from Murcia, made from the small, round, sweet *ñora* pepper, is, like that of Extremadura, highly regarded. Artichokes, tomatoes, lettuces, cucumbers, onions, snow peas, green beans, eggplants, and such fruits as cherries, apricots, plums, figs, pears, dates, and prickly pears are among the many other foods grown in the gardens and orchards of the region and exported to the rest of the country and beyond.

The local seafood, like the fruits and vegetables, is exceptional here. The large, tender-fleshed shrimp from the salty waters of the Mar Menor are both prized and, primarily because of high demand, scarce. Shrimp and *dorada* (gilt-head bream), caught in the same waters, are commonly baked in salt, and the results are spectacular. The method is simple: the fish is buried in coarse salt and cooked at a high temperature, with nothing else added. When the salt crust is cracked open, the seafood is tender and succulent but never salty. Both the shrimp and the bream are also often grilled or fried, as are other locally caught fish, including red mullet, sardines, monkfish, and hake.

While seafood stars in the Levante, beef and veal play supporting roles, though residents do enjoy panfried or grilled steaks and fillets. Chicken, rabbit, and pork are sometimes roasted and stewed, but they more commonly punctuate paellas and other rice dishes. Inland, near the mountains, where the land is less fertile and the sea is distant, game and goat are prepared.

Almond trees, abundant in the region since the time of the Moors, are undemanding, thriving both inland and along the coast. Alicante is the leader in the production of *turrón*, an almond-and-honey nougat that comes in two traditional varieties: *turrón duro*, hard bars of chopped almonds mixed with honey, and *turrón blando*, soft bars made by mixing ground almonds with honey. *Turrón* (page 294) is a favorite sweet across Spain, especially at Christmastime, and though many contemporary varieties exist—made with hazelnut, pine nut, coconut, and even chocolate—the original almond versions remain the most sought-after at holiday time.

Noteworthy cheeses from Valencia include Alicante, a small, round goat's milk cheese; La Nucía, made from goat's or sheep's milk, or a combination, and named for a small seaside town; Servilleta (from Spanish for "napkin"), which is also made from goat's or sheep's milk, or a blend, and is traditionally molded in cloth; and the mixed-milk Tronchón from northern Valencia, which is produced in neighboring Teruel, in Aragón, as well. In Murcia, two well-known goat's milk cheeses are made, the pure white fresh Queso de Murcia and the aged Queso de Murcia curado, which is washed with red wine from Jumilla or Yecla during the ripening process, yielding a purplish red rind.

Half a dozen areas—Yecla, Jumilla, and Bullas in Murcia, and Valencia, Alicante, and Utiel-Requena in Valencia—make up the main wine-producing regions of the Levante, and for the most part, the same grapes are grown throughout, with white wines made primarily from Macabeo, Merseguera, Malvasía, Airén, and Pedro Ximénez, and red wines from Monastrell, Garnacha Tinta, Tempranillo, Merlot, and Syrah. Though neither Murcia nor Valencia has a history of producing more than ordinary wine, in recent years, money and time have been invested in the local industry with some positive results. Two of the most notable developments are the red wines of Jumilla built on the Monastrell grape and some fine fruity rosés from Utiel-Requena.

Cork oak tree, stripped

CHAPTER 2

The Spanish Kitchen

DON'T GET DISCOURAGED thinking that you will need many hard-to-find ingredients or special equipment to cook good Spanish food. Most of the recipes in this book require only common pots and pans and everyday staples already in your pantry. Even when a specialty ingredient is called for, there is usually an acceptable substitute. I have often found myself cooking in a remote place where I could not find a specific ingredient or the ideal kitchen tool. That the food still turned out well is less a testament to my resourcefulness than it is to the remarkable durability of these recipes, most of which evolved over centuries in which home cooks needed to put food on the table with the materials at hand. If I suggest you use a *cazuela* (terracotta casserole) and you don't have one, a cast-iron skillet of similar size will do the job. When a recipe calls for Spanish rice, another short-grain rice, such as Arborio from Italy, is a fine substitute. Regular paprika can stand in for *pimentón*, prosciutto for *jamón serrano*.

In the typical Spanish kitchen, you would find the following specialty items, none of which is difficult to acquire in North America (see Sources).

ACEITE DE OLIVA (Olive Oil)

When Spain, then known as Hispania, was part of the Roman Empire, it was its main supplier of olive oil, shipping the oil in amphorae to the most distant outposts of the realm. But Spain's production was not just a question of volume. In his early-first-century cookbook, *De re coquinaria*, the wealthy and extravagant Roman merchant and gastronomist Apicius called specifically for Spanish olive oil in many of his recipes. Today, Monte Testaccio, a hundred-foot-high hill composed entirely of broken Spanish amphorae, stands on the shore of Rome's Tiber River, evidence of that long-ago popularity.

Nowadays, just as it was two millennia ago, Spain's olive oil industry is an important player in the international market, turning out fully one-fourth of the world's total production. To ensure the quality of Spanish oil, regulatory councils, or Denominaciones de Origen (DOs), within each producing region watch over its manufacture, affixing a DO label only if the oil meets the strict standards of the council.

The terminology used to distinguish the qualities of olive oil can be confusing to the uninitiated. The term *aceite de oliva* generically refers to the oil or juice obtained from olives. In the language of the trade, however, olive oil is divided into Aceite de Oliva Virgen (virgin olive oil, or oil that has not undergone any treatment other than washing, decanting, centrifuging, and filtering) and Aceite de Oliva (oil made from a blend of virgin and refined olive oils).

According to the European Union regulations of November 2003, virgin olive oils are further subdivided

Apron and garlic hanging on the author's kitchen door outside Ronda, Andalusia

into two categories: *extra virgen* (extra virgin olive oil), which has an acidity of less than 0.8 percent, and *virgen* (virgin olive oil), which has an acidity of less than 2 percent. The acidity is determined by measuring the percentage of free fatty acids, which are created when the molecular structure of the oil has degraded. When an olive oil is categorized as *extra*, it means that the oil must contain less than 0.8 gram of free fatty acids per 100 grams of olive oil.

Picking olives at their peak of ripeness and pressing them as soon as possible assures the lowest level of acidity, but does not necessarily yield a premium oil. For that reason, virgin olive oils are also judged on their organoleptic characteristics, that is, on whether they have excellent taste and aroma. To minimize subjectivity in the tasting process, *catadores*, or professional testers, follow an official method called a panel test, which is determined and controlled by the regulatory councils of each Denominación de Origen.

One can easily find parallels to wine tasting among the official terms employed to classify olive oils. *Frutado* describes the aroma of oil, which largely depends on the olive variety used. Each variety has its characteristic *frutado*, with notes reminiscent of almonds, apples, citrus, figs, tomatoes, or even freshly cut green grass. In taste, olive oils range from very subtle and sweet to lightly piquant with a slightly bitter aftertaste. Just as with grapes, many factors, including the soil, the climate, and the ripeness of the fruit at harvest, affect the aroma and flavor of the oil.

Directly below Aceite de Oliva Virgen is what the trade calls Aceite de Oliva, which is made from a blend of *extra virgen* or *virgen* and refined *lampante* olive oils. Because they have an acidity level of higher than 2 percent and/or defects in aroma and taste, *lampante* oils must be treated with chemicals, heat, or other means to eliminate the offending characteristics. The refined oil is odorless and tasteless, and so, before it is sold, it must be blended with *extra virgen* or *virgen* oil to create Aceite de Oliva. The amount of virgin oil added can range from 15 to 40 percent, depending on the criteria of the producer. The more virgin oil added to the blend, the more taste and aroma it will have.

In addition to the distinctions between *extra virgen*, *virgen*, and regular olive oil, there are also many single-varietal oils to choose from, all of which have different characteristics. They can appear either as *extra virgen* or *virgen* oils, depending on their acidity, though most bottles sold in the United States will be *extra virgen*. You can select a specific varietal oil according to how you will be using it. Just as oysters go beautifully with Champagne, and oxtails with a full-bodied red, a gazpacho is complemented by a Hojiblanca oil, and fried fish marries well with a Picual. Following are short descriptions of five of the main Spanish single-varietal oils and their characteristics.

The Spanish olive oils with the strongest personality come from the pointy Picual olive, which is named for its shape. These Andalusian olives produce some of the most stable olive oils in the world because of their high oleic acid content and polyphenol count, properties that make them ideal for high-heat cooking. Picual oils made from olives grown in the mountains are slightly sweeter, with a fresh pleasant flavor, while those pressed from olives cultivated in the plains tend to have more body, with fig and fresh wood undertones. These oils are primarily used for deep-frying, popular in southern Spain, and are also suitable for use in salads and gazpachos. They are rich in antioxidants as well.

Cornicabra oils from central Spain are fruity, with undertones of avocado, almonds, and apples. Their initial sweetness on the tongue is perfectly balanced by a slightly bitter and pungent aftertaste in the throat. They are delicious in cooked dishes, such as salt cod recipes, *escabeches* (marinated foods), and meat and fish stews, as they are in salads. Their stable molecular structure makes them well suited for frying, too.

Empeltre oils from Aragón and Arbequina oils from Catalonia tend to be sweeter, which doesn't mean sugary, but simply lacking the pungent character of other varieties. Both have a subtle almond aftertaste. Taken together, these characteristics make them suitable for use in mayonnaise sauces, for seasoning salads, for scrambling or frying eggs, for preparing delicate white fish such as hake, or even for frying pastries. Because of its molecular structure, Arbequina in particular is more delicate than other varieties and thus more prone to oxidize, so store it away from light in a cool spot.

Although delicate, Hojiblanca oils from Andalusia have a range of flavors, from an initial sweetness with aromatic undertones of freshly cut green grass to slightly pungent and peppery notes with hints of fresh apples and almonds. Because these oils are highly aromatic, they are wonderful additions to grilled meats and fish. Simply drizzle a little oil directly from the bottle on top just before serving. Hojiblanca oils are also perfect to use in gazpachos, salads, soups, purées, and even dough. One of the less stable varieties, this oil is not suitable for frying and should be stored in a cool, dark cupboard to preserve its fruity character and prevent or delay oxidation.

:: :: ::

I recommend *extra virgen* or *virgen* oils for drizzling on cooked foods or salads. They are higher priced but their superior aroma and taste are appreciated when they are used raw. Regular Aceite de Oliva is well suited to frying and other cooking applications. Incidentally, the term *light* or *lite* found on olive oil bottles in U.S. supermarkets is by no means an indication of the oil's quality or fat content. Instead, the labeling indicates that the oil contains only 5 percent virgin olive oil or less; the other 95 percent is odorless, tasteless refined oil. Simply put, it is an attempt to mislead the shopper into thinking that he or she is choosing a low-fat oil over the "regular" alternative.

When frying at high temperatures (between 280° and 360°F), olive oil produces a golden crust on a food's surface, preventing the food from absorbing too much fat. Frying should never be done at low temperatures, because the food will absorb too much oil, rendering it greasy. Because olive oil expands when heated, be sure to use deep, wide, high-sided pots for frying. Foods should be added gradually to avoid cooling the oil suddenly, and the pan should never be crowded, or the temperature of the oil will drop below optimal level. Also, between batches, always allow the oil to return to the original temperature before adding more food. When used to fry potatoes, croquettes, or bread, the oil can be reused up to four or five times. Let cool and then strain after each use. The high oleic acid and polyphenol content that makes olive oil thermally stable also gives it a significantly longer shelf life than most other oils. In discussing the specific varietal oils, I have advised you to store the more delicate ones away from the light and in a cool place, a sound rule for all olive oils.

VINAGRE (Vinegar)

Although the word *vinegar* is derived from the Latin *vinum acre*, or "sour wine," vinegar making is not restricted to a grape base, as store shelves lined with bottles of malt vinegar, rice vinegar, cider vinegar, and the like illustrate. But Spanish cooks primarily use only wine vinegars, probably because of our country's huge wine industry. We add them to salads and cold soups, such as the Andalusian gazpacho, use them for preserving raw foods, and they are an indispensable ingredient in the *escabeche* dishes (page 73) typical of Castile.

Spain's most distinctive and noteworthy vinegar—and my favorite—is Vinagre de Jerez, or sherry vinegar. For a long time, sherry vinegars were a well-kept secret among winemakers in the Jerez region. According to wine expert and food writer Paz Ivison, who was born and raised in Jerez, local winemakers didn't like to acknowledge that any of their barrels "had gone," or spoiled into vinegar, so consumption was restricted to family and close friends.

Fortunately, thanks in part to the establishment of its own Denominación de Origen in 1933, sherry vinegar is highly valued and enjoyed in Spain and abroad.

According to the DO regulations, Vinagre de Jerez must be aged in oak or chestnut casks for at least six months, and Vinagre de Jerez Reserva for a minimum of two years. Quality varies depending on the aging method and the wine used as the base. Aging can be static—that is, the vinegar is aged in the same barrel from beginning to end—or the *solera* method can be used, in which small quantities of young vinegar are periodically added to barrels that contain aged vinegar.

Intensely aromatic and complex, sherry vinegars are darker, stronger, and thicker than red wine vinegars. Pungently sweet and wood-scented notes are characteristic, and the taste is joyful, or *alegre*, as we say in Spanish. They produce outstanding vinaigrettes when combined with extra virgin olive oil, and add a distinctive flavor to gazpachos and sauces.

JAMONES DE ESPAÑA
(Spanish Cured Hams)

Good proof that *jamón* is a staple of the Spanish kitchen is the sheer number and variety of *jamoneros*—the special devices made to hold an entire ham for easy slicing—found in bars and in many households across the country. Two main categories of Spanish ham exist, *jamón serrano* (ham from the sierra, or mountains) and *jamón ibérico* (ham from the *ibérico* pig). The names are somewhat misleading, however, since all hams were originally cured by cool, dry mountain breezes and known generically as *jamón serrano*. Today, the differences lie primarily in the breed, the diet, and the curing times. Both varieties are extraordinary.

Jamón Serrano

Jamón serrano is made from white-coated pigs. Different breeds are used depending on the region, although Duroc-Jersey, Landrace, and Large White are preferred. Jamón de Teruel in Aragón and Jamón de Trevélez in Granada are perhaps the best known of these hams,

although most regions in Spain also produce excellent hams. The dark red, firm meat is marbled with whitish fat, and it ranges from sweet to slightly salty. It tastes best when sliced thin, and no part of the ham is wasted: the tougher ends are often diced and used for cooking, and the bones go into soups and stews.

The pigs are fed generous amounts of grain, and after slaughtering, their hams and shoulders are kept covered with coarse salt for an average of fourteen days. The salt is rinsed off with lukewarm water, and then the hams and shoulders are hung and air cured for at least eight months and up to twenty months or longer, depending on different grades in quality. Artisanal hams are cured in cool, naturally ventilated *secaderos*, or drying warehouses. But because of high demand, most hams are cured in large industrial sites where the humidity and temperature are electronically controlled. Hams typically lose about 30 percent of their weight in the curing process, so the average ham weighs about fourteen pounds when it is sold.

The *jamón serrano* available in the United States comes from pigs slaughtered in Denmark or Holland, where several slaughterhouses have been approved by the United States Department of Agriculture (USDA). The hams are then transported in refrigerated trucks to Spain for curing. Numerous stores in North America sell *jamón serrano*, and there are many online vendors. If necessary, other dry-cured ham, such as prosciutto, can be substituted in recipes calling for *jamón serrano*.

Jamón Ibérico

For the time being, it is necessary to travel to Spain to taste this phenomenal contribution to the culinary world. Widely acclaimed by foreigners and worshipped by Spaniards, *jamón ibérico* has no paragon. It is produced from the black-coated *ibérico* pig, also commonly called *cerdo negro* (black pig) or *pata negra* (black foot), though the latter is not quite accurate since not all *ibérico* pigs are black hoofed and some non-*ibérico* pigs are. According to the Denominación de Origen, *jamones ibérico* can be made from crossbred pigs, but in order to qualify, the

Hanging cured hams

hybrids must be at least 75 percent *ibérico* and the balance must be Duroc-Jersey.

A semidomesticated breed that over time has adjusted beautifully to Spain's south and southwest, the *ibérico* pig lives in the *dehesas* of the provinces of Ciudad Real, Toledo, Cáceres, Badajoz, Sevilla, Huelva, and Córdoba. These vast grazing meadows and woodlands of oak and cork, the perfect habitat for the celebrated pigs, are usually fenced. During most of the year, the pigs feed on grass, herbs, olives, and roots, but during the *montañera*, the final fattening period in the fall months prior to slaughter, their diet is strictly controlled. The quality grades of the hams directly reflect what pigs eat during the *montanera*: *bellota* (first class) hams are from pigs fed only on acorns, *recebo* (second class) hams are from pigs given a diet that combines acorns and grain, and *pienso* (third class) hams are from pigs that consume only grain. *Bellota* hams are unsurpassable; their meat is dark red and very aromatic, with an intensely nutty flavor and velvety, nonfibrous texture. It is finely marbled with a fat that is both delicious and beneficial to your health. Thanks to the pig's acorn diet, a majority of its fat, similar to olive oil, is oleic acid, which reduces bad cholesterol (low-density lipoproteins, or LDLs) and enhances the production of good cholesterol (high-density lipoproteins, or HDLs).

The fattened pigs are slaughtered in winter. They usually weigh almost four hundred pounds, and the resulting hams will weigh anywhere from twelve to twenty pounds, with the shoulders a little less. As with *jamón serrano*, the hams and shoulders from the pigs are completely drained of blood and then covered with coarse salt for about two weeks. After washing off the salt with lukewarm water, the hams and shoulders are dried and stored in cool rooms for four to six weeks. They are then hung in *bodegas* (cool cellars) for curing, which will take, depending on the weight, a minimum of nine months for hams and five months for shoulders. Good *jamón ibérico* is cured for as long as two and a half years. Toward the end of the estimated maturation time, a tester inserts a pencil-like object made of bone into the ham to check the quality—almost like checking a cake for doneness. Depending on

the aroma, the hams will be released or left a little longer for further curing. Like the *jamón serrano*, the *jamón ibérico* loses about 30 percent of its initial weight in curing.

The national demand for *jamón ibérico* is so large and the production is so limited—it accounts for only about 5 percent of Spain's cured ham production—that its high price is understandable. This is also probably the reason why the majority of the *jamón ibérico* producers are not interested in trying to file a request with the USDA to approve their slaughterhouses so they can export to the United States. The ham alone is worth a trip to Spain.

CHORIZO

Chorizo is unquestionably the national sausage of Spain. Usually made with pork, it is prepared in a variety of ways and comes in many shapes and sizes. Because the quality of the meats used determines the quality of the final product, chorizos made with meat from the *ibérico* pig, especially those raised in Extremadura and Salamanca, are prized as both cold cuts and for cooking. La Rioja is also known for its excellent, slightly spicy chorizo, which is an essential ingredient in *patatas a la riojana* (stewed potatoes with chorizo). Smoked chorizos from Asturias, used in *fabadas* and other bean stews, have a delicious, mildly spicy taste with a smoky finish. Venison chorizos from the mountains, particularly the Pyrenees, are increasingly popular and have a pleasant gamy flavor.

Depending on the type of chorizo, the meat is usually chopped and mixed with larger or smaller quantities of fat; seasoned with salt, garlic, *pimentón*, and herbs; and then stuffed into casings. *Pimentón* is typical, although sometimes crushed *choricero* peppers, named for the important role they play in the making of chorizo, are used in its place. To make spicy chorizo, crushed *guindillas seca* (small dried hot chiles) are added to the mix. Once the mixture is in the casings, the ends of each casing are tied to form a long single sausage, or they are tied and the filled casing is twisted to form a chain of three- to four-inch links.

Fresh chorizos are preserved in lard or olive oil and are used mainly for cooking. Air-cured chorizos are usually consumed as cold cuts on sandwiches or as tapas. Before

CHORIZOS Y MORCILLAS
DE "NAXEDA"
ESPECIALES DE LA CASA

hanging the chorizos to dry, some producers, mainly in northern Spain, briefly smoke the sausages. Curing times depend on the thickness of the sausages and on the desired texture. The longer they are cured, the firmer their final texture will be.

Few Spanish chorizos are exported to North America, but several North American companies produce Spanish-style chorizos (see Sources). Although these products are made from leaner meats and are therefore not as flavorful, they are a good approximation. Mexican chorizos, however, are not good substitutes. Unlike Spanish chorizos, these are often fresh, rather than cured, and very spicy, and usually they must be turned out of their casings before they are cooked.

MORCILLA (Blood Sausage)

The varieties of *morcillla* are both regionally defined and nearly countless, although pork blood, lard, and condiments are always part of the mix. Some versions include rice and onion, as in the famous *morcilla* of Burgos; others

Various sausages, including morcilla *(blood sausage) and* chorizo, *in Gijón, Asturias*

add *pimentón* and black pepper for spiciness, as in the recipes of Navarra and La Rioja; and still others are laced with almonds, pine nuts, and raisins, like those of Catalonia and Valencia. Some *morcillas* are creamier, while others are firmer; some are smoked, like the sausages of Asturias that are indispensable to the famed *fabada asturiana*, and others are dry cured.

Spain's customary slaughtering season is during the coldest months of the year, which is also the traditional—and many would say still the best—time to buy artisanal fresh *morcillas*. Smoking and other curing methods, along with modern storage techniques, extend the shelf life of many other handcrafted blood sausages. Commercial brands, in contrast, are available year-round. Butcher shops and delicatessens in North America specializing in Spanish foods typically carry house-made *morcillas*, or they can be purchased online (see Sources).

BACALAO (Salt Cod)

Every region in Spain boasts local specialties made with *bacalao* (salt cod), but Basque cooks are the true masters. It may seem curious that the Basques developed a passion for preserved fish, given their proximity to the sea. But Basque fishermen were great seafarers—whalers originally—and they preserved their catch to make the long journey home. Soon after discovering the rich cod fishing grounds off the shores of Newfoundland, they determined that the cod's lean meat was more suitable for salting and drying than whale meat was, and that cod tasted even better after it was cured and desalted than it did when it was fresh. Salt cod subsequently became a favorite staple back home, particularly inland, since it was the safest option for overland transport before the advent of refrigeration.

Salt cod is an acquired taste, but once you develop a fondness for it, you may find it difficult to go back to fresh cod. Its light saltiness and firm texture may at first be a surprise to the palate, but, if properly prepared, it almost always seduces in the end. Some Spaniards—me among them—love it so much that they even go so far as to buy fresh cod to cure, only to rehydrate it immediately for use in their favorite salt cod dishes. (The term *bacalao* refers to salt cod in general, while *bacalao fresco* refers to the fresh fish.)

When I don't salt my own cod, I usually buy the entire flat, triangular piece known as a *bacalada*. With few exceptions, good salt cod is difficult to find in North America. Even in Canada, an important participant in the international salt cod trade, good salt cod is rarely stocked in retail stores. It is worth the extra effort to try to locate it, however. In the United States, salt cod is usually sold by Portuguese vendors, although Italian and Greek shops often carry it as well. (You can also purchase it online; see Sources.) Sometimes the entire *bacalada* is available, but more often it is sold already cut into small pieces (or sometimes even shredded) without the skin. If possible, purchase cod with the skin on, as the gelatin plays a critical role in some preparations, such as *bacalao al pil-pil*, in which it helps to emulsify the sauce.

I use different parts of the *bacalada* to cook different

dishes. The meat is thickest, up to two inches or more, at the point at which the backbone ran through the center of the piece. It becomes thinner toward the edges, and pieces from the tail and the outer rim are the thinnest. The thinner pieces can be used when you need to shred the cod for a recipe, such as croquettes. If you are using the fish for a cod salad that calls for pieces that will yield flakes that are as large as possible and are simply prepared (that is, not cooked with flour and milk or a similar preparation), the thicker parts are preferred.

The soaking times for desalting will vary with how thick the cod is. For example, the 2-inch-thick fillets necessary to create the big flakes for the salad will need to soak for thirty-six to forty-eight hours. On the other hand, if you are making *bacalao al pil-pil* (page 210), you should use fillets that are $1^1/_2$ inches thick. In this case, the fillets remain whole, and though you want them to be succulent, they should not be too thick. Pieces this size will need to soak for twenty-four to thirty-six hours. The thinner pieces, used for recipes calling for shredded cod, need to soak for only twenty-four hours.

Select a deep bowl for soaking the cod, so that it will be fully submerged in the water, and always soak it in the refrigerator. Soaking at room temperature is tricky: if the weather is warm, the water and salt will evaporate more quickly and the suggested soaking times will not be accurate. Also, if a room is very hot, as is often the case in central and southern Spain in the summertime, you risk spoilage. Once you have begun the soaking, change the water every six to eight hours.

When the cod has been soaked properly, the fillets will be considerably thicker and flexible. Taste a tiny piece toward the end of the prescribed soaking time to see whether the cod has soaked long enough. It is ready when it still tastes slightly salty. If it tastes too salty, soak it a little longer. Use the reconstituted cod right away, if possible, or store it for no longer than two days in the refrigerator. You can store unsoaked salt cod in a cool, dark place or in the refrigerator for up to several weeks—or even longer.

If you love salt cod as much as I do, consider salting your own fresh cod. The process, although somewhat time-consuming, gives you additional control over the level of saltiness. Buy a whole cod or just half. Ask your fishmonger to fillet it for you (this way you can avoid the nuisance of the central bone, which makes cutting the fillets more difficult) and to keep the skin intact. (Incidentally, the popular Spanish saying *cortar el bacalao*—"to cut the cod"—means to be in command or to be the boss.) Select a baking pan or dish large enough to hold the fillet, or the fillets side by side, and cover the bottom with coarse salt. Place the fillet or fillets on top—skin up or skin down makes no difference—and bury the cod with more coarse salt. The fish should be completely covered on all sides with salt. Place the cod, uncovered, in the refrigerator for forty-eight hours. Every twelve hours, carefully pour off any liquid that the fish has released, disturbing the cod as little as possible. The salt tends to dissolve when the liquid is poured off, so add more salt as needed to encase the fish.

When the cod is ready, lift it out of the salt and rinse it briefly under cold running water. At this point, you can store it for up to a week before desalting it and using it. You desalt it the same way you desalt commercially salted cod, including changing the water every six to eight hours. The only difference is that the soaking time will be shorter. A freshly cured fillet about $1^1/_2$ inches thick needs to soak for only twenty-four hours. Be careful not to soak it too long, or it will be bland. Again, test a small piece cut from an edge to judge the saltiness.

PIMIENTOS (Peppers)

Given that Spain was the first European country to receive peppers from the New World, it is not surprising that many varieties of the *Capsicum annuum* species are grown there and that peppers figure prominently in regional cuisines. Peppers intended for frying (*pimientos para freir*) are usually picked while still green, at a length of four inches or less, and are generally sweet and have very thin skins. The mild and delicious *pimiento de Guernica*, called *Gernikako piperrak* in Basque, a particularly popular frying pepper, is highly valued across Spain. The Gernika and others like it are also allowed to ripen, that is, turn red, and then they are dried in the sun, crushed, and used in the making of chorizos. Another favorite frying pepper is Galicia's *pimiento de Padrón*. It is only about two inches long and can sometimes be surprisingly hot. Part of the fun of eating *pimientos de Padrón* is that you never know who at the table will end up with tearing eyes. Grown throughout Spain, *pimientos para asar* (bell peppers), large peppers harvested both red and green, are used mostly for roasting or stewing.

Piquillos

Pimiento del Piquillo de Lodosa is one of Spain's most important contributions to the culinary world. Originally from Navarra and now carefully protected by its own DO, this extraordinary pepper is enjoyed across Spain and exported worldwide. When cooking at culinary events as far away as Australia or Argentina, I have always been able to find *piquillos* in local stores.

Piquillos are triangular, about three inches long, with an acute peak at the bottom. It is this distinctive peak, known as *pico* or *piquillo* in Spanish, that has given the peppers their name. Contrary to the misleading association with the word *picante*, which means "hot," these peppers, although sometimes mildly spicy, are not at all hot. *Piquillos* are harvested by hand, roasted in wood-burning ovens, which imparts an intense aroma, and then peeled by hand, exposing their bright red, shiny flesh. They are then slipped into jars or cans, always free of artificial preservatives or other chemicals. Outside Lodosa and the surrounding area, fresh *piquillos* are often difficult to find. Even locals buy them canned or jarred, primarily because the wood-burning ovens of the *piquillo* farms are far better than household ovens, and also for the convenience.

One reason for the popularity of *piquillos* is their versatility. They can be eaten straight from the jar, mixed with vinaigrette in salads, sautéed in olive oil and garlic as a side dish, stuffed with meat or fish, or made into a sauce. And regardless of how you prepare them, they are always wonderful. Fortunately, they are widely available in specialty-foods stores across North America.

Pimentón

Pimentón, a powder made from dried red peppers, is the famed paprika of Spain and is a staple in kitchens across the country. It comes in three basic types: *dulce* (literally "sweet," though a better description is mild), *agridulce* (bittersweet), and *picante* (hot). It is used to season everything from fried foods, soups, and stews to meats and fish. But perhaps its most important role is in Spanish charcuterie: about 75 percent of the *pimentón* produced is destined for sausage making.

Murcia is known for its *pimentón*, but the best is from the La Vera valley in Extremadura. Farmers there cultivate different peppers for each of the three types of *pimentón*: cherry-shaped peppers yield the orange-red mild powder, while long, slender dark red peppers are used for the bittersweet paprika. The hot paprika is the product of a variety of elongated peppers. These specially selected varieties, fertile soil, and excellent growing conditions all contribute to a fine product, but the real secret to La Vera *pimentón* comes later. In October, the area is full of activity: The peppers have ripened and are handpicked. Next to the fields are small, simple smokehouses, with concrete floors and wooden grids several feet above them. An oak

fire is laid on the concrete floor, and the peppers are spread on the grid above the fire. The smoldering fire—only smoke, never flames—is maintained for ten to fifteen days, filling the surrounding countryside with the scent of smoking peppers. This is why *pimentón* from Extremadura has a characteristic aroma and a rich, deep flavor that are not present in *pimentón* made from sun-dried peppers. The smoked-dried peppers are seeded and stemmed and then slowly ground between millstones.

Pimentón is increasingly available in specialty-foods markets in North America, and is also sold online (see Sources). While I recommend having all three types—sweet, bittersweet, and hot—on hand, you can get by with just the sweet variety, adding a pinch of hot red pepper flakes when a recipe calls for hot *pimentón*. Although common paprika can be used in place of *pimentón*, it is neither as complex nor as aromatic.

Choriceros and Ñoras

Various green peppers that grow in the Basque Country and in some neighboring areas are known as *choriceros*, from their original use as a seasoning for chorizos. Smaller than green bells or even what are known as Italian peppers in the United States, these flavorful peppers are typically the length of a finger and have a thin skin and pungent aroma. *Choriceros* from the area surrounding Gernika are considered the best. In the summer,

A spoonful of pimentón *from La Vera, Extremadura*

we pick them green and eat them fried, always leaving some behind on the plants to ripen to a deep red later in the season, at which point they are harvested and hung to dry in the sun, usually until November. The dried peppers are then soaked in hot water before they are added to soups, stews, or sauces.

Gernika has a traditional and popular farmers' market on Mondays. It is only minutes away from Mundaka, where I spent wonderful summer vacations with my family, and during those visits, we went to the market every week. It was there, as a young girl, that I met my friend Felisa Madariaga, who sold fantastic peppers. Today, she is still famous throughout the area for her peppers, and I never miss a chance to visit her stand.

Other regions have their own equivalents to the *choriceros* of the Basque Country, everyday peppers that are used in many dishes. *Ñoras*, from Murcia, are smaller, darker, and almost round—like a huge cherry with a flat bottom. They are typically dried in the sun and used whole in cooking or ground to make *pimentón*.

Choricero peppers are difficult to find in North America, though they are available through online specialty retailers, as are *ñoras* (see Sources). Ancho chiles are a good substitute.

ESPARRAGOS DE NAVARRA
(Asparagus from Navarra)

White and green asparagus are harvested in spring, and we enjoy them thoroughly throughout their short season. Fortunately, the canning industry acquires much of the production of white asparagus, making it available year-round. Labeled Esparragos de Navarra, canned white asparagus produced in Navarra's Ribera del Ebro region is one of Spain's most prized *conservas*.

The region is known for its excellent produce: the soil is rich, the plants are carefully selected, the water for irrigation is of good quality, and the nights are cold, all of which make for outstanding growing conditions. The famed asparagus are not a product of large plantations. They are instead grown by more than five thousand small farmers across the region. At the moment when the soil

around each plant starts to bulge and open a little, the asparagus are ready to be harvested. In the early morning hours, workers handpick the tender white stalks from under the earth. Because the stalks and tips have never been exposed to the sun, they remain white, instead of turning green. They are quickly taken to the canning plants, where they are first washed to remove all traces of soil, and then manually peeled and any fibrous parts are stripped away. Next, they are briefly blanched and then classified and sorted according to their size. The size depends on the age of the plant: the older the plant, the larger the stem size. (Plants remain for only seven to eight years, and are then replaced with new ones.) The tips of all spears, regardless of size, must be compact and tightly closed. Finally, the blanched and graded spears are slipped into jars or cans.

Canned white asparagus are deliciously tender and have a pleasing, subtle bitterness. Larger spears are preferred for salads or are served alone with a little vinaigrette or mayonnaise. Smaller spears make an ideal tapa when served with hard-boiled eggs or salmon, or they are sometimes added to mixed-vegetable dishes or soups or cooked in *salsa verde* to accompany hake or monkfish.

AZAFRÁN (Saffron)

Saffron, the stigmata of a small, purple crocus, is the most expensive spice on the planet and one of the most important culinary riches of Spain. It was taken to Spain by the Moors, during their westward push, and in the thirteenth century, Alfonso X of Castile wrote in his *Primera crónica general* that Spain was "joyful in saffron." Today, such countries as Iran, Greece, India, and Morocco all produce fine saffron, but many respected authorities consider Spanish saffron the finest because of its particularly high concentration of aromatic and flavoring oils.

The extraordinary price of saffron becomes understandable when you consider how labor-intensive its production is. Each plant contains only one flower with three stigmata. These valuable vibrant red stigmata on yellowish orange styles are handpicked and then meticulously dried before they are ready for consumption. You need some five thousand flowers to produce a single ounce of saffron threads.

The harvest takes place in the fall, when fields in La Mancha and Bajo Aragón, two of the country's major saffron areas, are covered with the flowers. It is a visual thrill to drive alongside these otherwise arid stretches during harvesttime, when they look like velvety lilac sheets for as far as the eye can see.

For fifteen to twenty days, toward the end of October and into the beginning of November, when the crocuses are in full bloom, the flowers, known as *las rosas del azafrán*, are handpicked at dawn and transported in baskets to nearby villages. There, women known as *roseras* pluck out the stigmata, which are then taken to facilities where any dust or floral waste is removed by hand and they are safely stored to dry.

Saffron is sold either as whole stigmata (or threads), or powdered. Both forms are excellent, but the flavor and aroma of the powder dissipates more quickly over time. To make sure you have purchased high-quality, authentic saffron threads, immerse a few in water or milk. It will take a little while for true saffron to tint the liquid, while imitation saffron, an imposter treated with artificial dye, will color the liquid immediately. (Be wary of inexpensive powdered saffron, as it is sometimes mixed with other ingredients to extend it.) Store saffron threads in an airtight container in a dry place away from light for up to two years. Powdered saffron should be used within six months.

Somewhat bitter tasting at first, saffron has an exotic and pungent aroma that vaguely recalls dried grass. Always use it sparingly in your cooking; too much can overpower other flavors and ruin a dish. Saffron is more popular in southern Spain than in the north, and it is used mainly in paellas and other rice dishes, fish soups, and meat and fish stews. Before adding saffron to most dishes, crush the threads in a mortar and then soak them in a little warm liquid. Just a pinch of saffron will be enough to season a paella for four people. A small box goes a long way and is worth its price!

ARROZ (Rice)

The three main rice-growing regions of Spain are located in the east, along the Mediterranean, and each has its own DO: Arroz del Delta del Ebro in the Catalan province of Tarragona; Arroz de Valencia in the Valencian provinces of Castellón, Valencia, and Alicante; and Arroz de Calasparra in the province of Murcia and neighboring Albacete, near the southern border of Castile. The preferred varieties, each of them yielding round, short or medium grains, are Bahía, Senia, Leda, Balilla, and Bomba. All are considered ideal for paella and other Spanish rice dishes because they absorb large quantities of liquid and the flavors of other ingredients.

Spain's *maestros arroceros*, or "rice masters," are highly discerning when selecting from among these varieties. They prefer Bomba for cooking paellas because the grain is harder and stays whole. They generally use the other varieties, although suitable for making paellas, for rice casseroles. Home cooks typically have a favorite rice for everyday cooking, using it for both their paellas and all their other rice dishes. They are seldom aware of the variety, reaching instead for the brand that they have grown to like.

Spanish rice, in particular the Bomba variety, is increasingly available in the United States and Canada. Italian Arborio rice and the Japanese short-grain rice used for sushi can be used in place of a Spanish rice. Never stir either of them during cooking, however, or you may break the grains, which will cause the finished dish to be sticky.

:: Equipment ::

Nearly every Spanish home kitchen is equipped with an array of *cazuelas* in different sizes, at least one medium-sized paella pan, and a mortar and pestle for grinding spices and other ingredients for sauces and *mojos*. You should have these, too, if you want to cook authentic Spanish dishes. Other everyday Spanish utensils, from blenders to food processors, knives to tongs, stew pots to saucepans, are essentially the same as those found in most North American kitchens. Simply put, you don't need a lot of specialized equipment to prepare a Spanish meal. That said, I recommend that you stock your kitchen with the following four pieces of equipment for ease in making the recipes in this book.

Cazuela

Cazuelas, lead-free, glazed earthenware casseroles, can be used both in the oven and on the stove top. In the past, these emblematic Spanish cooking vessels could not withstand the direct heat of a burner unless they were soaked in water for a full day before using, and even then a heat-diffuser was often advised. In contrast, the *cazuelas* manufactured nowadays work beautifully on the stove top even over high heat.

For cooking such dishes as *gambas al ajillo* (page 69), the ideal size is about 5 inches in diameter. Even if I am cooking for four, I prefer to use four small *cazuelas*, known as *cazuelitas*, rather than one large one, because they match the size of the burners, ensuring that the heat is evenly distributed. For moist rice dishes, such as *arros brut* (page 195) or *arroz de la huerta* (page 187), *cazuelas* measuring between 10 and 15 inches in diameter are ideal. When using these large *cazuelas* on the stove top, be sure to rotate them in a circular motion on the burner periodically to help distribute the heat evenly.

If you don't have a *cazuela*, a cast-iron skillet, a sauté pan, or another type of flameproof earthenware casserole, all of a similar size, can be used in its place. However, given their relatively modest cost, *cazuelas* are excellent investments if you are even modestly serious about cooking Spanish food. As a precaution, soak a newly purchased *cazuela* in cold water overnight before using it for the first time on the stove top, and always heat it gradually, even when cooking over high heat; abrupt changes in heat level can cause cracking.

Paella Pan

Stainless-steel paella pans are both beautiful and superior to regular steel paella pans. But considering that they also cost twice as much, I prefer steel pans. Always choose a pan according to the size of the paella you are making; a pan too large or too small for the amount of ingredients will result in uneven cooking. I recommend a 13-inch pan for a paella to serve four, a 15-inch pan for a paella to serve six, and an 18-inch pan for serving eight.

Food Mill

A food mill is indispensable for certain sauces. Though a blender or food processor are useful for many tasks, they tend to crush and beat food particles, which can alter color and consistency. In contrast, a food mill, which usually comes equipped with interchangeable plates with holes of different sizes, purées a sauce by gently passing it through the disk. It also neatly traps any seeds and peels in the mill, rather than whirring them into the sauce. You will be using the medium-holed plate for most of the recipes in this book. In a pinch, a medium-mesh sieve can be used, though the results will not be as good.

Mortar and Pestle

Mortars are typically made out of stone, marble, cast iron, or wood. I grew up in a kitchen with a marble mortar, but in recent years I have used mortars made of other materials with success. If you are new to working with a mortar, you will find that when you use it to grind garlic, dried peppers, almonds or other nuts, and saffron or other spices, you have better control over the final texture of the ingredients.

Pa amb tomaquet
i oli d'oliva amb:
Anxoves de 2,85
l'Escala
Truita Francesa 2,00
Queso Manchego 2,10
Atún 2,00
Jamón Serrano 2,40
Xoriço Ibéric 1,80
Llonganissa 1,80
Ibérica
Beicon 2,10

:: CHAPTER 3 ::

Tapas

TAPAS, MONTADITOS, PINCHOS (*pinxtos* in Basque), *banderillas, raciones, cazuelitas, pulguitas*—all are variations on the same theme: small servings of food eaten before a meal. While today Spaniards rarely have to explain the nature of tapas to visitors, the meaning that the term has taken on outside of Spain doesn't convey the full sense of the ritual that is such an important part of our daily existence.

Many cuisines offer foods meant to awaken the appetite. Variously called antipasti, hors d'oeuvres, or mezes, among countless other names, these dishes are typically eaten at restaurants or at home just before, or as part of, a meal—or in the case of trendy small-plates restaurants, as meals themselves. In Spain, however, eating tapas is a separate dining experience that, in principle, does not substitute for a meal. And Spaniards do not eat tapas at home. In fact, the term *tapas* and its various regional equivalents have come to imply the act of going out: *de tapeo* means barhopping, or the art of eating while standing.

Even small villages have clusters of bars with inviting counters full of finger foods and a sea of cured hams hanging from the ceiling. Happy patrons walk in, usually in groups, and, depending on the region, order a *zurito* (minibeer) or a fino sherry along with an array of tapas. Each bar has its specialty or specialties, and Spaniards are particular about what they eat where. After completing the first round of lively conversation and small plates, the group moves on to the next bar, often only footsteps away.

In the tapas bars of Andalusia, small *cazuelas* of sizzling garlic shrimp and platters of deep-fried little fish served with fino are familiar sights, while in the Basque Country, typical *pintxos* include sliced bread topped with baby eel salad and sautéed mushrooms skewered on toothpicks. Equally popular in every region is *tortilla española*, the potato and onion omelet that appears in a trio of guises: a *ración* (larger appetizer-sized portion), a *montadito* (a small slice of bread with a topping), or a *pulguita* (a tiny bread roll, usually no longer than three inches, split and filled). Platters of sliced *jamón ibérico*, commonly offered as *raciones*, are also beloved across Spain.

The recipes in this chapter are my favorite tapas, drawn from around the country. All of them, with the exception of clearly recognizable snacks like almonds and olives, yield larger portions than the typical tapa, and can be eaten as first courses.

::
53

LEFT: *Tapas of the day, Barcelona* PAGES 54–55, FROM LEFT TO RIGHT: *Typical Zaragoza bar with* toro *motif; a tapas bar in Sevilla; artisanal goat cheese in the small (two men, three hundred goats) Peña Remoña* quesería *in the Picos de Europa, Cantabria; a barrel of manzanilla sherry at La Gitana in Sanlúcar de Barrameda, Andalusia*

LA GITANA

TORTILLA ESPAÑOLA ::
Potato and Onion Omelet

As its name suggests, *tortilla española* is one of our national dishes, much like paella or gazpacho. There is no prescribed time of day to eat *tortilla*. Indeed, we are just as likely to have it as a snack along with a coffee in the morning as we are to have it as a tapa with a glass of wine in the evening. This ubiquitous dish is subject to variations, too: it can be cooked until the egg and potato mixture is just set and still very moist or until it is firm and dry, it can be made with or without onion, and it can be thick or thin. No matter how it is prepared, it is a favorite of nearly every Spaniard. In bars, it is usually served in bite-sized squares pierced with a toothpick or placed on top of small bread slices. Cut into wedges and served with a salad, *tortilla española* also makes a nice light lunch or dinner. :: **Serves 6**

1 cup olive oil

1 yellow onion, chopped

4 boiling potatoes, about 2 pounds total weight,
    cut crosswise into ¹/₂-inch-thick slices

Salt

4 eggs

In a 9-inch nonstick skillet, heat the olive oil over medium-high heat. (You need to use a skillet here, which has sloped sides, rather than a sauté pan, which has straight sides, so that you can easily slide the *tortilla* in and out of the pan.) Add the onion and sauté for about 5 minutes, or until lightly golden.

Add the potatoes and decrease the heat to medium. The hot oil should cover the potatoes and onion about halfway. Fry the potatoes, turning them every 5 minutes or so, for about 20 minutes total, or until they are fork-tender. Season with salt.

Increase the heat to high and cook the potatoes, turning them frequently with a slotted spoon, for 2 minutes longer, or until they are crisp and golden outside and soft inside. Using the slotted spoon, lift the potatoes and onion from the pan and drain on paper towels. Pour the oil in the pan into a heatproof container and reserve. Set the skillet aside.

In a large bowl, lightly beat the eggs until blended. Add the fried potatoes and onion and let rest for a few minutes to allow the eggs to permeate the potatoes.

Return the skillet to high heat and add 1 tablespoon of the reserved olive oil. When the oil is almost smoking, tilt the pan to distribute it evenly over the bottom and sides. Slide in the egg-potato mixture, moving the pan in a gentle circular motion to prevent it from sticking and burning, and cook for about 30 seconds. Decrease the heat to medium-low and cook, shaking the pan gently on the heat, for about 3 minutes longer, or until the eggs are set around the rim.

Invert a flat plate or lid slightly wider than the pan on top of the pan. (If it is your first *tortilla*, have someone play the drums!) With one hand firmly holding the pan handle, and the other on the plate or lid, lift the pan slightly and flip it over with a quick and determined move. Lift off the empty pan and place it back on the stove over high heat, and set the plate with the half-cooked *tortilla* on the counter.

Add another tablespoon of the reserved olive oil to the skillet. (Cover and save the remaining oil for making future *tortillas*.) When the oil is almost smoking, again tilt the pan to coat it evenly with the oil. Slide the *tortilla*, uncooked side down, back into the pan. Shake the pan gently to distribute the *tortilla* evenly, decrease the heat to medium-low, and cook for about 3 minutes, or until the eggs are set around the rim. (If you prefer a firm omelet, allow it to cook a minute or so longer.)

Slide the *tortilla* onto a plate to cool. You can serve it warm or at room temperature. Cut it into small squares and pierce each square with a toothpick if you are serving it as a tapa, or cut it into 6 wedges if you are serving it as an appetizer (or even as a light main course with salad).

TORTILLA SACROMONTE ::
Gypsy Omelet with Ham and Chorizo ::
(Andalusia)

Sacromonte is an area of Granada Province where many gypsies used to live. Today their presence is greatly reduced, but the region is still famous for its caves, which now harbor establishments that stage flamenco shows exclusively for the flood of tourists who visit here. This omelet, a popular classic from the region, combines full-flavored chorizo and ham with lamb brains and kidneys in a complex and memorable dish.

In the United States, these lamb variety meats are usually only readily available during the Easter season, when spring lamb is in the butcher shops, so you will need to order them in advance from your butcher. Although the ingredients differ from those used to make Potato and Onion Omelet (page 56), the method is basically the same. :: Serves 6

3 ounces lamb kidneys (about 3 lobes)

Salt

1 (3-ounce) lamb brain

5 tablespoons olive oil

1 small (2-ounce) chorizo, finely chopped

8 eggs

3 ounces jamón serrano or other dry-cured ham, finely chopped

2 preserved whole piquillo peppers, finely chopped, or 1 red bell pepper, roasted, peeled, seeded, and finely chopped

1/2 cup fresh or frozen shelled English peas, boiled until tender and drained

Halve the kidneys lengthwise, place in a bowl of lightly salted water, and let stand for 30 minutes. Drain and rinse under cold water. Chop finely and drain on paper towels.

Rinse the brain under cold water. Place in a small saucepan, add water to cover, and salt the water lightly. As soon as small bubbles appear, lift out the brain with a slotted spoon. Drain on paper towels and cut into small pieces.

In a 9-inch nonstick skillet, heat 3 tablespoons of the olive oil over medium-high heat. (You need to use a skillet here, which has sloped sides, rather than a sauté pan, which has straight sides, so that you can easily slide the *tortilla* in and out of the pan.) Add the kidneys and sauté, stirring several times, for 5 minutes, or until just cooked through. Using the slotted spoon, transfer the kidneys to a dish and set aside.

Heat the oil remaining in the skillet over medium-high heat. Add the brain and sauté for 2 to 3 minutes, or until just cooked through. Using the slotted spoon, transfer the brain to the dish holding the kidneys.

Heat the oil remaining in the skillet over high heat. Add the chorizo and sauté for 2 minutes, or until bright colored and lightly golden. Using the slotted spoon, transfer the chorizo to the dish with the kidneys and brain. Discard the oil remaining in the pan and set the pan aside.

In a large bowl, lightly beat the eggs. Add the sautéed kidneys, brain, and chorizo; *jamón serrano*; *piquillo* peppers; and peas and mix well. Season with salt.

Return the skillet to high heat and add 1 tablespoon of the remaining olive oil. When the oil is almost smoking, tilt the pan to distribute it evenly over the bottom and sides. Slide in the egg-kidney mixture, moving the pan in a gentle circular motion to prevent it from sticking and burning, and cook for about 30 seconds. Decrease the heat to medium-low and cook, shaking the pan gently on the heat, for about 3 minutes longer, or until the eggs are set around the rim.

Invert a flat plate or lid slightly wider than the pan on top of the pan. With one hand firmly holding the pan handle, and the other on the plate or lid, lift the pan and flip it over with a quick and determined move. Lift off the empty pan and place it back on the stove over high heat, and set the plate with the half-cooked *tortilla* on the counter.

Add the remaining 1 tablespoon olive oil to the skillet over high heat. When the oil is almost smoking, again tilt the pan to coat it evenly with the oil. Slide the *tortilla*, uncooked side down, back into the pan. Shake the pan gently to distribute the *tortilla* evenly, decrease the heat to medium-low, and cook for about 3 minutes, or until the eggs are set around the rim. (If you prefer a firm omelet, allow it to cook a minute or so longer.)

Slide the *tortilla* onto a plate to cool. You can serve it warm or at room temperature. Cut it into 20 small squares and pierce each square with a toothpick if you are serving it as a tapa, or cut it into 6 wedges if you are serving it as an appetizer (or even as a light main course with salad).

TORTILLITAS DE CAMARONES ▪▪
Crisp Shrimp Fritters ▪▪ (Andalusia)

I have eaten these crisp, delicious shrimp fritters only in Andalusia, where deep-frying reigns supreme. They are at their best when made with chickpea flour, but all-purpose flour is an acceptable substitute. Manolo, the owner of La Tirana Restaurant in Marbella, taught me how to make them. For the best results, fry only a few fritters at a time, so that the oil temperature doesn't drop. (A constant high temperature keeps the *tortillitas* from absorbing excess oil.) Even though the shrimp are minced, I recommend using small shrimp, which are more tender than large ones. And if you were shopping for the shrimp to make these fritters in Andalusia or in the Canary Islands, you would ask for *camarones*, just as you would in most of Central or South America, whereas everywhere else in Spain, you would ask for *gambas*. ▪▪ Serves 6

1/2 pound small shrimp, peeled

1 1/2 cups chickpea or all-purpose flour

1 tablespoon chopped fresh flat-leaf parsley

3 scallions, white part and a little of the tender
    green tops, finely chopped

1/2 teaspoon sweet pimentón or paprika

Salt

Olive oil for deep-frying

In a saucepan, combine the shrimp with water to cover and bring to a boil over high heat. As soon as the water starts to boil, quickly lift out the shrimp with a slotted spoon and set aside. Scoop out 1 cup of the cooking water and let cool. Discard the remaining water. When the shrimp are cool, cover and refrigerate until needed.

To make the batter, combine the flour, parsley, scallions, and *pimentón* in a bowl or a food processor. Add a pinch of salt and the cooled cooking water. Mix or process well until you obtain a texture slightly thicker than a pancake batter. Cover and refrigerate for 1 hour.

Remove the shrimp from the refrigerator and mince finely. The pieces should be the size of coffee grounds. Remove the batter from the refrigerator, add the shrimp, and mix well.

Pour the olive oil to a depth of about 1 inch into a heavy sauté pan and heat over high heat until it is almost smoking. Add 1 tablespoon of the batter to the oil for each fritter and, using the back of the spoon, immediately flatten the batter into a round about 3 1/2 inches in diameter. Do not crowd the pan. Fry, turning once, for about 1 minute on each side, or until the fritters are golden and very crisp with what Spanish cooks call *puntillas*, or lacelike formations, on the borders. Using a slotted spoon, lift out the fritters, holding them briefly over the pan to allow the excess oil to drain, and transfer to an ovenproof platter lined with paper towels to drain further. Keep the fritters warm in a low oven. Fry the rest of the batter in the same way, always making sure the oil is very hot before frying more fritters.

When all the fritters are fried, arrange them on a platter and serve immediately.

SOLDADITOS DE PAVÍA ::
Salt Cod Fritters :: (*Madrid*)

Some people believe these cod fritters earned their unusual name, "soldiers of Pavía," because the pale yellow batter recalled the color of the uniforms worn by the Spanish troops of Emperor Charles V, who defeated the French in the battle of Pavía, near Milan, in 1525. The Spanish soldiers were cheered on their return to Spain; perhaps this recipe was made in their honor.

In Madrid, where these fritters are particularly popular, they are made exclusively with salt cod, while in Sevilla, where they are also quite popular, they are called *la pavía* when they are made with hake, and *el pavía* when they are made with cod. Either fish makes a satisfying tapa. :: **Serves 6**

1 pound salt cod, desalted (page 46), or
    fresh hake fillet

Salt

Freshly ground black pepper

Juice of 1 lemon

6 tablespoons olive oil, plus extra for deep-frying

1 tablespoon sweet pimentón or paprika

1 teaspoon saffron threads

$1/2$ cup warm water

$1/2$ cup all-purpose flour

2 tablespoons active dry yeast

Discard any skin and bones from the fish and then cut the fish into strips $2^1/_2$ inches long by $1/_2$ inch wide. Season with salt and pepper. In a shallow bowl, whisk together the lemon juice, the 6 tablespoons olive oil, and the *pimentón*. Add the fish, turn to coat evenly, cover, and marinate in the refrigerator for 2 hours.

To make the batter, in a bowl, soften the saffron in the warm water. Add the flour, yeast, and a pinch of salt and mix well. Set aside for 30 minutes to allow the batter to rise.

Pour the olive oil to a depth of about 1 inch into a wide, deep, heavy pot and heat over high heat. When the oil is hot, working in batches, dip a few of the fish strips into the batter and slip them, one at a time, into the hot oil. Do not allow them to touch one another during frying. Fry, turning at least once, for 2 to 3 minutes, or until golden. Using a slotted spoon, lift out the fish strips, holding them briefly over the pot to allow the excess oil to drain, and transfer to an ovenproof platter lined with paper towels to drain further. Keep the fish warm in a low oven. Fry the rest of the fish strips in the same way, always making sure the oil is very hot before adding more fish.

When all the fish is fried, arrange on a platter and serve immediately.

CROQUETAS DE JAMÓN SERRANO
:: Jamón Serrano Croquettes

Croquetas are a common sight on bar counters and in homes across Spain, served as a tapa, a light lunch, or a dinner along with a salad. The *jamón serrano* in this recipe could be replaced with chopped hard-boiled eggs, shredded salt cod, minced shrimp, chopped chorizo, cheese, or just about any vegetable. Start the preparation the previous day to allow the béchamel time to set. It will make the mixture easier to handle when shaping the *croquetas*.

:: Serves 6

> 2 tablespoons olive oil, plus extra for deep-frying
>
> 4 tablespoons unsalted butter
>
> 3 heaping tablespoons all-purpose flour
>
> 1¹/₂ cups whole milk, heated
>
> 3 ounces jamón serrano or other dry-cured ham, finely chopped
>
> Salt
>
> 2 eggs
>
> 2 tablespoons fine dried bread crumbs

Lightly oil a shallow 8-inch square dish.

In a saucepan, heat the 2 tablespoons olive oil and the butter over medium heat. When the butter has melted, add the flour and, using a wooden spoon or whisk, mix well. Continue to stir or whisk for about 2 minutes, or until the flour is well blended.

Add ¹/₂ cup of the milk and increase the heat to medium-high. Bring the mixture to a boil and add the remaining 1 cup milk. Cook, stirring constantly with the spoon or whisk, for about 5 minutes, or until the mixture begins to thicken. Decrease the heat to medium and cook, stirring constantly to prevent lumps from forming, for about 10 minutes, or until thickened.

Add the *jamón serrano*, season lightly with salt (remember, the ham is already salty), and stir until evenly distributed. Cook for 1 minute longer and then pour the contents of the pan into the prepared dish. Spread the mixture evenly. Let cool down for a bit and then cover and refrigerate for at least 2 hours, but preferably overnight to allow the mixture to set.

Break the eggs into a bowl and beat lightly until blended. Spread the bread crumbs on a dinner plate. With 2 spoons, shape the béchamel-ham mixture into walnut-sized croquettes. Roll each croquette in the bread crumbs, shaking off any excess crumbs, and then dip into the beaten egg. Lift each croquette from the egg and roll it again in the bread crumbs, coating it evenly. Lay the croquettes in a single layer on a platter. Refrigerate for 30 minutes before frying.

Pour the olive oil to a depth of about 2 inches into a wide, deep, heavy pot and heat over high heat. When the oil is almost smoking, slip 5 or 6 croquettes into the oil, pressing on them gently with a slotted spoon to submerge them, and fry, turning them gently, for about 2 minutes, or until they are golden on all sides. Using the slotted spoon, lift out the croquettes, holding them briefly over the pot to allow the excess oil to drain, and transfer to an ovenproof platter lined with paper towels to drain further. Keep the croquettes warm in a low oven. Fry the rest of the croquettes in the same way, always making sure the oil is very hot before adding more croquettes.

When all the croquettes are fried, arrange on a platter and serve immediately.

PA AMB TOMÀQUET ::
Toasted Bread Rubbed with Tomato and Olive Oil :: (Catalonia)

You could have lengthy discussions with a Catalan about whether this signature tapa is similar to its cousin *pa amb oli* (right) from the Balearic Islands; whether garlic is to be rubbed on both sides of the bread, on just one side, or not at all; and whether to drizzle the bread with olive oil first and then with tomato, or the reverse. In my experience, Catalans prefer a white country-style bread, rather than the dark loaf typically used for *pa amb oli*, and they usually skip the garlic. The wonderful anchovies from L'Escala, a fishing village in northern Catalonia, are often used as a topping, but I prefer *jamón serrano*. Make sure your tomatoes are perfectly ripe. :: **Serves 6**

6 (3/4-inch-thick) slices white country-style bread
Extra virgin olive oil for drizzling
3 tomatoes, halved crosswise
Salt
6 thin slices jamón serrano or other dry-cured ham (optional)

Preheat the oven to 350°F.

Place the bread slices on a baking sheet and toast in the oven for 5 to 8 minutes, or until golden and crisp. Remove from the oven and immediately drizzle olive oil on both sides of each slice. Rub each slice on both sides with the cut side of a tomato half, pressing a little to squeeze some of the pulp and seeds onto the bread. Sprinkle the tomato with salt and top each bread slice with a slice of ham, if desired. Serve while the bread is still warm and crisp.

PA AMB OLI ::
Bread with Olive Oil :: (Balearic Islands)

Pa amb oli means "bread with oil" in Majorcan, and it is as commonly eaten in the Balearic Islands as *pa amb tomàquet* is in Catalonia. But while the Majorcans usually add the tomato to their bread and then the olive oil, most Catalans do the reverse. Both preparations can be served at breakfast, as a snack at any time, or as an accompaniment to lunch or dinner. As with *pa amb tomàquet,* this recipe can be embellished with a topping of *jamón serrano*, anchovies, or cheese. :: **Serves 6**

6 (3/4-inch-thick) slices dark rye bread
1 clove garlic, halved (optional)
3 tomatoes, halved crosswise
Extra virgin olive oil for drizzling
Salt

Preheat the oven to 350°F.

Place the bread slices on a baking sheet and toast in the oven for 5 to 8 minutes, or until golden and crisp. Remove from the oven and immediately rub 1 side of each slice with a cut side of the garlic, if desired. Then rub the same side of each slice with the cut side of a tomato half, pressing a little to squeeze some of the pulp and seeds onto the bread. Drizzle olive oil over the tomato and sprinkle with salt. Serve while the bread is still warm and crisp.

PANTUMACA :: Bread with Olive Oil, Tomato, and Jamón Serrano

The following recipe is my own adaptation of the Catalan and Balearic dishes *pa amb tomàquet* and *pa amb oli*. You might call it a shortcut—you can chop the tomatoes in a food processor, which is faster than rubbing a tomato half over each slice—but even Catalans I know have approved of it. I also modified the Catalan spelling of the dish, making it phonetic. For a tasty variation, mix the chopped ham with 1 tablespoon Mayonnaise (page 306) and spread it on the toasted bread. :: **Serves 6**

3 tomatoes, finely minced

1/2 clove garlic, finely minced

4 thin slices Jamón serrano or other dry-cured ham, finely chopped

Salt

2/3 cup extra virgin olive oil

12 (1/2-inch-thick) slices baguette

Preheat the oven to 350°F.

In a bowl, stir together the tomatoes, garlic, and ham. Season sparingly with salt. Add the olive oil and mix well.

Place the bread slices on a baking sheet and toast in the oven for 5 minutes, or until golden and crisp. Immediately spoon the tomato mixture on top of each bread slice, dividing it evenly. Serve while the bread is still warm and crisp.

PATATAS ALIOLI :: Boiled Potatoes with Alioli :: *(Catalonia)*

Patatas alioli is a classic tapa that can be found in many bars even outside Catalonia or the Balearic Islands, where *alioli* originated. The creamy garlic and oil sauce is easy to make and can be prepared in advance. To prevent the potatoes from absorbing too much water, wait to peel and cut them until after they are boiled. :: **Serves 6**

3 boiling potatoes, about 1 1/2 pounds total weight

1/2 cup Alioli (page 306)

1 1/2 teaspoons chopped fresh flat-leaf parsley

In a saucepan, combine the potatoes with water to cover and bring to a boil over medium-high heat. Decrease the heat to low and cook, uncovered, for 20 to 30 minutes, or until fork-tender. Drain and let cool.

Peel the cooled potatoes and cut them into small, irregular chunks about the size of chestnuts.

In a bowl, combine the potatoes and the *alioli*, folding gently until completely blended. Sprinkle with the parsley and serve at room temperature.

PATATAS BRAVAS ::
Fiery Potatoes :: (*Madrid*)

In the heart of Madrid near the Puerta del Sol, there are several bars named Las Bravas, all of which belong to the same owners. For decades, they have been known to make the best *bravas* sauce in all of Spain, and in my own sampling, I have yet to find a version that rivals it. Their most famous tapa is *patatas bravas*, but they also serve the spicy sauce with a number of other dishes, including octopus and shrimp. On my many visits to each of these bars, I have tried to convince the bartenders and cooks to share the recipe with me, but they guard the secret closely. When I found out that the owners had patented the sauce (number 357942), I knew I had to give up. This recipe is my best attempt at approximating it. If you are using paprika in place of the hot *pimentón*, add an extra pinch of hot red pepper flakes. I also love to serve these fried potatoes *(patatas fritas)* without the sauce as an accompaniment to meat or fish.

:: **Serves 6**

3 boiling potatoes, about 1^1/$_2$ pounds total weight

Olive oil for frying

Salt

1 teaspoon hot pimentón or paprika

^{1}/$_2$ teaspoon hot red pepper flakes

^{1}/$_2$ teaspoon Tabasco sauce

1 teaspoon red wine vinegar

^{1}/$_2$ cup Tomato Sauce (page 321)

In a saucepan, combine the potatoes with water to cover and bring to a boil over medium-high heat. Decrease the heat to low and cook, uncovered, for 20 to 30 minutes, or until fork-tender. Drain and let cool.

Peel the cooled potatoes and cut them into small, irregular chunks about the size of chestnuts.

Pour olive oil to a depth of 1^1/$_2$ inches into a wide, deep, heavy pot and place over high heat. When the oil is almost smoking, add the potatoes and fry for 1 to 2 minutes, or until golden. Using a slotted spoon or wire skimmer, lift out the potatoes, holding them briefly over the pot to allow the excess oil to drain, and transfer to an ovenproof platter lined with paper towels to drain further. Sprinkle with salt and keep the potatoes warm in a low oven. Pour the oil in the pot into a heatproof container and reserve.

In a small saucepan or skillet, heat 3 tablespoons of the reserved oil over low heat. Add the *pimentón*, red pepper flakes, Tabasco sauce, and vinegar and mix with a wooden spoon or spatula until well blended. Remove from the heat.

In a blender or food processor, combine the tomato sauce and the *pimentón* mixture and process (on medium speed if using a blender) for 1 or 2 minutes, until the sauce is pale orange.

In a bowl, mix together the potatoes and the sauce. Serve hot.

ACEITUNAS ALIÑADAS ::
Marinated Olives

Wherever olives are picked in Spain, most families have perfected their own special *aliño*, or marinade for them. Small farmers usually take their harvest to the mills of the olive-oil cooperatives, but they also keep some olives to marinate, which are served later during the year as table olives. I was lucky that Mari Rueda, who lives near me in Ronda, taught me her recipe. If you are fortunate enough to have access to raw olives, this is a wonderful way to preserve them. :: **Makes 2 pounds**

    2 pounds freshly picked olives
    6 cloves garlic, coarsely chopped
    1 red bell pepper, seeded and coarsely chopped
    1 cup red wine vinegar
    1 tablespoon dried oregano
    1 tablespoon salt

Place the olives on a large, sturdy cutting board and strike them firmly with a small hammer until their skins break. Place them in a deep bowl and cover them with cold water. Leave the bowl in a cool place for about 4 weeks, changing the water daily, to remove the natural bitterness of the fresh olives. Toward the end of 4 weeks, try one. If you don't taste any bitterness, the olives are ready to marinate.

Now you are ready to add a tasty note to the olives. Drain the olives and set aside. In a blender or food processor, combine the garlic and two-thirds of the bell pepper and process until a paste forms. Very finely chop the remaining one-third of the bell pepper; the pieces should be about the size of rice kernels.

In a bowl or widemouthed jar, combine the vinegar, oregano, salt, pepper paste, chopped pepper, and drained olives and mix well. Cover and let rest for 1 week in the refrigerator before serving. They will keep for months—until the next harvest.

ALMENDRAS FRITAS ::
Fried Almonds

Vino español, literally "Spanish wine," is the name given to a social event of considerable importance, such as a gathering to celebrate the publication of a new book, a ceremony commemorating the unveiling of a prominent statue or the opening of a new building, or an embassy party hosted by the ambassador to introduce someone new to the community. Typically such get-togethers are relatively brief (about an hour) and the beverages and foods served at them are simple: just the choice of white, red, or sherry wines accompanied by fried almonds and olives.

Subtly sweet and pleasantly crisp, *almendras fritas* are easy to prepare but hard to stop eating. They are a great addition to any party, formal or otherwise, and also are a wonderful light snack with a little wine before lunch or dinner. Spain's Marcona almonds, prized all over the world, are rounder, flatter, and richer than American-grown almonds. They are available in specialty-foods stores and by mail order and are sold blanched or fried and salted. Look for blanched almonds for this recipe. Toasting them before frying makes the almonds particularly crisp and tender. :: **Makes 1 cup**

    1 cup blanched Marcona almonds
    2 tablespoons olive oil
    1/2 teaspoon salt

Preheat the oven to 350°F.

Spread the almonds on a baking sheet in a single layer. Place in the oven and toast, stirring every 3 minutes, for 10 minutes, or until an even pale gold. Remove from the oven.

In a large skillet, heat the olive oil over medium heat. Add the almonds and sprinkle with the salt. Sauté, stirring constantly, for about 5 minutes, or until golden and crisp.

Remove from the heat and let rest in the pan until cool. Serve at room temperature.

BOQUERONES EN VINAGRE ::
Marinated Anchovies :: *(Madrid)*

Although *boquerones* are eaten all over Spain, they are most popular in the bars of Madrid. When I moved to Madrid from Bilbao in the 1980s, I noticed, particularly on Sundays before lunchtime, how many people ordered these marinated anchovies along with a beer or other beverage and a plate of homemade potato chips. An anchovy on a chip, I soon learned, is a great combination.

When it comes to anchovies, freshness is of extreme importance because smaller fish, particularly anchovies or sardines, keep fresh for a shorter time. Make sure that the fish are shiny, silvery, and slippery, rather than dull, and that they don't smell fishy. In Europe, anchovies are in season during the spring and summer. Some of the best fishmongers in the United States carry anchovies imported from Spain, Portugal, and Italy, where the fish are plentiful. I have sometimes even been able to buy them in the United States the day after they were caught. If you cannot secure these imports, fresh anchovies of different species (and sometimes genus) are caught off the Atlantic and Pacific coasts of the United States and can be prepared the same way.

A secret to making the anchovies pristinely white is to sprinkle them with hydrogen peroxide as they marinate in the vinegar. This is an uncommon ingredient, but the hydrogen peroxide widely available over the counter is in a weak solution (3 percent) that is safe to ingest in small quantities. (The hydrogen peroxide also degrades to water and oxygen as it whitens the fish, long before you eat it.) Start the preparations the previous day, since the fish needs to marinate overnight. :: **Serves 6**

Illustrated on page 75

1/2 pound fresh anchovies
1 cup white wine vinegar
1/4 teaspoon hydrogen peroxide (optional)
1/3 cup extra virgin olive oil
1 clove garlic, minced
1 tablespoon finely chopped fresh flat-leaf parsley
Salt

Rinse the anchovies under running cold water. Working with 1 fish at a time, and using your thumb, break the neck and remove and discard the head. Slide your index finger into the belly opening, pull out the viscera, and discard. Then, using your fingers, separate the 2 fillets. Carefully lift away the central bone, which will be attached to 1 fillet, and discard it. Rinse the anchovy fillets again and pat dry with paper towels. Repeat with the remaining fish.

Place the fillets in a shallow dish and cover them with the vinegar. If desired, sprinkle the hydrogen peroxide evenly over the anchovies to make them whiten more quickly. Cover and refrigerate for at least 6 hours or preferably overnight.

Lift the anchovy fillets from the vinegar. By now, they should look nearly white. Place them in a single layer on a plate and pour the olive oil evenly over the top. Sprinkle with the garlic and parsley and season with salt. The anchovies are best when eaten right away, but you can keep them for a day or two in the refrigerator.

Variation

I have seen an interesting *montadito* in different areas of Spain called *matrimonio*, or "marriage." To prepare one, top a thin baguette slice with 1 freshly marinated anchovy fillet and 1 anchovy fillet canned in oil, placing them side by side. The combination of flavors is superb—a perfect marriage.

BOQUERONES FRITOS :: Deep-Fried Fresh Anchovies :: (*Andalusia*)

Anchoas, boquerones, bocartes—all mean essentially the same thing: anchovies. *Anchoas* is the general term used in Spain for both canned and fresh anchovies. *Bocartes* is the distinctive, old-fashioned name by which fried anchovies are known in the north, specifically in the Basque Country and in neighboring Cantabria. In most of southern Spain and in Madrid, the term *boquerones* is used for both marinated and deep-fried anchovies.

The deep-fried anchovies of coastal Andalusia are best enjoyed in one of its delightful seaside bars, where the dish can be savored along with a glass of chilled dry sherry. Sanlúcar de Barrameda, a fishing village near Cádiz at the mouth of the Guadalquivir River on the Atlantic coast, is an ideal spot for such a pairing, as it is the home of Manzanilla sherry. I remember having unforgettable *boquerones* in Bajo de Guia, Sanlúcar's seaside promenade that is lined with terraced bars. While there, you can look over the mouth of the river into the Coto de Doñana National Park, famous for its flourishing bird populations, and watch the sun set behind Portuguese soil. :: **Serves 6**

¹/₂ pound fresh anchovies
Salt
¹/₂ cup all-purpose flour
Olive oil for deep-frying

Rinse the anchovies under running cold water. Working with 1 fish at a time, and using your thumb, break the neck and remove and discard the head. Slide your index finger into the belly opening, pull out the viscera, and discard. Then, using your fingers, separate the 2 fillets. Carefully lift away the central bone, which will be attached to 1 fillet, and discard it. Rinse the anchovy fillets again and pat dry with paper towels. Repeat with the remaining fish.

Place the anchovies in a colander and sprinkle them evenly with salt. Add the flour, again coating the fish evenly and shaking the colander to discard any excess flour.

Pour the olive oil to a depth of about 2 inches into a wide, deep, heavy pot and heat over high heat. When the oil begins to smoke, decrease the heat to medium-high. Working in batches, add the anchovies and fry for about 5 minutes, or until golden and crisp. Using a slotted spoon or wire skimmer, lift out the anchovies, holding them briefly over the pot to allow the excess oil to drain, and transfer to an ovenproof platter lined with paper towels to drain further. Keep the anchovies warm in a low oven. Fry the rest of the anchovies in the same way, always making sure the oil is very hot before adding more anchovies.

When all the anchovies are fried, arrange on a platter and serve immediately.

Small bait crabs in the isolated fishing village of Majanicho, Fuerteventura (Canary Islands)

BIENMESABE ::
Deep-Fried Marinated Fish :: (Andalusia)

This is a classic dish served in homes, restaurants, and taverns across Andalusia. In the province of Cádiz, it is called *bienmesabe*, meaning "it tastes good to me," whereas in the rest of Andalusia it is known as *pescado en adobo*. (Oddly enough, *bienmesabe* doubles as the name for an almond dessert from the Canary Islands and a different dessert from Antequera in Andalusia.) *Cazón*, or dogfish (a small shark with a rough skin, also called a tope shark), is typically used by local cooks, but monkfish is a more readily available—and quite delicious—substitute. The recipe also works beautifully with scrod, hake, or scallops. Chickpea flour creates a particularly crunchy coating. Start the preparations the previous day, since the fish needs to marinate for 24 hours. :: **Serves 6**

MARINADE

1 cup olive oil

2 cups red wine vinegar

2 cloves garlic, peeled but left whole

1 tablespoon sweet pimentón or paprika

1 teaspoon dried oregano

1 teaspoon salt

1 bay leaf

1 pound monkfish fillet, cut into 1-inch cubes

5 black peppercorns

1 cup fine dried bread crumbs

1 cup chickpea or all-purpose flour

Olive oil for deep-frying

To make the marinade, in a blender or food processor, combine the olive oil, vinegar, garlic, *pimentón*, oregano, salt, and bay leaf and process for 1 to 2 minutes, or until a reddish mixture forms.

Place the monkfish pieces in a nonreactive bowl and add the marinade and the peppercorns. Cover and refrigerate for 24 hours, turning the mixture periodically with a wooden spoon.

Sift the bread crumbs through a fine-mesh sieve over a shallow bowl, discarding all but what passes through the sieve. Add the flour and stir to mix well.

Remove the fish cubes from the marinade, pressing them with your fingers to remove the excess liquid, and pat dry. Reserve the marinade.

Add the fish cubes to the crumb mixture and toss until evenly coated. Place the coated fish in a colander or sieve and shake to remove any excess coating.

Pour the olive oil to a depth of about 2 inches into a wide, deep, heavy pot and heat over high heat. When the oil begins to smoke, decrease the heat to medium-high. Working in batches, add the fish chunks and fry for about 1 minute, or until golden and crisp. Using a slotted spoon, lift out the fish chunks, holding them briefly over the pot to allow the excess oil to drain, and transfer to an ovenproof platter lined with paper towels to drain further. Keep the fish warm in a low oven. Fry the rest of the fish chunks in the same way, always making sure the oil is very hot before adding more fish.

When all the fish chunks are fried, arrange on a platter and serve immediately.

GAMBAS A LA PLANCHA ::
Pan-Grilled Shrimp

Spaniards love to eat grilled shrimp at the counter of a good tapas bar while sipping a glass of chilled fino sherry or cold beer. The bars are often crowded, leaving little or no space for proper eating, and I find it fascinating to watch the locals skillfully manage to eat shrimp with one hand while holding a drink in the other. Look for medium-large whole shrimp and leave the heads on for cooking. Sucking the juices from the flavor-packed heads of the cooked shrimp is considered the best part. ::
Serves 6

1/3 cup olive oil

Juice of 1 lemon

2 teaspoons coarse salt

24 medium-large shrimp (about 1 pound) in the shell
    with heads intact

In a bowl, whisk together the olive oil, lemon juice, and salt until well blended. Dip the shrimp briefly into the mixture to coat lightly.

Heat a dry skillet over high heat. When the pan is very hot, working in batches, add the shrimp in a single layer without crowding. Sear for 1 minute. Decrease the heat to medium and continue cooking for 1 minute longer. Turn the shrimp, increase the heat to high, and sear for 2 more minutes, or until golden. Keep the shrimp warm on an ovenproof platter in a low oven. Cook the rest of the shrimp in the same way.

When all the shrimp are cooked, arrange on a platter and serve immediately.

GAMBAS AL AJILLO ::
Sizzling Garlic Shrimp :: (Andalusia)

Shrimp served sizzling in this spicy garlic-infused oil are irresistible. The recipe works best with medium or small shrimp (36 to 40 to a pound) because the high heat required tends to burn the outside of larger shrimp before the inside cooks through. I like to reserve the shells (and the heads, if they were intact) to prepare fish stock; you can freeze them and prepare stock when you need it, and the fish stock can be frozen as well.

The shrimp taste best when cooked in individual *cazuelas*, but if you don't have them, you can prepare the shrimp in a single large skillet. :: **Serves 4**

Illustrated on page 75

3/4 cup olive oil

2 cloves garlic, finely minced

2 teaspoons hot red pepper flakes

1 pound small or medium shrimp, peeled

1 teaspoon salt

Chopped fresh flat-leaf parsley for garnish

Place 4 small *cazuelas* (page 51), each about 5 inches in diameter, on the stove, add 3 tablespoons olive oil to each, and turn the heat to high. When the oil is hot, divide the garlic and red pepper flakes evenly among the *cazuelas* and cook, stirring, for 30 seconds. Divide the shrimp into 4 equal portions and add 1 portion to each *cazuela*. Cook over very high heat for 1 minute, season with the salt, again dividing evenly, and stir constantly while the shrimp begin to sizzle and turn pink. Cook for 1 more minute, or until nearly opaque throughout, and remove from the heat. The shrimp should be slightly undercooked, as they will continue to sizzle in the heat of the dish for up to 1 minute.

Sprinkle the shrimp with the parsley and serve sizzling.

GAMBAS CON GABARDINA ::
Battered Shrimp

"Coated" shrimp (literally "with a gabardine") are generally served in Spain at cocktail parties as finger food, which is the reason for leaving the shell segment on the tail, and they are also a mainstay of tapas bars around the country. I like to use medium-large shrimp for this recipe (20 to 24 to a pound). The smaller ones are more difficult to handle when applying the batter, and very large shrimp remain undercooked when the batter reaches the optimum golden color. :: **Serves 6**

1 pound medium-large shrimp in the shell
Salt
1/2 cup all-purpose flour
1/2 cup light beer
1 teaspoon saffron threads
Olive oil for deep-frying

If the shrimp have their heads intact, remove them. Peel away the shells, leaving the shell section at the tip of the tail intact. Season with salt and refrigerate until needed. Discard the shells and heads or slip them into the freezer for making stock.

Place the flour in a bowl. Add the beer a little at a time, stirring until you have a thick, creamy batter. Add the saffron threads, mix well, and let rest at room temperature for 30 minutes.

Pour the olive oil to a depth of 2 to 3 inches into a wide, deep, heavy pot and heat over high heat. When the oil begins to smoke, decrease the heat to medium-high. Working with 1 shrimp at a time, and holding it by its tail, dip the shrimp into the batter, allowing the excess to drip off, and slip it into the hot oil. Working in batches so that the shrimp don't touch one another, fry, turning at least once, for 2 to 3 minutes, or until golden. Using a slotted spoon, lift out the shrimp, holding them briefly over the pot to allow the excess oil to drain, and transfer to an ovenproof platter lined with paper towels to drain further. Keep the shrimp warm in a low oven. Fry the rest of the shrimp in the same way, always making sure the oil is very hot before frying more shrimp.

When all the shrimp are fried, arrange on a platter and serve immediately.

ALMEJAS EN SALSA VERDE ::
Clams in Salsa Verde :: *(Basque Country)*

Salsa verde, or "green sauce," is one of the most commonly used sauces in the Basque Country. The base is typically made from clam stock, and the cooked clams are incorporated into the final presentation, sometimes with the addition of fish such as hake, monkfish, or grouper, as in Hake Fillets with Clams in Salsa Verde (page 221). Serve with plenty of bread for sopping up the delicious sauce. :: **Serves 6**

24 Manila or small littleneck clams

1 tablespoon coarse sea salt

4 cups water

1/3 cup olive oil

2 cloves garlic, finely minced

1/2 teaspoon hot red pepper flakes (optional)

1 tablespoon all-purpose flour

1 1/2 teaspoons table salt

2 tablespoons chopped fresh flat-leaf parsley

1/2 cup dry white wine

Scrub the clams under cold running water, discarding any that fail to close to the touch. In a large bowl, combine the clams, coarse salt, and water to cover and let stand for at least 30 minutes or up to 2 hours so that the clams release any sand trapped in their shells. Drain.

In a large saucepan, combine the clams with the 4 cups water and bring to a boil over medium-high heat. Cover and cook for about 5 minutes, or until they open. As the clams cook, uncover the pan occasionally and stir them with a wooden spoon to encourage them all to open at about the same time. Drain the clams, reserving the cooking liquid. Discard any clams that have not opened.

In a large *cazuela* (page 51), heat the olive oil over high heat. Add the garlic and red pepper flakes, if using, and sauté, stirring, for 1 to 2 minutes, or until the garlic begins to turn golden. Sprinkle the flour over the garlic and stir with a wooden spoon until the mixture is well blended. Add 3 cups of the reserved cooking liquid and the table salt, parsley, and wine. Decrease the heat to medium and boil gently, stirring occasionally, for 5 minutes, or until the sauce thickens slightly. Add more cooking liquid if you prefer a thinner sauce.

Add the clams to the sauce, rotate the *cazuela* in a circular motion over the burner to mix all the ingredients, and boil gently for 2 minutes, or until the sauce looks whitish green and the clams are heated through.

Spoon the clams and sauce into *cazuelitas* or small bowls and serve immediately.

Grape vines protected by volcanic rock shelters in Lanzarote's La Geria valley (Canary Islands)

NAVAJAS A LA PLANCHA ::
Pan-Grilled Razor Clams :: *(Cantabria)*

When we were children, my brothers and I had great fun catching all manner of creatures from the sea. When the tide was out, we would take a package of salt to sprinkle into certain little holes in the hard sand just at the edge of the water. If we were lucky, a *navaja* (razor clam) would poke out from the sand and, with a quick grasp and joyful cheers, we would deposit the long, narrow mollusk into our bucket. Today, I content myself with seeking out these extraordinary shellfish in the market. They bring back memories and, simply prepared this way, they are wonderful. Razor clams are most abundant on the beaches of Cantabria, although they are found and treasured in many other areas of Spain as well. :: **Serves 6**

24 razor clams, about 2^1/$_2$ pounds

2 tablespoons coarse sea salt

^{1}/$_3$ cup extra virgin olive oil

Juice of 1 lemon

2 cloves garlic, minced

1 tablespoon chopped fresh flat-leaf parsley

Discard any clams that fail to close to the touch. Scrub the clams under cold running water. In a large bowl, combine the clams, coarse salt, and water to cover and let stand for at least 30 minutes or up to about 2 hours so that the clams release any sand trapped in their shells. Drain.

In a shallow dish, combine the olive oil and lemon juice and mix well. Heat a large skillet over high heat. Baste the clams with the olive oil mixture, and place 6 clams in a single layer on the hot pan. After about 2 minutes, turn the clams with kitchen tongs onto their opposite side and leave for 2 minutes longer, or until they open completely. Transfer the clams to a wide serving dish. Repeat with the remaining clams, working in batches of 6 clams until all have been opened. Discard any that fail to open.

Stir the garlic and parsley into the remaining olive oil mixture and sprinkle over the clams before serving. The clams taste best when served hot, but they are also good at room temperature.

MEJILLONES A LA MARINERA ::
Mussels in White Wine Sauce :: *(Galicia)*

This straightforward recipe for mussels in wine is a favorite among Galicians. Together with a glass of chilled Albariño wine, these mussels make a delightful midday snack at bar counters across the region. Common blue-black mussels are fine for this recipe, but if you can find the succulent green-lipped mussels from New Zealand, by all means use them. :: **Serves 6**

^{1}/$_4$ cup olive oil

1 yellow onion, finely chopped

1 clove garlic, finely chopped

2 tomatoes, halved crosswise, grated on the large holes of a handheld grater, and skins discarded

3 pounds mussels, scrubbed and debearded

1 cup dry white wine

Salt

2 tablespoons chopped fresh flat-leaf parsley

In a stockpot, heat the olive oil over medium heat. Add the onion and garlic and sauté for about 5 minutes, or until soft. Add the tomatoes and cook for 1 minute longer.

Discard any mussels that fail to close to the touch and add the mussels and wine to the stockpot. Increase the heat to high, cover, and cook for about 5 minutes, or until the mussels start to open. Decrease the heat to low, sprinkle with a little salt and the parsley, re-cover, and cook, shaking the pan occasionally to shift the mussels about, for 5 minutes longer, or until all the mussels open.

Discard any mussels that have not opened, transfer to a serving dish, and serve immediately.

:: Escabeche ::

Escabeches, or *escabechados*, are foods that are fried or steamed and then cooked or sometimes just stored in a mild brine. They can turn up as tapas or main courses and are served cold or at room temperature. For centuries before the arrival of refrigeration and canning, this technique was used for preserving foods. In his wonderful book *Catalan Cuisine*, Colman Andrews explains that the word *escabeche* comes from the Perso-Arabic *sikbāj*, or "vinegar stew," a reminder of one of many culinary traditions the Moors introduced to the Spanish.

Partridge, quail, pheasant, chicken, trout, sardines, tuna, and mussels are among the foods most commonly prepared *en escabeche*. The brines generally include vinegar; olive oil; and wine, stock, or water; or a combination. These liquids are often, but not always, added in equal parts. Because sherry vinegar is strong flavored, it is not commonly used. If you use it in place of the red wine or white wine vinegar in an *escabeche* recipe, add only half the amount called for and make up the difference with water, wine, or stock. The simplified chicken *en escabeche* recipe on page 241 is an exception to this rule.

To give you an idea of the typical ingredient proportions, here is an example of a basic *escabeches* that would be suitable for 1 chicken: Combine 1 cup red or white wine vinegar; 1 cup olive oil; $^1/_2$ cup dry white wine; $^1/_2$ cup water; 1 yellow onion, thinly sliced; 4 cloves garlic, halved; 10 black peppercorns; 1 teaspoon sweet *pimentón* or paprika; 2 bay leaves; 1 rosemary sprig; 1 teaspoon salt, and 1 teaspoon sugar. Cut the chicken into serving pieces, brown them in a skillet, add the marinade, and simmer over low heat for 30 minutes or so until cooked through.

If you are cooking small items, such as sardines, mussels, or bite-sized chunks of chicken, reduce the cooking time to 10 minutes. If you are preparing large pieces, such a whole partridge, increase the cooking time to 1 to $1^1/_2$ hours. Let the food cool completely in the *escabeches* brine and then store in the brine at cool room temperature for a day or so or in the refrigerator for up to a week.

MEJILLONES EN ESCABECHE ::
Mussels in Vinegar and Wine ::
(Castilla–La Mancha)

En escabeche is a traditional method of preserving foods that was frequently used before refrigeration (see box). Castilla–La Mancha is known for its superb *escabeches*, of which this is just one good example. The mussels will keep in the refrigerator for up to a week. :: **Serves 6**

3 pounds mussels, scrubbed and debearded

$^1/_2$ cup dry white wine

2 cups olive oil

2 yellow onions, cut into thin rings

1 head garlic, halved crosswise

2 bay leaves

10 black peppercorns

1 tablespoon sweet pimentón or paprika

1 teaspoon salt

$^1/_2$ cup sherry vinegar

Discard any mussels that fail to close to the touch. In a stockpot, combine the mussels with water to cover and add the wine. Bring to a boil, decrease the heat to low, and cook, shaking the pot occasionally so that the mussels shift about, for about 10 minutes, or until the mussels open. Drain the mussels into a colander or large sieve. Discard any mussels that have not opened. Let cool.

Remove the mussels from their shells and discard the shells and any remaining beards. Set the mussels aside.

In a nonreactive deep sauté pan or wide saucepan, heat the olive oil over medium heat. Add the onions, garlic, bay leaves, and peppercorns and cook, stirring occasionally, for about 10 minutes, or until the onion is soft. Using a slotted spoon, discard the garlic. Add the *pimentón*, salt, and vinegar to the pan. Be careful, as the vinegar may make the oil spatter. Mix well and decrease the heat to low.

Add the mussels, mixing well, and simmer for about 5 minutes. Remove from the heat and allow the mussels to cool in the brine. Transfer to a bowl, cover, and refrigerate until cold.

Serve the mussels cold with toothpicks for spearing or on decorative spoons.

MEJILLONES DE LA TRAINA :: Mussels in Tomato Sauce :: (Cantabria)

La Traina is a restaurant and bar in Argoños, not far from the Cantabrian town of Laredo on the Bay of Biscay. Like many bars in the area—and throughout Spain—La Traina serves a number of tapas and other small dishes. But what makes the place stand out is that it has its own *vivero*, or nursery, of shellfish where beautiful lobsters, spider crabs, and *nécoras* (tasty, small regional crabs) are raised. When I visit the Viesca sisters, longtime friends in the village of Liendo, a quick drive to the nearby La Traina is a must to enjoy mussels with tomato sauce, a house specialty. :: **Serves 6**

3 pounds mussels, scrubbed and debearded
1/2 yellow onion, finely chopped
1/2 green bell pepper, seeded and finely chopped
1/2 red bell pepper, seeded and finely chopped
2 cups Tomato Sauce (page 311)
1/4 cup Sherry Vinaigrette (page 314)

Discard any mussels that fail to close to the touch. In a stockpot, combine the mussels with water to cover. Bring to a boil, decrease the heat to low, and cook, shaking the pot occasionally so that the mussels shift about, for about 10 minutes, or until the mussels open. Drain the mussels into a colander or large sieve. Discard any mussels that have not opened. Let cool.

Remove the mussels from their shells, placing the mussel meats in a bowl and discarding the shells along with any remaining beards.

Add the onion, green and red peppers, tomato sauce, and vinaigrette to the mussels and mix well. Cover and refrigerate until well chilled.

Spoon the mussels and sauce onto 6 small plates, dividing evenly. Spoon any sauce remaining in the bottom of the bowl evenly over the mussels and serve.

TIGRES :: Mussels in a Spicy Tomato Sauce :: (Basque Country)

In my hometown of Bilbao, these mussels are called *tigres* because of their fieriness. Spaniards aren't particularly fond of spicy-hot food, but the tomato sauce on these mussels is an exception. I fondly remember the crowded little bars in the old part of Bilbao, where orders of *tigres* would emerge by the dozens from the tiny kitchens. We devoured the mussels and everyone dropped the empty shells right onto the floor, where periodically they would be raked up. This tapa is not as popular today in the bars as it once was, but I like it so much that I make it whenever I find fresh mussels. :: **Serves 6**

3 pounds mussels, scrubbed and debearded
1 cup Tomato Sauce (page 311)
1 teaspoon hot red pepper flakes, or 1/2 teaspoon Tabasco sauce

Discard any mussels that fail to close to the touch. In a stockpot, combine the mussels with water to cover. Bring to a boil, decrease the heat to low, and cook, shaking the pot occasionally so that the mussels shift about, for about 10 minutes, or until the mussels open. Drain the mussels into a colander or large sieve. Discard any mussels that have not opened. Let cool.

Remove the mussels from their shells, discarding any remaining beards, and reserve half of the shells, discarding the balance. Place a mussel in each shell half and arrange on a platter.

In a small saucepan, heat the tomato sauce over medium heat until hot. Add the red pepper flakes and mix well. Spoon a little of the spicy sauce onto each mussel and serve hot or at room temperature.

Mussels in Tomato Sauce, Marinated Anchovies (page 66), and Sizzling Garlic Shrimp (page 69)

PULPO A FEIRA ::
Boiled Octopus :: *(Galicia)*

Though it originated in Galicia or the neighboring region of León, *pulpo a feira*, as it is known in Galician, or *pulpo a la gallega*, as it is called in Castilian, is now popular throughout Spain. It is usually served on wooden plates with *cachelos*, potatoes that have been boiled or roasted in embers with their skins on. Frozen octopus works particularly well, since the freezing tenderizes the otherwise quite tough meat, so that is what I suggest you use here. If you prefer to use a fresh octopus, you will need to practice the almost tribal tradition of beating the animal with a rock or meat mallet to rid it of its rubbery texture. The size of the most commonly available octopus is about three pounds; smaller ones, while more tender, are not suited to this preparation, since the tentacles would be too small when cut into rings. Another option is to freeze fresh octopus for about two weeks to tenderize it. :: **Serves 6**

4 quarts water

6 tablespoons coarse sea salt

1 frozen octopus, about 3 pounds, thawed overnight in the refrigerator

1 pound new potatoes, boiled with their skins on and kept warm

1 cup extra virgin olive oil

2 tablespoons hot pimentón or paprika plus a pinch of hot red pepper flakes

In a large stockpot, combine the water and 5 tablespoons of the salt and bring to a boil. While the water is heating, rinse the octopus under running cold water. Using sharp kitchen scissors, cut out the mouth and the eyes.

With a long fork, pierce the octopus to get a good grip and dip it into the boiling water. Lift it out immediately and, when the water returns to a boil, dip it briefly again. Repeat this dipping procedure 3 or 4 times, or until the tentacles have curled. (Dipping the octopus into boiling water helps to tenderize it.) Submerge the octopus in the water and let it boil over medium heat for about 2 hours, or until it is tender when pierced with a knife.

Turn off the heat and let the octopus rest in the hot water for 10 minutes. Lift the octopus from the water and cut it into pieces with the scissors: the tentacles into $1/2$-inch-thick rings and the body into small chunks. Divide the octopus pieces evenly among 6 plates.

Cut the potatoes crosswise in $1/2$-inch-thick slices and surround the octopus pieces with the potato slices. Drizzle the octopus and potatoes with the olive oil and sprinkle with the *pimentón* and the remaining 1 tablespoon salt. Serve the dish while the octopus and potatoes are still warm.

PULPITOS FRITOS ::
Pan-Seared Baby Octopus :: (*Andalusia*)

Spaniards have a weakness for minuscule fish of all kinds. Squid, cuttlefish, and octopus are plentiful in Mediterranean waters, and baby octopus, no larger than 1 1/2 inches, are extremely tender and tasty. In the United States, they are sometimes difficult to find, but I often have success in Italian and Asian markets. :: **Serves 6**

1 pound baby octopus

Salt

1/2 cup olive oil

3 tablespoons freshly squeezed lemon juice

1 small clove garlic, finely chopped

1 teaspoon chopped fresh flat-leaf parsley

Rinse the octopus under running cold water and pat dry. Sprinkle with salt.

To make a marinade, combine the olive oil, lemon juice, garlic, and parsley in a bowl and mix well. Slip the octopus into the marinade and turn several times. Let rest for 30 minutes.

Heat a dry skillet over high heat. When the skillet is very hot, add the octopus in a single layer and sear, stirring constantly, for 1 minute. Decrease the heat to medium and cook, turning with a slotted spoon, for about 5 minutes longer, or until browned on all sides. Serve immediately.

PULPO EN VINAGRETA ::
Octopus Salad :: (*Galicia*)

When I make Boiled Octopus (page 76), I usually boil two octopuses at the same time and keep one to make this fantastic salad. While I keep the suction cups of the octopus intact for *pulpo a feira*, for this dish I remove them to give the salad a "cleaner" appearance. :: **Serves 6**

4 quarts water

4 heaping tablespoons coarse sea salt

1 frozen octopus, about 3 pounds, thawed overnight in the refrigerator

1/2 cup Sherry Vinaigrette (page 314)

1 tomato, peeled, seeded, and cut into very small dice

1 green bell pepper, seeded and cut into very small dice

In a large stockpot, bring the water and salt to a boil. While the water is heating, rinse the octopus under cold running water. Using sharp kitchen scissors, cut out the mouth and the eyes.

With a long fork, pierce the octopus to get a good grip and dip it into the boiling water. Lift it out immediately and, when the water returns to a boil, dip it briefly again. Repeat this dipping procedure 3 or 4 times, or until the tentacles have curled. (Dipping the octopus into boiling water helps to tenderize it.) Submerge the octopus in the water and let it boil over medium heat for about 2 hours, or until it is tender when pierced with a knife.

Turn off the heat and let the octopus rest in the hot water for 10 minutes. Lift the octopus from the water and cut it into pieces with the scissors: the tentacles into 1/2-inch-thick rings, removing the suction cups if you dislike their appearance, and the body into small chunks.

In a large bowl, combine the octopus, vinaigrette, tomato, and bell pepper. Mix well, cover, and refrigerate until cold. Serve cold in large scallop shells or on individual plates.

CARACOLILLOS :: Sea Snails ::
(Basque Country)

Sea snails always remind me of my youth, when I competed with my younger brothers, Angel and Iñigo, in harvesting them. During our school years, we always spent long summer months in Mundaka, a beautiful fishing village near Bilbao. When we didn't accompany our father in his boat to go fishing, my brothers and I went to Mundaka's beach, Laidatxu, to collect all sorts of treasures from the sea. Because I was a little older (which at that age also meant a littler taller), I could reach higher on the rocks, capturing the sea snails "glued" out of my brothers' reach. My older and also braver brothers, Manu and Vale, didn't bother with our childish occupation. They instead explored for a more precious capture, *percebes* (gooseneck barnacles, page 234), which nowadays are scarce and costly.

Simply boiled in salt water, sea snails have an intense taste of the sea. Many bars in the Basque Country offer them, sometimes wrapped in *cucuruchos* (paper cones), along with the pins necessary to extract the bodies from the shells. To eat them, hold one snail between two fingers. With a pin in your other hand, remove and discard the round, brownish, translucent protection that covers the opening. Pierce the body with the pin and, with your fingers still holding the snail, rotate the shell until the morsel is pulled free. With my fast and greedy moves—a necessity in a large family—I also beat my brothers when eating them.

Sea snails may be difficult to find in some areas in the United States. Look for them in Italian and Chinese fish shops. :: **Serves 6**

4 cups water
2 tablespoons coarse sea salt
1 pound sea snails

In a saucepan, combine the water, salt, and snails and bring to a boil over high heat. Decrease the heat to medium and boil the snails for 15 minutes. Remove from the heat and let cool in the water. Eat the snails warm or cold.

Row boats in Bermeo, Basque Country, near where the author spent her childhood summers

ALBÓNDIGAS EN SALSA ESPAÑOLA :: Beef Meatballs in Onion and Carrot Sauce :: (*Madrid*)

My children love meatballs served with *arroz blanco* (page 186) for dinner, so I often cook these at home. Most bars, particularly in Madrid, offer *albóndigas* as a tapa because it is a perfect dish for serving in *cazuelitas* (page 51) at the counter. I usually order a plate of *patatas fritas* (Fiery Potatoes, page 64, prepared without the sauce) for scooping up the extra sauce from the meatballs.

I use exclusively beef for meatballs, but a combination of beef and pork is also good. You can cook them in different ways as well. You can brown them as directed, add the sauce, and finish them on the stove top over medium-low heat for 10 minutes. Or, instead of frying the meatballs in olive oil, you can bake them in a 450°F oven for 10 minutes before adding the sauce, and then decrease the temperature to 325°F, add the sauce, and cook for another 10 minutes. My preferred sauce is the delicious carrot-and-onion mix known as *salsa española*, but some bars serve meatballs with a tomato sauce (page 311). :: **Serves 8**

1 slice white country-style bread

$1/3$ cup whole milk

$1^1/4$ pounds lean ground beef

2 cloves garlic, finely minced

$1/4$ yellow onion, finely chopped

1 egg

2 teaspoons chopped fresh flat-leaf parsley

1 teaspoon salt

2 tablespoons all-purpose flour, or as needed

$1/3$ cup olive oil

2 cups Onion and Carrot Sauce (page 311)

In a shallow bowl, combine the bread and milk and let soak for about 10 minutes. Meanwhile, in another bowl, combine the beef, garlic, and onion and mix thoroughly.

Add the soaked bread and any milk remaining in the bowl, the egg, parsley, and salt to the meat mixture and mix well with a wooden spoon or spatula.

Preheat the oven to 350°F. Spread the 2 tablespoons of flour in a shallow dish. Oil your hands and form about 60 meatballs, each $1^1/2$ inches in diameter, shaping them neatly with your palms. Roll the meatballs in the flour, coating them lightly and evenly and shaking off any excess. Add more flour to the bowl if needed.

In a large skillet, heat the olive oil over medium-high heat. Add the meatballs and fry, turning frequently, for about 5 minutes, or until evenly browned on all surfaces.

Transfer the meatballs to a baking dish and pour the sauce evenly over them. Place in the oven for 15 minutes, or until the meatballs are cooked through and the sauce is hot. Serve hot or warm.

Potato and Onion Omelet (page 56), olives, and Beef Meatballs in Onion and Carrot Sauce

CHAPTER 4

Cold Soups and Salads

DURING THE HOT summer months, Spaniards look forward to their cuisine's rich array of cold soups and salads. Gazpacho, the quintessential Spanish cold soup, is eaten mainly but not exclusively in Andalusia, the southernmost region of the peninsula, where it is enjoyed almost daily. Descendants of mixtures of bread and olive oil enjoyed by the Romans, gazpachos have evolved over the centuries into far more elaborate concoctions, such as *ajo blanco* (almond gazpacho), velvety *salmorejo*, and *porra*, which is more of a dip than a soup. But the most beloved gazpacho both within and beyond Spain is the refreshing and nutritious *gazpacho andaluz*, which marries tomatoes with sweet peppers and cucumber. The evolution of these cold Andalusian soups continues today with such inventive versions as the cherry gazpacho of Ronda's famed restaurant Tragabuches.

Dried (day-old) bread, a humble ingredient common to many cuisines, plays an important role in gazpachos. Rather than discarding stale bread, resourceful home cooks use it to thicken these soups, in smaller quantities when making traditional tomato gazpacho and in larger amounts for *salmorejos* and *porras*. I prefer not to add bread to my *gazpacho andaluz*, provided the tomatoes are ripe and flavorful. Of course, if you do not have dried bread on hand, fresh can be used, with the same good results. Be sure to use sturdy country-style bread with a dense crumb.

Salads range from uncomplicated combinations to more elaborate compositions. With the exception of the seasoned lettuce or escarole leaves that usually accompany roasted lamb or goat, salads are served before the main course. *Ensalada mixta*, a simple mix of lettuce, tomatoes, and onions, is common to all regions and also serves as a base to which hard-boiled eggs, potatoes, tuna, and/or olives are added. Specialty ingredients such as salt cod, baby eels, avocados, asparagus, cheeses, or roasted red bell peppers give more complex salads their regional character. One of the most distinctive preparations is Catalan *xató*, which combines escarole, salt cod, tuna, and anchovies and tosses them with a *picada*, a classic sauce of the region made from dried red peppers and hazelnuts or almonds, or both. Not surprisingly, salads made with citrus begin many meals in orange country—Valencia and surrounding areas—while the frequent use of cheeses such as Cabrales in Asturian salads arises out of that region's venerable cheese-making tradition.

The key to making good cold soups and salads is to use only the finest and freshest ingredients. Tomatoes, in particular, should always be very ripe. If you must postpone making a gazpacho or salad because the tomatoes aren't ideal, do so, or you will be disappointed. Properly dried greens is another salad essential. Excess moisture will make a salad wilt more quickly and will dilute the dressing. Finally, and of utmost importance, use only the best extra virgin olive oil available, ideally of Spanish origin. It is precisely in these cold preparations that superior quality is most apparent.

PAGE 82: *Windows full of preserves in Barcelona* ABOVE, FROM LEFT TO RIGHT: *Buying seafood in Barcelona's Boqueria market; harvesting olives in Extremadura; fruit in Barcelona's Boqueria market*

AJO BLANCO ▪ Cold Almond and Garlic Soup ▪ (*Andalusia*)

Also known as white gazpacho, *ajo blanco* is a perfect cold summer soup: easy to make, healthful, and distinctive. The Arabs who ruled Andalusia for almost eight hundred years introduced almonds to the Iberian Peninsula, and this dish probably originated with their reign. Though highly popular in Andalusia, it is little known in the rest of Spain and virtually unknown in the United States. I serve it garnished with grapes, but thin apple slices are also common. ▪ Serves 6

2 cloves garlic, coarsely chopped

1½ cups blanched almonds

1 day-old country-style bread roll, about 3 ounces, torn into pieces and soaked in 1 cup water for 10 minutes, or 1 fresh roll, torn into pieces

1½ teaspoons salt

6 tablespoons sherry vinegar

½ cup extra virgin olive oil

4 cups water

12 green grapes, seeded and halved, for garnish

½ cup sliced almonds, toasted

In a blender, process the garlic until puréed. Add the blanched almonds and process until finely ground. Add the soaked bread and any remaining water (or the fresh bread), salt, vinegar, and olive oil and blend for 2 minutes, or until a smooth paste forms. Add the water and blend for 2 minutes longer, or until smooth. Transfer to a bowl, cover, and refrigerate for at least 4 hours, or until well chilled.

Just before serving, stir the soup well, reaching to the bottom of the bowl. Taste and adjust the seasoning with salt. Ladle into chilled soup plates, garnish with the grapes and toasted almonds, and serve.

GAZPACHO ANDALUZ ▪ Traditional Tomato Gazpacho ▪ (*Andalusia*)

This is my favorite gazpacho recipe for picnics. You must use very ripe, peak-of-season tomatoes for the best results. I prefer not to add bread because I like a thinner soup that I can serve in cups as a beverage. If you want a slightly thicker consistency, tear 2 day-old small country-style bread rolls, each weighing about 2½ ounces, into pieces, soak in 1 cup water for 10 minutes, and add the soaked bread and any remaining water to the blender with the rest of the ingredients. (Or, you can add 2 fresh rolls, torn into pieces, and omit the water.) If you like, garnish the soup with additional finely chopped tomatoes, cucumbers, or peppers, or all three. ▪ Serves 4

6 tomatoes, coarsely chopped

½ cucumber, peeled, seeded, and cut into chunks

2 cloves garlic, chopped

1 small green bell pepper, seeded and cut into chunks

½ cup water

½ cup extra virgin olive oil

3 tablespoons sherry vinegar

1 tablespoon salt

In a large bowl, combine the tomatoes, cucumber, garlic, bell pepper, water, olive oil, vinegar, and salt and mix well. Working in batches if necessary, add the tomato mixture to a blender or food processor and process at high speed until smooth. For an especially smooth texture, pass the puréed mixture through a food mill fitted with the medium plate. Transfer to a bowl, cover, and refrigerate for at least 4 hours, or until well chilled.

Just before serving, taste the soup and adjust the seasoning with salt. Ladle into chilled soup plates or cups and serve.

SALMOREJO CORDOBÉS ▪
Thick Cordoban Gazpacho ▪ (Andalusia)

Similar to a traditional tomato gazpacho but richer and smoother, this delightful cold soup is typical of the Córdoba table. My friend Maria Antonia Marín de Alfonso is a classic Cordoban beauty, and one could easily picture her stepping out of a painting by Julio Romero, the famous Cordoban painter of the early twentieth century. Maria Antonia has prepared many dishes for me, and this is a special one. In Córdoba, they use dried country-style bread; plain rolls will also work. ▪ **Serves 6**

Illustrated on page 95

- 6 tomatoes, coarsely chopped
- 2 cloves garlic, chopped
- 1/4 cup sherry vinegar
- 1 cup extra virgin olive oil
- 1 tablespoon salt
- 2 day-old country-style bread rolls, about 3 ounces each, torn into pieces and soaked in 1 cup water for 10 minutes, or 2 fresh rolls, torn into pieces
- 1 egg yolk (optional)
- 3 hard-boiled eggs, peeled and finely chopped
- 3 ounces jamón serrano or other dry-cured ham, finely chopped

In a large bowl, combine the tomatoes, garlic, vinegar, olive oil, salt, and soaked bread and any remaining water (or fresh bread) and mix well. Working in batches if necessary, add the tomato mixture to a blender or food processor and process at high speed until smooth. For an especially smooth texture, pass the puréed mixture through a food mill fitted with the medium plate, and then, if desired, return it to the blender or processor, add the egg yolk, and process until thoroughly incorporated. Transfer to a bowl, cover, and refrigerate for at least 4 hours, or until well chilled.

Just before serving, taste the soup and adjust the seasoning with salt. Ladle into chilled soup plates, garnish with the chopped eggs and ham, and serve.

Variation

In my take on *salmorejo*, I omit the bread, which makes the soup even smoother and silkier than you would commonly find it in Córdoba. And instead of adding the olive oil with the other ingredients, I purée the other ingredients first and then add the oil slowly, much as I do when making mayonnaise. Before adding the oil, pass the mixture through a food mill to remove any trace of peels or seeds and return it to the blender or food processor (in batches, if necessary). Then, with the motor running, add the oil in a thin, slow, steady stream and process until incorporated.

PORRA ANTEQUERANA ▪
Tomato and Bread Dip ▪ *(Andalusia)*

Antequera is one of the main cities in the beautiful foothills of the Sierra de Chimenea in the province of Andalusia. It is an important center for the production of olive oil, and when you drive around the countryside, the air bears a fruity aroma. At the Parador of Antequera, I once tasted a delightful *porra*—a distinctive dip that is the town's contribution to the Andalusian culinary canon—and the chef graciously allowed me to watch him prepare it afterward.

Porra and *salmorejo* are similar preparations. The difference lies mainly in the amount of bread added. *Salmorejo* is made with less bread, making it only a moderately thick soup, while the bread-laden *porra* has the consistency of a dense purée. The bread used in Antequera, or in Archidona, the other Andalusian village that claims to be the original home of *porra*, is *pan candela*, a particularly dense country-style loaf. Also, while *salmorejo* is typically presented as a first course, *porra* is usually served in a small *cazuela* (or a few *cazuelas* if the dinner party is large) in the center of the table, along with bread for dipping, as an appetizer to share before the balance of the meal arrives. Guests enjoy just a small taste for the superb flavor and not to fill the stomach, unlike in the past when *porra* was the whole lunch for a peasant or field worker. If you prefer, you can divide the mixture into individual portions, and you can also substitute canned tuna for the garnish of chopped eggs and *jamón serrano*.
▪ **Serves 6 to 8**

6 tomatoes, coarsely chopped

2 cloves garlic, chopped

$1/4$ cup sherry vinegar

1 cup extra virgin olive oil

1 tablespoon salt

4 day-old country-style bread rolls, about 3 ounces each, torn into pieces and soaked in 2 cups water for 10 minutes, or 4 fresh rolls, torn into pieces

3 hard-boiled eggs, peeled and finely chopped

3 ounces jamón serrano or other dry-cured ham, finely chopped

In a large bowl, combine the tomatoes, garlic, vinegar, olive oil, salt, and soaked bread and any remaining water (or fresh bread) and mix well. Working in batches if necessary, add the tomato mixture to a blender or food processor and process at high speed until pale orange and smooth. Taste and adjust the seasoning with salt. At this point, the dip can be transferred to a bowl, covered, and refrigerated for a few hours before serving.

Spoon the dip into a serving bowl or small individual bowls and garnish with the eggs and ham. Serve cool—not chilled—or at room temperature.

AJOTOMATE ▪ Tomato Salad ▪ (*Murcia*)

When you order a tomato salad in Murcia, you can expect this delicious dish. Pounding one of the tomatoes and integrating it into the vinaigrette increases the subtlety of the dressing. I like to use perfectly ripe beefsteak tomatoes for their intense flavor and aroma. ▪ **Serves 4**

Illustrated on page 134

> 2 cloves garlic, peeled but left whole
> 1 teaspoon salt
> 5 tomatoes, peeled
> 2 tablespoons red wine vinegar
> Pinch of freshly ground black pepper
> 1 teaspoon cumin seeds
> 1/2 teaspoon sweet pimentón or paprika
> 6 tablespoons extra virgin olive oil

Using a mortar and pestle, mash the garlic with the salt until a paste forms. Coarsely chop 1 of the tomatoes and add it to the mortar. Pound the tomato together with the garlic paste until well blended. Add the vinegar, pepper, 1/2 teaspoon of the cumin seeds, and the *pimentón* to the mortar and pound until smooth. Add the olive oil and stir with the pestle to mix well with the rest of the ingredients, forming a vinaigrette.

Cut the remaining tomatoes crosswise into 1/2-inch-thick slices. Arrange them on a serving platter in a single layer, overlapping them as little as possible. Pour the vinaigrette over the tomatoes, sprinkle with the remaining 1/2 teaspoon cumin seeds, and serve.

ENSALADA MIXTA ▪ Mixed Salad with Tomatoes, Potatoes, Tuna, and Eggs

My mother used to prepare this everyday salad for us several times a week, usually as a first course for lunch. Today, I often have it as a main course, especially during the summer when I want a light lunch. Numerous variations on this pleasing salad are found across Spain, with such additions or substitutions as preserved white asparagus or green bell peppers. If you see *ensalada mixta* on a restaurant menu, however, it is usually a simpler affair, made with only lettuce, tomato, and onion. ▪ **Serves 6**

> 1 head Boston or romaine lettuce, torn into
>   bite-sized pieces
> 3 tomatoes, peeled and cut into wedges
> 4 scallions, including the tender green tops,
>   cut crosswise into 1/2-inch-long pieces, or
>   1 small yellow onion, thinly sliced
> 4 small boiling potatoes, about 1 pound total weight,
>   boiled, peeled, and cut into small chunks
> 1 (3-ounce) can white albacore tuna in olive oil,
>   drained and flaked
> 12 green or black olives
> 1/2 cup Sherry Vinaigrette (page 314)
> 2 hard-boiled eggs, peeled and cut into wedges
> 6 anchovy fillets in olive oil

In a large bowl, combine the lettuce, tomatoes, scallions, potatoes, tuna, and olives and mix well. Drizzle all but about a spoonful of the vinaigrette over the salad and mix gently with the ingredients. Garnish the salad with the egg wedges and the anchovies, sprinkle the remaining vinaigrette on the eggs, and serve.

PIPIRRANA DE JAÉN ▪
Tomato Salad of Jaén ▪ (Andalusia)

Pipirrana means "frog's piss," and I have no idea how this pleasant salad got that name. This version is from Jaén, hometown of my friend Manolo Cacho, who shared his family's recipe with me. I have tasted versions of *pipirrana* from other areas of Andalusia (such as the variation that follows), but I find his, which, unlike the others, calls for mayonnaise, to be the best. It is appealing summer fare, when tomatoes are at their best. ▪ **Serves 6**

> 2 pounds tomatoes, peeled, finely chopped, and
>   2 tablespoons juice reserved
> 1/2 green bell pepper, seeded and finely chopped
> 1 teaspoon salt
> 2 hard-boiled eggs, peeled, halved, and yolks and
>   whites separated
> 2 cloves garlic, peeled but left whole
> 1 slice day-old country-style bread, broken into chunks
> 3 tablespoons extra virgin olive oil
> 1 tablespoon sherry vinegar
> 1 tablespoon Mayonnaise (page 306)
> 1 (3-ounce) can white albacore tuna in olive oil,
>   drained and flaked

In a large bowl, combine the tomatoes (reserve the juice), bell pepper, and salt and mix gently. Set aside.

Using a mortar and pestle, pound together the hard-boiled egg yolks, garlic, and bread until a coarse paste forms. Add the olive oil, vinegar, and reserved tomato juice and stir with the pestle to incorporate. Add the mayonnaise and continue to stir with the pestle—always in the same direction to prevent the dressing from breaking—until the dressing has the texture of a creamy paste.

Add the dressing to the bowl holding the tomatoes and bell pepper and mix well. Cover and refrigerate for at least 1 hour, or until chilled.

Finely chop the egg whites. Divide the salad among 6 plates and sprinkle evenly with the egg whites and tuna. Serve chilled.

PIPIRRANA ▪ Tomato, Cucumber, and
Green Pepper Salad ▪ (Andalusia)

Here is the most common version of the Andalusian *pipirrana*, served in almost every restaurant and a favorite in most households. *Piriñaca*, a similar salad, adds tuna and hard-boiled eggs. ▪ **Serves 6**

> 2 pounds tomatoes, peeled and finely chopped
> 1 small green bell pepper, seeded and finely chopped
> 1 small yellow onion, finely chopped
> 2 cucumbers, peeled and thinly sliced
> 1/2 cup black olives
> 1/2 cup Sherry Vinaigrette (page 314)

In a large bowl, combine the tomatoes, bell pepper, onion, cucumbers, and olives and mix well. Drizzle with the vinaigrette and toss to coat evenly. Cover and refrigerate for at least 1 hour, or until chilled. Serve chilled.

ENSALADA DE ESPÁRRAGOS SOBRE PIQUILLOS :: Salad of White Asparagus over Piquillo Peppers :: (Navarra)

The main ingredients for this salad are both classic *conservas* (preserved foods) of Navarra. The bright red color and deep smoky taste of the *piquillo* peppers juxtaposed with the shiny whiteness and delicate flavor of the asparagus create an arresting, delicious presentation. The accompanying garnish—a favorite in my home—is a little laborious to prepare but worth it; the smaller the pieces are (ideally the size of a rice kernel), the better the garnish tastes and looks. :: **Serves 4**

GARNISH

1 hard-boiled egg, peeled and finely minced

2 preserved whole piquillo peppers, finely minced

3 scallions, white part only, finely minced

10 green olives, pitted and finely minced

Pinch of salt

2 tablespoons sherry vinegar

$1/4$ cup extra virgin olive oil

SALAD

8 preserved whole piquillo peppers, halved lengthwise

16 preserved white asparagus or cooked fresh white asparagus spears

$1/3$ cup Sherry Vinaigrette (page 314)

1 tablespoon chopped fresh flat-leaf parsley

To make the garnish, in a bowl, combine the egg, *piquillo* peppers, scallions, olives, salt, and vinegar and mix well. Add the olive oil in a slow stream, folding it into the rest of the ingredients with a spatula. Cover and refrigerated until well chilled.

To make the salad, unfold the pepper halves, yielding 16 triangles. Have ready 4 salad plates. Place 4 of the pepper halves on the upper half of each plate, forming a semicircle and with their peaks pointing toward the rim of the plate. Cut the thicker ends of each asparagus stalk crosswise into two or three $1/4$-inch-thick slices and set the slices aside. Arrange 4 of the asparagus spears so that the cut ends are together at the bottom of each plate, with the tips fanning out on top of the peppers. Distribute the asparagus slices around the bottom of each plate. Spoon the garnish into the empty spaces between the spears and the *piquillo* peppers, drizzle the salads with the vinaigrette, sprinkle with the parsley, and serve.

Jars of preserved white asparagus from Navarra

ENSALADA DE PIMIENTOS ROJOS ASADOS ▪ Roasted Red Pepper Salad ▪ (Castilla y León)

My friend Ester Garcia is a talented tailor and clothes designer, but as with many Spanish women who are successful in various nonculinary professions, she is also an accomplished home cook. Two of her best dishes are her *pollo en escabeche* (page 241) and this salad of roasted peppers. She calls the salad simply *asadillo*, which is the name used in her village of Salamanca; everywhere else it is known as *ensalada de pimientos rojos asados*. Try it as an appetizer or as a side dish for meats or fish. ▪ **Serves 6**

6 red bell peppers

1 tomato

1 yellow onion, peeled but left whole

Extra virgin olive oil for brushing vegetables,
    plus 1/3 cup

1 clove garlic, peeled but left whole

1 teaspoon cumin seeds, plus a few extra seeds
    (optional)

1 teaspoon salt

2 tablespoons sherry vinegar

Preheat the oven to 500°F.

Arrange the bell peppers, tomato, and onion on a rimmed baking sheet or in a roasting pan and brush on all sides with olive oil. Place in the oven and roast for 15 minutes. Turn the vegetables and continue roasting for 15 minutes longer, or until the skins begin to blacken. Remove from the oven, cover, and let cool (trapping the heat makes the vegetables sweat, which makes them easier to peel).

Place a colander inside a large bowl, and place the cooled peppers in the colander. Working with 1 pepper at a time, peel off the blackened skin and discard, and then remove and discard the stem and seeds. As you work, the juices from the pepper will pass through the colander into the bowl. When all the peppers are done, cut them lengthwise into 1/2-inch-wide strips and place in a bowl. Strain the captured juices through a fine-mesh sieve placed over a measuring cup. Reserve 1/2 cup of the pepper juices, discarding the rest. Peel the tomato, cut it into small pieces, and add to the bowl. Cut the onion into thin strips and add to the bowl. Mix the vegetables together and set aside.

Using a mortar and pestle, pound together the garlic, 1 teaspoon cumin seeds, and salt until a coarse paste forms. Add 2 tablespoons of the pepper juices, the 1/3 cup olive oil, and the vinegar and stir with the pestle until a thick vinaigrette forms.

Add the vinaigrette and the remaining 6 tablespoons pepper juices to the bowl with the vegetables and mix well. Add more cumin seeds if you want the salad to have a sharper bite. Serve immediately, or cover and refrigerate and serve cold.

ZORONGOLLO ▪ Red Pepper and Tomato Salad ▪ (*Extremadura*)

The name of this salad, and even the sound of the name, is uncommon even to many Spaniards, but this simple mix of red peppers and tomatoes from Extremadura is a variation on the roasted pepper salad of Castilla y León and other similar salads served all over Spain. Many years ago, I ate it at a local inn in Puebla de la Reina in Badajoz, and it is still served the same way there today. Start the salad the night before, as it needs to sit overnight for the juices to achieve a gelatin-like consistency. Serve as an accompaniment to meats or fish. ▪ **Serves 6**

3 tomatoes

3 red bell peppers

Extra virgin olive oil for brushing, plus $1/3$ cup

2 cloves garlic, peeled but left whole

$1/2$ teaspoon salt

1 tablespoon sherry vinegar

Preheat the oven to 500°F.

Arrange the tomatoes and bell peppers on a rimmed baking sheet or in a roasting pan and brush on all sides with olive oil. Place in the oven and roast for 15 minutes. Turn the vegetables and continue roasting for 15 minutes longer, or until the skins begin to blacken. Remove from the oven, cover, and let cool (trapping the heat makes the vegetables sweat, which makes them easier to peel).

Peel the tomatoes and reserve 1 tomato; cut the remaining 2 tomatoes into quarters and place them in a bowl. Place a colander inside a bowl, and place the cooled peppers in the colander. Working with 1 pepper at a time, peel off the blackened skin and discard, and then remove and discard the stem and seeds. As you work, the juices from the pepper will pass through the colander into the bowl. When all the peppers are done, cut them lengthwise into $1/4$-inch-wide strips and add to the bowl holding the tomato quarters. Strain the captured juices through a fine-mesh sieve held over the bowl holding the vegetables and stir gently to mix.

Using a mortar and pestle, mash the reserved tomato, the garlic, and the salt until a coarse paste forms. Add the garlic mixture, the $1/3$ cup olive oil, and the vinegar to the bowl with the roasted vegetables and mix well. Cover and let rest overnight in the refrigerator.

The next day, serve the salad at room temperature.

ENSALADA DE AGUACATE CON GAMBAS SOBRE VINAGRETA DE SALMOREJO ▪ Avocado and Shrimp Salad with Salmorejo Vinaigrette ▪ (Andalusia)

When avocados are ripe, I always make this salad. It is not a traditional recipe, but it is my favorite way to put an abundance of avocados and leftover *salmorejo* in the refrigerator to practical—and delicious—use. I first ate the salad in a restaurant in Málaga some years ago and have been making it ever since. The rich avocados and the refreshing, slightly tangy vinaigrette are a perfect match. ▪ **Serves 4**

4 cups water

1¹/₂ teaspoons salt

1 bay leaf

4 black peppercorns

12 small shrimp in the shell

2 avocados

³/₄ cup Salmorejo Vinaigrette (page 315)

1 tablespoon finely minced tomato

1 tablespoon finely minced green bell pepper

In a small pot, bring the water to a boil over high heat. Add the salt, bay leaf, and peppercorns and then the shrimp. When the water is boiling again, remove the shrimp immediately and submerge them in ice water. Peel the shrimp and halve each lengthwise. Set aside.

Using a sharp knife, halve 1 avocado lengthwise, cutting around the large central pit. Rotate the halves in opposite directions and gently pull them apart; one half will retain the seed. With a swift but gentle motion, strike the pit with the heel of the blade; the blade should lodge in it easily. Using a gentle rocking action, free the pit from the avocado half. Repeat with the remaining avocado. Carefully peel the avocado halves with your fingers. Or, if the avocado is ripe enough, you can use a spoon to scoop out the flesh from the skin. In either case, make sure you keep the shape of each avocado half intact. Place each half, cut side down, in the center of a plate. Starting at the bottom of the avocado, make vertical incisions ¹/₄ inch apart along the length of the avocado, leaving about 1 inch at the stem end uncut. Fan the slices slightly.

Spoon the vinaigrette around the avocado halves. Surround each avocado with shrimp halves, cut side down. Sprinkle each plate with the tomato and bell pepper and serve.

Avocado and Shrimp Salad with Salmorejo Vinaigrette,
served with Thick Cordoban Gazpacho (page 87)

ENSALADILLA RUSA ⁛ Russian Salad

It is hard to imagine a bar in Spain that doesn't serve *ensaladilla rusa* as a tapa, and many restaurants offer it as a first course. The mayonnaise-bound salad originated in Russia in the nineteenth century, and is said to have been created by a French chef resident in Moscow, where it is still known as *salat Olivier*. It soon migrated to France, Spain, and elsewhere, with local variations, and remains popular not only in its birthplace, but in its adopted homes as well. ⁛ **Serves 4**

3 medium boiling potatoes, about 1¹/₂ pounds
    total weight

2 small carrots, halved crosswise

2 hard-boiled eggs

10 green Manzanilla olives or other green olives,
    pitted and cut into quarters

¹/₂ cup fresh or frozen shelled English peas, boiled
    until tender and drained

1 red bell pepper, roasted, peeled, seeded, and
    cut into small pieces

2 (3-ounce) cans white albacore tuna in olive oil,
    drained and flaked

1¹/₂ cups Mayonnaise (page 306)

Salt and freshly ground black pepper

In a saucepan, combine the potatoes and carrots with water to cover and bring to a boil over medium-high heat. Decrease the heat to low and cook, uncovered, for 20 to 30 minutes, or until the potatoes are fork-tender. The carrots will be ready in less time; remove them as soon as they are tender and let the potatoes finish cooking. Drain and set aside to cool.

Peel the potatoes, carrots, and hard-boiled eggs and cut them into small irregular chunks about half the size of a grape. In a large bowl, combine the potatoes, carrots, eggs, olives, peas, and bell pepper. Add the tuna and gently mix together all the ingredients with a spatula until evenly combined. Then gently fold in the mayonnaise to coat evenly. Season to taste with salt and pepper.

Cover and refrigerate the salad until serving. Serve cold or at room temperature.

ENSALADA DE NARANJAS ⁛ Orange Salad with Onions ⁛ (*Levante*)

With the abundance of oranges in Spain's Valencian Community, the fruit enjoys a prominent place in salads, sauces, cakes, and sherbets of the region. The combination of pungent onion, sweet orange, and salty olive makes this salad one of interesting counterpoints. ⁛
Serves 6

4 large oranges

1 red onion, very thinly sliced crosswise

¹/₂ cup black olives

Pinch of sugar

Juice of 1 lemon

¹/₄ cup extra virgin olive oil

Working with 1 orange at a time, cut a thin slice off the top and bottom and stand the orange upright on a cutting board. Using a sharp knife, and following the contour of the fruit, cut off the orange peel and the white pith beneath it in wide strips. Holding the orange in one hand over a bowl, cut along both sides of each segment, freeing it from the membrane and allowing it drop into the bowl. When all the segments are freed, use the tip of the knife to dislodge and discard any visible seeds. Repeat with the remaining 3 oranges.

In a large bowl, combine the orange segments, onion, olives, sugar, and lemon juice. Mix gently, taking care not to tear the orange segments. Drizzle the olive oil over the salad. Serve at room temperature, or cover and refrigerate and serve cold.

ENSALADA DE ENDIVIAS CON CABRALES Y NARANJAS ▪
Endive Salad with Cabrales Cheese and Oranges ▪ *(Asturias)*

Cabrales is a spectacular blue cheese from Asturias that is famous throughout Spain and is becoming better known abroad. Salty and intensely flavored, it is a treat whether served alone with bread and cider or wine or added to a salad, as in this recipe. Valdeón, a more subdued blue from Castilla y León, is a fine substitute for the Cabrales.
▪ **Serves 4**

24 large Belgian endive leaves, each 3 to 4 inches long (from 3 or 4 heads)

2 ounces Cabrales, Valdeón, or other blue cheese, at room temperature

3 tablespoons plain yogurt

3 tablespoons sliced almonds, toasted

3 large oranges

1 tablespoon finely chopped fresh flat-leaf parsley

Carefully cut off a horizontal slice from the base of each endive leaf so that the leaf will remain upright and the cheese filling will not spill out of the base.

In a bowl, combine the cheese and the yogurt. Using a fork, mash together until a smooth paste forms. Line up the leaves, hollow side up, on a tray, and place 1 teaspoon of the mixture into each leaf. Sprinkle the almonds evenly on top of the cheese mixture.

Working with 1 orange at a time, cut a thin slice off the top and bottom and stand the orange upright on a cutting board. Using a sharp knife, and following the contour of the fruit, cut off the orange peel and the white pith beneath it in wide strips. Holding the orange in one hand over a bowl, cut along both sides of each segment, freeing it from the membrane and allowing it drop into the bowl. When all the segments are freed, use the tip of the knife to dislodge and discard any visible seeds. Repeat with the remaining 2 oranges.

Arrange 6 filled endive leaves on each of 4 plates. Tuck the orange segments attractively around them. Sprinkle the parsley over the filled leaves and orange segments and serve.

ENSALADA DE ANGULAS ▪
Baby Eel Salad ▪ *(Basque Country)*

If there was one thing that I missed eating regularly when I lived in the United States, it was a dish of baby eels. I consoled myself thinking that even if I lived in Spain, I wouldn't have been able to enjoy them as frequently as I once did because of their current scarcity and corresponding astronomic price. For that reason and because they are in season during winter, *angulas* are often served as a special course for Christmas Eve dinner or for Christmas Day lunch, usually as a forerunner to *besugo al horno* (baked sea bream) or another dish. In *angulas a la bilbaina*, the classic preparation, the eels are served sizzling in garlic and oil; this salad is a more contemporary treatment, wonderful in its own right.

Frozen baby eels are a fine, if still expensive, substitute. Place them in a colander over a bowl and thaw them in the refrigerator overnight. They are parboiled before they are frozen and can be eaten as is once they are thawed. Avoid canned baby eels, popular in some Central American countries. I find them too oily, rubbery, and lacking the fresh taste that even the frozen eels deliver. ▪ **Serves 4**

2 cloves garlic, halved

$1/2$ pound frozen baby eels, thawed overnight in the refrigerator and patted dry

$1/2$ cup extra virgin olive oil

2 tablespoons freshly squeezed lemon juice

Salt

2 cups loosely packed mixed young, tender salad greens

$1/4$ cup Sherry Vinaigrette (page 314)

1 tablespoon chopped fresh flat-leaf parsley

Rub the garlic, cut side down, on the inside of a bowl and discard. Add the baby eels and the olive oil to the bowl, and gently swirl them around the bowl to infuse them with some of the garlic flavor. Add the lemon juice, season sparingly with salt, and stir to blend the flavors.

Place the greens in another bowl, drizzle with the vinaigrette, and toss to coat. Put the baby eels in the center of a serving plate, or divide among 4 plates, and arrange the greens around them. Garnish with the parsley and serve.

XATÓ ∷ Escarole Salad with Anchovies, Salt Cod, and Tuna ∷ (*Catalonia*)

You will find this salad in the southernmost Catalan province of Tarragona, where several villages claim it as their own. I learned how to prepare it from my Catalan friend Marisa Escribano when I stayed with her one summer in La Pera, in L'Empordà in northern Catalonia. After trying her version, it was clear to me why *xató* often inspires extreme displays of proprietorship. The only change to Marisa's original recipe that I sometimes make is to substitute Black Olive Vinaigrette (page 314) for the whole olives and basic vinaigrette.

The salad calls for a *picada*, a kind of sauce or paste usually made from garlic, parsley, tomato, and nuts and ground in a mortar. *Picadas* are added to soups, stews, or, as here, salads. This particular one includes dried peppers and resembles *salsa romesco*, although it is neither cooked nor does it contain onion and wine. The recipe yields more than you will need for the salad; spread the extra *picada* on grilled fish or use it to make another salad. ∷ Serves 4

PICADA

2 dried ñora, choricero, or ancho chiles

Boiling water as needed

6 tablespoons extra virgin olive oil

1 slice white country-style bread

1 clove garlic, peeled but left whole

10 hazelnuts, blanched and skins removed

1 tomato

1 tablespoon chopped fresh flat-leaf parsley

1 tablespoon red wine vinegar

Pinch of salt

SALAD

1 head escarole or other mildly bitter green, such as frisée and/or curly endive

2 tablespoons extra virgin olive oil

8 anchovy fillets in olive oil, halved crosswise

2 ounces white albacore tuna in olive oil, flaked

2 scallions, white part only, sliced

5 ounces salt cod, desalted (page 46)

1/4 cup Sherry Vinaigrette (page 314)

20 black olives, pitted

To make the *picada*, in a heatproof bowl, combine the dried chiles with boiling water to cover and let stand for 30 minutes, or until soft. Drain the chiles, slit them open, and scrape off the flesh with the edge of a knife, discarding the seeds, skins, and stems. Set the flesh aside.

In a frying pan, heat 3 tablespoons of the olive oil over medium-high heat. Add the bread and fry, turning once, for 2 or 3 minutes on each side, or until golden. Remove from the pan, let cool slightly, and break into several pieces.

Using a mortar and pestle, grind together the garlic and the hazelnuts until a paste forms. Add the fried bread and the flesh of the chiles and mash the mixture a little more. Cut the tomato in half crosswise and, using the large holes of a handheld grater held over the mixture, grate the tomato halves, discarding the skin. Add the parsley, the remaining 3 tablespoons olive oil, the vinegar, and salt. Continue to grind until the mixture is a smooth paste.

To make the salad, tear the escarole leaves into bite-sized pieces. Add 1/4 cup of the *picada* to a large bowl and stir in the olive oil to thin it a bit. (Reserve the remaining *picada* for another use.) Add the escarole, anchovies, tuna, and scallions. Using your fingers, break the cod into flakes as large as possible, discarding any skin or bones, and add to the bowl. (Don't worry if you cannot get large flakes; the salad will still be very good.) Stir gently to mix well.

Divide the salad among 4 plates. Drizzle the vinaigrette and distribute the olives evenly over the top. Serve immediately.

ENSALADA DE ATÚN FRESCO ∷
Fresh Tuna Salad with Greens and Piquillo Peppers ∷ (Basque Country)

This delicious salad, so simple to prepare, was a favorite appetizer at my restaurant Marichu. When I was young, my friends and I used to catch so many albacore in the summertime that it was necessary to come up with new ideas on how to prepare them. This salad is one of my favorite ways to use the prized fish, and the ingredients are a familiar pairing in the Basque Country. If you cannot find albacore, any good-quality fresh tuna will do.

∷ Serves 4

1/2 pound albacore belly or steak

Coarse salt for sprinkling, plus 1 teaspoon

3 tablespoons olive oil

1 tablespoon freshly squeezed lemon juice

2 cups loosely packed Boston, romaine, or other green lettuce leaves (1/2 head)

1/2 cup Sherry Vinaigrette (page 314)

8 preserved whole piquillo peppers or 2 red bell peppers, roasted and peeled

2 scallions, including the tender green tops, cut on the diagonal into 1/2-inch pieces

If using albacore belly, cut along its layered grain into 2-inch slabs. If using steak, cut into 1-inch-thick pieces, discarding the bone. Sprinkle the pieces lightly with salt. In a bowl, combine the olive oil, lemon juice, and the 1 teaspoon salt and mix well. Add the tuna and toss to coat it evenly with the olive oil mixture.

Heat a stove-top grill pan or a frying pan over high heat. When the pan is hot, remove the tuna pieces from the oil mixture, reserving the oil mixture, and place them in a single layer in the pan. Sear for 30 seconds. Decrease the heat to medium, sear for 1 minute longer, and then turn the slices over. Sear for 2 minutes longer, while spooning some of the oil mixture on the top. The tuna should be just opaque throughout. (Although the tuna belly is cut into thicker pieces than the steak, it is more delicate than the steak, so both will cook in the same amount of time.) Transfer to a shallow dish and let cool.

Tear the lettuce leaves into bite-sized pieces and put them in a bowl. (Don't cut the leaves with a knife, or they will wilt more quickly.) Drizzle with 1/4 cup of the vinaigrette and toss to coat the lettuce evenly. Divide the greens among 4 plates.

Halve the *piquillo* peppers lengthwise. Unfold each half to yield 2 triangles. If using roasted red bell peppers, slice each pepper into 8 triangular pieces. Place 4 of the pepper triangles on the center of each bed of greens, with their peaks pointing to the plate rim in a star pattern.

When the tuna has cooled, use your fingers to break it into large flakes. Place the tuna on the center of each plate without covering the peppers completely. Sprinkle with the scallions, drizzle the remaining 1/4 cup vinaigrette over the salad, and serve.

ESQUEIXADA ∷ Salt Cod with Onion, Tomato, Red Pepper, and Olives ∷ (Catalonia)

Esqueixada is a quintessential Catalan salad (*esqueixar* is Catalan for "to tear"). The main ingredient is always cod. Some versions also include green bell peppers; others eliminate the peppers altogether. I make mine with red only. ∷ **Serves 6**

1 pound salt cod, desalted (page 46)

1 yellow onion, sliced into very thin rings

1 cup extra virgin olive oil

2 tomatoes, cut into 1-inch dice

1 red bell pepper, seeded and cut into
   ¹/₄-inch-wide strips

¹/₂ cup black olives

²/₃ cup Sherry Vinaigrette (page 314)

Tear the cod into small pieces, discarding any skin or bones. In a bowl, combine the cod and onion, and pour in the olive oil to cover. Cover and refrigerate for at least 1 hour or for up to a few hours.

Drain the cod and onion and transfer to a large bowl. Add the tomatoes, bell pepper, and olives and mix well. Drizzle with the vinaigrette and toss to coat evenly. Cover and refrigerate until well chilled and serve cold.

Fishing on the Mediterranean

CHAPTER 5

Vegetable Dishes and Other First Courses

CARDOONS, SWISS CHARD, eggplants, zucchini, asparagus, and other vegetables, whether cooked alone or as part of a more elaborate presentation, are typically served as a first course in Spain, rather than as an accompaniment to a main course. (A main-course accompaniment is usually roasted or fried potatoes, potato purée, or white rice.) Since some of these vegetables dishes, such as the mixed-vegetable *menestra de verduras* from Navarra, require a lengthy preparation—often far longer than grilled meats or fish—it's fitting that they receive special attention at the table. However, many of these first courses could indeed make wonderful accompaniments in the American sense. For example, in Spain, the classic La Mancha stew, a simple blend of tomatoes and peppers, is often served with fried or scrambled eggs as a first course for lunch or dinner, but it would go well with grilled fish or meat as a side dish, too.

And the versatility of these dishes, despite their prescribed place on the Spanish menu, does not end there. Most of these first courses can be served as main courses by simply increasing the portion size. You will find fried egg dishes listed here because we typically eat them for lunch or dinner as a first course, but they would make a wonderful special breakfast or brunch. Similarly, the two pâtélike spreads, one of pork liver and the other of hare and partridge and both from Castilla–La Mancha, are usually eaten at the beginning of a meal, as are such regional specialties as crayfish cooked in a spicy sauce from La Rioja and sautéed frog legs from Extremadura. But all of these recipes could be scaled up to serve as a main course, or you could present a selection of them as an informal tapas menu.

::
103

LEFT: *The author's brother dipping* papas arrugadas *(wrinkled potatoes) into* mojo picón *at a bar in Teguise, in the center of Lanzarote (Canary Islands); baskets of eggs brought to market, Barcelona* PAGES 104-5, FROM LEFT TO RIGHT: *Grilling* calçots *(long spring onions) over coals; buying wine at the co-op in Gandesa, Catalonia; a sign for anchovies, Catalonia; outdoor-grill chef, Getaria, Basque Country*

ACELGAS REHOGADAS CON PASAS Y PIÑONES ▪ Sautéed Swiss Chard with Raisins and Pine Nuts ▪ (Catalonia)

In Catalonia, this is an everyday first course, with spinach sometimes standing in for the Swiss chard. Cooks in the Balearic Islands combine these same ingredients to make the filling for *cocarrois* (page 149), their traditional vegetable turnovers. The *jamón serrano* can be left out, since the original recipe is strictly vegetarian, but it gives the dish greater complexity. ▪ **Serves 6**

Pictured opposite

2 cups water

1¹/₂ teaspoons salt

2 pounds Swiss chard, stems removed and leaves coarsely chopped

¹/₄ cup olive oil

1 (¹/₄-inch-thick) slice jamón serrano or other dry-cured ham, about 3 ounces, finely diced

¹/₄ cup pine nuts

¹/₄ cup raisins, soaked in hot water to cover for 1 hour to soften and drained

In a large saucepan, bring the water to a boil over high heat. Add the salt and the Swiss chard, cover, and cook for 15 minutes, or until tender. Drain the chard in a colander, pressing on it firmly with the back of a spoon to remove any excess liquid.

In a skillet, heat the olive oil over high heat. Add the *jamón serrano* and sauté, stirring, for 1 to 2 minutes to color lightly. Add the pine nuts, stir well, and then add the Swiss chard and the raisins, again mixing well. Cook briefly, stirring, until all the ingredients are heated through.

Serve immediately, or remove from the heat, set aside, and reheat later just before serving.

CALÇOTS A LA BRASA CON SALSA ROMESCO ▪ Grilled Scallions with Romesco Sauce ▪ (Catalonia)

On a visit to the village of Valls in Catalonia, I was invited to an unforgettable *calçotada*, an early spring celebration of the delicious *calçots*, large green onions that are grilled and dipped in nutty *romesco* sauce. *Calçotadas* are happy events that typically bring together friends and family members. In *Catalan Cuisine*, Colman Andrews goes into admirable depth on the process of growing, cooking, and eating *calçots*, which look similar to leeks but are much sweeter and more tender. In the United States, I use the largest scallions available, and the recipe works beautifully. I usually serve the *calçots* before grilling fish or meat for a barbecue lunch or dinner.

Valls is also known throughout Spain for its *castellets*, or human castles, a fascinating spectacle that I watched on the village square just before the *calçotada*. Every Friday evening, the young people in town train in the amazingly daring art of creating human columns, sometimes as many as eight levels high. A large circle of as many as twenty men form the ground level, and another group of between sixteen and eighteen young men climb onto their shoulders. Groups of youngsters climb atop this second level, forming ever higher interlocked levels, until the castle is crowned by a six- or seven-year-old boy, who scampers like a monkey over backs and shoulders to crown the top. The finished tower is a majestic sight—as long as you can keep from imagining your own children swaying at the peak! ▪ **Serves 4**

24 large scallions, ends trimmed

2 cups Romesco Sauce (page 310)

Prepare a hot fire in a charcoal grill.

Place the scallions directly over the fire and grill, turning them occasionally, for about 10 minutes, or until they are blackened on the outside and tender inside. Remove the scallions from the grill, wrap tightly in newspaper, slip into a large plastic bag, and let cool for 1 hour.

Unwrap the scallions, and remove and discard the outer burnt layer. Serve them with the sauce for dipping.

ALCACHOFAS CON TIRABEQUES ▪
Seared Artichoke Hearts with Snow Peas ▪
(Murcia)

Tirabeques, or snow peas, are common in the vegetable gardens of Murcia. Here, they are combined with tender artichoke hearts to create a first course favored by local cooks. ▪ **Serves 4**

> Juice of 2 lemons
>
> 1 tablespoon coarse salt
>
> $^1/_2$ cup plus 3 tablespoons extra virgin olive oil
>
> 4 large artichokes, about $^3/_4$ pound each
>
> 1 pound snow peas, trimmed and strings removed
>
> $^1/_4$ pound jamón serrano or other dry-cured ham, finely minced (optional)
>
> Parsley Oil (page 315) for garnish

In a large bowl, combine the lemon juice, salt, and the $^1/_2$ cup olive oil. Mix well.

Working with 1 artichoke at a time, peel off the leaves completely until you get to the core. (Reserve the leaves for use in the delicious snack recipe that follows.) Using a small, sharp-edged spoon, scoop out the fuzzy choke that remains and discard. Cut off the stem flush with the bottom, and trim around the bottom of each artichoke, removing the tough outer layer. Cut the bottoms crosswise into thin slices, and toss the slices into the lemon mixture. Repeat with the remaining artichokes. Add the snow peas to the artichokes and toss well.

Heat a large, dry nonreactive skillet over high heat. When the surface is very hot, lift the artichoke slices from the marinade with a slotted spoon and place them in a single layer in the pan. Sear for 1 minute. Decrease the heat to medium and sear for another minute, or until the slices are nicely browned at the edges. Raise the heat to high, turn the artichokes, and cook for 2 more minutes, again lowering the heat to medium after a minute. Remove the artichokes from the skillet, set aside, and keep warm. Repeat until you have cooked all of the slices.

Return the skillet to high heat. When the surface is very hot, lift the snow peas from the marinade with the slotted spoon and place in the pan. Cook, stirring them constantly, for about 2 minutes, or until bright, shiny, and tender-crisp. Remove the snow peas from the skillet, set aside, and keep warm.

Heat the remaining 3 tablespoons olive oil in the skillet over high heat. Add the ham and fry, stirring constantly, until lightly browned, about 1 minute. Using the slotted spoon, transfer to paper towels to drain.

Distribute the snow peas evenly among individual plates, arrange the artichoke slices over the snow peas, and sprinkle the ham on top. Drizzle the parsley oil around the rim of the plate. Serve immediately while the vegetables are still warm.

Artichoke Leaves

In a nonreactive saucepan, combine the artichoke leaves with 2 quarts water and 1 tablespoon salt and bring to a boil over high heat. Decrease the heat to medium and cook for 30 minutes, or until the leaves turn brownish green and are tender. (To test for doneness, taste the base of a leaf.) Drain the leaves, reserving the water. Toss the leaves with Sherry Vinaigrette (page 314) and eat them as a snack, scraping the meat off the bottom of the leaves with your front teeth.

Pour the reserved cooking water into a pitcher, add a little lemon juice and a touch of extra virgin olive oil, mix well, and refrigerate. Drink it in the morning on an empty stomach. The Spanish believe it is a great diuretic.

GAZPACHO DE TRIGUEROS ∷ Asparagus with Eggs ∷ (Extremadura)

Trigueros, or slim wild asparagus, are difficult to find outside of Spain, but this classic recipe can be prepared with cultivated asparagus. Although its name might lead you to think this dish is similar to a tomato gazpacho (page 86), it is more of a soupy vegetable dish than a true soup. For the best flavor, serve at room temperature. ∷ **Serves 6**

> 1 pound asparagus spears
> 1/4 cup olive oil
> 4 hard-boiled eggs, peeled
> 2 tablespoons red wine vinegar
> 6 cups water
> 2 cloves garlic, coarsely chopped
> 1 slice day-old country-style bread, torn into pieces
> 2 teaspoons salt

Snap off the tough end of each asparagus spear by bending it; it will break where it begins to be fibrous. Discard the ends and cut the spears on a severe diagonal into 1/4-inch-thick strips.

In a large sauté pan, heat the olive oil over high heat. Add the asparagus and sauté for about 5 minutes, or until slightly undercooked. Using a slotted spoon, remove the asparagus to a bowl. Reserve the oil in the pan.

Halve 2 of the hard-boiled eggs, remove the yolks, and set aside the whites. Finely chop the removed yolks along with the remaining 2 whole eggs and transfer to a large bowl. Add the vinegar, half of the asparagus, the reserved oil, and 1 cup of the water to the bowl and mix well with a wooden spoon.

In a blender or food processor, combine the remaining asparagus, the garlic, bread, and 1 cup of the water and process until smooth. Transfer to the bowl holding the eggs and asparagus. Add the remaining 4 cups water and the salt and stir gently to incorporate. Taste and adjust the seasoning.

Coarsely chop the reserved egg whites and sprinkle on top. Serve at room temperature in individual bowls.

ESCALIVADA ∷ Roasted Eggplant, Onion, and Pepper with Olive Oil ∷ (Catalonia)

Catalonians eat this dish as a first course or as an accompaniment to meats. The special characteristic of these roasted vegetables is their smoky flavor, since orthodoxy demands roasting them over embers (the Catalan word escalivar means "to roast over ashes or embers"). I have prepared them in the oven with good results. ∷ **Serves 4**

> 4 small eggplants
> 4 spring onions or large scallions
> 4 red bell peppers
> 2 tomatoes
> Extra virgin olive oil for brushing, plus 1/3 cup
> 2 cloves garlic, thinly sliced
> Salt

Prepare a hot fire in a charcoal grill, or preheat the oven to 500°F.

Brush the eggplants, onions, bell peppers, and tomatoes with olive oil. If using a grill, place the vegetables directly over the fire and grill, turning frequently, for 15 to 30 minutes, or until the skins blacken and the vegetables are tender. The variation in timing depends on the heat of the fire, and some vegetables, such as the tomatoes, may be ready before the others. If using an oven, arrange the vegetables on a rimmed baking sheet or in a roasting pan and roast, turning every 10 minutes, for 30 minutes, or until the skins blacken and the vegetables are tender. Remove the vegetables from the grill or oven, wrap in newspapers, slip into 1 or more plastic bags, and let cool for 1 hour.

Unwrap the vegetables. Peel the eggplants, peppers, and tomatoes, and peel away the outer layer of the onions. Split the bell peppers in half, discard the seeds and stems, and cut lengthwise into strips about 11/2 inches wide. Transfer to a bowl. Trim the stems from the eggplants and core the tomatoes, and then cut them into strips of the same size as the pepper strips and add to the bowl. Trim the onions, cut into rings, and add to the bowl along with the garlic.

Add the 1/3 cup olive oil, season with salt, and toss to mix well. Serve at room temperature.

BERENJENAS RELLENAS ::
Stuffed Eggplants :: *(Balearic Islands)*

The eggplants grown on Majorca are smaller than those from the mainland and are a particularly pretty purple, lighter than the eggplants commonly seen in the United States. I typically serve one whole eggplant to each guest for a first course, though occasionally I double the amount because the eggplants are so delicious. They also taste wonderful reheated the following day.

I use bread crumbs in this recipe because I have never been able to find the omnipresent Majorcan Quely crackers in the United States. But any island cook would forgive that shortcoming (and maybe not even notice the difference). :: **Serves 6**

1 cup olive oil

6 small eggplants, about 1 pound total weight, stem end trimmed and cut in half lengthwise

Salt

1 large yellow onion, finely chopped

1 clove garlic, finely chopped

1/2 pound lean ground pork

1/2 pound lean ground beef

1/2 teaspoon chopped fresh marjoram

Freshly ground black pepper

1 tablespoon fine dried bread crumbs

1/2 cup Majorcan Tomato Sauce (page 312)

In a deep skillet, heat the olive oil over medium-high heat until very hot. Season the eggplant halves with salt. Working in batches, fry the eggplant halves, cut side down, for about 5 minutes, or until browned. Decrease the heat to medium, turn the eggplants, and fry them on the round side for another 5 minutes, or until they have shrunken slightly and the flesh is tender. Using a slotted spoon, transfer the eggplants to paper towels to drain and pat them dry with additional towels to remove any excess oil. Let cool completely. Repeat with the remaining eggplant halves.

Discard all but 2 tablespoons of oil from the pan and return the pan to medium heat. Add the onion and garlic and sauté, stirring often, for 10 minutes, or until softened. Add the pork, beef, and marjoram, season with salt and pepper, and mix well, using the edge of a wooden spatula or spoon to break up the ground meat into bits. Sauté, stirring occasionally, for another 10 minutes, or until the meat is crumbly and cooked through. Transfer the mixture to a bowl.

Preheat the oven to 400°F. Lightly oil a rimmed baking sheet.

Using a spoon, carefully remove the pulp of each eggplant half, taking care not to break the skin, and add the pulp to the meat mixture; reserve the eggplant shells for filling. Mix the eggplant pulp with the meat and taste and adjust the seasoning. Spoon the mixture into the empty eggplant halves. Transfer the stuffed eggplants to the prepared baking sheet. Sprinkle the tops evenly with the bread crumbs, and cover with about 2 teaspoons of the tomato sauce.

Bake the eggplants for 10 minutes, or until heated through. Place 2 eggplant halves on each plate and serve immediately.

CALABACINES RELLENOS DE CARNE ▪ Zucchini Stuffed with Ground Meats ▪ (Murcia)

Zucchini are abundant in many parts of Spain, but especially in Murcia and Aragón. They are cooked in soups, sautéed for side dishes, combined with other vegetables as in the *pisto* on page 118, or filled with ground meat and baked as in this Murcian recipe. ▪ **Serves 4**

4 small zucchini, halved lengthwise

1/3 cup olive oil

1 yellow onion, finely chopped

2 tomatoes, halved crosswise, grated on the large holes of a handheld grater, and skins discarded

5 ounces lean ground pork

5 ounces lean ground beef

Salt

Freshly ground black pepper

2 tablespoons fine dried bread crumbs

2 tablespoons grated aged Manchego or other aged hard cheese such as Parmesan

Preheat the oven to 300°F. Lightly oil a rimmed baking sheet.

Using a sharp-edged spoon, remove the pulp from each zucchini half, taking care to leave a thin layer inside the skin so that the shells look like small canoes. Finely chop the pulp and set it and the shells aside.

In a sauté pan, heat the olive oil over medium heat. Add the onion and tomatoes and sauté, stirring frequently, for 10 minutes, or until softened. Add the pork, beef, and zucchini pulp, season with salt and pepper, and mix well, using the edge of a wooden spatula or spoon to break up the ground meats into bits. Increase the heat to high and sauté for 5 minutes, or until the meat is crumbly and cooked through. Transfer the mixture to a bowl and let cool.

Spoon the meat mixture into the cavities of the zucchini halves. Transfer the stuffed halves, filled side up, to the prepared baking sheet. Sprinkle evenly with the bread crumbs and then with the cheese.

Bake the zucchini for 30 minutes, or until the shells are tender and the stuffing is heated through. Place 2 zucchini halves on each plate and serve immediately.

ZARANGOLLO MURCIANO ▪ Stewed Zucchini with Onion ▪ (Murcia)

This simple dish, which combines the ubiquitous zucchini of Murcia with onions, is a favorite of Murcian cooks, who prepare it both with and without eggs. When zucchini flowers, which are less commonly at hand and expensive, are in the market, they are usually stuffed and fried. ▪ **Serves 6**

1/2 cup extra virgin olive oil

2 cloves garlic, minced

3 yellow onions, finely chopped

2 pounds zucchini, peeled and cut into small dice

Salt

Freshly ground black pepper

1 teaspoon chopped fresh oregano, or 1/2 teaspoon dried oregano

6 eggs (optional)

In a large sauté pan, heat 1/4 cup of the olive oil over medium heat. Add the garlic and onions and cook, stirring often, for 5 minutes. Decrease the heat to medium-low and cook for about 15 minutes, or until soft and translucent.

Meanwhile, heat the remaining 1/4 cup olive oil in another sauté pan over medium heat. Add the zucchini and cook, stirring often, for 15 minutes, or until they have softened and released their juices. Remove from the heat and drain off any liquid released during cooking. Transfer the zucchini to the pan with the onions.

Season the mixture with salt and pepper, add the oregano, and cook over medium heat, stirring often, for 5 minutes to blend the flavors. If desired, break the eggs onto the vegetables and cook over medium heat for about 5 minutes, or until the whites are set.

Remove from the heat and serve hot or at room temperature.

CARDO EN LECHE ::
Cardoon Stewed in Milk :: *(Aragón)*

Cardoon is popular in Aragón and Navarra. Its flavor is roughly a cross between artichoke and celery, and it looks somewhat like a large bunch of celery, although it is paler, almost whitish, and the stalks are not as dense. Cardoons are in season from October until February, but they are at their best after the first frost, in December, when the outer leaves are tender and mild, unlike the tough, bitter leaves of cardoons harvested earlier in the season. Some cooks add flour to the cooking water to help whiten the stalks, though often, particularly in Navarra, plain water is used. This recipe from Aragón calls for cooking the cardoons with milk and almonds, which nicely balance the flavor of the vegetable. :: **Serves 4**

1 bunch cardoon, about 2 pounds total weight

2 quarts water

1 tablespoon salt

2 tablespoons all-purpose flour

6 tablespoons olive oil

1 small yellow onion, finely minced

1 clove garlic, peeled and left whole

12 blanched almonds

1 tablespoon chopped fresh flat-leaf parsley

1 cup whole milk

Remove and discard the tough outer stalks of the cardoons. Wash the tender inner stalks under running cold water. With a knife, scratch off any impurities and pull off the threads, if any, from the edges. Cut the stalks crosswise into 3-inch-long pieces.

In a large saucepan, bring the water to a boil over high heat. Add the salt and 1 tablespoon of the flour and mix well. Add the cardoon pieces, decrease the heat to medium, and cook for 1 hour, or until tender. Drain the cardoon pieces, reserving 1 cup of the cooking liquid, and set aside.

In the same saucepan, heat the olive oil over medium-high heat. When it is hot, add the onion, decrease the heat to medium, and sauté for 5 minutes, or until soft. Add the remaining 1 tablespoon flour and stir to incorporate. Add 1/2 cup of the reserved cooking liquid, mixing well, and cook for 5 minutes. It should be a uniformly whitish mixture.

Meanwhile, in a mortar or a blender, combine the garlic, almonds, and parsley and pound with a pestle or process until well mashed. Add 1 tablespoon of the milk and pound or process until a paste almost forms. Transfer this mixture to the pan with the onion mixture, add the remaining milk, and stir with a wooden spoon to blend the ingredients evenly.

Add the cardoon pieces to the pan, decrease the heat to medium, and cook, shaking the pan occasionally, for about 5 minutes, or until the flavors are well blended. Add some or all of the remaining 1/2 cup cooking liquid if you prefer a thinner sauce.

Transfer to a serving dish and serve immediately.

HABAS RONDEÑAS ▪
Fava Beans with Jamón Serrano and
Hard-Boiled Egg ▪ (*Andalusia*)

This classic dish from Ronda—the enchanting Andalusian town that enamored the poet Rilke, Orson Welles, and the Bloomsbury writers, among many others—is a marvelous use of fresh fava beans. While watching over the construction of our house in Ronda, my husband and I stayed at the *cortijo* (an Andalusian farmstead) of our friends Gracia and Rafael Mazarrasa. Gracia maintains a vegetable garden from which we often harvested fava beans for this appetizer.

Once you shell the beans, you need to boil them to remove their tough outer skin. The process is time-consuming, but I find it a therapeutic break—a time to think quietly. You can, of course, enlist someone to help you to make the time pass more quickly. If you instead use dried fava beans, I recommend buying the split ones available in Middle Eastern markets; they are already skinned and they cook faster than whole dried beans. ▪ **Serves 6**

2 teaspoons salt

3 pounds fresh fava beans in the shell, or
   1$^1/_2$ pounds dried split fava beans

$^1/_4$ cup olive oil

1 yellow onion, finely chopped

1 clove garlic, minced

1 ($^1/_4$-inch-thick) slice jamón serrano or other
   dry-cured ham, about 3 ounces, finely diced

3 hard-boiled eggs, peeled

1 tablespoon chopped fresh flat-leaf parsley

Fill a saucepan with water and bring to a boil. Add the salt and the beans and boil for 15 minutes if using fresh favas and 30 minutes if using dried favas. Drain, reserving 1 cup of the cooking water. Peel the fresh beans to uncover their sparkling green color.

In a sauté pan, heat the olive oil over medium heat. Add the onion and garlic and sauté, stirring frequently, for about 10 minutes, or until the onion is soft and lightly caramelized. Add the *jamón serrano* and sauté for 2 minutes, or until its fat turns shiny. Add the beans and the reserved cooking liquid, cover, decrease the heat to medium-low, and cook for 15 minutes, or until the beans are tender.

Cut each egg lengthwise into 8 wedges, or chop the eggs coarsely. Add the eggs to the beans and mix well. Serve hot, garnished with the parsley.

MENESTRA DE VERDURAS NAVARRA ▪ Vegetable Medley ▪ (Navarra)

This recipe is one of the irreplaceable dishes on the menu of my favorite restaurant in Madrid, the acclaimed Príncipe de Viana. I had the honor of spending one week in its kitchen, where I worked closely with the owner, Chelo Oyarbide, a remarkable woman from Navarra who generously shared some of her culinary secrets with me.

You use only the stems of the Swiss chard in *menestra*. Cut away the greens and save them for making Sautéed Swiss Chard with Raisins and Pine Nuts (page 107). You will be using three pots simultaneously because the vegetables must be cooked separately, but the result more than justifies a crowded stove top. ▪ **Serves 6**

> 6 preserved or fresh white asparagus spears
>
> 3 quarts water
>
> Salt
>
> 6 Swiss chard stems
>
> 1/2 pound romano (flat) beans or regular green beans, ends trimmed
>
> 6 small artichokes
>
> 1 lemon, halved
>
> 1 tablespoon plus 1 teaspoon all-purpose flour
>
> 2 cups fresh or frozen shelled English peas
>
> 1/4 cup olive oil
>
> 4 thin slices jamón serrano or other dry-cured ham, minced

If using preserved asparagus, drain them and reserve 1 cup of the brine; set the asparagus and brine aside separately. If using fresh asparagus, cut off about 1 inch from the base of each spear and then peel the spears with a vegetable peeler.

Pour 1 quart of the water into a saucepan and bring to a boil over high heat. Salt the water lightly and add the Swiss chard stems, beans, and, if you are using them, the fresh asparagus. Cook for 20 minutes, or until the asparagus are tender, and then lift the asparagus out with a wire skimmer

or tongs. Continue cooking the chard stems and beans for 10 minutes longer, or until very tender. Drain, reserving 1 cup of the cooking liquid, and set aside to cool. When cool enough to handle, cut the chard stems and the beans into thin strips.

Meanwhile, working with 1 artichoke at a time, peel off the tough outer leaves. Cut off the stem flush with the bottom, and cut off the top one-third of the leaves. Rub the trimmed artichoke with a lemon half. Repeat with the remaining artichokes, rubbing them each with the same lemon half. In a second saucepan, bring 1 quart of the water to a boil over medium-high heat. Add 1 tablespoon of the flour and the remaining lemon half and stir to mix. (The lemon prevents the artichokes from turning dark, and the flour counterbalances the acidity of the lemon and makes the artichokes more tender.) Add the artichokes, decrease the heat to medium, cover, and cook for 20 minutes, or until tender when pierced with the tip of a knife. Drain.

Preheat the oven to 350°F.

In a third saucepan, bring the remaining 1 quart water to a boil over medium-high heat. Salt the water lightly, add the peas, decrease the heat to medium-low, and boil gently for about 5 minutes, or until tender. Drain.

Put the vegetables in separate piles on an ovenproof platter and place in the oven. Meanwhile, in a small skillet, heat the olive oil over medium heat. Add the *jamón serrano* and sauté, stirring often, for 1 minute, or until the fat glistens. Using a slotted spoon, lift the ham from the pan and sprinkle it evenly over the vegetables. Return the pan with the oil to high heat and stir in the remaining 1 teaspoon flour. Add the reserved 1 cup brine (or the cooking liquid if you used fresh asparagus), stirring to mix well, and bring to a boil. Cook, stirring often, for about 2 minutes, or until the liquid turns opaque.

Pour the sauce over the vegetables, heat through in the oven for 2 minutes, and serve immediately.

SAMFAINA ▪ Vegetable Stew ▪
(Catalonia)

Samfaina, also known as *chanfaina*, is a vegetable stew that resembles French ratatouille—or maybe ratatouille resembles *samfaina*, as some Catalans would say. In Salamanca, cooks make a rice dish called *chanfaina*, but it has nothing to do with this Catalan vegetable dish. *Samfaina* is sometimes eaten alone as a first course, but more often it is served as an accompaniment to chicken or meats, or even as a filling for *canelones* or ravioli. ▪

Serves 4

> 1 eggplant
> 1 red bell pepper
> 1 yellow onion
> 1 large tomato
> Olive oil for brushing vegetables, plus 6 tablespoons
> 1 clove garlic, thinly sliced
> 1 large zucchini, cut into ¹/₂-inch cubes
> 2 teaspoons salt

Prepare a hot fire in a charcoal grill, or preheat the oven to 500°F.

Brush the eggplant, bell pepper, onion, and tomato with olive oil. If using a grill, place the vegetables directly over the fire and grill, turning frequently to avoid burning, for 15 to 30 minutes, or until the skins blacken and the vegetables are tender. The variation in timing depends on the heat of the fire, and some vegetables, such as the tomato, may be ready before the others. If using an oven, arrange the vegetables on a rimmed baking sheet or in a roasting pan and roast, turning every 10 minutes, for 30 minutes, or until the skins blacken and the vegetables are tender. Remove the vegetables from the grill or oven, wrap in newspaper, slip into 1 or more plastic bags, and let cool for 1 hour.

Meanwhile, in a large sauté pan, heat the 6 tablespoons olive oil over medium-high heat. Add the garlic and sauté, stirring often, for 2 to 3 minutes, or until golden. Add the zucchini, decrease the heat to medium, and cook, stirring

occasionally, for 15 minutes, or until they have softened and released their juices. Remove from the heat.

Unwrap the vegetables. Peel the eggplant, bell pepper, and tomato. Split the bell pepper in half, remove and discard the seeds and stem, and cut the flesh into 1-inch squares. Transfer to the sauté pan holding the zucchini. Trim the stem from the eggplant and core the tomato, and then cut them into 1-inch cubes and add to the pan. Remove the outer layer from the onion, cut the onion into rings, and add to the pan.

Place the sauté pan over high heat, season with salt, and cook, stirring occasionally, for 5 minutes, or until the liquid evaporates. Taste and adjust the seasoning. Serve warm.

Sautéed Salt Cod in Vegetable Stew

This stew is also combined with salt cod to make a heartier dish known as *bacalao con samfaina*. For the best result, look for cod pieces 1¹/₂ inches thick. Desalt 1¹/₂ pounds salt cod (page 46) and cut into 6 pieces. In a large skillet, heat ¹/₄ cup olive oil over medium heat. When the oil is hot, add the cod and fry, turning once or twice, for 5 minutes, or until lightly golden. Using a slotted spoon, transfer the cod to a plate. Reserve the oil in the pan. When the cod is cool enough to handle, remove the skin and any errant bones. Return the pan with the oil to medium heat, add 2 cups of the cooked vegetables, and cook for about 5 minutes to heat through. Add the cod pieces, mix well with the vegetables, and cook for 5 minutes longer, or until heated through and the flavors are blended. Serve hot. Serves 6.

PISTO MANCHEGO ORIGINAL ▪▪
The Original Vegetable Stew of La Mancha
▪▪ (Castilla–La Mancha)

Manolo López Camerana, a respected authority on Manchego cooking, insisted I mention that contemporary *pistos* have little in common with the original one, which never included the onions, zucchini, and sometimes eggplants you see today. This dish must have been a novelty during the years following the discovery of America, since both peppers and tomatoes came from the New World. The formula for the amount of vegetables you need is simple: use twice the weight of tomatoes as peppers. In La Mancha, this dish is served as a first course the day after it is made. ▪▪ **Serves 4**

6 tablespoons olive oil

1 pound small green sweet peppers, seeded and
finely chopped

2 pounds tomatoes, coarsely chopped

Pinch of sugar

Salt

In a sauté pan, heat 5 tablespoons of the olive oil over high heat. Add the peppers, decrease the heat to medium, and sauté, stirring frequently, for about 10 minutes, or until softened. Set aside.

Add the tomatoes to a second sauté pan and bring to a boil over high heat. Boil for 5 minutes, stirring constantly. Decrease the heat to medium and cook the tomatoes for 15 minutes, or until most of the liquid has evaporated. Add the remaining 1 tablespoon olive oil and the sugar, season with salt, and cook for 10 minutes longer, or until the tomatoes resemble a thick purée.

Add the peppers to the tomatoes, mix well, and cook for 5 minutes to blend the flavors. Let cool, cover, and refrigerate to allow time for the flavors to develop.

The next day, reheat the vegetables and serve warm.

PISTO MANCHEGO COMÚN ▪▪
The Common Vegetable Stew of
La Mancha ▪▪ (Castilla–La Mancha)

This variation on the classic *pisto* of La Mancha (left) is beloved across Spain, and even though it departs from the recipe of old, Don Quixote would probably still approve. We usually serve it as a first course with fried eggs or scrambled eggs, or alone. ▪▪ **Serves 6**

1/2 cup olive oil

1 pound small green sweet peppers, seeded and
finely chopped

1 yellow onion, finely chopped

4 zucchini, peeled and diced

Salt

1 cup Tomato Sauce (page 311)

In a sauté pan, heat 5 tablespoons of the olive oil over high heat. Add the peppers and onion, decrease the heat to medium, and sauté, stirring frequently, for about 10 minutes, or until softened. Set aside.

Place a second sauté pan over medium heat and add the remaining 3 tablespoons olive oil. When it is hot, add the zucchini, season with salt, and cook, stirring often, for 15 minutes, or until they have softened and released their juices. Remove from the heat and drain off any liquid released during cooking.

Transfer the zucchini to the pan with the peppers and onion and place over low heat. Add the tomato sauce, mix well, and cook, stirring occasionally, for 5 minutes longer to blend the flavors.

Taste and adjust the seasoning. Serve warm.

PIMIENTOS DEL PIQUILLO REHOGADOS ▪ Sautéed Piquillo Peppers ▪ (*Navarra*)

Piquillo peppers require little extra work because they are already roasted and bursting with flavor straight out of the jar. I often serve them as a side dish with meats, sautéing them in olive oil, garlic, and a little milk. The addition of the milk is not traditional, but I have found that it combines with the oil to make a whitish and surprisingly delicious sauce. ▪ **Serves 4**

6 tablespoons olive oil

1 clove garlic, thinly sliced

1 (10-ounce) jar preserved whole piquillo peppers (about 18 peppers)

Salt

¹/₄ cup whole milk

In a sauté pan, heat the olive oil over high heat. Add the garlic and sauté for about 2 minutes, or until it begins to turn golden. Add the *piquillo* peppers, decrease the heat to medium-low, season with salt, and stir briefly to blend the ingredients. Add the milk, decrease the heat to low, and cook, swirling the pan occasionally, for about 5 minutes, or until the sauce turns whitish and the flavors are blended. Serve immediately.

Light rain at dusk on the streets of Sevilla, Andalusia

FLAN DE PIMIENTOS DEL PIQUILLO CON MERLUZA Y GAMBAS ▪ Piquillo Pepper Flan with Hake and Shrimp ▪ (La Rioja)

I first had this dish many years ago in La Rioja, at the house of a friend of my mother's, and have made it ever since. It can be prepared in advance, and therefore I often serve it to guests, either at room temperature with mayonnaise, as in this recipe, or warm with a tomato sauce (page 211). ▪ **Serves 4**

1/2 cup olive oil

1/2 yellow onion, chopped

1 leek, white part only, cut into thick rings

10 preserved whole piquillo peppers, coarsely chopped, or 3 red bell peppers, roasted, peeled, seeded, and coarsely chopped

12 shrimp, peeled and coarsely chopped

1/4 pound hake or cod fillet or scallops, coarsely chopped

Salt

2 eggs

1/2 cup heavy cream

1/2 cup Mayonnaise (page 306)

6 tablespoons freshly squeezed orange juice

1 tablespoon finely chopped fresh flat-leaf parsley

In a sauté pan, heat the olive oil over medium-high heat. Add the onion and leek, decrease the heat to medium, and sauté, stirring often, for about 10 minutes, or until tender. Add the *piquillo* peppers and continue to cook for about 15 minutes, or until the vegetables are soft and have a stewlike quality.

Preheat the oven to 375°F. Lightly oil a round baking dish 8 inches in diameter and at least 6 inches deep.

Season the shrimp and hake with salt and add them to the sauté pan, stirring them in with the vegetables. Decrease the heat to low and sauté, stirring occasionally, for 5 minutes, or until the seafood is opaque. Remove the pan from the heat, transfer the mixture to a bowl, and let cool to lukewarm.

Fill a teakettle with water and bring to a boil. Meanwhile, in a bowl, beat the eggs until blended, add the cream, and mix well. Add the lukewarm seafood mixture to the bowl and mix well. Transfer the mixture to a blender and process until a coarse purée forms. Pour the purée into the prepared baking dish and cover tightly with aluminum foil.

Place the covered baking dish in a roasting pan and pour boiling water into the roasting pan to reach one-third of the way up the sides of the baking dish. Bake the flan for 30 minutes, or until set. Carefully remove the baking dish from the water bath and place on a rack. Uncover and let cool to room temperature. (Once the flan is cool, it can be re-covered and refrigerated for several hours; bring to room temperature before serving.)

To unmold, run a knife blade around the inside of the baking dish to loosen the sides of the flan, then invert a flat plate a couple of inches larger than the baking dish over the top and invert the dish and plate together. Lift off the dish.

In a small bowl, whisk together the mayonnaise and orange juice. Sprinkle the flan with the parsley and surround it with dollops of the orange-flavored mayonnaise. Cut the flan into wedges and serve each slice with a little of the mayonnaise.

PAPAS ARRUGADAS ::
Wrinkled Potatoes :: *(Canary Islands)*

2 pounds baby red potatoes

¹/₂ pound coarse salt

1 cup Green Mojo or Spicy Red Mojo (page 309)

In the Canaries, as in most Latin American countries, the name for potato is *papa*, rather than *patata*, the common term in the rest of Spain. The Canaries were a port of call for ships laden with goods from the New World on their way home to Spain, hence the linguistic connection.

Cooked in heavily salted water, *papas arrugadas* are served as a tapa or as a side dish with meats and fish, and are eaten with the skin on, dipped in one of the islands' classic *mojos*. It is not easy to achieve the distinctive "wrinkling." For best results, use small potatoes, preferably baby red potatoes or baby creamers. The salt extracts moisture from the potatoes but will not make them taste salty. Placing small, clean, uniform stones on the bottom of the pan will prevent the bottom layer of potatoes from sticking to the pan and burning once the water is completely evaporated. Only when the water has evaporated will the potatoes begin to wrinkle—a trick one typically learns only from the locals. :: **Serves 6**

Select a heavy stockpot or saucepan about 8 inches in diameter and at least 5 inches deep and cover the bottom completely with small stones. Place the potatoes on top of the stones and add enough water so that the tops of the potatoes are just peeking out. Sprinkle with the salt. Bring to a boil over high heat; cover, leaving a little corner uncovered to allow steam to escape; and boil for 30 minutes, or until most of the water has evaporated but still covers the stones.

Remove the lid and place a clean kitchen towel on top of the potatoes. (Unlike the lid, the towel allows the remaining water to evaporate slowly.) Decrease the heat to the lowest setting and cook for about 20 minutes longer, or until the water evaporates completely. Remove the pot from the stove and let rest, covered with the towel, for 30 minutes, or until the potatoes are nicely wrinkled and have cooled somewhat but are still warm.

Serve warm with the *mojo* of your choice.

Papas arrugadas *(wrinkled potatoes) at a bar in Teguise, in the center of Lanzarote (Canary Islands)*

PATATAS A LA IMPORTANCIA ▪▪
Potatoes of Importance ▪▪ *(Two Castiles)*

The potatoes in this dish gain "importance" when fried in a simple batter of flour and egg. The dish used to be common in many homes, especially in Madrid, and although many younger families have forgotten about it, *patatas a la importancia* is still a classic among the older crowd. It is a wonderful appetizer, but it can also be served as a small meal, especially for children. Although you can fry the potatoes, arrange them on a platter, top them with the hot sauce, and serve them right away, they taste a bit better if you heat the fried potatoes and the sauce together on the stove top or in the oven. ▪▪ **Serves 4**

Harvest of Canary Island potatoes in Lanzarote

3 medium white boiling potatoes, about 1¹/₂ pounds total weight

Salt

3 tablespoons all-purpose flour

2 eggs

¹/₂ cup olive oil

2 cups Onion and Carrot Sauce (page 311)

In a large saucepan, combine the potatoes with water to cover and bring to a boil over medium-high heat. Decrease the heat to low and cook, uncovered, for about 20 minutes, until the potatoes are fork-tender. Drain and let cool completely.

Peel the potatoes and cut them crosswise into ¹/₂-inch-thick slices. Season the slices with salt. Spread the flour in a shallow dish. Coat the potato slices on both sides with the flour and shake off any excess. In a small bowl, beat the eggs until blended.

In a skillet, heat the olive oil over high heat. Working in batches, dip the potato slices into the beaten egg, allowing the excess to drip off, and arrange them in a single layer in the hot oil. Decrease the heat to medium and fry, turning once, for 1 minute on each side, or until golden. Transfer to paper towels to drain and pat the tops of the slices dry with additional paper towels. Repeat with the remaining potato slices.

Layer the potatoes in a *cazuela* (page 51), cover with the sauce, and quickly reheat over medium heat on the stove top. Or, layer the potatoes in a baking dish, cover with the sauce, and heat in a preheated 400°F oven for about 10 minutes, or until piping hot. Serve immediately directly from the dish.

HUEVOS AL MODO DE SOLER ::
Fried Eggs with Sobrasada in Creamy Sauce
:: (Balearic Islands)

Fried eggs in oil are a favorite across Spain. This rendition features the delicious *sobrasada* from Majorca (page 124), the pâtélike sausage made from the local black pig. Chorizo can be used in its place. :: **Serves 4**

1³/4 cups olive oil, plus 2 tablespoons if using chorizo

¹/2 cup fresh or thawed frozen shelled English peas

1 carrot, peeled and thinly sliced

1 leek, white part only, sliced

1 cup whole milk

¹/2 teaspoon sugar

1 teaspoon salt

8 thin slices sobrasada or chorizo, about 2 ounces total weight

8 eggs, at room temperature

In a sauté pan, heat 6 tablespoons of the olive oil over medium heat. Add the peas, carrot, and leek and sauté for 5 minutes, or until tender. Add the milk, sugar, and salt and stir well. Decrease the heat to low, cover, and cook for 20 minutes, or until the vegetables are very soft. Pass the mixture through a food mill fitted with the medium blade or process in a food processor until smooth. Keep warm.

In a small, dry skillet, cook the *sobrasada* over high heat for about 30 seconds on each side, or until the surface is shiny. If using chorizo, heat the 2 tablespoons olive oil in a small skillet before adding the slices, and then cook as directed for the *sobrasada*. Place 2 slices of the sausage in the center of each plate; transfer to a low oven.

Heat 1 cup of the olive oil in the same skillet. When the oil is hot, fry the eggs one at a time as described on page 125, or two at a time using your preferred technique. When you finish cooking each egg, place it on top of a sausage slice (2 eggs to a plate). As you fry the eggs, gradually replenish the frying oil with the remaining 6 tablespoons olive oil, adding a little before you fry each egg.

When you have finished cooking all of the eggs, spoon the sauce on top and serve immediately.

:: Spanish Fried Eggs ::

Spanish cooks fry eggs often, usually as part of a lunch or dinner, rather than for breakfast. And we Spanish dislike eggs when the white is not completely set, but we also love the yolk to be runny, so we can dip small pieces of bread into it.

At my parents' home in Bilbao, my father has a collection of paintings from his late friend Pelayo Olaortua, who visited our house many times. Several of these paintings are extraordinary still lifes of fried eggs, a food that Pelayo was particularly adept at preparing. His technique, which he shared with me, results in perfectly set whites and runny yolks.

Begin by using eggs at room temperature. Heat 1 cup olive oil in a small skillet. Break the eggs and separate the whites into individual small bowls, keeping the yolks in their shells. When the oil is hot, slide the first white into the pan and fry it over high heat for 30 seconds, or until it begins to bubble. Using a slotted spatula, "wave" a little of the hot oil over the white and then form a little indentation in the center with the spatula's edge. Now, carefully slide the yolk into this hollow and continue distributing some hot olive oil on top for 15 seconds. Lift the egg from the oil with a slotted spatula and transfer to a plate. The yolk will be runny and shiny, but the white will be completely set, with *puntillas* (golden lacelike formations) around the edges. Reheat the oil for 15 seconds before frying the next egg.

Be sure to cook only 1 egg at a time so the oil will maintain the proper heat, and add additional oil as needed. You can keep the cooked eggs in a low oven while preparing the rest.

:: Sobrasada ::

Residents of the Balearic Islands are unabashed partisans for their distinctive red *sobrasada* sausage. It is made from the meat of the local *porc negre*, or "black pig," which is related to the *ibérico* pig of the mainland, but is slightly larger with a longer neck and meatier cheeks, and it is seasoned with a hot *pimentón* ground from the local red peppers. The meat and seasonings are stuffed into casings, and the sausages are then hung to cure in the open air, usually for between one month and eight months, with the timing determined by the size and shape of the casing. All of the casings are from the pig as well, and they can range from long and thin to short and stout to very large, depending on whether the smallest intestine, the colon, or even the stomach is used.

Although from the outside *sobrasada* looks like a sausage, the texture inside is more like a soft pâté. When eaten on its own, it is usually spread on toast, rather than cut into slices as you would a chorizo or *salchichón*. It is also used to flavor other dishes, and is a popular topping for *cocas*, the typical flatbreads of the islands.

The late Spanish gastronomist Nestor Luján considered *sobrasada* the best pâté in the world. I agree with him. Its unique texture is due to the humid and salty Mediterranean air on the islands, conditions that are terrible for curing the hams so coveted on the mainland but are ideal for curing this sublime delicacy.

Because of the increasing demand for *sobrasada* both in the Balearics and in Catalonia, where it is also popular, some farmers are using the meat of light-coated European pigs to make the sausage, creating a less expensive but still tasty product. For the adventurous reader with the desire to try something special, here are the proportions for the primary ingredients for homemade *sobrasada* that I learned from my Majorcan friends: 65 percent pork tenderloin and 35 percent fatback and lard in equal portions. Finely mince the meat, fatback, and lard and season with salt, pepper, and hot *pimentón*. Fill natural or artificial casings with the mixture and cure your sausages in a cool place of about 50°F. For thinner sausages (about two inches in diameter) allow a minimum of two months for curing; for thicker sausages (between three and five inches in diameter), allow four to five months.

Since you will not be using meat from the *porc negre*, this *sobrasada* can only roughly approximate the real thing. But the next time you travel to Majorca, make sure you taste this unique and delicious sausage, checking first for the label that depicts the black pig, a guarantee of authenticity.

HUEVOS CON TORREZNOS ::
Fried Eggs with Crispy Fatback and
Cured Ham :: *(Extremadura)*

Extremadura is a paradise for lovers of pork products. The exquisite *torreznos*, or fatback from the *ibérico* pig, is not available in the United States, but I have had good results making this dish with fatty bacon or an end cut of domestic fatback, which usually contains streaks of lean meat. :: **Serves 4**

1¹/₂ cups olive oil

¹/₄ pound fatback with streaks of lean meat or fatty bacon, cut into large dice

4 thin slices jamón serrano or other dry-cured ham

8 eggs, at room temperature

Salt

A black-footed pig grazing on acorns

In a skillet, heat 3 tablespoons of the olive oil over high heat. Add the fatback and fry, turning constantly, for 5 minutes, or until crispy and golden brown. Using a slotted spoon, transfer the fatback to a dish and place in a low oven. Reserve the oil in the skillet.

Return the skillet to high heat. Add 2 slices of the *jamón serrano* and sauté, turning once, for 30 seconds on each side, or until the fat edging the ham glistens. Transfer to the dish holding the fatback. Repeat with the remaining 2 ham slices.

Heat 1 cup of the olive oil in another skillet over high heat. When the oil is hot, fry the eggs 1 at a time as described at right, or 2 at a time using your preferred technique. When you finish cooking each egg, transfer it to a plate and keep warm in a low oven (2 eggs to a plate). As you fry the eggs, gradually replenish the frying oil with the remaining 5 tablespoons olive oil, adding a little before you fry each egg.

When you have finished cooking the eggs, season them with salt.

Distribute the crispy fatback and ham evenly among the plates and serve immediately.

HUEVOS EN SALMORREJO ::
Poached Eggs with Asparagus and Pork ::
(Aragón)

This is a wonderful dish to prepare for a homey lunch or dinner on a cold winter day. Lourdes Plana, a proud Aragonese who is a food writer and editor and the director of the acclaimed annual gastronomic event known as Madrid Fusión, gave me her family recipe. The original calls for marinated pork tenderloin, which is easily purchased in butcher shops in Aragón but not in their American counterparts, and fresh sausages—a combination typical of the Daroca region of Aragón. Marinating the pork yourself is simple, but you will need to plan a day in advance. You can also use tenderloin that has not been marinated and the dish will still be excellent. :: **Serves 4**

MARINATED PORK

1/2 clove garlic

1/4 teaspoon salt

1 heaping tablespoon sweet pimentón or paprika

1/4 cup olive oil

1/2-pound piece pork tenderloin

8 fresh or preserved white asparagus spears

Salt

1/3 cup olive oil

1/2 pound fresh seasoned pork sausages,
    cut into 1/2-inch-thick slices

1 clove garlic, minced

1 tablespoon chopped fresh flat-leaf parsley

1 1/2 teaspoons all-purpose flour

1 1/2 teaspoons sweet pimentón or paprika

1 teaspoon red wine vinegar

4 eggs

To marinate the pork, in a mortar, combine the garlic and salt and mash with a pestle until a paste forms. Add the *pimentón* and olive oil and mash until the paste is an intense, uniform red. Rub the paste evenly over the tenderloin, wrap tightly in plastic wrap and then aluminum foil, and refrigerate for 24 hours. The next day, unwrap the tenderloin, cut crosswise into 1/2-inch-thick slices, and set aside.

If using preserved asparagus, drain them and reserve 1 cup of the brine; set the asparagus and brine aside separately. If using fresh asparagus, cut off about 1 inch from the base of each spear and then peel the spears with a vegetable peeler. Fill a saucepan with enough water to cover the asparagus once they are added and bring to a boil over high heat. Salt the water lightly, add the asparagus, decrease the heat to medium-low, and cook for 10 to 15 minutes, or until the stems test quite tender when pierced with the tip of a knife. Drain the asparagus, reserving 1 cup of the cooking liquid, and set the asparagus and liquid aside separately.

In a *cazuela* (page 51) about 12 inches in diameter, heat the olive oil over medium heat. Add the tenderloin and sausage slices and sauté, turning as needed, for 5 minutes, or until lightly browned. Using a slotted spoon, transfer the meats to a plate and set aside. Leave the oil in the pan.

Return the *cazuela* to medium-high heat, add the garlic and parsley, and sauté, stirring often, for 1 to 2 minutes, or until slightly golden. Add the flour and cook, stirring often, for 3 minutes, to blend the ingredients thoroughly. Remove from the heat and stir in the *pimentón* until evenly mixed.

Return the *cazuela* to low heat, add the meats, season with salt, and add the reserved asparagus brine or cooking liquid, mixing well. Cook for 5 minutes, stirring occasionally. Sprinkle the vinegar over the top of the mixture. Lay 4 asparagus spears, parallel and touching one another, across the center of the pan. Lay the other 4 spears, again parallel and touching one another, across the center of the pan, positioning them perpendicular to the first spears, forming a cross. Now break 1 egg into each of the 4 quadrants created by the cross. Season the eggs with salt, cover, and cook over low heat for 5 minutes, or until the whites are set and the yolks are still soft.

Place the *cazuela* in the center of the table. Transfer 1 egg and 2 asparagus to each plate and then distribute the meats and sauce evenly among the 4 plates. Serve immediately.

MORTERUELO DE CUENCA ::
Terrine of Hare and Partridge ::
(Castilla–La Mancha)

Morteruelo is a rich and ancient dish from Cuenca, a province of Castilla–La Mancha, east of Madrid. It is a pâtélike spread of game meats, usually served during winter on toasted bread. Since Castilla–La Mancha is large, variations of this recipe exist in different areas. In neighboring Albacete Province, for example, there is a similar dish known as *ajo mataero* (page 128), and in La Solana, in Ciudad Real Province, the local version is called *ajo pringue*. What these dishes have in common is the slow cooking of the meats and the addition of torta, the local flatbread, to make a robust nourishment for shepherds. Today, the recipe has been revived and is widely served in restaurants specializing in traditional cooking. I usually make *morteruelo* when I expect a large number guests on a given day. But if you don't finish it at a single sitting, you can refrigerate the leftovers for several days. :: **Serves 10**

1/2 hare or 1 small rabbit, about 3 pounds,
    cut into 8 pieces

1 partridge, about 3/4 pound, cut into quarters

1 pound boneless pork loin, in a single piece

1/2 pound jamón serrano or other dry-cured ham,
    in a single piece

1 ham bone from a dry-cured ham (optional)

Salt

Freshly ground black pepper

3/4 pound pork liver, in a single piece

2/3 cup olive oil

8 cloves garlic, peeled

1/2 pound bacon, finely chopped

1 teaspoon ground cinnamon

1 heaping tablespoon sweet pimentón or paprika

Pinch of ground cloves

Pinch of caraway seeds

1/2 pound country-style bread, thinly sliced
    and toasted

In a large stockpot, combine the hare, partridge, pork loin, *jamón serrano*, and ham bone, if using. Season with salt and pepper, add cold water to cover, and bring to a boil over high heat, skimming off any foam that forms on the surface. Decrease the heat to medium-low and cook, skimming as needed, for $1^1/_2$ to 2 hours, or until the meats are tender. Add water as necessary to keep the meats covered while cooking.

Scoop the meats out of the pot and set aside to cool to room temperature. Strain the cooking liquid through a fine-mesh sieve placed over a saucepan and reserve. When the meats are cool, remove and discard any bones. Shred the meats into fine pieces and set aside.

Bring the reserved cooking liquid to a boil and add the pork liver. Season with salt, decrease the heat to medium, and boil gently for 15 minutes, or until the liver turns pale. Lift the liver from the pot and let cool to room temperature. Strain the cooking liquid again and reserve about 4 cups. Grate the cooled liver on the large holes of a handheld grater and reserve.

In a large sauté pan, heat the olive oil over medium heat. Add the garlic and sauté, stirring often with a wood spoon, for about 5 minutes, or until golden. Remove and discard the garlic. In the same oil, fry the bacon over medium heat, stirring often, for 5 minutes, or until lightly browned. Add the cinnamon, *pimentón*, cloves, and caraway seeds and stir well. Add the shredded meats and grated liver and sauté, stirring occasionally, for 5 minutes, or until well blended.

Add the 4 cups reserved cooking liquid, mix well, and cook over medium heat for 15 minutes, stirring frequently. Slowly add the toasted bread a slice at a time, breaking it up with the wooden spoon until completely incorporated into the rest of the ingredients. Cook and stir for 10 minutes longer, or until the mixture acquires a smooth, creamy, pâtélike texture.

Serve at room temperature.

AJO MATAERO ▪ Country Pâté of Pork Liver ▪ (Castilla–La Mancha)

This delicious pâté from Albacete, a medieval town famous for its knives, is a typical first course for family lunches. It is served on a plate placed in the middle of the table, and everyone takes a portion and spreads it on toasted bread slices. Although this pâté is a little coarser than the hare and partridge terrine on page 127, both dishes are seasoned with cloves and cinnamon, common accents in savory dishes from this area of Spain. ▪

Serves 6

1/2 pound pork liver, cut into small strips

1 1/2 teaspoons salt

1/2 teaspoon freshly ground black pepper

1/4 cup olive oil

1/4 pound unsmoked bacon, coarsely chopped

1/4 pound country-style bread, sliced and toasted

2 cups water

1 clove garlic, peeled but left whole

1/2 teaspoon ground cinnamon

1 1/2 heaping teaspoons sweet pimentón or paprika

1/2 teaspoon dried oregano

Pinch of ground cloves

1/4 cup pine nuts

Season the liver with 1 teaspoon of the salt and the pepper. In a sauté pan, heat the olive oil over high heat. When it is hot, add the liver and bacon, decrease the heat to medium and cook, stirring, for 5 minutes, or until lightly browned. Using a slotted spoon, transfer the liver and bacon to a bowl and set aside.

Return the pan to medium heat, add the bread slices, and cook briefly, turning as needed, for a few minutes, or until the bread slices have soaked up the remaining oil and are lightly browned. Add the water, increase the heat to high, and bring to a boil. Decrease the heat to medium-low and cook, stirring occasionally, for 15 minutes, or until the mixture turns into a soupy porridge.

Meanwhile, in a blender or mortar, combine the garlic, cinnamon, *pimentón*, oregano, cloves, and a spoonful of the fried liver. Process or pound with a pestle for several minutes until a pastelike consistency forms.

Add the paste and the remaining 1/2 teaspoon salt to the bread mixture and continue to cook over medium-low heat, stirring frequently, for 15 minutes, or until thickened. Add the pine nuts and the bacon and liver, mix well with the rest of the ingredients, and cook for 10 minutes longer, or until all the liquid has evaporated and the mixture has a chunky, pâtélike texture.

Spoon the pâté onto a serving plate, shaping it into an attractive mound. Serve warm or at room temperature.

CANGREJOS A LA RIOJANA ■
Crayfish in Spicy Sauce ■ (La Rioja)

Susan Spicer, chef and owner of the famed Bayona restaurant in New Orleans, used to own the wonderful delicatessen Spices, and once invited me to give some cooking classes there. I thought it would be fun to prepare Spanish-style crayfish for an audience so familiar with the crustacean, even if it generated controversy as people compared my recipe to their treasured local versions. I added a whole tablespoon of red pepper flakes to the sauce, and as I gasped for air, steam practically came out of my ears. But the New Orleanians were happy—just the right amount of heat for the local palate.

Deveining live crayfish isn't for the faint of heart. My husband cannot bear to watch me when I commence the operation, but when the crayfish are on the table, he doesn't hesitate to help himself to a few. ■ **Serves 4**

1 pound live crayfish
1 (750-milliliter) bottle dry white wine
1 cup Tomato Sauce (page 311)
1 tablespoon hot red pepper flakes
Salt

Put the crayfish in a large colander and rinse them under running cold water. Take care that they don't wander off or pinch you with their little claws. To devein them, hold a crayfish tight with 2 fingers behind its head, where it joins the tail. The tail has 3 flippers at the end. Grab the middle flipper and (it is at this point that my husband walks away) twist it as you pull it out to remove the intestine. Discard the flipper and intestine. Repeat the operation with the rest of the crayfish.

In a stockpot, combine the wine and crayfish and bring to a boil over high heat. Boil for 10 minutes, or until the crayfish turn bright red. Drain the crayfish into a colander and rinse under running cold water. The crayfish will have released some grit during boiling, so rinse thoroughly.

Transfer the crayfish to a *cazuela* (page 51) about 15 inches in diameter. Add the tomato sauce and red pepper flakes, season with salt, and stir to mix the ingredients. Place over medium heat and cook, stirring occasionally, for 5 minutes, or until heated through and the flavors are blended. Serve immediately.

BOYITORI ❖ Salt Cod with Potatoes and Onions ❖ (Valencian Community)

This first course from the coastal area of the province of Alicante is ideal for the cold days of winter when the catch of fresh fish is scarce. It is also served during Lent. ❖ **Serves 4**

> **¹/₃ cup olive oil**
>
> **2 russet potatoes, about 1 pound total weight, peeled and cut into chestnut-sized pieces**
>
> **2 yellow onions, cut into quarters**
>
> **1 pound salt cod, desalted (page 46)**
>
> **1 tablespoon chopped fresh flat-leaf parsley**
>
> **Salt (optional)**

In a sauté pan, heat the olive oil over medium-high heat. Add the potatoes and onions and sauté for 5 minutes, or until lightly browned.

Meanwhile, cut the cod into small pieces, leaving the skin on but removing any errant bones.

When the potatoes and onions are ready, decrease the heat to medium, add the salt cod, and sauté for 5 minutes. Add water to cover, bring the mixture to a boil, and cook, uncovered, for 15 to 20 minutes, or until the potatoes are tender.

Ladle into warmed soup plates and sprinkle with the parsley and a little salt, if desired. Serve immediately.

PERICANA ❖ Cod Skins with Dried Peppers and Tomatoes ❖ (Valencian Community)

I often wonder how unusual preparations like this one came to be. As with many traditional recipes, this dish probably arose out of a home cook's resourceful use of scraps from another preparation. The combination of cod skins, dried chiles, and tomatoes may not sound appealing, but it's a delicious snack and quite original. If you ever receive an invitation to dine at a home in the village of Alcoy, inland from the busy beach area of Benidorm, there is a good chance that *pericana* will appear before the main course.

To obtain the necessary amount of cod skin, you will need to desalt about ¹/₂ pound of salt cod. When the cod is ready, gently pull off the skin; it will come away in small pieces of a suitable size for this recipe. Since only the skin is needed, you can use the skinned cod to make fritters (page 60) or another dish calling for skinned cod. ❖ **Serves 6**

> **¹/₃ cup plus 3 tablespoons olive oil**
>
> **4 dry-packed sun-dried tomatoes, cut into quarters**
>
> **4 dried ñora, choricero, or ancho chiles, halved and stems and seeds removed**
>
> **¹/₂ cup salt-cod skins from ¹/₂ pound salt cod, desalted (page 46)**
>
> **Salt**
>
> **12 thin slices baguette**

In a skillet, heat ¹/₃ cup of the olive oil over medium-high heat. Add the tomatoes and peppers and sauté for 10 minutes, or until slightly softened. Transfer to a bowl and set aside.

Using tongs, hold the skin pieces, in batches, over the flame of a gas stove or wood fire for about 10 seconds, or until curly and slightly burned. Transfer the skins to the bowl with the peppers and tomatoes and mix well.

Season the mixture with salt, drizzle with the remaining 3 tablespoons olive oil, toss lightly, and then spoon onto the bread slices. Serve immediately.

ANCAS DE RANA ENTOMATÁS ::
Sautéed Frog Legs in Tomato Sauce ::
(Extremadura)

Toño Pérez is the talented chef and owner of the highly regarded restaurant Atrio in Cáceres. He began as a pioneering young chef preparing innovative Extremaduran cuisine, but over the years his dishes have become classics. Years ago, we cooked together for a special event in Chicago and became friends. His magnificent *Gusto y gustos de Extremadura* is a treasure trove of delicious recipes and gorgeous photography of this rugged region of Spain.

This dish is a specialty of northern Extremadura, home to an abundance of rivers and creeks and also frogs. In his recipe, Toño uses a local wild thistle, *cardillo*. I have substituted chard stems and spearmint in its place. ::

Serves 6

24 pairs frog legs

Salt

Freshly ground black pepper

$1/2$ cup olive oil

2 cloves garlic, thinly sliced

4 Swiss chard stems, cut on the diagonal into
$1/4$-inch-wide strips

4 tomatoes, peeled and finely chopped

2 tablespoons chopped fresh spearmint

1 tablespoon chopped fresh oregano

Rinse the frog legs under running cold water and pat dry on paper towels. Separate each pair into 2 legs, and then loosen the meat of each leg by pulling it up, but keeping the meat on the bone to form a lollipop shape. Season the legs with salt and pepper.

In a skillet, heat the olive oil over high heat. Working in batches, fry the frog legs in a single layer, turning gently as needed, for 5 minutes, or until browned on all sides. Using a slotted spoon, transfer to a plate and set aside.

Return the pan to high heat and add the garlic and Swiss chard stems to the oil remaining in the pan. Cook, stirring, for 5 minutes, or until the stems are tender and almost translucent. Add the tomatoes, mint, and oregano, season with salt, decrease the heat to low, and cook, stirring several times, for 10 minutes, or until the tomatoes have softened. Return the frog legs to the pan, stir gently, and cook for 2 to 3 minutes, or until all the ingredients are well blended.

Spoon the vegetables onto the center of individual plates, dividing them evenly, and arrange 8 frog legs on top of each mound. Serve immediately.

MIGAS EXTREMEÑAS ▪ Shepherds' Bread Crumbs ▪ (*Extremadura*)

This humble dish is a good example of the frugality practiced in rural Spanish kitchens. Originally a typical breakfast for shepherds and hunters before they took off in the morning, *migas* today is a fashionable first course served for lunch and dinner at renowned restaurants and popular taverns.

I learned this *migas* recipe during my stays on an estate in Extremadura. While everyone else slept happily into the late morning, I arose early, curious to see what was cooking in the nearby house where the estate keeper lived. Numerous times, I watched his wife prepare this dish in the fireplace for our breakfast. The memory of dipping spoonfuls of *migas* into a *café con leche* are still very alive in my memory.

In other parts of Spain, such as the Pyrenees, cooks add chorizo or bacon to the *migas*, or serve them as a first course for lunch or dinner with fried eggs garnished with grapes. For breakfast, though, this version from Extremadura is my favorite. The main ingredients are patience and care, because if you don't work the bread thoroughly in the pan, it will not be transformed into deliciously crisp, golden brown crumbs. You will need to begin the recipe the previous evening, since the thinly sliced bread needs to sit overnight. ▪ **Serves 4**

1 pound day-old country-style bread or baguette, very thinly sliced
4 tablespoons water
1 teaspoon salt
$1/2$ cup extra virgin olive oil
4 cloves garlic, thinly sliced
1 tablespoon sweet pimentón or paprika

Place the bread slices in a large bowl, sprinkle with 3 tablespoons of the water and the salt, cover with a cloth, and let stand overnight.

The next day, in a large skillet, heat the olive oil over medium-high heat. Add the garlic and sauté, stirring often, for 2 to 3 minutes, or until golden. Remove from the heat and stir in the *pimentón*.

Return the pan to medium heat and add the bread slices, mixing well to blend the ingredients. With the edge of a large metal spoon, break up the mixture while gradually adding the remaining 1 tablespoon water by drops. Cook, continuing to stir and break up the bread, for 20 to 30 minutes, or until the crumbs are the size of rice kernels and are golden and crisp. Serve hot.

MOLLEJAS SALTEADAS ▪
Sautéed Sweetbreads in Parsley and Garlic
▪ (Madrid)

Many people think of sweetbreads as an exotic ingredient served only at upscale restaurants, but they are actually simple to prepare at home. Lamb sweetbreads are harder to find than those from a calf; if using them, omit the first step in this recipe in which the sweetbreads are simmered for 10 minutes, as the more delicate lamb sweetbreads don't require it. ▪ **Serves 4**

1 pound calf sweetbreads

1 yellow onion, halved

1 leek, halved crosswise

Salt

3 cloves garlic, minced

2 tablespoons chopped fresh flat-leaf parsley

1/2 cup fine dried bread crumbs

1/4 cup olive oil

In a large saucepan, combine the sweetbreads with water to cover by 1 inch. Add the onion and leek and bring to a boil over high heat. Decrease the heat to medium-low and simmer for 10 minutes, or until the sweetbreads turn whitish. Drain and discard the onion and leek.

Rinse the sweetbreads under cold running water. Trim away any fat and peel off the outer membrane. Pat dry on paper towels. Dice the sweetbreads into 1-inch cubes.

Season the sweetbread cubes with salt and sprinkle with the garlic and parsley. Spread the bread crumbs in a shallow dish. Roll the sweetbreads in the bread crumbs to coat evenly on all sides.

In a skillet, heat the olive oil over high heat. Add the sweetbreads and sauté, stirring gently, for 5 to 6 minutes, or until golden brown and crispy. Serve immediately.

Afternoon among beer and tapas in Zaragoza, Aragón

:: CHAPTER 6 ::

Bread Pies and Pastas

ITALIAN PASTA IS served in nearly every home in Spain, but pasta with a distinctive Spanish imprint is not part of our culinary tradition. The existing pasta dishes are either legacies of Arabic cooking or, more recently, adaptations of Italian dishes. One of these, *canelones*, the stuffed pasta rolls of Catalonia, was such a beloved import that it has long since been integrated into the local cuisine, earning the status of "permanent alien resident." Castellón, the most northern province in the Valencian Community, is also home to *fideuá*, a dish made with an elbow-shaped pasta of Moorish decent known as *fideos*. *Fideuá* is essentially paella prepared with pasta rather than rice, so you will find the recipe for it in chapter 8 with the paellas.

Spain's bread pies also find their origins in remote lands and times. *Empanada gallega*, which in one form or another appears at almost every Galician meal, or even between meals, is thought to be a descendant of an ancient bread pie prepared in Babylon with quail, while *pastel de carne* from Murcia is probably an adaptation of the Moroccan *b'stecya*, a well-known pigeon-filled pie made with *warqa*, a pastry similar to phyllo. Galicians fill their empanadas with various ingredients, from chorizo and pork to scallops and peppers, and sometimes even serve them as desserts, such as the apple-filled *empanada de manzana* on page 281. Empanadas are also popular in the Balearic Islands, where they are typically filled with lamb.

I've heard more than a few Catalonians claim that *cocas*, or *coques* in Catalan, are the forerunners of modern-day pizza, and indeed these flatbreads have been made in the region for centuries. *Cocas* are distinct from pizzas in that they are traditionally not topped with cheese and are usually, though not exclusively, served at room temperature, either before a meal or as a midday snack. Versions from the mainland are usually oval, while those from the Balearics are typically rectangular. Toppings include an array of vegetables (parsley, Swiss chard, and peppers are classics), *sobrasada* (page 124), sardines, or sweet ingredients such as apricots.

135

Bread Pie with Pork and Chorizo (page 147), served with Tomato Salad (page 89)

ABOVE, FROM LEFT TO RIGHT: *Sweet cocas at a market in Catalonia; sign in Santillana del Mar, Cantabria, for local delicacies; pouring beer among Basque* pintxos *(tapas) in a Bilbao bar*

CANELONES ⧉ Cannelloni with Ground Meats, Truffle, and Béchamel Sauce ⧉ (Catalonia)

Sicily and Naples were under Spanish rule for centuries, and members of the court moved freely within the Habsburg empire, carrying their tastes and recipes with them. This is probably the reason that *canelones* became popular, especially in Barcelona and Madrid. In Catalonia, special *canelones* are served on Saint Stephan's Day, December 26. This recipe is a festive version of *canelones* that has been prepared for generations on this holiday at the home of my friend Maria Angeles Fuster in the medieval town of Cardona, west of Barcelona. Maria Angeles was kind enough to ask her mother, Elvira, for the recipe. I invited Maria Angeles and her husband, Valentín, for dinner one night. Valentín didn't know of our recipe exchange, so imagine my joy when he exclaimed after the first bite, "These *canelones* are incredibly good, just like my mother-in-law's!" Maria Angeles and I started laughing and then shared our secret. ⧉ **Serves 4**

1 (3-ounce) lamb brain (optional)

Salt

1/2 cup olive oil

1 yellow onion, finely chopped

1/2-pound piece pork tenderloin, cut into chickpea-sized pieces

1/2 pound veal fillets, cut into chickpea-sized pieces

1/2 pound boneless chicken breast, cut into chickpea-sized pieces

2 chicken livers, coarsely chopped

Freshly ground black pepper

1 black truffle, shaved

2 1/2 cups Béchamel Sauce (page 310)

16 (4 by 5-inch) rectangles fresh or dried pasta

1/2 cup whole milk

1/2 cup grated aged Manchego or Parmesan cheese

1/2 teaspoon freshly grated nutmeg

If using the lamb brain, rinse under cold running water. Place in a small saucepan, add water to cover, and salt the water lightly. As soon as small bubbles begin to appear, lift out the brain with a slotted spoon. Drain on paper towels and cut into chickpea-sized pieces. Set aside.

In a large skillet, heat the olive oil over medium heat. Add the onion and sauté for 5 minutes, stirring occasionally. Decrease the heat to low and cook the onion for another 10 minutes, or until tender and translucent. Add the pork, veal, chicken, chicken livers, and lamb brain, if using, to the skillet. Season with salt and pepper, mix well, and cook over medium heat for about 15 minutes. At this point, the meats will be cooked through and the flavors will have blended. Remove from the heat.

Transfer the contents of the skillet to a food processor and pulse to achieve an almost puréelike mixture, with a bit of texture. Transfer the mixture to a bowl, add the truffle and 1 cup of the béchamel sauce, and mix well with a spatula. Set aside and allow the mixture to cool to room temperature before filling the pasta.

Fill a stockpot three-fourths full of water and bring to a boil over high heat. Add salt to the water, and then add the pasta, decrease the heat to medium to maintain a gentle boil, and cook for 5 to 8 minutes, or until done. The timing will depend on how thick and dry the fresh pasta is. When it is ready, it should be flexible, white, and shiny. If using dried pasta, cook according to the package instructions. Using a slotted spoon, transfer the pasta to a bowl filled with cold water. When the pasta is cool, drain and lay the rectangles, with a 5-inch side facing you, on a clean, wide work surface.

Preheat the oven to 400°F. To make the rolls, spoon about 2 tablespoons of the filling in a strip across the center third of each rectangle. Fold the edge closest to you over the filling, and then bring the edge farthest from you over the filling, overlapping the first edge. Each *canelón* should be about 4 inches long and 2 inches in diameter.

Place the *canelones*, seam side down, in a flameproof baking dish just large enough to accommodate them in a single layer. In a saucepan, combine the remaining 1 1/2 cups béchamel sauce with the milk. Mix well with a whisk, place over medium heat, and heat, stirring constantly, until hot. Pour the béchamel mixture evenly over the *canelones* and sprinkle with the cheese and nutmeg.

Bake the *canelones* for 15 minutes, or until heated through. Turn the oven to the broiler setting and then broil the *canelones* for a few minutes, or until golden on top. Serve immediately.

CANELONES MARIJÓS ▪
Cannelloni Stuffed with Spinach and Tuna with Béchamel and Tomato Sauce ▪
(Madrid)

Marijós was my mother-in-law. I was very young when I joined her family, and she influenced my cooking a great deal. She taught me many dishes, including this one for *canelones* stuffed with tuna, which my children still associate with their grandmother. I served these *canelones* at my restaurant in New York, too, where they were very popular. I know my mother-in-law would have been pleased to see how much my customers enjoyed them. Thank you, Marijós! ▪ **Serves 4**

Salt

16 (4 by 5-inch) rectangles fresh or dried pasta

1 pound spinach, boiled, drained, and finely chopped

12 ounces canned tuna in olive oil

3 cups Tomato Sauce (page 311)

2¹/₂ cups Béchamel Sauce (page 310)

¹/₂ cup grated Manchego or Parmesan cheese (optional)

¹/₂ teaspoon freshly grated nutmeg (optional)

Fill a stockpot three-fourths full of water and bring to a boil over high heat. Add salt to the water, and then add the pasta, decrease the heat to medium to maintain a gentle boil, and cook for 5 to 8 minutes, or until done. The timing will depend on how thick and dry the fresh pasta is. When it is ready, it should be flexible, white, and shiny. If using dried pasta, cook according to the package instructions. Using a slotted spoon, transfer the pasta to a bowl filled with cold water. When the pasta is cool, drain and lay the rectangles, with a 5-inch side facing you, on a clean, wide work surface.

In a bowl, combine the spinach and tuna and mix well. Add 1 cup of the tomato sauce and ¹/₂ cup of the béchamel sauce and mix thoroughly.

Preheat the oven to 400°F. To make the rolls, spoon about 2 tablespoons of the filling in a strip across the center third of each rectangle. Fold the edge closest to you over the filling, and then bring the edge farthest from you over the filling, overlapping the first edge. Each *canelón* should be about 4 inches long and 2 inches in diameter.

In a baking dish large enough to accommodate the *canelones* in a single layer, cover the bottom with the remaining 2 cups tomato sauce. Place the *canelones*, seam side down, on top of the sauce. Heat the remaining 2 cups béchamel sauce over medium heat, stirring constantly, until hot. Pour the sauce evenly over the *canelones*. Sprinkle with the cheese and nutmeg, if desired.

Bake the *canelones* for 15 minutes, or until heated through. Turn the oven to the broiler setting and then broil the *canelones* for a few minutes, or until golden on top. Serve immediately.

COCA ▪ Crusty Flatbread ▪
(Balearic Islands and Catalonia)

Cocas are crusty, mainly square or rectangular flat-breads prized by everyone who lives in or visits the Balearics. They are also highly popular in Catalonia, where they are known as *coques* and are typically oval.

Every Majorcan household has a designated baking sheet for making *cocas* that accommodates a consistent amount of dough. For this recipe, you will need a 10 by 15-inch rimmed baking sheet. If you want to serve *cocas* with a variety of toppings at one meal—recipes for a quartet of topping combinations follow—double or triple the dough recipe as needed. ▪ **Makes one 10 by 15-inch flatbread**

DOUGH

2 teaspoons active dry yeast

$1/_3$ cup lukewarm water (90° to 100°F)

$1/_3$ cup olive oil

1 egg

$1/_2$ teaspoon salt

$1^1/_2$ cups all-purpose flour

$1^1/_2$ teaspoons lard or unsalted butter, at room temperature

To make the dough, in a small bowl, dissolve the yeast in the lukewarm water and let stand for about 5 minutes, or until foamy. In a large bowl, combine the yeast mixture, olive oil, egg, salt, and $1/_2$ cup of the flour. Using a rubber spatula or your hands, begin mixing the ingredients together, adding the remaining flour a little at a time until completely incorporated. Add the lard, working it into the dough, and then knead the dough well in the bowl until it is smooth and elastic, about 5 minutes. Cover the bowl with a damp kitchen towel and let the dough rest for 30 minutes.

Lightly oil a 10 by 15-inch baking sheet with 1-inch sides. Using your fingers, spread the dough evenly over the bottom and up the sides of the pan, forming a low rim around the edges. Pierce the dough with fork tines in several places to prevent bubbles from forming. The *coca* dough is now ready to be topped.

COCA AMB TRAMPÓ ▪ Crusty Flatbread with Tomato, Pepper, and Onion Salad

Trampó, a mixture of ripe tomatoes, green bell peppers, and white onion, usually seasoned with salt and extra virgin olive oil but no vinegar, is the most common salad on the islands. The salad also shows up on top of this equally popular *coca*.

2 pounds tomatoes, peeled and minced

1 green bell pepper, seeded and minced

1 small white onion, minced

$1^1/_2$ teaspoons salt

6 tablespoons extra virgin olive

Coca dough–lined baking sheet (above)

Preheat the oven to 400°F. In a sieve, combine the tomatoes, bell pepper, and onion and let drain for 10 minutes. (This step prevents the topping from making the crust soggy.) Transfer the vegetables to a bowl, add the salt and olive oil, and toss to combine.

Distribute the topping evenly over the surface of the dough. Bake in the oven for 30 minutes, or until the edge of the dough is firm when tested with a fingertip or toothpick. Serve hot or at room temperature, cut into squares or rectangles.

COCA DE PEREJIL :: Crusty Flatbread with Parsley

This *coca*, with its shades of green, is beautiful to look at, particularly when served alongside a *coca amb trampó* (page 140).

2 bunches flat-leaf parsley, stems removed

1 bunch scallions, tender green tops only, coarsely chopped

6 large Swiss chard leaves, coarsely chopped

1¹/₂ teaspoons salt

6 tablespoons extra virgin olive oil

Coca dough–lined baking sheet (page 140)

Preheat the oven to 400°F. In a bowl, combine the parsley, scallions, Swiss chard, salt, and olive oil and toss to combine.

Distribute the topping evenly over the surface of the dough. Bake in the oven for 30 minutes, or until the edge of the dough is firm when tested with a fingertip or toothpick. Serve hot or at room temperature, cut into squares or rectangles.

COCA DE PIMIENTOS ROJOS Y TOMATES :: Crusty Flatbread with Roasted Red Bell Peppers and Tomatoes

In summertime, when red bell peppers are in season, local cooks regularly make this *coca*. The color and the sweetness of the peppers and tomatoes make it both tasty and attractive. Brushing the peppers and tomatoes with olive oil before roasting simplifies peeling.

4 pounds red bell peppers

2 tomatoes

¹/₂ cup extra virgin olive oil

2 cloves garlic, coarsely chopped

1 teaspoon salt

¹/₂ teaspoon freshly ground black pepper

Coca dough–lined baking sheet (page 140)

Preheat the oven to 500°F. Brush the peppers and tomatoes with 2 tablespoons of the olive oil. Arrange them on a rimmed baking sheet or in a roasting pan and roast, turning every 10 minutes, for 30 minutes, or until the skins blacken and the vegetables are tender. Remove the vegetables from the oven, wrap in newspapers, slip into 1 or more plastic bags, and let cool for 1 hour.

Preheat the oven to 400°F. Peel the peppers and tomatoes. Split the peppers in half, remove and discard the stems and seeds, and cut the flesh lengthwise into ¹/₂-inch-wide strips. Place the pepper strips in a large sieve or a colander. Core the tomatoes, cut in half crosswise, and squeeze gently to force out the seeds. Cut the tomatoes into small pieces, add to the peppers, mix well, and let drain for 10 minutes. (This step prevents the topping from making the crust soggy.)

Transfer the vegetables to a bowl, add the garlic, salt, pepper, and the remaining 6 tablespoons olive oil, and toss to combine.

Distribute the topping evenly over the surface of the dough. Bake in the oven for 30 minutes, or until the edge of the dough is firm when tested with a fingertip or toothpick. Serve hot or at room temperature, cut into squares or rectangles.

COCA DE CEBOLLA CON MIEL ❖
Crusty Flatbread with Onion and Honey

The combination of tangy onion and sweet honey together with raisins and pine nuts provides an interesting contrast of flavors and textures. Serve this *coca* as a snack, an appetizer, or even as an unusual dessert.

1 tablespoon salt

3 yellow onions, thinly sliced

$^{1}/_{2}$ cup honey

$^{1}/_{2}$ cup raisins

$^{1}/_{2}$ cup pine nuts

Coca dough–lined baking sheet (page 140)

In a large bowl, combine the salt and enough water to cover the onions once they are added. Stir until the salt dissolves, add the onions, and let stand for 1 minute. Drain the onions in a large sieve or colander, rinse well, and let stand in the sieve for 30 minutes.

Preheat the oven to 400°F. Pat the onions dry with a paper towel. Transfer the onions to a bowl, add the honey, and mix well. Add the raisins and pine nuts and toss to combine.

Distribute the topping evenly over the surface of the dough. Bake in the oven for 30 minutes, or until the edge of the dough is firm when tested with a fingertip or toothpick. Serve hot or at room temperature, cut into squares or rectangles.

A jar of artisanal honey from Catalonia

EMPANADA GALLEGA ::
Bread Pie :: (Galicia)

Empanadas, bread pies stuffed with shellfish, fish, or meats, are iconic of Galician cuisine. The crusts and fillings vary from place to place, and nearly every Galician family, restaurant, and tavern claims to have the secret formula for making the best version. Of the many empanadas I have tasted in this beautiful northwestern region, those made by my friend Menchu Briz are my favorite—his crust is consistently delicate and delicious. This is the recipe for his dough; pair it with one of the four empanada fillings that follow. The dough and the filling can be prepared in advance and refrigerated for up to a day before assembling the empanada. Empanadas are ideal for when you have to feed a large family or party. Serve them alone or with a salad. :: **Makes one 10 by 15-inch or 9 by 12-inch pie**

DOUGH

2 teaspoons active dry yeast

$^1/_2$ cup milk, heated to lukewarm (90°F to 100°F)

1 egg

$^1/_2$ teaspoon sugar

1 teaspoon salt

2 tablespoons unsalted butter, at room temperature

$2^1/_2$ cups all-purpose flour

Oil or lard for preparing pan

Empanada filling of choice (recipes follow)

1 egg, lightly beaten

To make the dough, in a small bowl, dissolve the yeast in the lukewarm milk and let stand for about 5 minutes, or until foamy. In a large bowl, whisk together the yeast mixture, egg, sugar, salt, and butter. Add half of the flour, and mix with a rubber spatula or wooden spoon until completely incorporated. Add the rest of the flour a little at a time, mixing with the spatula until the dough becomes too difficult to work. Turn out the dough onto a lightly floured work surface and knead until smooth and elastic but not sticky, about 10 minutes.

Place the dough in a large bowl, cover with a damp kitchen towel, and let rise at room temperature for $1^1/_2$ hours, or until about doubled in size.

Preheat the oven to 450°F. Brush a 10 by 15-inch or a 9 by 12-inch baking sheet with 2-inch sides with oil.

Punch down the dough and divide into 2 portions, one slightly larger than the other (the larger portion will form the bottom crust, and the smaller portion the top crust). Using a rolling pin, roll out the larger portion into a sheet about $^1/_4$ inch thick and about the same size as the baking sheet. Drape the dough sheet over the rolling pin and transfer it to the prepared baking sheet. Using your fingers, gently press the dough evenly over the bottom and all the way up the sides of the pan. Pierce the dough with fork tines in several places to prevent bubbles from forming.

Spread one of the empanada fillings over the dough, layering it as indicated in the filling recipe. Roll out the second piece of dough into a thin sheet slightly smaller than the bottom crust. Carefully lay it over the filling. Using your fingers, press the edges of the top and bottom crusts together, sealing them to form a rim. Trim any excess dough (see note). Pierce the top of the dough several times with a fork to allow steam to escape during baking. Brush the empanada with the beaten egg.

Place the empanada in the oven and bake for 30 minutes, or until nicely browned. Remove from the oven and let cool in the pan on a rack. Serve warm or at room temperature, cut into squares.

NOTE: If you want to decorate the empanada, as illustrated on page 146, you can use the dough trimmings from the edges. Before you brush the empanada with the beaten egg, shape the trimmings into thin strips long enough to extend across the empanada on the diagonal. Lay them parallel and press the ends of the strips onto the rim of the empanada. Lay a single thin strip perpendicular to the other strips, running it kitty-corner the length of the pan. Then brush the empanada with the beaten egg.

EMPANADA DE BERBERECHOS ::
Bread Pie with Cockles and Peppers

Berberechos are bivalves known as cockles in English. They are similar to Manila clams, although smaller and with vertical crevices on both shells. Manila clams or smal littleneck clams can be substituted.

    1/2 cup olive oil
    1 yellow onion, finely chopped
    1 green bell pepper, seeded and finely chopped
    1 red bell pepper, seeded and finely chopped
    2 cloves garlic, minced
    Salt
    Empanada dough (opposite)
    1 pound cockles or Manila clams, steamed open and
        shells discarded
    2 tablespoons Tomato Sauce (page 311, optional)

In a sauté pan, heat the olive oil over high heat. Add the onion, bell peppers, and garlic and sauté for 5 minutes, stirring frequently. Decrease the heat to medium low, season with salt, and cook, stirring occasionally, for about 30 minutes, or until the vegetables are soft and tender. Transfer the vegetables to a bowl and let cool completely, then drain them well in a sieve to remove any excess liquid. (The filling should never be hot or have too much liquid when you spread it on the dough, or it will make the crust soggy.)

Line the baking sheet with the bottom empanada crust as directed on page 144. Spread the vegetables evenly over the crust. Distribute the cockles over the vegetables and top evenly with the tomato sauce. Roll out the top crust, cover the filling, and bake and serve as directed.

EMPANADA DE SARDINAS ::
Bread Pie with Sardines and Onions

In Galicia, the small local sardines called *xoubas* are traditionally used for making this empanada. I have occasionally found small sardines from Portugal in U.S. markets, and some domestic fisheries—particularly on the Pacific coast—are making a comeback, so fresh sardines are increasingly available.

    1/3 cup olive oil
    3 yellow onions, cut into thin rings
    2 cloves garlic, minced
    Salt
    1 pound small fresh sardines
    Empanada dough (opposite)
    2 tablespoons Tomato Sauce (page 311, optional)

In a sauté pan, heat the olive oil over high heat. Add the onions and garlic and sauté for 5 minutes, stirring frequently. Decrease the heat to medium, season with salt, and cook, stirring occasionally, for about 15 minutes, or until the onions are soft and tender and lightly caramelized. Transfer the onion mixture to a bowl to cool. (The filling should never be hot or have too much liquid when you spread it on the dough, or it will make the crust soggy.)

Rinse the sardines under cold running water. Working with 1 sardine at a time, cut off the head and fins and scrape away any scales. Slit the fish open along its belly and remove the viscera. Slip your index finger inside the fish and run it the length of the backbone so that the fish opens flat like a book. Carefully remove the backbone, keeping the halves of the fish connected. Rinse the fish well again and pat dry with a paper towel. Repeat with the remaining fish.

Line the baking sheet with the bottom empanada crust as directed on page 144. Spread the onion mixture evenly over the crust. Arrange the sardines in a single layer over the onion and top evenly with the tomato sauce. Roll out the top crust, cover the filling, and bake and serve as directed.

EMPANADA DE LOMO ::
Bread Pie with Pork and Chorizo

This robust meat filling is typically made with pork loin or tenderloin, but chicken and beef are fine substitutes. Tomato sauce is used in most empanada fillings, but always with restraint, as too much would make the dough soggy.

Pictured opposite

1/3 cup olive oil

1 yellow onion, finely chopped

2 cloves garlic, minced

Salt

1 pound boneless pork loin or pork tenderloin, cut into narrow strips

2 chorizos, about 1/4 pound each, finely chopped

1 tablespoon sweet pimentón or paprika

Empanada dough (page 144)

2 tablespoons Tomato Sauce (page 311)

In a sauté pan, heat half of the olive oil over high heat. Add the onion and garlic and sauté for 5 minutes, stirring frequently. Decrease the heat to medium, season with salt, and cook, stirring occasionally, for about 15 minutes, or until the onion is soft and tender and lightly caramelized. Transfer the onion mixture to a bowl to cool.

Return the sauté pan to high heat and add the remaining oil. Add the pork loin and chorizo and sauté for 5 minutes, stirring frequently. Decrease the heat to medium, sprinkle with the *pimentón*, and continue to cook the meats, stirring occasionally, for 5 minutes, or until tender. Transfer to the bowl holding the onion, stir to combine, and let cool completely. (The filling should never be hot or have too much liquid when you spread it on the dough, or it will make the crust soggy.)

Line the baking sheet with the bottom empanada crust as directed on page 144. Spread the meat mixture evenly over the crust and and top evenly with the tomato sauce. Roll out the top crust, cover the filling, and bake and serve as directed.

EMPANADA DE VIEIRAS ::
Bread Pie with Scallops and Peppers

In the same way that the sight of a paella brings to mind its place of origin, the Valencia region, scallops and especially their shells evoke the Galician town of Santiago de Compostela, where the tomb of Saint James has drawn pilgrims from far away since the Middle Ages. The shell, the symbol of the pilgrimage, can be found on the facades of historic buildings and churches along the route.

1/2 cup olive oil

1 yellow onion, finely chopped

1 green bell pepper, seeded and finely chopped

1 red bell pepper, seeded and finely chopped

2 cloves garlic, finely minced

1 pound sea scallops, halved crosswise

Salt

Empanada dough (page 144)

In a sauté pan, heat the olive oil over high heat. Add the onion, bell peppers, and garlic and sauté for 5 minutes, stirring frequently. Decrease the heat to medium-low and cook for about 30 minutes, or until the vegetables are soft and tender. Add the scallops, season with salt, mix well with the rest of the ingredients, and cook for 1 minute. Transfer the vegetables and scallops to a bowl and let cool completely, then drain them well in a sieve to remove any excess liquid. (The filling should never be hot or have too much liquid when you spread it on the dough, or it will make the crust soggy.)

Line the baking sheet with the bottom empanada crust as directed on page 144. Spread the vegetable and scallop mixture evenly over the crust. Roll out the top crust, cover the filling, and bake and serve as directed.

EMPANADA DE CORDERO ⠿
Majorcan Bread Pie with Lamb ⠿
(Balearic Islands)

Unlike their large, leavened Galician kin, Majorcan empanadas are single servings and the dough is made without yeast. These tartletlike bread pies are usually stuffed with lamb, though I have made them with chicken as well and they taste equally delicious. ⠿ **Makes 12 small turnovers**

FILLING

1 pound lean lamb, preferably from the leg,
    cut into 1-inch dice
1/4 pound bacon or fatback, finely chopped
Salt
Freshly ground black pepper

DOUGH

2/3 cup lukewarm water (90° to 100°F)
1 egg yolk
2/3 cup olive oil
1 cup (1/2 pound) lard or unsalted butter,
    at room temperature
1 teaspoon salt
3 cups all-purpose flour, plus 1/2 cup for sprinkling

To make the filling, pat the lamb dry with a paper towel to soak up any surface moisture. Add the lamb and bacon to a large bowl, season with salt and pepper, and stir to combine. Set aside.

To make the dough, combine the lukewarm water, egg yolk, olive oil, lard, and salt in a large bowl. Using your hands or a wooden spoon, mix the ingredients until thoroughly combined. Then begin adding the 3 cups flour, 1/2 cup at a time, working in each addition before adding the next one. When all the flour has been fully incorporated, the dough will be flexible and moist but not sticky. This step will take about 10 minutes.

Preheat the oven to 400°F. Oil a rimmed baking sheet.

Divide the dough into 12 equal pieces (about 1 1/2 ounces each) and shape each piece into a ball. Sprinkle each ball with a little flour and knead for about 1 minute. Working with 1 ball at a time, cut off one-fourth of it and reserve to make the top crust. Place the larger portion on a sheet of parchment paper and, using your hands, shape it into a round tartlet shell about 3 inches in diameter with 2-inch sides. Repeat with the remaining balls.

Fill each empanada base tightly with about 2 heaping tablespoons of the meat mixture. With each portion of reserved dough, use your fingers to make a round 3 inches in diameter and place on top of the filling. Using your fingertips, firmly press together the edges of the top and bottom crusts, fluting them attractively and sealing them closed. As each empanada is finished, place it on the prepared baking sheet. Pierce the empanadas with the tip of a sharp knife or with fork tines so that steam can escape during baking.

Bake the empanadas for 50 minutes, or until the pastry is lightly browned and the filling is cooked through. Transfer to a wire rack to cool. Serve warm or at room temperature.

COCARROIS ∷ Vegetable Turnovers ∷ (Balearic Islands)

The *cocarrois* of Majorca are similar to the island's *empanadas de cordero* (page 148), except that the dough is enriched with sugar and orange juice. And while the empanadas look like tartlets with a top crust, *cocarrois* are half-moons. These turnovers typically contain a vegetable filling; the addition of pine nuts and raisins in this recipe is a legacy of the former Moorish rulers. ∷ **Makes 20 small turnovers**

FILLING

2 bunches scallions, white part only, finely chopped

8 Swiss chard leaves, stems removed and leaves finely chopped

1 bunch flat-leaf parsley, coarsely chopped

4 large cauliflower florets, about 6 ounces total weight, cut into very small florets

1/2 cup pine nuts

1/4 cup raisins

2 tablespoons extra virgin olive oil

1 tablespoon salt

1 teaspoon freshly ground black pepper

DOUGH

1/2 cup lukewarm water (90° to 100°F)

2 egg yolks

2/3 cup olive oil

1/2 cup (1/4 pound) lard or unsalted butter, at room temperature

1/4 cup sugar

1/2 cup freshly squeezed orange juice

3 cups all-purpose flour, plus 1/2 cup for sprinkling

To make the filling, combine the scallions, chard, parsley, cauliflower, pine nuts, raisins, olive oil, salt, and pepper in a large bowl and toss to mix well. Set aside.

To make the dough, combine the water, egg yolks, olive oil, lard, sugar, and orange juice in a large bowl. Using your hands or a wooden spoon, mix the ingredients until thoroughly combined. Then begin adding the 3 cups flour, 1/2 cup at a time, working in each addition before adding the next one. When all the flour has been fully incorporated, the dough will be flexible and moist but not sticky. This step will take about 10 minutes.

Preheat the oven to 400°F. Oil a rimmed baking sheet.

Divide the dough into 20 equal pieces (about 1 ounce each) and shape each piece into a ball. Sprinkle each ball with a little flour and knead for about 1 minute. To fill and shape each turnover, using a rolling pin, roll out a ball of dough on a lightly floured work surface into a round about 5 inches in diameter. Put 1 heaping tablespoon of the filling on the lower half of the round and fold the upper half over to form a half-moon. With your fingers, seal the dough by gently pinching together the edges. As each turnover is finished, place it on the baking sheet. Pierce the turnovers with the tip of a sharp knife or fork tines in a few places so that steam can escape during baking.

Bake the turnovers for about 50 minutes, or until the pastry is lightly browned and the filling is heated through. Transfer to a wire rack to cool. Serve warm or at room temperature.

PASTEL DE CARNE ▪
Puff Pastry Meat Pie ▪ (Murcia)

This meat pie from Murcia is a great way to use leftover meat from a beef or pork roast or from your Thanksgiving turkey. You will need a total of about $3/4$ pound meat, whether you are using all ground beef or part ground beef and roasted meat. Leaving out the brains would be a departure from the original recipe, but most Murcianos would approve, as long as you honor tradition by crowning the top with a pastry rosebud. ▪

Makes one 9-inch pie

> 1 ($1/2$-pound) package frozen puff pastry, or $1/2$ pound homemade puff pastry
>
> All-purpose flour for rolling out the pastry
>
> 2 (3-ounce) lamb brains (optional)
>
> Salt
>
> $1/4$ cup olive oil
>
> $1/2$ pound ground beef
>
> Freshly ground black pepper
>
> 1 (3-ounce) chorizo, finely diced
>
> $1/4$ pound roast beef, pork, or turkey leftovers, shredded, or an additional $1/4$ pound ground beef
>
> 2 hard-boiled eggs, peeled and coarsely chopped
>
> 2 eggs, beaten, plus 1 egg, beaten, for brushing

Roll out the puff pastry on a floured surface until it is about $1/4$ inch thick and almost doubled in size. Cut off a 5-inch square and set it aside in the refrigerator. Divide the rest of the puff pastry into 2 pieces, one slightly larger than the other. Use the larger piece to line a round 9-inch cake pan with 2-inch sides, pressing it against the bottom and sides to cover completely and trimming away the overhang. (The pastry is quite flexible, and no matter what the original shape, it can be easily molded into the shape of the cake pan.) Set the pastry-lined pan and the remaining pastry sheet aside in the refrigerator with the reserved pastry square.

If using the lamb brains, rinse under cold running water. Place in a saucepan, add water to cover, and salt the water lightly. As soon as small bubbles begin to appear, lift out the brain with a slotted spoon. Drain on paper towels and cut into small pieces. Set aside.

Preheat the oven to 350°F.

In a sauté pan, heat the olive oil over high heat. Add the ground beef and cook, stirring frequently, for about 5 minutes, or until the meat breaks up and browns slightly. Add the brains, stir gently to mix with the meat for about 1 minute, and season with salt and pepper. Transfer to a bowl and let cool to room temperature.

When the meat has cooled, add the chorizo, roast leftovers, hard-boiled eggs, and the 2 beaten eggs to the bowl. Using a rubber spatula, stir until well mixed. Transfer the mixture to the pastry-lined cake pan, spreading it evenly.

Trim the slightly smaller piece of puff pastry if needed to yield a round a little larger than 9 inches in diameter and carefully lay it over the filling, forming the top crust. Using your fingers, firmly press the edges of the top and bottom crusts together to seal them.

To make a pastry rosebud with the 5-inch pastry square, cut it into 8 uniform petal shapes. Arrange the petals so that their bases overlap and press together firmly. The top, viewed from above, has the appearance of a just-opening rosebud. Place the pastry flower in the center of the top crust, and brush the entire top crust and the rose with the 1 beaten egg.

Bake the pie for 30 minutes, or until nicely golden. Transfer to a wire rack to cool. Serve warm or at room temperature, cut into wedges.

Bread left to cool in old wooden dressers in a traditional bakery outside Girona, Catalonia

CHAPTER 7

Warm Soups
and Legume Stews

SCORES OF SOUPS and legume stews, called *platos de cuchara*, literally "dishes eaten with a spoon," are beloved across the country. Many of them are regional variations of national favorites, and in this chapter, I have included recipes that reflect that diversity. They range from clear soups to soups based on bread or potatoes to bean soups to *cocidos*, the hearty chickpea stews that are a meal-in-a-pot and are found in various guises in every region.

Among the clear soups you will find are a trio built on seafood, yet each made distinctive by the addition of a particular ingredient, such as the bitter orange in *caldillo de perro*, the mayonnaise in *gazpachuelo de Málaga*, and the saffron in *sopa de pescado*. You will also discover *sopa de picadillo*, a chicken broth laced with *jamón serrano*, chicken, and mint. All these soups are eaten as a first course.

So are a variety of bread-based soups, including the simple but delicious *sopa de ajo*, a fragrant garlic soup known as *sopa castellana* in central Spain. Its main ingredient is day-old bread, evidence of the frugality of Spanish cooks, and despite its humble makings, it is offered today in many restaurants. Two other bread soups, *zurrukutuna*, which includes salt cod, and *sopas mallorquinas*, which marries bread slices and a gardenful of vegetables, are somewhat heartier, yet are still first courses.

Even substantial bean and lentil soups, such as *pochas*, *alubias de Tolosa*, *fabada*, *fabes con alemjas*, and *caldo gallego*, arrive at the table before the main dish, some of them quite rich because of the addition of various sausages. I used to offer two superb potato stews, *marmitako* with tuna and *patatas a la Rioja* with chorizo, as main courses at my restaurant in Manhattan because they are so filling. But they, too, are traditional first courses.

The *cocidos*, in contrast, are meals in themselves. Each region boasts its own version of this chickpea stew, from the *cocido madrileño* and *cocido maragato* of the Castiles to the Catalan *escudella* and the Canarian *puchero de lujo*. Although ingredients vary from region to region, the concept is the same: a robust stew served as a whole meal in three stages. The first course is the broth that results from cooking the meats and chickpeas, the second features the chickpeas and vegetables, and the final course is the meats. (The exception to this progression is *cocido maragato*, which is served in the reverse order.) Some *cocidos* include a *relleno* or *pelota*, literally "stuffing" or "meatball." They are made from bread crumbs, garlic, and parsley or from ground meat or sausages, are added to the stew toward the end of cooking, and are served with the meat course.

Some dishes call for specialty meats, sausages, and even legumes that are not easy to find outside of Spain. For instance, *fabes* from Asturias, the buttery white beans that melt in your mouth, are difficult, though not impossible, to buy elsewhere, but I have had good results using white lima beans in their place. *Lacón*, semicured pork shoulder from Galicia; *cecina*, salted beef from León; and special regional varieties of chorizo and *morcilla* (blood sausage) are not available in the United States either. But tracking down generic Spanish chorizo and *morcilla* will allow you to come close to the original *platos de cuchara*.

153

PAGE 152: *Sign for wine grapes in Priorat, Catalonia; La Boqueria market, Barcelona*
ABOVE, FROM LEFT TO RIGHT: *Mushrooms at the market in San Sebastián, Basque Country; public water fountains in Grazalema, Andalusia; Catalan melons for sale at a weekly rural market*

SOPA DE PICADILLO ⸫
Consommé with Hard-Boiled Eggs, Jamón Serrano, and Mint ⸫ *(Andalusia)*

I never tire of eating this simple delight. When I am preparing stock specifically for this soup, I usually reserve a chicken breast to simmer, shred, and add to the pot. If you are using homemade frozen stock or store-bought stock, it is fine to omit the chicken breast. ⸫ **Serves 4 as a first course**

5 cups Chicken Stock (page 304)

1 (¼-inch-thick) slice jamón serrano or other dry-cured ham, about 3 ounces, finely diced

1 (4-ounce) boneless, skinless chicken breast, boiled and finely shredded (optional)

2 hard-boiled eggs, peeled and finely chopped

¼ cup dry sherry

1 tablespoon chopped fresh mint

In a large saucepan, bring the stock to a boil over high heat. Add all the ingredients, cook for 2 minutes, and serve immediately.

Old jamón *delivery truck parked in Extremadura*

CALDILLO DE PERRO :: Fish Soup with Bitter Orange :: (Andalusia)

The touch of bitter orange gives this fish soup an original flavor. Outside Andalusia, it is unusual to find bitter orange in any recipe, mainly because the trees are planted primarily in this part of Spain. This soup is typical of the ancient city of Cádiz, which is also known as *La Tacita de Plata*, or "Little Silver Cup." Theory holds that the name comes from the fact that Cádiz, which sits on a cup-shaped bay, turns silvery in the setting sun.

Bitter oranges are not widely available in the United States, where farmers usually sell their entire crop to marmalade producers. If you cannot find them in your market, a mixture of regular orange juice and lemon juice is a good approximation. :: **Serves 6 as a first course**

6 cups Fish Stock (page 304)

Zest of 1 bitter orange, or of $1/2$ lemon and $1/2$ regular orange, cut into wide strips

1 tomato, cored and halved

1 yellow onion, halved

$1/2$ green bell pepper, seeded and coarsely chopped

1 flat-leaf parsley sprig, plus chopped parsley for garnish

1 clove garlic, peeled but left whole

1 slice day-old country style bread or baguette, about 1 ounce, soaked in water to cover and squeezed dry

Pinch of saffron threads

$1^1/2$ pounds hake, cod, or whiting fillets, cut into small pieces

Salt

Juice of 1 bitter orange, or of $1/2$ lemon and $1/2$ regular orange

In a stockpot, combine the fish stock, orange zest, tomato, onion, bell pepper, and parsley sprig and bring to a gentle boil over medium heat. Decrease the heat to low and cook for 15 minutes to blend the flavors. Strain the stock through a fine-mesh sieve placed over another saucepan. Discard the orange zest and parsley and set the vegetables aside.

In a small, dry skillet, roast the garlic over high heat, turning as needed, for 3 minutes, or until colored on all sides. Remove from the heat.

In a blender or food processor, combine $1/2$ cup of the reserved stock with the reserved tomato, onion, and bell pepper; the roasted garlic; bread; and saffron. Process until a smooth purée forms. Add the purée to the remaining stock, mix well, place over medium heat, and bring to a simmer.

Season the fish pieces with salt and add to the pan. Decrease the heat to low and cook for about 5 minutes, or until the fish turns opaque.

Remove from the heat, add the orange juice, stir gently, and let rest for 5 minutes. Ladle into warmed bowls, sprinkle with the chopped parsley, and serve.

SOPA DE PESCADO ::
Fish Soup :: (Basque Country)

This fish soup was a specialty at my restaurant in New York. In fact, it was so popular that I found it impossible to take if off the menu in favor of another fish soup. The original recipe is from Larruskain, a village near Markina, where my family comes from. Over many years of cooking it, I have diverged little from the traditional recipe, which was included in my first book, *The Basque Table*. There are some differences, however, including using tomato sauce instead of fresh tomato, fish stock in place of water, and whole shrimp, rather than halved. I have also added a touch of saffron, for both color and flavor.

:: **Serves 6 as a first course**

$^1/_2$ pound Manila or small littleneck clams

1 tablespoon coarse salt

$^1/_2$ cup olive oil

1 small yellow onion, finely chopped

2 small carrots, finely julienned, and cut into 2-inch segments

1 leek, white part only, thinly sliced

$^1/_2$ pound monkfish fillet, cut into small chunks

$^1/_2$ pound medium shrimp, peeled

1 teaspoon salt

2 tablespoons unbleached all-purpose flour

6 cups Fish Stock (page 304)

Pinch of saffron threads

$^1/_2$ cup dry white wine

$^1/_3$ cup Tomato Sauce (page 311) or Biscayne Sauce (page 313)

1 pound mussels, scrubbed and debearded

Scrub the clams under cold running water, discarding any that fail to close to the touch. In a large bowl, combine the clams, coarse salt, and water to cover and let stand for at least 30 minutes or up to 2 hours so that the clams release any sand trapped in their shells. Drain.

Meanwhile, in a large sauté pan, heat the olive oil over medium-high heat. Add the onion, carrots, and leek, decrease the heat to low, and sauté for 10 minutes, or until the vegetables are soft.

Sprinkle the monkfish and shrimp with the salt. Spread the flour in a shallow plate and coat the monkfish on all sides, shaking off any excess flour. Add the monkfish and shrimp to the pan holding the vegetables and cook over low heat, stirring, for about 5 minutes, or until the monkfish is opaque and the shrimp turn pink. Add the stock, increase the heat to medium-high, and bring to a boil. Add the saffron and wine, stir gently, and decrease the heat to low. Add the tomato sauce, stir gently to mix all the ingredients well, and simmer for 1 to 2 minutes to heat thorough. Remove from the heat and set aside.

In a large saucepan, combine the clams and mussels with water just to cover and bring to a boil over medium-high heat. Cover and cook for about 5 minutes, or until they open. As the clams and mussels cook, uncover the pan occasionally and stir them with a wooden spoon to encourage them all to open at about the same time. Drain the mollusks, discarding any that have not opened. Remove the meats from the shells and discard the shells.

Add the clams and mussels to the soup, stir gently, and return to medium-low heat. Bring to a simmer and cook gently for about 2 minutes to heat through. Ladle into warmed bowls and serve immediately.

GAZPACHUELO DE MÁLAGA ▪
Seafood Stew with Mayonnaise, Málaga Style ▪ *(Andalusia)*

Typical of the province of Málaga, this fish stew is made with monkfish, flounder, shrimp, mussels, clams, and potatoes. If you cannot find flounder, sole is a good substitute, as is rockfish. What makes this soup so special and appealing is the unusual combination of the mayonnaise and the fish stock. Add more liquid at the end if you like your soup thinner. ▪ **Serves 4 as a first course**

8 Manila or small littleneck clams

1 teaspoon coarse salt

8 mussels, scrubbed and debearded

1 cup water

$1/3$ cup olive oil

1 clove garlic, minced

8 small shrimp with heads intact, peeled with heads and shells reserved

1 small flounder, about $1/2$ pound, filleted and cut into small pieces, with backbone reserved

$1/3$ cup dry white wine

2 small boiling potatoes, about $1/2$ pound total weight, peeled and cut into small chunks

1 bay leaf

$1/2$ teaspoon saffron threads

1 teaspoon red wine vinegar

$1/2$ teaspoon salt

$1/2$ pound monkfish fillet, cut into chunks

1 tablespoon mayonnaise, homemade (page 306) or store bought

1 tablespoon chopped fresh flat-leaf parsley

Scrub the clams under cold running water, discarding any that fail to close to the touch. In a large bowl, combine the clams, coarse salt, and water to cover and let stand for at least 30 minutes or up to 2 hours so that the clams release any sand trapped in their shells. Drain.

In a small saucepan, combine the clams, mussels, and 1 cup water and bring to a boil over medium-high heat. Cover and cook for about 5 minutes, or until they open. As the clams and mussels cook, uncover the pan occasionally and stir them with a wooden spoon to encourage them all to open at about the same time. Drain the mollusks, reserving the liquid, and discard any that have not opened. Remove the meats from the shells and discard the shells. Strain the liquid through a fine-mesh sieve and set aside.

In a medium-sized saucepan, heat the olive oil over low heat. Add the garlic and sauté briefly for 2 to 3 minutes, or until lightly golden. Do not allow it to brown. Add the shells and heads of the shrimp and the bone of the flounder. Mix well and add the wine and water to cover. Bring to a gentle boil over low heat and cook for 5 minutes. Add the reserved cooking liquid from the mollusks and cook for 1 minute longer. Strain the contents of the pan through a fine-mesh sieve placed over a clean saucepan and discard the contents of the sieve. You should have 4 to 5 cups liquid.

Bring the strained liquid to a boil over high heat and add the potatoes, bay leaf, saffron, and vinegar. Decrease the heat to medium, add the salt, and cook for 10 minutes, or until the potatoes are almost tender. Add the shrimp, monkfish, and flounder, and cook for 5 minutes longer, or until the shrimp turn pink and the fish is opaque. Remove from the heat and add the mussels and clams.

Ladle a little of the liquid into a small bowl and stir in the mayonnaise. Return the mixture to the soup and stir to distribute evenly. Ladle into warmed soup plates, sprinkle with the parsley, and serve at once.

SOPA DE AJO ▪ Bread and Garlic Soup with Poached Eggs ▪ (*Madrid*)

Every region in Spain has a version of this humble dish that arose from the need to nourish large families with small means. It is especially comforting on cold winter days and nights. Known as *sopa castellana* in Madrid and both Castiles, it is also said to be a great hangover remedy, and in Madrid and elsewhere you will find places that serve this curative soup late at night or in the early morning hours. For the best results, the bread should be quite dry, so, if possible, slice it the night before and keep it covered with a kitchen towel.

On a trip to Spain with the acclaimed photographer Richard Avedon, I dined with him at Casa Lucio, a popular restaurant in the old part of Madrid, where the kitchen adds eggs and thin strips of *jamón serrano* to the soup. I ordered us each a bowl of *sopa de ajo* as an appetizer; the late Mr. Avedon loved it so much he asked for a second serving. ▪ **Serves 6 as a first course**

1/3 pound day-old country-style bread

1/2 cup olive oil

6 cloves garlic, peeled but left whole

1 tablespoon sweet pimentón or paprika

4 cups hot water

1 teaspoon salt

1/2 teaspoon hot red pepper flakes (optional)

6 eggs

Slice the bread as thinly as possible and, if you have the time, let it rest overnight covered with a kitchen towel.

In a large *cazuela* (page 51), heat the olive oil over medium heat. Add the garlic and fry for 5 minutes, or until golden. Add the bread slices and cook, turning often, until they absorb all the oil. Add the *pimentón*, mix well with the bread, and then add the water, salt, and red pepper flakes. Cook, stirring often, for at least 15 minutes, or until the ingredients are well blended, the bread slices are broken up, and the soup is fairly thick.

Working quickly, break the eggs one at a time into a cup and slide each egg into the pan to rest on the surface of the soup. Shake the pan a little and cook for 3 to 5 minutes, or until the whites are set and the yolks are still soft.

Ladle the soup into warmed bowls, including 1 egg with each serving. Serve immediately.

SOPA MENORQUINA ■
Bread and Olive Oil Soup with Egg Yolks ■
(Balearic Islands)

The renowned baritone Joan Pons and his wife, Nina, are from Minorca. During the New York opera season, they spend extended periods of time in the city, and when I lived there, they often visited my restaurant. I used to bombard them with questions about the cuisine of Minorca, and on one occasion, they graciously shared some of their favorite recipes with me. This simple and delightful soup is one of them. ■ **Serves 4 as a first course**

4 cups water

3 tablespoons olive oil

2 cloves garlic, peeled but left whole

Leaves from 2 flat-leaf parsley sprigs

Pinch of fresh or dried thyme

1 teaspoon salt

1/2 pound day-old country-style bread or baguette, thinly sliced and toasted

4 egg yolks

In a saucepan or small stockpot, bring the water to a boil over high heat. Add the olive oil, garlic, parsley, thyme, and salt. Decrease the heat to medium and cook for about 5 minutes.

Distribute the bread slices evenly among the soup plates or bowls. Place 1 egg yolk on top of the bread in each bowl. Ladle the hot broth over the top. Serve immediately.

ZURRUKUTUNA ■ Bread Soup with
Salt Cod ■ (Basque Country)

Salt cod is the star of this hearty winter soup, which is basically a simple garlic soup dressed up with the popular fish. The name comes from the onomatopoeic Basque word *zurrup*, a "sip" or "slurp," and *kutuna*, which means "pleasant." ■ **Serves 6 as a first course**

1 pound salt cod, desalted (page 46) and cut into 4 or 5 pieces

1/3 cup olive oil

1 large yellow onion, finely chopped

3 cloves garlic, finely chopped

1/2 tablespoon sweet pimentón or paprika

1/2 pound day-old country-style bread or baguette, thinly sliced and toasted

2 teaspoons salt

Heat a stove-top grill pan or frying pan over high heat (or you can use a charcoal grill). Add the cod pieces and cook, turning several times, for about 10 minutes, or until golden. Transfer to a dish and, when cool enough to handle, discard the skin and any bones and shred the fish with your fingers into threads.

In a large saucepan, heat the olive oil over high heat. Add the onion and sauté for 5 minutes, or until golden. Decrease the heat to medium and add the garlic, *pimentón*, and cod and stir with a wooden spoon until well mixed. Add water to cover by 1 inch and cook over medium heat for about 30 minutes, or until the flavors are well blended.

Add the bread, break it up with the spoon, and mix well with the other ingredients. Add the salt and simmer for 5 minutes longer, or until the ingredients are fully blended. The soup should be fairly chunky and without much liquid.

Ladle the soup into warmed bowls and serve.

SOPAS MALLORQUINAS :: Majorcan Vegetable Soup :: (Balearic Islands)

Even though it is called *sopas*, this isn't a soup in the traditional sense because it contains almost no liquid. In the Balearic Islands and other parts of Spain, *sopas* is also the word given to thin slices of bread that are used in dishes such as this one, and most bakers in the islands sell the bread already sliced in plastic bags. The ingredients for this soup should be plentiful and vary with the season. This is a typical spring version. A *greixonera*, the *cazuela* of the islands, is used for the baking step, but a typical Spanish *cazuela* or a baking dish can be used in its place.

:: **Serves 8 as a first course**

1/2 cup olive oil

1 tablespoon lard (optional)

1 yellow onion, coarsely chopped

2 cloves garlic, finely minced

2 tomatoes, coarsely chopped

2 cups firmly packed coarsely chopped green cabbage

1 cup firmly packed coarsely chopped Swiss chard

1 cup small cauliflower florets

4 cups Vegetable Stock (page 305) or water

1 cup snow peas

1/2 cup fresh or thawed frozen shelled English peas

1 tablespoon sweet pimentón or paprika

Salt

12 very thin slices day-old whole-grain country-style bread

In a large saucepan or stockpot, heat the olive oil and lard, if using, over medium heat. Add the onion and garlic and sauté for 5 minutes, or until softened. Do not allow them to color. Add the tomatoes and cook, stirring occasionally, for 5 minutes, or until they begin to soften.

Add the cabbage, Swiss chard, and cauliflower in layers. Pour the stock over the vegetables, cover, and cook for about 5 minutes longer, or until the vegetables lose some of their volume. Add the snow peas and English peas, sprinkle with *pimentón*, and season with a little salt. Cover, decrease the heat to low, and cook for about 10 minutes, or until all the vegetables are fork-tender. Taste and adjust the seasoning with salt.

Line a *greixonera*, *cazuela* (page 51), or round baking dish (each 12 inches in diameter) with the bread slices. Using a slotted spoon, lift the vegetables from the pan and place them on top of the bread. Pour the cooking liquid from the pan over the vegetables.

Place in the oven and bake for about 10 minutes, or until the vegetables and bread are evenly mixed with the liquid. Spoon into warmed bowls or soup plates and serve immediately.

LENTEJAS A LA EXTREMEÑA ⊞
Lentil Soup with Jamón Serrano and White Wine ⊞ *(Extremadura)*

Brown lentils are a Spanish kitchen staple, and each region has its own variation of lentil soup. I particularly like this version, which calls for *jamón serrano* and wine. Elsewhere in Spain, lentil soups made with ham usually call for a few drops of vinegar to be added just before serving, but in Extremadura, cooks traditionally add wine to the lentils as they cook. Outside of Spain, many cooks simmer their lentils for a much shorter time, but I have always cooked my lentils as described here, and they turn out good every time. ⊞ **Serves 4 as a first course**

$^1/_2$ **pound (1 rounded cup) brown lentils**

1 head garlic, unpeeled

$^1/_3$ **cup olive oil**

$^1/_4$ **pound jamón serrano or other dry-cured ham, finely diced**

1 yellow onion, finely chopped

2 tomatoes, peeled and chopped

1 tablespoon sweet pimentón or paprika

$^1/_2$ **cup dry white wine**

$^1/_2$ **teaspoon salt**

Rinse the lentils in a colander under cold running water. In a saucepan, combine the lentils with water to cover by 2 inches and bring to a boil over high heat. Decrease the heat to medium-low and cook, uncovered, for 30 minutes. Add the garlic, decrease the heat to low, and continue to cook, uncovered, for 1 hour, or until the lentils are very tender.

About 15 minutes before the lentils are ready, in a skillet, heat the olive oil over medium heat. Add the *jamón serrano* and onion and fry, stirring often, for 5 minutes, or until the onion is soft. Add the tomatoes and cook, stirring occasionally, for 10 minutes longer, or until they start to break down. Add the *pimentón* and wine, mix well, and transfer the contents of the pan to the pan holding the lentils.

Add the salt, stir with a wooden spoon, and cook the lentils for 5 minutes to blend the flavors. Remove the head of garlic if you wish and discard. Serve the soup at once in warmed soup plates.

Winter fields near Zafra in Extremadura

LENTEJAS DE ARAGÓN ::
Lentil Soup :: (Aragón)

The addition of the sweet Cariñena wine makes these lentils different and delicious. Known in France as Carginan Noir, Cariñena grapes are grown in Aragón and Catalonia, where they are commonly combined with Garnacha (Grenache) grapes (and sometimes others) to produce superb wines. When used as a monovarietal, Cariñena wines are traditionally aged in wooden casks using the *solera* process to yield sweet wines. Muscatel or similar dessert wines are good substitutes. :: **Serves 4 as a first course**

3/4 pound (about 1 1/2 cups) brown lentils

1 small ham bone

1/4 pound white mushrooms, trimmed and coarsely chopped

Juice of 1/2 lemon

1/3 cup olive oil

1 leek, white part only, cut into 1-inch-thick slices

1 yellow onion, finely chopped

1 tomato, peeled and chopped

2 (3-ounce) morcillas

1/2 teaspoon salt

1/3 cup Cariñena or other sweet wine

Rinse the lentils in a colander under cold running water. In a large saucepan, combine the lentils, ham bone, and water to cover by 2 inches and bring to a boil over high heat. Decrease the heat to medium-low and cook the lentils, uncovered, for 1 hour.

After the lentils have cooked for about 30 minutes, in a bowl, combine the mushrooms and lemon juice, toss to coat evenly, and let stand for 30 minutes.

In a skillet, heat the olive oil over medium heat. Add the leek and onion and cook, stirring, for 5 minutes, or until the onion has softened. Add the tomato and cook, stirring occasionally, for about 10 minutes, or until it starts to break down. Add the sausages and mushrooms, mix well, decrease the heat to medium-low, and continue to cook, stirring occasionally, for about 10 minutes, or until all the ingredients have softened and are well blended.

When the lentils have cooked for 1 hour, transfer the contents of the skillet to the pot. Add the salt and cook over low heat, stirring gently every now and again, for 30 minutes longer to blend the flavors and finish cooking the lentils.

Add the wine and stir gently to mix well. Ladle into warmed bowls and serve at once.

ALUBIAS ROJAS DE TOLOSA ::
Red Bean Stew of Tolosa :: *(Basque Country)*

Tolosa, located about twenty miles south of San Sebastián, in the Basque Country, becomes lively on Saturdays, the town's market day. People from all over the area flock there for the exceptional local produce. The dried red beans of the region are particularly flavorful and thus highly prized. If you should visit Tolosa one day, seek out one of the numerous bars or restaurants there that serves this red bean stew, which is traditionally accompanied with the spicy-hot pickled peppers known as *guindillas*. My favorite place to eat it is Herriko Etxea, a tavern in Albiztu, only minutes away by car from Tolosa.

These famed dried red beans, as well as dried white ones, are called *alubias* in the Basque Country and in neighboring areas in northern Spain. In the rest of the country, however, dried beans are usually called *judías*, literally, "Jewish." I find it surprising that *lubia*, Arabic for "bean" (*al* is the article), is used in precisely those parts of Spain where the Moors had relatively little influence—a curiosity for which I have no explanation. :: **Serves 8 as a first course**

1 1/2 pounds dried red kidney beans

6 tablespoons olive oil

1/2 yellow onion, finely chopped

5 ounces salt pork, in one piece

3 (3-ounce) chorizos

6 cups water

Salt

1 small head green cabbage, coarsely chopped

3 (3-ounce) morcillas

1 clove garlic, thinly sliced

8 pickled guindilla chiles or peperoncini

Rinse the beans in a colander under cold running water. Place in a bowl, add water to cover by 2 inches, and let soak for at least 8 hours or up to overnight.

Drain the beans, place in a stockpot, and add water to cover by 1 inch. Add 2 tablespoons of the olive oil, the onion, and the salt pork and bring to a boil over high heat. Decrease the heat to medium-low and cook, uncovered, at a gentle boil, stirring occasionally.

After the beans have cooked for 1 hour, add the chorizos. Add warm water if needed to keep the beans covered, and continue to boil gently for 1 hour longer, or until the beans are tender.

Meanwhile, in a saucepan, bring the 6 cups water to a boil over high heat. Salt the water lightly, add the cabbage, and cook for about 20 minutes, or until the cabbage has lost its volume. Decrease the heat to medium, add the *morcillas*, and cook for 20 minutes longer, or until the *morcillas* are fork-tender. Lift the sausages from the pot and keep them warm on a serving platter. Drain the cabbage, squeezing it thoroughly to eliminate any excess liquid.

In a sauté pan, heat the remaining 4 tablespoons olive oil over medium heat. Add the garlic and sauté for 2 to 3 minutes, or until golden. Add the cabbage and turn several times in the oil and garlic to heat through and blend the flavors. Transfer the cabbage to a serving platter and keep warm.

When the beans are tender, remove the chorizos and salt pork to the platter holding the *morcillas*. Slice the sausages and salt pork into 2-inch pieces. (For ease, you can transfer the meats to a cutting board for slicing and then return them to the platter.)

Transfer the beans to a warmed serving bowl and place on the table along with the platter of sausages and salt pork and the platter of cabbage. Offer the *guindillas* on the side.

POCHAS A LA RIOJANA ▪ Fresh White Beans and Pork Stew ▪ (*La Rioja*)

In Spanish, *pocha* or *pocho* is a colloquial term used to describe something wilted or worn down, or sometimes even sick. Why this contradictory name was given to fresh, young shelling beans is a mystery to me. In Logroño, the capital of La Rioja, these same beans are called *caparrones*, so don't be surprised if you see *caparrones*, rather than *pochas*, on a menu when you visit that region.

I have never seen *caparrones* in the United States, but you can substitute other white shelling beans, such as white lima, flageolet, or cannellini. You will need to buy about 1¹/₂ pounds beans in the pod to yield 1 pound shelled. ▪ **Serves 6 as a first course**

1 pound shelled white shelling beans
1 small yellow onion, halved
¹/₂ pound spareribs
3 (3-ounce) chorizos
¹/₄ pound bacon, in one piece
1 fresh ham hock
1 teaspoon salt

In a stockpot, combine the beans and onion with water to cover by 2 inches. Bring slowly to a boil over medium heat. Add the spareribs, chorizos, bacon, and ham hock. When the water returns to a boil, add the salt, cover, decrease the heat to low, and cook at a very gentle boil for 2 hours.

Lift the meats and sausages from the pot. Remove the meat from the hock and cut it into small pieces. Cut the chorizos and bacon into small pieces, and arrange all the meats and the spareribs on a warmed platter.

Transfer the bean stew to a warmed serving bowl and serve immediately with the platter of meats.

CALDO GALLEGO ▪ White Bean Soup with Greens and Meats ▪ (*Galicia*)

Restaurant chefs in Galicia usually prepare this soup with many ingredients in multiple pots. But at home, most Gallegos make a straightforward recipe: just one stockpot in which everything is cooked together, with the ingredients added according to the time required to cook them. When turnip greens are out of season, they use cabbage instead. ▪ **Serves 6 as a first course**

¹/₂ pound (1 rounded cup) dried white cannellini or Great Northern beans
¹/₂ pound bacon, in one piece
1 pound turnip greens or green cabbage, chopped
2 (3-ounce) chorizos
1 pound boiling potatoes, peeled and cut into large chunks
1 teaspoon salt

Rinse the beans in a colander under cold running water. Place in a bowl, add water to cover by 2 inches, and let soak for at least 8 hours or up to overnight.

Drain the beans, place in a stockpot, and add the bacon and water to cover by 1 inch. Bring to a boil over high heat, decrease the heat to medium-low, and cook, uncovered, for 1 hour. Add the greens and cook, stirring occasionally, for 30 minutes longer, adding water as needed to keep the beans fully covered with liquid. Add the chorizos and potatoes, season with salt, and cook for 30 minutes longer, or until the potatoes are fork-tender.

Lift the bacon and the chorizos from the pot and cut into small pieces. Divide the bacon and sausage pieces evenly among 6 warmed soup plates. Ladle the soup on top and serve immediately.

FABADA ASTURIANA ▪ White Bean Stew with Sausages ▪ (*Asturias*)

This classic stew of Asturias is made with ingredients that rarely travel beyond the region's borders: *fabes*, the outstanding creamy white beans from La Granja; *compango*, a smoked sausage; the local *morcilla*; and *lacón*, cured pork shoulder. The beans are available in the United States, though not widely, and the specialty meats are not, but I have found that the stew can be made with white lima beans, any Spanish chorizos and *morcillas*, and fresh or cured ham hock with excellent results.

Asturias is not only the place of origin for *fabada asturiana*, however. It is also the birthplace of the brave Don Pelayo, who in Covadonga began the Reconquista, the centuries-long process of recovering the land from the Moors that later would be unified as Spain. ▪ **Serves 8 as a first course**

2 pounds dried fabes or white lima beans

1 pound fresh or cured ham hock or salt pork, in one piece

4 (3-ounce) chorizos

4 (3-ounce) morcillas

1 teaspoon salt

Rinse the beans in a colander under cold running water. Place in a bowl, add water to cover by 3 inches, and let soak for at least 8 hours or up to overnight. If using a cured ham hock, place it in a bowl with warm water to cover and let soak for 8 hours or up to overnight.

Drain the beans, and the ham hock, if soaked, and place them in a large stockpot. Add the sausages and water to cover by 1 inch. Bring to a boil over medium heat, cover, decrease the heat to low, and cook at a steady slow boil for about 1 hour. Gently move the pot often but do not stir the contents (to avoid breaking the beans), and add more water if necessary to keep the beans just covered at all times.

After the beans and sausages have cooked for 1 hour, add the salt, re-cover, and continue cooking at a gentle boil for about 1 hour longer, or until the beans are fork-tender. During this second hour, add cold water by the spoonful every 15 minutes to interrupt the boil. This helps soften the beans and prevents their skins from loosening. Remove from the heat and let rest for 10 minutes before serving.

Lift the sausages and ham hock from the pot. Slice the sausages into 1-inch pieces and chop the meat from the hock coarsely. Transfer the meats to a warmed serving platter. Transfer the beans to a serving bowl. To serve, ladle the beans into individual soup plates and place the sausages and meat alongside in the same plate.

POTE ASTURIANO ❚❚ White Bean and Cabbage Stew ❚❚ (Asturias)

My friend Santiago Botas, the olive oil expert, gave me this recipe for hearty *pote asturiano*. It is his mother's recipe, who, although she is a Basque, has lived for many years in Asturias. I have used cannellini and Great Northern beans in this traditional Spanish dish and they both work well. ❚❚ **Serves 6 as a first course**

1 pound dried cannellini or Great Northern beans

1/2 pound fresh or cured ham hock or salt pork, in one piece

2 (3-ounce) chorizos

4 cups water

2 cups finely shredded green cabbage

2 teaspoons salt

2 (3-ounce) morcillas

1 pound russet potatoes, peeled and cut into large chunks

2 tablespoons olive oil

1 clove garlic, peeled but left whole

1 1/2 teaspoons sweet pimentón or paprika

Rinse the beans in a colander under cold running water. Place in a bowl, add water to cover by 3 inches, and let soak for at least 8 hours or up to overnight. If using a cured ham hock, place it in a bowl with warm water to cover and let soak for 8 hours or up to overnight.

Drain the beans, and the ham hock, if soaked, and place them in a large stockpot. Add the chorizos and water to cover by 1 inch. Bring to a boil over medium heat, cover, decrease the heat to low, and cook at a gentle boil for 1 hour. Add water if necessary to keep the beans covered at all times.

Meanwhile, in a saucepan, bring the 4 cups water to a boil over high heat. Add the cabbage and 1 teaspoon of the salt, decrease the heat to medium, and cook, uncovered, for 20 minutes, or until the cabbage is tender. Drain well and set aside.

After the beans have cooked for 1 hour, season them with the remaining 1 teaspoon salt and add the *morcillas*. Stir gently to mix the ingredients and cook for 30 minutes over low heat. Add the potatoes and cabbage and more water if needed to cover and cook for 30 minutes, or until the potatoes are fork-tender.

Just before the potatoes are ready, in a small skillet, heat the olive oil over medium heat. Add the garlic and sauté for 2 to 3 minutes, or until golden. Using a fork, mash the garlic into the oil, and then discard the garlic. Add the *pimentón*, mix well with the oil, and fry for 1 minute. Add the contents of the skillet to the stew and cook over low heat for 5 minutes longer. Remove from the heat and let stand for 10 minutes before serving.

Lift the sausages and ham hock from the pot. Cut the sausages and the meat from the hock into small pieces and divide the meats among 6 warmed soup plates. Ladle the stew over the meats and serve immediately.

FABES CON ALMEJAS ▪ White Bean Stew with Clams ▪ (*Asturias*)

In Asturias, fresh clams and big, buttery white beans known as *fabes* are abundant, and both ingredients are highlighted in this favorite dish of the region. The clams are prepared in a *salsa verde* and then mixed with the cooked beans. White limas are a satisfying substitute in the absence of the *fabes*. ▪ **Serves 6 as a first course**

1 pound dried fabes or white lima beans

1/2 leek, white part only, sliced

1/2 green bell pepper, seeded, in one piece

1/2 red bell pepper, seeded, in one piece

1/4 cup olive oil

1/2 yellow onion, chopped

1 tablespoon sweet pimentón or paprika

Salt

1/2 recipe Clams in Salsa Verde (page 71)

Rinse the beans in a colander under cold running water. Place in a bowl, add water to cover by 3 inches, and let soak for at least 8 hours or up to overnight.

Drain the beans and place them in a large stockpot with the leek, bell peppers, and water to cover by 2 inches. Bring to a boil over high heat and cook rapidly for 2 to 3 minutes, skimming any foam from the surface as it forms. Decrease the heat to low and simmer gently, uncovered, for about 2 hours, adding cold water by the spoonful to interrupt the boil every 15 minutes. This helps soften the beans and prevents their skins from loosening. Gently move the pot often but do not stir the contents (to avoid breaking the beans), and add more water if necessary to keep the beans just covered at all times. The beans are done when they are fork-tender.

Just before the beans are ready, in a small skillet, heat the olive oil over medium-high heat. Add the onion and sauté for about 10 minutes, or until the onion has softened. Add the *pimentón* and cook, stirring, for about 2 minutes longer. Remove from the heat.

When the beans are cooked, remove the bell peppers and discard them. Add the onion mixture, stir gently to mix, and season the stew to taste with salt.

Add the sauce from the clams to the bean stew and stir gently to mix. Ladle the stew into warmed soup plates and then divide the clams evenly among the plates. Serve immediately.

POTAJE DE BERROS :: Watercress and Sweet Corn Soup :: (Canary Islands)

Two of my brothers, Vale and Iñigo, live in the Canary Islands, and so do my husband's mother and sister, Laurette and Silvia. Every time I visit my relatives, we enjoy ourselves by going on excursions and dining in and out. One popular dish we often have, both at home and in restaurants, is this wonderful puréed soup.

Because the Canaries were the last bits of Spain the conquistadors saw on their journeys to the New World, and the first land they saw on their return home, produce from the Americas, such as potatoes and corn, usually arrived on the islands before they were introduced to the mainland. This recipe originated as a way to use some of these new ingredients. :: **Serves 6 as a first course**

1/2 cup olive oil

1/2 yellow onion, chopped

1 clove garlic, sliced

4 ripe tomatoes, peeled and chopped

Leaves from 2 bunches watercress

2 small carrots, peeled and chopped

1/4-pound piece pumpkin or winter squash, peeled, seeded, and cut into chunks

2 small boiling potatoes, about 1/2 pound total weight, peeled and cut into chunks

2/3 cup dried white beans, rinsed, soaked at least 8 hours or up to overnight in water to cover, and drained

2 cups Chicken Stock (page 304)

Salt

4 cups water

1 cup fresh or frozen corn kernels

In a stockpot, heat the olive oil over medium heat. Add the onion, garlic, and tomatoes and sauté for 15 minutes, or until the onion is tender and the tomatoes have softened.

Set aside some of the watercress leaves for garnish and add the rest to the pot along with the carrots, pumpkin, potatoes, and white beans. Mix well, add the stock and 1 1/2 teaspoons salt, bring to a simmer, decrease the heat to medium-low, and cook, uncovered, for about 45 minutes. Add the water, increase the heat to medium, and cook for about 10 minutes longer, or until the beans are tender.

Meanwhile, in a small saucepan, combine the corn with water to cover, salt the water lightly, and bring to a boil over high heat. Cover, decrease the heat to low, and cook for about 15 minutes, or until the corn is very tender. Drain and reserve the corn for garnish.

When the beans are tender, remove from the heat. Working in batches, transfer to a blender or food processor and purée until smooth. Reheat gently in a clean saucepan if the soup is no longer hot. Season to taste with salt.

Ladle into warmed soup plates or bowls, garnish with the corn and watercress leaves, and serve immediately.

CALDO DE PAPAS Y HUEVOS ▪
Potato Soup with Eggs ▪ *(Canary Islands)*

The eggs in this simple potato soup from the Canaries are added in two ways: first, the beaten egg is stirred in, turning the broth opaque, and then whole eggs are added at the last moment with just enough time to allow them to set before the soup is served. The additions of *pimentón* and saffron are modern embellishments to this traditional component of a farmer's midday meal. ▪

Serves 6 as a first course

2 cloves garlic, peeled but left whole

1¹/₂ teaspoons salt

1 pound russet potatoes, peeled and cut into chunks

1 yellow onion, finely chopped

2 tomatoes, peeled and finely chopped

1 cilantro sprig

¹/₄ cup olive oil

1¹/₂ teaspoons sweet pimentón or paprika

Pinch of saffron threads

7 eggs

In a mortar, mash the garlic with about ¹/₂ teaspoon of the salt until a paste forms. Set aside.

In a large, wide saucepan, combine the potatoes, onion, tomatoes, cilantro, and olive oil and place over medium heat. Using a wooden spoon, stir all the ingredients once or twice to mix well. Add the garlic paste, *pimentón*, and saffron to the pan, stir to combine, and then add water to cover by 3 inches. Slowly bring to a boil and add the remaining 1 teaspoon salt. Decrease the heat to medium-low, cover, and cook for 30 minutes, or until the potatoes are fork-tender.

Break 1 egg and beat it lightly. Add to the pan and stir quickly for 30 seconds, or until the liquid turns opaque. Working quickly, break the remaining 6 eggs one at a time into a cup and slide each egg into the pan to rest on the surface of the soup. Shake the pan a little and cook for 3 to 5 minutes longer, or until the whites are set and the yolks are still soft. The soup will be a little starchy and thick.

Ladle the soup into warmed bowls, including 1 egg with each serving. Serve immediately.

PATATAS A LA RIOJANA ▪
Potato and Chorizo Stew ▪ *(La Rioja)*

When the acclaimed French chef Paul Bocuse was asked to prepare a banquet for the hundredth anniversary of a famous winery in La Rioja, he shared this dish with the kitchen staff and apparently requested a second and then third serving for himself! Even when made with chorizos produced in the United States, it is delicious. ▪

Serves 6 as a main course

3 pounds russet potatoes

¹/₃ cup olive oil

1 yellow onion, finely chopped

1 clove garlic, finely minced

3 (3-ounce) chorizos, casings removed and cut into 1-inch-thick slices

1¹/₂ tablespoons sweet pimentón or paprika

¹/₂ teaspoon hot red pepper flakes

1 teaspoon salt

Peel the potatoes. To "crack" the potatoes into chestnut-sized pieces, make a small cut in each potato and then break it open the rest of the way. Set the potato pieces aside.

In a large saucepan, heat the olive oil over medium heat. Add the onion and garlic and sauté for 10 minutes, or until softened. Add the chorizos and cook, stirring, for about 1 minute. Add the potatoes, *pimentón*, red pepper flakes, and salt and stir to mix the ingredients. Add water to cover by 1 inch and bring to a boil. Cover, decrease the heat to medium-low, and cook slowly for 30 minutes, or until the potatoes are fork-tender.

Remove from the heat. Mash a piece or two of the potato against the side of the pot with the back of a spoon to thicken the soup. Stir once, re-cover, and let stand for 10 minutes.

Stir again, ladle into warmed bowls, and serve immediately.

MARMITAKO ▪ Fresh Tuna and Potato Stew ▪ (Basque Country)

Marmita translates as "pot" or "casserole" in Basque, while the suffix *ko* is the genitive case, so that *marmitako* literally means "from the pot." Of course, just about everything in Basque cooking comes "from the pot," but only this venerable dish goes by that name. Originally it was cooked on board fishing boats (and it still is), but for decades now it has appeared on restaurant menus in the Basque Country, sometimes even prepared with salmon. The stew is soupy but thick, especially when the potatoes are "cracked open" to yield more starch. You can prepare *marmitako* up to the point at which the tuna is added, and then reheat the stew up to a day later and add the tuna. ▪ **Serves 6 as a main course**

2 dried choricero or ancho chiles

1 pound fresh bonito or other tuna fillet

Coarse salt

4 russet potatoes, about 2 pounds total weight

1/3 cup olive oil

1 yellow onion, finely chopped

1 clove garlic, minced

1/2 green bell pepper, seeded and cut lengthwise into narrow strips

2 tablespoons Biscayne Sauce (page 313), or 1 tablespoon sweet pimentón or paprika

In a heatproof bowl, combine the dried chiles with boiling water to cover and let stand for 30 minutes, or until soft. Drain the chiles, slit them open, and scrape off the flesh with the edge of a knife, discarding the seeds, skins, and stems. Set the flesh aside.

Cut the tuna into small pieces. Sprinkle the pieces with coarse salt and set aside.

Peel the potatoes. To "crack" the potatoes into chestnut-sized pieces, make a small cut in each potato and then break it open the rest of the way. Set the potato pieces aside.

In a stockpot, heat the olive oil over medium-high heat. Add the onion, garlic, and bell pepper, and the flesh from the chiles, stir well, and cook, stirring occasionally, for 5 minutes, or until the onion and bell pepper have begun to soften and all the ingredients are well blended.

Add the potatoes and Biscayne sauce and mix well. Season with a little coarse salt and add water to cover by 2 inches. Bring to a boil, cover, decrease the heat to medium-low, and cook for about 30 minutes, or until the potatoes are fork-tender.

Add the tuna pieces to the pot and simmer for 5 minutes, or until the tuna is opaque. Remove from the heat and let stand for 30 minutes before serving. If the soup is very clear because the potatoes didn't release enough starch, mash a piece or two against the side of the pot with the back of a spoon and shake the pot a little.

Reheat gently to serving temperature (if your pot retains heat well, the stew may still be piping hot and you won't need to reheat it). Ladle into warmed bowls and serve at once.

COCIDO MADRILEÑO ▪ Madrid-Style Chickpea, Meat, and Vegetable Stew ▪ (Madrid)

This *cocido* has its origin in the much older *olla podrida*, a stew containing legumes, meats, and sausages that was cooked for long hours over low heat. *Adafina*, the equivalent Sephardic dish popular in every Jewish quarter in Spain, is cooked at the lowest heat all Friday night until dawn on Saturday, so the dish is ready for the Sabbath.

Though undeniably humble in origin, *cocidos* gained respectability during the years the Habsburgs ruled Spain, when aristocrats and peasants alike were drawn to these bountiful dishes. Today, Madrid offers a long list of prominent establishments that prepare excellent *cocidos*. My favorite, the legendary restaurant Lhardy, is steps away from Puerta del Sol, at the heart of the city. Its dining room is on the second floor, above its delicatessen, where you can also enjoy a wonderful consommé-like *caldo* made from the broth of the *cocidos* served in the dining room.

Some Madrileños add a *pelota*, a large dumpling made of ground pork or beef, or of bread crumbs, garlic, parsley, and egg, to their *cocidos*. It is slipped into the pot toward the end of cooking, and although I have not included one here, you will find a *pelota* in the *escudella* recipe on page 178. As noted earlier, *cocidos* are traditionally served in three courses, usually with the broth first, followed by the chickpeas and vegetables, and then finally the meats. You may alter the order, of course, if you like. ▪ **Serves 6 as a three-course meal**

1 pound dried chickpeas

MEATS

1 pound boneless beef shank, round, or chuck, in one piece

$1/2$ stewing hen or 1 small chicken, about 2 pounds, quartered

$1/2$ pound fatback or bacon, in one piece

2 small soup bones, preferably marrowbones

1 small ham bone (optional)

3 (3-ounce) chorizos

3 (3-ounce) morcillas

$1^1/2$ teaspoons salt

VEGETABLES

8 cups water

Salt

3 carrots, peeled and halved crosswise

3 russet potatoes, peeled and halved crosswise

1 head green cabbage, coarsely chopped

1 cup broken-up angel hair pasta (optional)

6 tablespoons olive oil

2 cloves garlic, thinly sliced

2 cups Tomato Sauce (page 311)

Country-style bread or baguette slices, toasted, if using marrowbones

Rinse the chickpeas in a colander under cold running water. Place in a bowl, add water to cover by 3 inches, and let soak for at least 8 hours or up to overnight.

To prepare the meats, in a large stockpot, combine the beef, stewing hen, fatback, soup bones, and ham bone with water to cover by 3 inches. Bring to a boil over high heat, boil for 10 minutes, and then skim the foam from the surface.

Drain the chickpeas and wrap them in a cheesecloth pouch tied with kitchen string (to make it easier to retrieve them for serving later). Add the chickpeas to the stockpot holding the meats. Cover, decrease the heat to medium-low, and simmer gently for about $1^1/2$ hours. Skim the foam from the surface every 30 minutes and add more water if necessary to keep the ingredients covered at all times.

Add the sausages and salt, decrease the heat to low, and cook for 30 minutes longer, or until the sausages are fork-tender. At this point, the chickpeas and the meats should be done.

Just before the chickpeas and meats are ready, cook the vegetables. In another stockpot or large saucepan, bring the water to a boil over high heat and then salt it lightly. Add the carrots, potatoes, and cabbage, decrease the heat to medium, and cook for 30 minutes, or until the carrots and potatoes are fork-tender.

(continued)

When the meats and chickpeas are ready, retrieve the cheesecloth pouch of chickpeas and set aside; keep warm. Lift out the beef, hen, fatback, soup bones, ham bone, and sausages and set aside; keep warm. Pour the broth through a fine-mesh sieve placed over a clean saucepan. Bring the broth to a boil over high heat and add the pasta, if using. Boil for about 5 minutes, or until the pasta is tender. Remove from the heat and keep warm.

When the vegetables are ready, drain them into a sieve or colander. Place the carrots and potatoes on a warmed platter and keep warm. Squeeze the cabbage thoroughly to eliminate any excess liquid. In a sauté pan, heat the olive oil over medium heat. Add the garlic and sauté for 2 to 3 minutes, or until golden. Add the cabbage and turn several times in the oil and garlic to heat through and blend the flavors. Transfer the cabbage to the platter holding the carrots and potatoes.

In a saucepan, heat the tomato sauce over medium heat until hot. Transfer to a serving bowl and keep warm.

Cut all the meats and sausages into pieces and arrange on a warmed serving platter. If the soup bones contain marrow, remove the marrow, spread it on the toasted bread, sprinkle with salt, and keep warm; otherwise, discard the bones. If you have used the ham bone, cut the meat from the bone and add it to the platter. Remove the chickpeas from the cheesecloth pouch and add them to the vegetable platter.

Serve the broth with pasta as the first course, reheating it if it has cooled. Serve the chickpeas, cabbage, potatoes, and carrots with the tomato sauce on the side as the second course. Serve the meats and sausages and the marrow-topped toast as the third course.

COCIDO MARAGATO :: León-Style Chickpea, Meat, and Vegetable Stew :: (*Castilla y León*)

Maragatería is a county in the province of León, well known in Spain for its beautiful medieval architecture and for its *cocido maragato*. The *cocido* owes much of its fame to its use of two local products, spicy chorizos and *cecina* (salted beef), and to the fact that it is the only Spanish *cocido* that is eaten in reverse order: the meats and sausages are served first, followed by the legumes and vegetables, and finally the soup.

Several theories account for this out-of-step dining sequence. One insists that the dish is easier to digest when eaten in this opposite order. Another was born in the mid-nineteenth century during the First Carlist War, when Spain was plagued with civil unrest during the struggle for the throne between the daughter and the brother of Ferdinand VII. Soldiers tired of being called unexpectedly to the battlefield during their meals, with the result that they were able to eat only the soup and never the succulent meats, decided to reverse the order. In yet another theory, the *arrieros*, porters who once crossed Spain, transporting goods on their donkeys, used to wait in Astorga, a town in Maragatería, for the fish to arrive from neighboring Galicia. The moment the fish appeared, the *arrieros* had to set out again, inevitably having enjoyed only the soup and never the meats.

In whichever order it is served, *cocido maragato* is a robust, satisfying dish. There is no substitute for *cecina*, the local superior beef cured in salt, but the stew is still flavorful without it. A *relleno*, a large dumpling made of chicken liver, chorizo, and *jamón serrano*, is added to the *cocido* toward the end of cooking. :: **Serves 6 as a three-course meal**

1 pound dried chickpeas

MEATS

1 pound fresh or cured ham hock or bacon, in one piece

$1/2$ pound boneless beef shank, round, or chuck, in one piece

$1/2$ stewing hen or 1 small chicken, about 2 pounds, quartered

1 pig ear (optional)

1 pig trotter (optional)

1/2 pound salt pork, in one piece

2 (3-ounce) chorizos

1 1/2 teaspoons salt

VEGETABLES

4 cups water

Salt

2 carrots, peeled and cut crosswise into 3 pieces

1 pound russet potatoes, peeled and cut into chunks

2 cups loosely packed, finely chopped cabbage

DUMPLING

1/2 (3-ounce) chorizo

2 eggs, lightly beaten

1 thin slice jamón serrano or other dry-cured ham, very finely chopped

1 chicken liver, finely chopped

1 clove garlic, finely chopped

2 tablespoons fine dried bread crumbs

1 cup broken-up angel hair pasta

3 tablespoons olive oil

1 clove garlic, thinly sliced

1 1/2 teaspoons sweet pimentón or paprika

Rinse the chickpeas in a colander under cold running water. Place in a bowl, add water to cover by 3 inches, and let soak for at least 8 hours or up to overnight. If using a cured ham hock, place it in a bowl with warm water to cover and let soak for 8 hours or up to overnight.

Drain the ham hock, if soaked. To prepare the meats, in a large stockpot, combine the ham hock, beef, stewing hen, pig ear and trotter if using, and salt pork with water to cover by 3 inches. Bring to a boil over high heat, boil for 10 minutes, and then skim the foam from the surface.

Drain the chickpeas and wrap them in a cheesecloth pouch tied with kitchen string (to make it easier to retrieve them later). Add the chickpeas to the stockpot holding the meats. Cover, decrease the heat to medium-low, and simmer gently for about 1 1/2 hours. Skim every 30 minutes and add more water if necessary to keep the ingredients covered.

Add the chorizos and salt, decrease the heat to low, and continue to cook for 30 minutes longer, or until the sausages are fork-tender. At this point, the chickpeas and the meats should be done.

Just before the chickpeas and meats are ready, cook the vegetables. In another stockpot, bring the water to a boil over high heat and then salt it lightly. Add the carrots, potatoes, and cabbage, decrease the heat to medium, and cook for 30 minutes, or until most of the water has cooked away and the potatoes are fork-tender.

To make the dumpling, remove the casing from the chorizo and mince the chorizo into pieces the size of lentils. Transfer to a bowl. Add the eggs, jamón serrano, chicken liver, chopped garlic, and bread crumbs. Mash the mixture well with a fork and shape it into a large ball with your hands, pressing it until it is tightly packed. Add to the stockpot holding the meats and cook for 10 minutes, or until cooked through.

When the meats and chickpeas are ready, retrieve the cheesecloth pouch of chickpeas and set aside; keep warm. Lift out all the meats and the dumpling and set aside; keep warm. Pour the broth through a fine-mesh sieve placed over a clean saucepan. Bring the broth to a boil over high heat and add the pasta. Boil for about 5 minutes, or until tender. Remove from the heat and keep warm.

When the vegetables are ready, drain them into a sieve or colander. Place the carrots and potatoes on a warmed platter and keep warm. Squeeze the cabbage thoroughly to eliminate any excess liquid. In a sauté pan, heat the olive oil over medium heat. Add the garlic and sauté for 2 to 3 minutes, or until golden. Sprinkle with the pimentón, mix well, and then add the cabbage and turn several times in the oil and garlic to heat through and blend the flavors. Transfer the cabbage to the platter holding the carrots and potatoes.

Cut the meats and sausages into pieces and slice the dumpling into 1-inch-thick slices. Arrange the meats, sausages, and dumpling slices on a large serving platter. Remove the chickpeas from the cheesecloth pouch and add them to the vegetable platter.

Serve the meats and sausages as the first course. Serve the chickpeas, cabbage, potatoes, and carrots as the second course. Serve the broth with the pasta as the third course, reheating it if it has cooled.

ESCUDELLA I CARN D'OLLA ▪
Catalan-Style Legume, Meat, and Vegetable Stew ▪ *(Catalonia)*

The Catalan *escudella* is unique among the *cocidos* of Spain because of its inclusion of two kinds of legumes, white beans and chickpeas. Meats used in the stew often include a combination of sausages, chicken, beef, and bacon, plus a dumpling made from ground pork and *butifarra blanca*, a Catalan white pork sausage. If the sausage is not available, you can double the amount of ground pork. *Butifarra negra*, a typical black sausage of the region flavored with mint, is cooked along with the vegetables. *Morcilla* can be used in its place. Unlike most other *cocidos*, this one is served in two courses, rather than three. ▪ **Serves 6 as a two-course meal**

LEGUMES

$1/2$ pound (1 rounded cup) dried chickpeas

$1/2$ pound (1 rounded cup) dried cannellini or
    Great Northern white beans

MEATS

1 pound boneless beef shank, round, or chuck,
    in one piece

$1/2$ stewing hen, or 1 small chicken, about 2 pounds,
    quartered

$1/4$ pound bacon, in one piece

1 pig ear (optional)

1 pig trotter (optional)

2 small soup bones, preferably marrowbones

DUMPLING

$1/4$ pound ground pork

$1/4$ pound butifarra blanca, about 2 small pieces,
    casings removed and finely minced

2 tablespoons fine dried bread crumbs

1 egg, lightly beaten

1 clove garlic, finely minced

1 tablespoon chopped fresh flat-leaf parsley

$1/2$ teaspoon ground cinnamon

$1/2$ teaspoon salt

Freshly ground black pepper

All-purpose flour for dusting

VEGETABLES AND BUTIFARRA NEGRA

1 large turnip, peeled and halved crosswise

1 carrot, peeled and halved crosswise

$1/2$ pound butifarra negra, about 3 pieces

$1/2$ pound russet potatoes, peeled and cut into
    large chunks

$1/2$ head green cabbage, coarsely chopped

1 cup broken-up angel hair pasta

Country-style bread or baguette slices, toasted,
    if using marrowbones

Rinse the chickpeas and white beans in a colander under cold running water. Place in a bowl, add water to cover by 3 inches, and let soak for at least 8 hours or up to overnight.

To prepare the meats, in a large stockpot, combine the beef, stewing hen, bacon, pig ear and trotter, if using, and soup bones with water to cover by 3 inches. Bring to a boil over high heat, boil for 10 minutes, and then skim the foam from the surface.

Pheasant and rabbit for sale in Barcelona's Boqueria market

Drain the chickpeas and white beans and wrap them in a cheesecloth pouch tied with kitchen string (to make it easier to retrieve them for serving later). Add the legumes to the stockpot holding the meats. Cover, decrease the heat to medium-low, and simmer gently for about $1^1/_2$ hours. Skim the foam from the surface every 30 minutes and add more water if necessary to keep the ingredients covered at all times.

When the meats and legumes are almost ready, make the dumpling. In a bowl, combine the pork, sausage, bread crumbs, egg, garlic, parsley, cinnamon, salt, and a few grinds of pepper. Mash the mixture well with a fork and shape it into a large ball with your hands, pressing it until it is tightly packed. Dust the ball on all sides with flour. Set aside.

After the meats and legumes have cooked for $1^1/_2$ hours, add the turnip, carrot, *butifarra negra*, potatoes, cabbage, and the dumpling. Season generously with salt and cook for 30 minutes longer over low heat, or until the potatoes are fork-tender.

Retrieve the cheesecloth pouch of legumes and set aside; keep warm. Lift out all the meats and the dumpling and set aside; keep warm. Pour the broth through a fine-mesh sieve placed over a clean saucepan. Bring the broth to a boil over high heat and add the pasta. Boil for about 5 minutes, or until tender. Remove from the heat and keep warm.

While the pasta is cooking, cut the meats and sausages into pieces and slice the dumpling into 1-inch-thick slices. If the bones contain marrow, remove the marrow, spread it on toasted bread, sprinkle with salt, and keep warm; otherwise, discard the bones. Arrange the meats, sausages, and dumpling slices on a warmed serving platter and keep warm. Place the legumes and vegetables on a separate warmed platter and keep warm.

Serve the broth with the pasta as the first course, reheating it if it has cooled. Serve the platters of meats and vegetables at the same time, along with the marrow-topped toast, as the second course.

PUCHERO DE LUJO CANARIO ::
Meat and Vegetable "Luxury" Pot ::
(Canary Islands)

It is appropriate that Canarians call this delightful *puchero*, with its extraordinary array of meats, vegetables, and even pears, *puchero de lujo*, or "luxury pot." To make it truly luxurious, some cooks add seven different kinds of meats, including lamb and poultry. :: **Serves 6 as a three-course meal**

$1/2$ pound (1 rounded cup) dried chickpeas

1 pound boneless beef shank, round, or chuck, in one piece

1 pound boneless pork loin, in one piece

4 cloves garlic, peeled but left whole

2 teaspoons salt

1 tomato, finely chopped

1 yellow onion, finely chopped

1 leek, white part only, thinly sliced

Pinch of dried thyme

Pinch of saffron threads

$1/2$-pound piece pumpkin or winter squash, peeled, seeded, and cut into large chunks

1 zucchini, peeled and halved crosswise

1 pound russet potatoes, peeled and cut into large chunks

1 sweet potato, peeled and cut into large chunks

2 firm Anjou or Bartlett pears, peeled, quartered lengthwise, and cored

1 chayote, peeled and quartered with seed discarded (optional)

1 ear corn, cut crosswise into 6 equal pieces

$1/2$ pound romano (flat) beans or regular green beans, trimmed and tied into a bundle with kitchen string

2 cups firmly packed, finely shredded green cabbage

1 cup broken-up long, thick pasta of choice

Green Mojo made with cilantro (optional, page 309)

Rinse the chickpeas in a colander under cold running water. Place in a bowl, add water to cover by 3 inches, and let soak for at least 8 hours or up to overnight.

In a large stockpot, combine the beef and pork with water to cover by 3 inches and bring to a boil over high heat.

Meanwhile, in a mortar, mash the garlic with $1/2$ teaspoon of the salt to form a paste. Drain the chickpeas and wrap them in a cheesecloth pouch tied with kitchen string (to make it easier to retrieve them for serving later).

When the meats are boiling, add the chickpeas, tomato, onion, leek, thyme, saffron, and the garlic paste to the pot. Mix well, cover, decrease the heat to medium-low, and simmer gently for about $1^1/2$ hours. Skim the foam from the surface every 30 minutes and add more water if necessary to keep the ingredients covered at all times.

Add the pumpkin, zucchini, russet and sweet potatoes, pears, chayote, corn, romano beans, and cabbage to the pot and mix well. Add the remaining $1^1/2$ teaspoons salt and add more water if needed to cover the ingredients. Re-cover and cook over medium-low heat for 30 minutes longer, or until the potatoes are fork-tender.

Retrieve the cheesecloth pouch of chickpeas and set aside; keep warm. Lift out the beef and pork and set aside; keep warm. Pour the contents of the pot into a large fine-mesh sieve or a colander placed over a saucepan. Set the sieve with its contents aside. Bring the broth to a boil over high heat and add the pasta. Boil for about 8 minutes, or until tender.

While the pasta is cooking, retrieve the vegetables and pears from the sieve and arrange them neatly on a warmed platter; add the chickpeas to the platter and keep warm. Cut the meats into pieces and arrange on another warmed serving platter; keep warm.

Serve the broth with the pasta as the first course. Serve the chickpeas, vegetables, and pears as the second course, followed by the meats as the third course. Accompany with the *mojo*, if desired.

A lighthouse outside El Cotillo, Fuerteventura (Canary Islands); a fishing boat in El Cotillo called "La Suerte" ("The Lucky")

CHAPTER 8

Rice Dishes

RICE IS COOKED all over Spain, but rice dishes are traditionally rooted in Levante, the large eastern region of the country that includes the autonomous communities of Valencia and Murcia and extreme southern Catalonia. This is also where nearly all of the rice in Spain is grown, much of which is turned into paella, the most famous of all Spanish rice dishes.

Paella vies with gazpacho as the country's most universally recognized dish. And just like gazpachos, paellas, when cooked elsewhere, often differ markedly from their authentic homeland versions. Many different variations of paella exist, of course, but Spanish cooks typically adhere to long-standing traditions when preparing them. For example, they might replace chicken with rabbit but never with partridge or duck, or they might add grouper instead of monkfish but never tuna. Onions, green and red sweet peppers, artichokes, and green beans are widely used, but never zucchini, eggplant, or asparagus. These same cooks—and restaurant chefs as well—may depart from tradition on when they serve paella, however. Traditionally it was served as a first course, with the rice the indisputable star of the dish. Nowadays, even in Spain, paella is increasingly served as a main course, with the result that the proportion of rice to the other ingredients

has diminished, though not to the extent often expected by foreign palates.

But other traditions are invariably followed. The rice is never washed before adding it to the pan, as it needs its starch to ensure the proper texture when cooked. When the liquid is combined with the rice, whether it is already in the pan and the rice is added to it or vice versa, it must always be at a boil. (Always keep a little extra hot liquid on hand, in case you have not controlled the heat properly and the paella is turning out a little dry.) Finally, once the rice and the liquid are together, the mixture is never stirred. The rice grains must remain whole, and even gentle stirring might break them up, or it can give the rice an undesirable sticky consistency.

Despite their prominence, paellas are not the only rice dishes of Spain. For example, there is the robust Majorcan *arros brut*, a mix of rice, game, and meats; Salamancan *chanfaina*, which marries rice, pig blood, and pig trotters in a *cazuela*; and the delightful deep green *arroz de la huerta*, from Zahara de los Atunes, at the southernmost tip of the country. Finally, *fideuá*, a delicious dish made in a paella pan but with pasta instead of rice, is also included in this chapter.

Just-harvested rice field in the Ebro delta, Catalonia; a typical seafood paella, Catalonia

ABOVE, FROM LEFT TO RIGHT: *An ancient Roman aqueduct outside of Tarragona, Catalonia; rice field in the Ebro delta, Catalonia; jars of high-quality anchovies for sale in Santoña on the coast of Cantabria*

ARROZ BLANCO ▪ White Rice

Plain white rice is the perfect accompaniment to anything cooked in or served with a sauce, such as Baby Squid in Black Ink Sauce (page 235). I use a little less water when cooking this rice than for other rice recipes. A smaller amount yields a slightly grainier texture, which is desirable with sauce-rich dishes. ▪ **Makes about 3 cups; serves 4 as a side dish**

1/4 **cup olive oil**

1 clove garlic, thinly sliced

1 cup Spanish rice

1²/₃ **cups water**

1/2 **teaspoon salt**

1 teaspoon chopped fresh flat-leaf parsley (optional)

In a small saucepan, heat the olive oil over medium heat. Add the garlic and sauté for 2 to 3 minutes, or until golden. Add the rice, stir with a wooden spoon to coat the kernels evenly with the olive oil, and then sauté for 1 minute. Add the water, increase the heat to high, bring to a boil, and boil, stirring occasionally, for about 30 seconds. Add the salt, cover, decrease the heat to low, and cook for about 15 minutes, or until the water is absorbed and the rice is tender.

Remove from the heat, uncover, and let rest for 5 minutes. If desired, sprinkle with the parsley before serving.

ARROZ DE ENFERMO ▪ Get-Well Rice ▪ *(Catalonia)*

Marisa and Javier Godó, friends who live in Barcelona, eat this mild rice soup whenever they are not feeling well. And they are not the only ones. Apparently everybody loves this comforting and homey dish when they are under the weather, and it is also a favorite of young children. Marisa and Javier like to add a little fresh ginger, which, although not indigenous to Spain, frequently appears in modern Spanish recipes and adds a wonderful flavor to this soup. ▪ **Serves 4 as a first course**

6 cups water

1/4 **cup olive oil**

2 cloves garlic

1-inch piece fresh ginger, peeled and halved

1 cup Spanish rice

1/2 **teaspoon salt**

Chopped fresh flat-leaf parsley for garnish

In a saucepan, bring the water to a boil.

Meanwhile, in a medium saucepan, heat the olive oil over medium heat. Add the garlic and ginger and sauté for about 5 minutes, or until the garlic is golden. Add the rice and stir to coat with the oil. Sauté for 1 minute and pour in the boiling water.

Decrease the heat to medium-low and cook, uncovered, for about 30 minutes, or until the rice kernels have swollen and are very tender and more than half the water is absorbed. The rice should be quite soupy.

Remove from the heat, add the salt, and let rest for 5 minutes. Remove and discard the garlic and ginger. Set the table with spoons and serve the rice in soup plates with parsley sprinkled on top.

ARROZ DE LA HUERTA ::
Green Vegetable Rice :: *(Andalusia)*

The charming fishing village of Zahara de los Atunes stands where Africa and Europe shake hands and the waters of the Atlantic and the Mediterranean meet. The area is renowned for the magnificent tuna that are caught as they pass through the strait (hence, the name of the village). The Romans already knew about the abundant tuna in these waters; the archeological site of Bolonia, only a few miles from Zahara, contains remnants of large areas once devoted to salting and storing the fish. Centuries later, the Arabs invented a system to trap the tuna in *almadrabas*, or "netted fences."

The tuna in Zahara are indeed excellent, but what has really captured my attention is a deep green and absolutely delectable rice dish. No fish is added, just vegetables, therefore the locals call it *arroz de la huerta*, "rice from the vegetable garden," or *arroz verde*, "green rice." This recipe was given to me by José María, who operates a well-known restaurant that bears his name in the middle of town. :: **Serves 6 as a first course**

1/2 lemon

2 small to medium artichokes

2 cups water

Salt

2 cups loosely packed spinach leaves

4 cups Vegetable Stock (page 305) or water

1/2 cup olive oil

1 clove garlic, finely minced

1 yellow onion, finely chopped

1 eggplant, finely diced

2 zucchini, finely diced

1 carrot, peeled and finely diced

1 cup small cauliflower florets

1 tomato, halved crosswise, grated on the large holes of a handheld grater, and skin discarded

2 cups Spanish rice

Squeeze the juice from the lemon half into a bowl filled with water and set aside. Working with 1 artichoke at a time, peel off the tough, dark outer leaves. Cut off the stem flush with the bottom, cut off the top two-thirds of the leaves, and quarter the artichoke lengthwise. Using a small, sharp knife or a spoon, remove and discard the fuzzy choke. Slip the quarters into the lemon water.

In a saucepan, bring the 2 cups water to a boil over high heat. Add 1/2 teaspoon salt and the spinach and cook for about 15 minutes, or until the spinach is tender and the water has turned deep green. Remove from the heat and set aside to cool.

Meanwhile, preheat the oven to 350°F. In a small saucepan, bring the stock to a boil. Decrease the heat to maintain a simmer.

In a large (about 15-inch) *cazuela* (page 51), heat the olive oil over medium heat. Add the garlic and onion and sauté for about 2 minutes, or until the onion begins to soften. Drain the artichokes, pat dry, and add to the *cazuela* along with the eggplant, zucchini, and carrot. Continue to cook, stirring occasionally, for 5 minutes to blend the ingredients well. Add the cauliflower and tomato and cook, stirring, for a minute or so to blend them with the rest of the ingredients.

Add the rice, mix it well with the vegetables, and then pour in the hot stock. Season with salt, stir to distribute the ingredients evenly, increase the heat to high, and cook for 5 minutes.

Meanwhile, transfer the cooled spinach and its cooking water to a blender or food processor and purée until smooth. Add the spinach purée to the *cazuela* and stir gently to combine.

Place the *cazuela* in the oven and bake for 12 minutes. The rice will absorb the stock and become tender.

Remove from the oven, cover with a lid or a kitchen towel, and let rest for 5 minutes before serving.

ARROZ NEGRO ▪ Black Rice ▪
(Valencian Community and Catalonia)

Arroz negro is popular along the entire Mediterranean coast of Spain, but especially in Castellón de la Plana, the extreme north of the Valencian Community, and in Tarragona, the most southern area of neighboring Catalonia. The original recipe is also known as *arroz de pobre*, or "poor man's rice," a reflection of its modest ingredients. Its simplicity—just flavorful rice with a little *alioli*—makes it a perfect first course. For a more substantial meal, add additional squid or any other fish or shellfish when you add the rice.

Some Catalan cooks make a version of this recipe that calls for sautéing a lot of onion until it is very dark before adding the rice. Although it is also called *arroz negro*, the resulting dish looks more grayish than black. ▪ **Serves 6 as a first course**

Pictured opposite

> 6 tablespoons Black Ink Sauce (page 312), with reserved chopped squid
>
> 4 cups Fish Stock (page 304)
>
> 2 cups Spanish rice
>
> 1 teaspoon salt
>
> 1 teaspoon freshly squeezed lemon juice
>
> 1 cup Alioli (page 306)

Make the black ink sauce as directed in the recipe, measure out the 6 tablespoons, and reserve the remainder for another use.

Pour the stock into a large (about 15-inch) paella pan and bring to a boil over high heat. Add the rice, ink sauce, chopped squid, and salt and mix well, distributing the rice evenly in the pan. Boil for 5 minutes, then decrease the heat to medium-low and cook for about 12 minutes longer, or until the rice has absorbed the liquid and is tender.

Remove from the heat and sprinkle with the lemon juice. Cover with a lid or a kitchen towel and let rest for 5 minutes before serving. Serve with the *alioli*.

ARROZ DE AYUNO ▪ "Fasting" Rice with Salt Cod and Artichokes ▪
(Castilla–La Mancha)

One of the legacies of the country's Catholic heritage, which prohibits the eating of meat on Fridays and during Lent, is the proliferation of salt cod dishes, such as this delightful "fasting" rice. In this recipe, the cod is cooked with the rice mixture without desalting first. ▪ **Serves 6**

> 1/2 lemon
>
> 6 small artichokes
>
> 1/2 pound salt cod (page 46), shredded and any skin or bones discarded
>
> 1/3 cup olive oil
>
> 2 tomatoes, halved crosswise, grated on the large holes of a handheld grater, and skins discarded
>
> 2 cloves garlic, finely minced
>
> 1 red bell pepper, seeded and cut into narrow strips
>
> 5 cups water
>
> 2 cups Spanish rice
>
> 1/2 cup fresh or thawed frozen shelled English peas
>
> Salt

Squeeze the juice from the lemon half into a large bowl filled with water and set aside. Working with 1 artichoke at a time, peel off the tough, dark outer leaves. Cut off the stem flush with the bottom, cut off the top two-thirds of the leaves, and quarter the artichoke lengthwise. Using a small, sharp knife or a spoon, remove and discard the fuzzy choke. Slip the quarters into the lemon water. When all the artichokes have been trimmed, drain and pat dry.

Rinse the shredded salt cod and pat dry. In a large (about 15-inch) paella pan, heat the olive oil over high heat. Add the tomatoes and garlic and sauté for 1 minute. Decrease the heat to medium, add the artichokes, bell pepper, and salt cod, and cook, stirring constantly, for about 10 minutes.

Meanwhile, in a saucepan, bring the water to a boil.

Add the rice to the paella pan and stir to mix well. Pour in the boiling water, decrease the heat to medium-low, scatter the peas over the top, and cook for 15 minutes longer. The rice will be tender at this point.

Remove the pan from the heat, cover, and let rest for 5 minutes. Taste and adjust the seasoning with salt and serve.

ARROZ A BANDA ▪
Fish-Flavored Rice ▪ (Valencian Community)

A banda means "on the side." This dish is arguably the best example of how much Spaniards, and especially Valencians, love rice. Here, the fish and shellfish lend their flavors to the broth in which the rice cooks, but the importance of the dish rests with the rice. As a result, the rice is served first, followed by the fish, shellfish, and potatoes as the main course. You can cook this dish on the stove top or in the oven. If your stove top nicely accommodates a 15-inch pan, it is the best choice. ▪

Serves 6 as a two-course meal

$2/3$ cup olive oil

6 russet potatoes, peeled and cut into chunks

2 yellow onions, cut into quarters

2 teaspoons sweet pimentón or paprika

8 cups water

Salt

$1/2$ pound grouper fillet, cut into small pieces

$1/2$ pound monkfish fillet, cut into small pieces

12 large shrimp in the shell with heads intact

$1/2$ pound squid, about 7 inches long, cleaned and with bodies cut into rings and tentacles halved if large (page 196)

2 cloves garlic, finely minced

2 tomatoes, halved crosswise, grated on the large holes of a handheld grater, and skins discarded

Pinch of saffron threads

2 cups Spanish rice

1 cup Alioli (page 306)

In a stockpot, heat $1/3$ cup of the olive oil over high heat. Add the potatoes, onions, and 1 teaspoon of the *pimentón* and fry, stirring often, for about 2 minutes, or until the ingredients are well mixed. Add the water, season with a little salt, and bring to a boil. Decrease the heat to medium and cook for about 10 minutes.

Sprinkle the grouper and monkfish with salt and add them and the shrimp to the stockpot. Cook for about 10 minutes longer, or until the seafood is cooked and the potatoes and onions are tender. Remove from the heat and discard the onions. Using a slotted spoon, lift the fish, shrimp, and potatoes from the pot and place them on a warmed serving platter; keep warm. Measure out 4 cups of the liquid from the pot and set aside.

Heat the remaining $1/3$ cup olive oil in a large (about 15-inch) paella pan over high heat. Add the squid, garlic, and tomatoes and cook, stirring constantly, for 5 minutes, or until the squid is lightly browned and tender. Using the slotted spoon, transfer the squid mixture to the serving platter with the other ingredients.

Add the remaining 1 teaspoon *pimentón* and the 4 cups reserved cooking liquid to the oil remaining in the pan and bring to a boil over high heat. Add the saffron and cook for about 2 minutes, or until it dissolves in the liquid. Add the rice, distributing it evenly in the pan and season with salt. Cook over high heat for 5 minutes. Decrease the heat to medium-low and cook for about 12 minutes longer, or until the liquid has been absorbed and the rice is tender. Alternatively, after the mixture has cooked on the stove top for 5 minutes, transfer the pan to a preheated 450°F oven for about 12 minutes.

Remove the pan from the stove top or oven, cover with a lid or kitchen towel, and let rest for 5 minutes before serving. Serve the rice as a first course, followed by the fish, shellfish, and potatoes. Pass the *alioli* at the table.

ARROZ AL CALDERO ::
Rice and Seafood Casserole :: (*Murcia*)

This rice dish resembles *arroz a banda* in that the rice is served with the fish alongside. It differs, however, in that it is not cooked in a paella pan, but instead in a pot, which gives the rice a softer, moister texture. Both dishes are made with many kinds of fish, most of which can be found in American fish markets. Here, I have substituted silver or striped mullet for the gray mullet and red snapper for the bream typically used in Spain. :: **Serves 6**

1/2 cup olive oil

3 dried ñora, choricero, or ancho chiles, quartered
    lengthwise and seeded

1 head garlic, unpeeled

8 cups water

Pinch of saffron threads

1/2 pound striped or silver mullet fillet, cut into small
    pieces

1/2 pound red snapper fillet, cut into small pieces

1/2 pound grouper fillet, cut into small pieces

1/2 pound monkfish fillet, cut into small pieces

1 1/2 teaspoons salt

2 tomatoes, halved crosswise, grated on the large holes
    of a handheld grater, and skins discarded

1 teaspoon sweet pimentón or paprika

2 cups Spanish rice

1 cup Alioli (page 306)

In a stockpot or large, wide saucepan, heat the olive oil over high heat. Add the chiles and garlic and fry, turning constantly, for about 5 minutes, or until the garlic is golden on all sides. Using a slotted spoon, remove the chiles and garlic and set aside. Reserve the oil in the pot.

In a saucepan, bring the water to a boil. Decrease the heat to maintain a simmer.

Meanwhile, peel the garlic. In a mortar, mash the garlic with the chiles, saffron, and 2 tablespoons of the simmering water until a paste forms. Set aside.

Season all the fish with the salt. Return the pot with the oil to high heat. When the oil is hot, add all the fish, and cook, stirring often, for about 5 minutes, or until they begin to turn opaque. Add the chile-garlic paste, tomatoes, and *pimentón* and stir gently to mix the ingredients. Add the simmering water, decrease the heat to medium, and cook, stirring occasionally, for 10 minutes, or until the fish is cooked through and the flavors are blended.

Remove from the heat and pour the contents of the pot through a fine-mesh sieve placed over a clean vessel. Transfer the fish from the sieve to a warmed serving platter and keep warm. Measure out 6 cups of the cooking liquid and return the liquid to the pot.

Place the pot over high heat and bring to a boil. Add the rice and cook for about 5 minutes, or until the liquid returns to a boil and the rice begins absorbing it. Decrease the heat to medium-low and cook for about 10 minutes longer, or until most of the liquid is absorbed and the rice is tender but still a little soupy.

Serve the rice in soup plates with the fish and the *alioli* on the side.

ARROZ CON COSTRA ▪ Crusty Rice with Spareribs and Chicken ▪ (*Murcia*)

This rice casserole is one of the signature dishes of Murcia, a region that excels in rice cookery. If you cannot find *butifarra blanca*, a white pork sausage of the region, bratwurst or a similar white sausage can be substituted, or you can omit the sausage. Ask your butcher to chop the spareribs coarsely; and be prepared to use your fingers to nibble on the rib bones. ▪ **Serves 6**

1/2 cup olive oil

1/2 pound spareribs, coarsely chopped

2 butifarras blancas, cut into 1-inch-thick slices (optional)

1/2 pound pork loin, cut into medium dice

6 chicken drumsticks

11/2 teaspoons salt

2 tomatoes, peeled and coarsely chopped

4 cups Beef Stock (page 000)

1 teaspoon sweet pimentón or paprika

2 cups Spanish rice

6 eggs, lightly beaten

Preheat the oven to 450°F.

In a large (about 15-inch) *cazuela* (page 51), heat the olive oil over medium-high heat. Add the spareribs, sausages, if using, pork, and chicken and fry, turning as needed, for about 10 minutes, or until lightly golden on all sides. Add the salt and tomatoes and mix well.

Meanwhile, in a saucepan, bring the stock to a boil. Decrease the heat to maintain a simmer.

Add the *pimentón* to the *cazuela* and stir quickly to combine with the meat-tomato mixture. Add the stock, increase the heat to high, and bring the stock back to a boil. Add the rice and stir with a wooden spoon until well mixed with the rest of the ingredients and evenly distributed in the *cazuela*. Decrease the heat to medium-low and cook, without stirring, for 2 minutes.

Place the *cazuela* in the oven and bake for 10 minutes, or until most of the stock is absorbed and the rice is nearly tender. Pour the eggs evenly over the surface of the rice and bake for about 5 minutes longer, or until the eggs form a crust on the surface. Serve immediately.

ARROZ AL FORNO ▪ Baked Rice with Chickpeas, Tomato, and Chorizo ▪ (*Valencian Community*)

To outsiders, it may sound unusual to combine three starches—rice, chickpeas, and potatoes—in a single recipe, but in Valencia, this is an everyday dish. I first tasted it at my friend Sali de Mesía's house in Marbella, and although she is a Canarian, I have always been praised by Valencians whenever I have served them her version. A head of garlic, which the Valencians call *la perdiz*, or "partridge," should always be set in the center of the dish before it is carried to the table.

You will need to start the dish the night before you plan to serve it to allow time for the chickpeas to soak. ▪

Serves 6

1/2 pound (1 rounded cup) dried chickpeas

4 cups Chicken Stock (page 304)

1 teaspoon salt

Pinch of saffron threads

1/2 cup olive oil

1 head garlic, unpeeled, halved crosswise

2 small russet potatoes, peeled and cut into 1/2-inch-thick slices

1 (3-ounce) chorizo, cut into 1/2-inch-thick slices

1 (3-ounce) morcilla, cut into 1/2-inch-thick slices

1 green bell pepper, seeded and cut in half lengthwise

1 large tomato, finely chopped

11/2 cups Spanish rice

Rinse the chickpeas in a colander under cold running water. Place in a bowl, add water to cover by 3 inches, and let soak for at least 8 hours or up to overnight.

Drain the chickpeas. In a saucepan, bring the stock to a boil over medium-high heat. Add the chickpeas, cover, decrease the heat to medium-low, and cook for about 1 hour or so, or until nearly tender. (They will still be a bit firm, but will cook again with the other ingredients.) Remove from the heat and pour the contents of the pot through a fine-mesh sieve placed over a clean vessel. Set the chickpeas aside. Measure out 3 cups of the cooking liquid, add the salt and saffron, and set aside.

In a large (about 15-inch) *cazuela* (page 51), heat 1/4 cup of the olive oil over medium-high heat. Add the garlic and fry, turning constantly, for about 5 minutes, or until the garlic is golden on all sides. Using a slotted spoon, remove the garlic and set aside for the garnish. Reserve the oil in the *cazuela*.

Decrease the heat to medium, add the potatoes, and fry, turning them occasionally, for about 5 minutes, or until they are evenly golden on the outside but still undercooked inside. Using a slotted spoon, transfer to a plate and set aside. Add the chorizo and *morcilla* to the same oil over medium heat and fry, turning them occasionally, for about 5 minutes, or until the sausages are evenly browned on the outside but still undercooked inside. Using the slotted spoon, transfer the sausages to the plate holding the potatoes. Discard the oil.

Preheat the oven to 500°F.

In the same *cazuela*, heat the remaining 1/4 cup olive oil over medium heat. Add the bell pepper and sauté for 5 minutes to flavor the oil. Remove and discard the pepper or reserve for another use. Add the tomato to the oil and sauté for 1 minute. Add the reserved potatoes, sausages, and chickpeas and cook, stirring, for 2 minutes, or until well blended.

Increase the heat to high and add the 3 cups reserved cooking liquid 1 cup at a time, stirring after each addition to combine well with the other ingredients before adding the next one. When all the liquid has been added and the mixture begins to boil, add the rice and mix well. Cook the rice for about 5 minutes, or until it begins to absorb the liquid.

Put the reserved garlic head in the center of the *cazuela* on top of the rice and place the *cazuela* in the oven. Bake for about 10 minutes, or until the liquid is absorbed and the rice is tender. If the rice is still quite moist and the kernels feels a bit hard, bake for a few more minutes.

Remove from the oven, cover with a lid or a kitchen towel, and let rest for 5 minutes before serving.

ARROZ CON ALUBIAS Y NABOS ::
Soupy Rice with White Beans and Turnips
:: *(Valencian Community)*

Arros amb fesols i naps is the proper name for this dish in Valenciano, the language of Valencia and the neighboring regions. It is typically served during the cold days of winter. :: **Serves 6**

1/2 pound (1 rounded cup) dried white cannellini or Great Northern beans

2 1/2 quarts water

1 pig trotter, quartered (optional)

1/2 pound boneless pork shoulder or shank, cut into medium dice

1/2 pound bacon, in one piece

6 (3-ounce) morcillas

1 teaspoon salt

1/3 cup olive oil

3 cloves garlic, peeled but left whole

1 yellow onion, chopped

4 turnips, peeled and chopped

1 teaspoon sweet pimentón or paprika

Pinch of saffron threads

1 1/2 cups Spanish rice

Rinse the beans in a colander under cold running water. Place in a bowl with water to cover by 2 inches and let soak for at least 8 hours or up to overnight.

Drain the beans. In a large stockpot, bring the 2 1/2 quarts water to a boil over high heat. Add the beans, pig trotter, if using, pork, bacon, *morcillas*, and salt, decrease the heat to medium, and cook, uncovered, at a gentle boil for 2 hours, or until all the meats are tender. Add more water if necessary to keep the ingredients covered at all times.

Meanwhile, in a sauté pan, heat the olive oil over high heat. Add the garlic and fry for 1 minute, or until it begins to color, then decrease the heat to medium. Add the onion and turnips and cook, stirring often, for 10 minutes longer, or until the onion and turnip soften. Add the *pimentón* and mix well with the vegetables.

When the beans and meats have been cooking for 2 hours, transfer the vegetables to the pot and mix well, being careful not to break up the meats. Ladle some of the broth into a cup, add the saffron, and let stand for a couple of minutes to dissolve. Add the rice and the dissolved saffron to the pot and stir gently to blend with the rest of the ingredients. Cook over medium heat for 20 minutes, or until the rice is tender but still quite soupy.

Using a slotted spoon, lift the trotter, meats, and sausages from the pot. Cut the trotter, sausages, and bacon into small pieces and arrange all the meats on a warmed serving platter. Serve the rice in warmed soup plates with the platter of meats alongside. Each diner adds meats to his or her serving as desired.

ARROS BRUT ▪ Majorcan Rice Casserole with Game and Meat ▪ (Balearic Islands)

Brut in Majorcan means "dirty," but don't let that put you off this wonderful dish. (Here, dirty refers to the many ingredients added to the rice.) *Arros brut* is time-consuming to prepare, but it is spectacular and is especially worth the effort if you are having a large group to dinner. You can omit or substitute any ingredients that are difficult to find. The recipe is prepared in a large *greixonera*, the local name for a *cazuela*, and although the result is similar to a paella, the rice is moister. ▪ **Serves 10**

$1/2$ lemon

4 small to medium artichokes

$2/3$ cup olive oil

1 partridge, cut into quarters

$1/2$ rabbit or $1/4$ hare, about $11/4$ pounds, cut into
 small pieces

1 young chicken (poussin) or Cornish hen, about
 $11/2$ pounds, cut into small pieces

1 squab, cut into small pieces

1 small pork tenderloin, about $1/2$ pound, cut into
 small pieces

$1/2$ pound spareribs, coarsely chopped by the butcher

Salt

Freshly ground black pepper

1 cup oyster mushrooms, trimmed and chopped

1 yellow onion, finely chopped

1 tomato, halved crosswise, grated on the large holes
 of a handheld grater, and skin discarded

2 cloves garlic, minced

$1/2$ cup dry red wine

$21/2$ quarts water

2 cups Spanish rice

1 cup fresh or frozen shelled English peas

Boiling water, if needed

PICADA

3 tablespoons olive oil

1 chicken liver

2 cloves garlic, peeled but left whole

1 tablespoon chopped fresh flat-leaf parsley

Pinch of salt

Squeeze the juice from the lemon half into a large bowl filled with water and set aside. Working with 1 artichoke at a time, peel off the tough, dark outer leaves. Cut off the stem flush with the bottom, cut off the top two-thirds of the leaves, and quarter the artichoke lengthwise. Using a small, sharp knife or a spoon, remove and discard the fuzzy choke. Slip the quarters into the lemon water. When all the artichokes have been trimmed, drain, pat dry, and set aside.

In a large (at least 15-inch) *cazuela* (page 51), heat the olive oil over medium-high heat. Working in batches, add the partridge, rabbit, chicken, squab, pork, and ribs and brown, turning as needed, for about 10 minutes for each batch, or until nicely browned on all sides. Return all the meats to the *cazuela* and season with salt and pepper.

Add the artichokes, mushrooms, onion, tomato, and garlic, mix well, and cook over medium heat, stirring occasionally, for another 5 minutes. Add the wine and 4 cups of the water and continue cooking over medium heat, stirring occasionally, for about 30 minutes, or until some of the liquid has evaporated.

In a saucepan, bring the remaining 6 cups water to a boil. When the meats and vegetables have cooked for 30 minutes, add the rice and peas to the *cazuela* and mix well with the rest of the ingredients. Increase the heat to high, pour in the 6 cups boiling water, mix well, and cook, without stirring, for 10 minutes.

While the rice is cooking, make the *picada*. In a small sauté pan, heat 2 tablespoons of the olive oil over high heat. Add the chicken liver and fry, turning once, for about 5 minutes, or until lightly browned on the outside and just cooked through. Transfer to a mortar and add the garlic, parsley, salt, and the remaining 1 tablespoon olive oil. Pound with a pestle until a paste forms.

When the rice has cooked for 10 minutes, decrease the heat to medium, add the *picada*, and mix gently but well. Continue to cook, without stirring, for 10 minutes longer, adding a little boiling water if necessary to keep the dish moist.

At this point the rice will be tender and the dish will be moist but not soupy. Serve immediately.

:: Cleaning Squid ::

I have caught thousands of baby squid by hand because one of my father's favorite summer activities in Mundaka was to go out fishing in his boat. *Poteras*, small, glittery, colorful, oval lures with tiny hooks attached in a circle at one end and the fishing line affixed to the other, are used for fishing for baby squid by hand. The shape and color of this clever device attract squid, and when one comes too close, the tiny hooks easily snare its tentacles, leaving the body intact as you haul in your catch.

Once you have located a good fishing spot—young squid usually swim in schools of several hundred—you simply drop the *poteras* into the water and, in no time, the tiny hooks latch onto a squid and you promptly pull the line in. If you are fast, you will catch dozens of them quickly, one at a time. When you remove the squid from the *poteras*, they squirt their ink at you in defense. Not surprisingly, this is an exciting experience for the young and curious.

Alas, cleaning squid is more tedious than fun, but once you get the hang of it, you can rapidly become an expert. Typically, the baby squid we catch in Spain are between four and five inches long, sometimes smaller. If you are a beginner, start with larger squid, so you can become familiar with the anatomy and because they are easier to handle.

Hold the squid over a colander, under a thin stream of cold running water, and begin peeling the pale brown skin from the body to expose the white and shiny flesh. This might be tricky at first, but it becomes easier with practice. The color of the flesh underneath the skin—the whiter, the better—is a good test of freshness. Not-so-fresh squid tends to turn a pale pink when peeled and should be discarded. As you peel, carefully tear off the small triangular winglets and reserve them in the colander. When you have finished peeling, pull the head and tentacles from the body (they come away together), cut away the eyes, and squeeze out and discard the beak (a tiny, hard ball) at the base of the head. Peel as much skin from the tentacles and head (this is a single piece) as possible and then add to the colander. Remove and discard the hard "quill" and all soft parts (the organs) from inside the body. If you plan to use the squid ink, locate the gland among the soft parts and carefully separate it. Squid, more often than not, have been frozen and yield very little, if any, ink. Cuttlefish are a much better source, or you can purchase squid ink in small jars or little plastic envelopes from your fishmonger.

Now comes an important step: turn the tiny body inside out like a sock. Take care not to tear the delicate flesh when you do this, especially if working with a smaller squid. Rinse the body well. This step allows thorough cleaning of the inside and, if you are stuffing the squid, it will cause the body's opening to shrink during cooking, so that the stuffing is held snugly in the cavity. If you are stuffing the squid in the style of Basque cooks (page 235), slip the reserved tentacles and the winglets into the body cavity. In recipes in which the body is cut into rings, the tentacles are usually added along with the rings. With practice, each squid should take no more than a few minutes to clean.

ARROZ CON CEBOLLA CONFITADA :: Rice with Caramelized Onion :: (Catalonia)

Catalans like to mix seafood and meats, which they call *mar y montaña* (sea and mountain), and this dish, a specialty of the Bajo Ampurdán area, in Girona Province north of Barcelona, is an excellent example of that tradition. I first tasted it at Can Pep, a restaurant in the beautiful beach town of Calella de Palafrugell, and was immediately smitten. My friend Angeles Villegas, who lives there, was kind enough to give me the recipe for her version. Like many other rice dishes from around the Mediterranean, this one is prepared in a *cazuela*, rather than in a paella pan. :: **Serves 6**

$1/2$ pound Manila or small littleneck clams

1 tablespoon coarse salt

$1/2$ cup olive oil

$1/2$ rabbit or small chicken, about $1 1/2$ pounds, cut into small pieces

2 yellow onions, grated

1 clove garlic, finely minced

$1/3$ cup sweet vermouth

2 cups water

$1/2$ teaspoon salt

$1/2$ teaspoon freshly ground black pepper

$1/2$ teaspoon sugar

4 cups Fish Stock (page 304)

2 tomatoes, halved crosswise, grated on the large holes of a handheld grater, and skins discarded

1 teaspoon sweet pimentón or paprika

Pinch of saffron threads dissolved in 1 tablespoon hot water

$1/4$ pound squid, about 7 inches long, cleaned and with bodies cut into rings and tentacles halved if large (page 196)

2 cups Spanish rice

$1/2$ pound medium shrimp in the shell with heads intact

Scrub the clams under cold running water, discarding any that fail to close to the touch. In a large bowl, combine the clams, coarse salt, and water to cover and let stand for at least 30 minutes or up to 2 hours so that the clams release any sand trapped in their shells.

Meanwhile, in a large sauté pan, heat the olive oil over medium-high heat. Add the rabbit and brown, turning as needed, for about 10 minutes, or until golden on all sides. Using a slotted spoon, remove the rabbit and set aside.

Decrease the heat to medium and add the onions, garlic, vermouth, water, salt, pepper, and sugar. Cook, stirring occasionally, for 20 minutes, or until the liquid has evaporated. Increase the heat to high and cook, stirring occasionally, for about 5 minutes longer, or until the onions are caramelized.

Meanwhile, preheat the oven to 350°F. In a saucepan, bring the stock to a boil. Decrease the heat to maintain a simmer.

When the onions are ready, add the tomatoes, *pimentón*, and saffron to the pan and mix well. Add the squid, decrease the heat to medium, and stir briefly to mix with the rest of the ingredients. Transfer the mixture to a large (about 15-inch) *cazuela* (page 51), place over high heat, add the rabbit and rice, and stir to combine. Pour in the hot stock and cook for 5 minutes without stirring.

Drain the clams. Place the clams and the shrimp on top of the rice, and place the *cazuela* in the oven. Bake for 12 minutes. The liquid will be absorbed, the rice will be tender, the clams will have opened, and the shrimp will turn pink.

Remove from the oven, cover with a lid or a kitchen towel, and let rest for 5 minutes before serving. Discard any clams that failed to open and serve.

CHANFAINA DE SALAMANCA ▪
Sunday Rice ▪ (Castilla y León)

The city of Salamanca, with its monuments built of golden sandstone, is home to one of Europe's oldest universities. While the city itself needs no introduction, this ancient and unusual dish does. *Chanfaina* is usually served on Sundays as a tapa at the city's bustling bars, where parents go with their children for a little snack before returning home for lunch. You will probably need to special order the blood and perhaps even the lamb tripe, liver, and trotters from a good butcher, although some Asian markets regularly carry pork blood. If you cannot find the blood, it can be omitted and the dish will still be quite good. If you go to Salamanca, do not miss the opportunity to try a dish of authentic *chanfaina* with a glass of the excellent red wine of the region. ▪ **Serves 4**

1/4 pound lamb tripe

2 1/2 cups Chicken Stock (page 304)

1/3 cup olive oil

1 clove garlic, minced

1 yellow onion, finely chopped

1/4 pound lamb or pork blood, cut into small cubes

2 lamb trotters, halved

1 lamb liver, about 2 ounces, coarsely chopped

1 tablespoon hot pimentón or paprika plus a pinch of hot red pepper flakes

1 cup Spanish rice

1 teaspoon salt

1 teaspoon cumin seeds

2 hard-boiled eggs, peeled and coarsely chopped

Preheat the oven to 400°F.

Rinse the tripe thoroughly under cold running water. In a saucepan, combine the tripe with water to cover and bring to a boil over high heat. Remove from the heat, drain, let cool, and cut into small pieces. Set aside.

In a small saucepan, bring the stock to a boil. Decrease the heat to maintain a simmer.

In a medium (about 12-inch) *cazuela* (page 51), heat the olive oil over medium heat. Add the garlic and onion and sauté for 5 minutes, or until the onion starts to soften. Add the blood cubes, tripe, trotters, liver, and *pimentón* and cook, stirring gently, for about 5 minutes to blend the ingredients well.

Pour the hot stock into the *cazuela*, mix well with the rest of the ingredients, and bring to a boil. Add the rice, distributing it evenly, and then season with the salt and sprinkle with the cumin seeds. Place in the oven and bake for 15 minutes. The rice will absorb the stock and be tender.

Remove from the oven and mix the eggs into the dish. Cover with a lid or kitchen towel and let rest for 5 minutes before serving.

OLLETA ▪ Pumpkin Chestnut Rice with Vegetables and Pork ▪
(Valencian Community)

Juan Francisco Seva, a good friend from the province of Alicante, describes this recipe, with its cured pork, sausage, chickpeas, pumpkin, and chestnuts, as typical cold-weather fare of the province's mountainous region.

▪ Serves 8

1 cup dried chickpeas

1/2 cup chestnuts

4 cups Vegetable Stock (page 305)

1/2 cup olive oil

2 cloves garlic, sliced

1/4 pound lean salt pork or bacon, in one piece, coarsely chopped

1 (3-ounce) morcilla, cut into 1/2-inch-thick slices (optional)

6 Swiss chard stems, diced

1/2-pound piece pumpkin, peeled, seeded, and cut into chunks

1 1/2 cups Spanish rice

1/3 cup wheat bran

1 teaspoon salt

Rinse the chickpeas in a colander under cold running water. Place in a bowl, add water to cover by 3 inches, and let soak for at least 8 hours or up to overnight. Drain, place in a saucepan, add water to cover by 2 inches, and bring to a boil over high heat. Decrease the heat to medium-low and cook for about 1 hour or so, or until nearly tender. (They will still be a bit firm, but will cook again with the other ingredients.) Drain and set aside.

Using the tip of a sharp paring knife, score the flat side of each chestnut with an X, cutting through the hard outer shell. In a small saucepan, combine the chestnuts with water to cover, bring to a boil, and boil for 5 to 8 minutes, depending on the size of the nuts. Drain and, while still warm, peel away the hard, spiny outer shell and the softer inner light brown membrane of each nut. Then quarter each chestnut and set aside.

In a small saucepan, bring the stock to a boil. Decrease the heat to maintain a simmer.

In a large (about 15-inch) *cazuela* (page 51), heat the olive oil over medium-high heat. Add the garlic, salt pork, *morcilla*, if using, chard stems, pumpkin, and chestnuts and cook, stirring occasionally, for about 10 minutes, or until the pork is lightly browned.

Decrease the heat to medium-low, add the rice, chickpeas, and wheat bran, and mix well with the rest of the ingredients. Add the hot stock a little at a time until completely incorporated. Season with the salt and continue cooking over medium-low for 15 minutes longer, or until most of the liquid is absorbed. The rice will be tender but still a little soupy.

Remove from the heat, cover with a lid or kitchen towel, and let rest for 5 minutes before serving.

PAELLA DE CARNE ▪ Meat Paella ▪
(Valencian Community)

This paella is my children's favorite dish. I usually make it on Sundays when everybody is at home. Roasting the garlic before adding it to the pan is an old trick that my friend Vicente Gironella shared with me more than twenty years ago. You can still taste the garlic, but it is mellower than when you use it raw. ▪ **Serves 4**

2 cloves garlic, unpeeled

3¹/₂ cups Chicken Stock (page 304)

1¹/₂ teaspoons sweet pimentón or paprika

Pinch of saffron threads

¹/₂ cup olive oil

¹/₂ green bell pepper, seeded and cut lengthwise into narrow strips

¹/₂ red bell pepper, seeded and cut lengthwise into narrow strips

¹/₄ pound beef tenderloin tip, cut into small pieces

¹/₄ pound boneless, skinless chicken breast, cut into small pieces

Salt

1 (3-ounce) chorizo, cut into ¹/₂-inch dice

1¹/₂ cups Spanish rice

1 lemon, cut into 4 wedges

Preheat the oven to 500°F. Place the garlic cloves in a small baking pan or dish and roast in the oven for 10 to 15 minutes, or until the skin is browned.

Meanwhile, in a small saucepan, bring the stock to a boil. Add the *pimentón* and a few of the saffron threads and decrease the heat to maintain a simmer.

When the garlic is ready, remove from the oven and leave the oven on. When the garlic is cool enough to handle, peel it, place in a blender or food processor, and add ¹/₂ cup of the simmering stock and the rest of the saffron. Process until well blended. Set aside.

In a large (about 15-inch) paella pan, heat the olive oil over medium-high heat. Add the bell pepper strips and cook, stirring often, for about 10 minutes, or until tender. Sprinkle the beef and chicken pieces with salt and add them along with the chorizo to the pan. Cook, stirring often, for about 5 minutes, or until the meats are lightly browned but still undercooked. Add the rice and stir to blend well with the rest of the ingredients, allowing the rice to absorb a little of the oil. Spread the mixture evenly in the pan. Pour the hot stock into the pan, increase the heat to high, and bring the mixture to a boil. Add the garlic mixture, stir gently to incorporate, and continue to boil for 5 minutes without stirring. Decrease the heat to medium and cook for 5 minutes longer. Because the bottom of the paella pan is most likely wider than the reach of the burner's heat, shift the pan from side to side on the burner to distribute the heat evenly. Do not stir the mixture. Taste the stock and season with salt, if necessary.

Transfer the pan to the oven and cook for 7 minutes longer. The liquid will be absorbed and the rice will be tender. Remove from the oven, cover with a lid or kitchen towel, and let rest for about 7 minutes before serving.

Serve with the lemon wedges on the side.

PAELLA DE PESCADOS Y MARISCOS :: Fish and Shellfish Paella :: (Valencian Community)

Seafood paella is arguably the best-known dish of Spanish cuisine. For the most successful result, you will need to seek out the freshest, best-quality fish and shellfish available, keeping in mind that fatty fish, such as salmon, trout, or tuna, are never used for paella because their relatively strong flavors would change the taste of the rice. A good fish stock is important, too, so take the time to make it from scratch. I usually make more than is needed and freeze the rest so I always have homemade stock on hand. :: **Serves 4**

1/2 pound Manila or small littleneck clams

1 tablespoon coarse salt

2 cloves garlic, unpeeled

4 1/2 cups Fish Stock (page 304)

Pinch of saffron threads

1 pound mussels, scrubbed and debearded

1 cup water

1/2 cup olive oil

1 small green bell pepper, seeded and cut lengthwise
    into narrow strips

1/2 pound monkfish or grouper fillet, cut into chunks

1/2 pound medium shrimp, peeled and halved crosswise

1/2 pound small squid, cleaned and with bodies cut into
    narrow rings and tentacles left whole (page 196)

1 1/2 teaspoons salt

2 cups Spanish rice

4 large shrimp in the shell with heads intact

1 teaspoon freshly squeezed lemon juice

1 lemon, cut into 4 wedges

Scrub the clams under cold running water, discarding any that fail to close to the touch. In a large bowl, combine the clams, coarse salt, and water to cover and let stand for at least 30 minutes or up to 2 hours so that the clams release any sand trapped in their shells.

Preheat the oven to 500°F. Place the garlic cloves in a small baking pan or dish and roast in the oven for 10 to 15 minutes, or until the skin is browned.

Meanwhile, in a small saucepan, bring the stock to a boil. Add a few of the saffron threads and decrease the heat to maintain a simmer.

When the garlic is ready, remove from the oven and leave the oven on. When the garlic is cool enough to handle, peel it, place in a blender or food processor, and add 1/2 cup of the simmering stock and the rest of the saffron. Process until well blended. Set aside.

In a large saucepan, combine the mussels, discarding any that fail to close to the touch, and the 1 cup water, bring to a boil over high heat, cover, and cook for about 5 minutes, or until they open. As the mussels cook, uncover the pan occasionally and stir them with a wooden spoon to encourage them all to open at about the same time. Using a slotted spoon, lift the mussels from the pan and set aside until cool enough to handle. Remove the meats from the shells, discarding the shells and any mussels that failed to open. Set the meats aside.

In a large (about 15-inch) paella pan, heat the olive oil over medium heat. Add the bell pepper and cook, stirring often, for about 10 minutes, or until tender. Add the monkfish, medium shrimp, squid, and salt and increase the heat to medium-high. Sauté for about 5 minutes, or until the shrimp are pink. Add the rice and stir to blend well with the rest of the ingredients, allowing the rice to absorb a little of the oil. Spread the mixture evenly in the pan. Pour the hot stock into the pan, increase the heat to high, and bring the mixture to a boil. Add the garlic mixture, stir gently to incorporate, and continue to boil for 5 minutes without stirring. Because the bottom of the paella pan is most likely wider than the reach of the burner's heat, shift the pan from side to side on the burner to distribute the heat evenly. Taste the stock and season with salt, if necessary.

Arrange the mussels and large shrimp neatly on top of the rice. Drain the clams and arrange them around the rim of the pan. Place the pan in the oven for 12 minutes. The liquid will be absorbed, the rice will be tender, and the clams will have opened.

Remove from the oven and discard any clams that failed to open. Sprinkle the lemon juice evenly over the top. Cover with a lid or kitchen towel and let rest for 7 minutes before serving. Serve with the lemon wedges on the side.

PAELLA VALENCIANA ▪▪
The "Original" Paella from Valencia ▪▪
(Valencian Community)

My friend Amadeo Peñalver, a successful painter who lives and works in New York, comes from a small village in the countryside one hour west of Valencia. He frequently returns to visit his family, who continue to live in the old house where he grew up. Every Valencian will say that his or her family's paella dates from the untraceable origins of the dish, and Amadeo is no exception, proudly claiming that his paella is the real one. While I have too many other Valencian friends to support Amadeo's claim, I can say that his paella is as definitive as any that I've had. If you cannot find fresh snails, leave them out. The paella will not be authentic, but it will still taste very good. ▪▪ **Serves 4**

1/2 pound (1 rounded cup) dried white lima beans

1/2 cup olive oil

12 fresh land snails

4 handfuls coarse salt

2 bay leaves

1 yellow onion, halved

3 1/2 cups Chicken Stock (page 304)

1 1/2 teaspoons sweet pimentón or paprika

Pinch of saffron threads

1 small chicken or rabbit, about 2 1/2 pounds, cut into small pieces

Salt

1/2 pound romano (flat) beans or regular green beans, ends trimmed and cut in half crosswise

1 tomato, peeled and finely diced or halved crosswise, grated on the large holes of a handheld grater, and skin discarded

1 1/2 cups Spanish rice

Rinse the lima beans in a colander under cold running water. In a bowl, combine the beans with water to cover by 2 inches and let soak for at least 8 hours or up to overnight.

Drain the beans, place in a saucepan, add 2 tablespoons of the olive oil and water to cover by 1 inch, and bring to a boil over high heat. Decrease the heat to medium-low and cook for 1 hour or so, or until tender. Drain and set aside.

Place the snails in a bowl, sprinkle with a handful of coarse salt, and let stand for 30 minutes. Transfer the snails to a colander and rinse under cold water. Repeat this process 3 more times, using a handful of salt each time. After the final rinsing, place the snails in a saucepan and add the bay leaves, onion, and water to cover by 2 to 3 inches. Place over high heat, bring to a boil, cover, decrease the heat slightly, and cook for 30 minutes. Drain and set aside.

Preheat the oven to 500°F.

In a saucepan, bring the stock to a boil. Add the *pimentón* and saffron and decrease the heat to maintain a simmer.

In a large (about 15-inch) paella pan, heat the remaining 6 tablespoons olive oil over medium-high heat. Sprinkle the chicken pieces with salt and add to the pan. Sauté for about 5 minutes, or until lightly browned but still undercooked. Add the reserved lima beans, the romano beans, snails, tomato, and rice and stir to blend well with the chicken, allowing the rice to absorb a little of the oil. Spread the mixture evenly in the pan. Pour the hot stock into the pan, increase the heat to high, bring the mixture to a boil, and boil for 5 minutes without stirring. Decrease the heat to medium and cook for 5 minutes longer without stirring. Because the bottom of the paella pan is most likely wider than the reach of the burner's heat, shift the pan from side to side on the burner to distribute the heat evenly. Taste the stock and season with salt, if necessary.

Transfer the pan to the oven and cook for 7 minutes longer. The liquid will be absorbed and the rice will be tender. Remove from the oven, cover with a lid or kitchen towel, and let rest for 7 minutes before serving. Serve immediately.

FIDEUÁ ▪ Seafood Pasta Paella ▪
(*Valencian Community*)

Unlike the many rice dishes cooked in a paella pan, *fideuá*, the equally good pasta dish cooked in the same pan, is little known in the United States. Like most paellas, *fideuá* comes from the Valencian Community, where it is very popular, though it is made in Catalonia as well. The pasta traditionally used for this dish is *fideos para fideuá*, which looks similar to 1/2-inch elbow macaroni and can be purchased in Spanish shops in the United States or by mail order. I like to use angel hair pasta, too. If you can only find monkfish fillet, make the broth with just the shrimp shells. ▪ **Serves 4**

1/2 pound Manila or small littleneck clams

1 tablespoon coarse salt

6 cups water

1 pound mussels, scrubbed and debearded

1/2 pound medium shrimp, peeled and halved crosswise, shells reserved

1/2-pound monkfish with bone intact, cut into small chunks, bone reserved

Pinch of saffron threads

Salt

1/2 cup olive oil

1/2 pound fideos para fideuá, 1/2-inch elbow macaroni, or angel hair pasta, broken into 2-inch lengths

1 clove garlic, minced

1 small green bell pepper, seeded and cut into narrow strips

1 small red bell pepper, seeded and cut into narrow strips

1/2 pound small squid, cleaned and with bodies cut into rings and tentacles left whole (page 196)

1 lemon, cut into 4 wedges

Scrub the clams under cold running water, discarding any that fail to close to the touch. In a large bowl, combine the clams, coarse salt, and water to cover and let stand for at least 30 minutes or up to 2 hours so that the clams release any sand trapped in their shells.

In a stockpot or large saucepan, bring the 6 cups water to a boil over medium-high heat. Add the mussels, discarding any that fail to close to the touch, cover, and cook for about 5 minutes, or until they open. As the mussels cook, uncover the pan occasionally and stir them with a wooden spoon to encourage them all to open at about the same time. Using a slotted spoon, lift the mussels from the pot and set them aside to cool. Add the shrimp shells and monkfish bone to the stockpot and simmer for 15 to 20 minutes to create a flavorful broth.

Meanwhile, when the mussels are cool enough to handle, remove the meats from the shells, discarding the shells and any mussels that failed to open. Set the meats aside.

When the broth is ready, strain it through a fine-mesh sieve placed over a clean vessel and discard the contents of the sieve. Measure out 4 cups, add the saffron and 1 1/2 teaspoons salt, and set aside.

Preheat the oven to 450°F.

In a large (about 15-inch) paella pan, heat the olive oil over medium-high heat. Add the pasta and cook, stirring often, for about 3 minutes, or until golden. Using a slotted spoon, remove the pasta and set aside. Reserve the oil in the pan.

Decrease the heat to medium, add the garlic and peppers to the pan, and cook, stirring often, for about 10 minutes, or until the peppers are tender.

Sprinkle the shrimp, monkfish, and squid with salt and add them to the vegetables. Increase the heat to medium-high and sauté for about 5 minutes, or until the shrimp turn pink. Add the 4 cups reserved broth to the mixture and bring to a boil. Decrease the heat to medium and distribute the fried pasta evenly in the paella pan. Drain the clams and place the clams and the shelled mussels on top of the pasta. Increase the heat to high and cook for 5 minutes, or until the contents of the pan is at an even, steady boil.

Transfer the pan to the oven and cook for 10 minutes longer. The liquid will be absorbed, the pasta will be tender, and the clams will have opened. Remove from the oven, discard any clams that failed to open, and serve with the lemon wedges on the side.

CHAPTER 9

Fish and Shellfish

SPANIARDS BELIEVE THAT some of their country's fish and shellfish taste best when eaten in their place of origin, such as the *angulas*, or baby eels, of the north; the *carabineros*, or jumbo red shrimp, of the south; and the *salmón* of Asturias. But salt cod, sometimes called the "inland fish," crosses all borders. Author and revered gastronomist Xavier Domingo calls salt cod together with pork the principal actors in the "ideological cuisine." In his book *El sabor de España*, Domingo points out that the historical prohibition of the consumption of meat on Fridays and during Lent by the Catholic Church prompted salt cod to become the food of choice of the pious and the cover of the nonpious throughout the country. In contrast, demonstrably eating pork at times other than Lent and on Fridays offered these same people the opportunity to show off their opposition to dietary restrictions observed by Jews. The result is that salt cod and pork alike are deeply engraved in the collective culinary memory of most Spaniards.

In this chapter, you will find a quartet of regional dishes that star salt cod. My favorite is the Basque *bacalao al pil-pil*, in which the hard dried fish turns velvety and delicious when simmered in a *cazuela* with olive oil. *Bacalao con alioli* from the Balearics pairs salt cod with the region's emblematic sauce, while in *tiznao* from La Mancha, salt cod and vegetables are grilled, chopped, and married with chiles and olive oil. Finally, *bacalao al ajoarriero chivite* from Navarra, named after the *ajoarrieros*, or "muleteers," who once transported salt cod along with other foods across Spain, calls for braising the cod with potatoes, tomatoes, and eggs.

The long coastline of our mainland, combined with our two archipelagos, the Balearics and the Canaries, ensures that fresh fish and shellfish are also ubiquitous elements of the Spanish table. This chapter showcases only a small number of the dishes that cooks and chefs throughout the country regularly prepare as seafood main courses, such as *suquet*, the seafood stew of Catalonia; *dorada a la sal*, fish baked in a salt crust from Murcia; and *chipirones en su tinta*, Basque-style squid in its own ink. Simpler grilled, pan-roasted, fried, and boiled fish are popular menu items as well, typically accompanied with *mojos*, vinaigrettes, or other sauces that add color, flavor, and a distinctive regional stamp.

A bowl of cleaned sardines ready for the grill

ABOVE, FROM LEFT TO RIGHT: *Tin of canned bonito del norte (albacore); fishing nets in L'Ampolla, Ebro delta; pulling a fish from a net in L'Escala, Catalonia*

::
209

BACALAO AL PIL-PIL ▪ Salt Cod in an Olive Oil Emulsion ▪ *(Basque Country)*

This dish is classic Basque fare. After you prepare the garnish and simmer the cod for several minutes, you make the sauce by engaging the cod in "a dance" with the olive oil to create an emulsion that looks very much like a mayonnaise. The dance is not without challenge, but even the patient novice cook can produce an excellent result.

To ensure success, bear in mind the following rules: Use only olive oil; other fats will not result in the superior emulsion this dish demands. Use the best salt cod you can find or salt it yourself (page 46). Use a *cazuela* or similar earthenware cooking vessel that can be used on the stove top. And finally, when you are ready to place the fish in the *cazuela* to begin the sauce, make sure the salt cod, olive oil, and *cazuela* are all lukewarm. ▪ **Serves 6**

2 pounds salt cod, desalted (page 46)

1¹/₂ cups olive oil

3 cloves garlic, thinly sliced

1 small dried hot chile, seeded and cut into rings

Drain the salt cod and pat dry with paper towels. Cut into 3-inch squares, leaving the skin intact. (When cooking later in olive oil, the skin will release the needed gelatin to help emulsify the sauce.)

In a 12-inch *cazuela* (page 51), heat the olive oil over medium heat. When the oil is hot, add the garlic and chile and fry, stirring occasionally, for 2 to 3 minutes, or until the garlic starts to turn golden. Using a slotted spoon, transfer the garlic and chile to a small bowl and reserve for garnish. Reserve the oil in the *cazuela*.

Decrease the heat to medium-low and add the cod pieces to the oil. Simmer for about 10 minutes, being careful not to let the oil become too hot. The oil should just barely sizzle around the edges of the fish pieces. Using a slotted spoon, transfer the cod to a plate and then pour the olive oil into a wide heatproof bowl to cool. When the cod is cool enough to handle, remove any errant bones, leaving the pieces as intact as possible.

Return the cod pieces, skin side up and in a single layer, to the *cazuela*. At this point, make sure that the *cazuela*, the cod, and the reserved olive oil are all lukewarm.

Place the *cazuela* over medium heat and begin by spooning 2 or 3 tablespoons of the olive oil over the cod. It is here that the dance begins: using both hands, rotate the *cazuela* in circular motions over the burner. Continue the motion until the first drops of oil start to emulsify. You will know that the emulsion is beginning when the oil drops turn pale and cling to one another. Eventually the whole sauce will turn pale white.

Continue to rotate the *cazuela*, interrupting only to add the olive oil gradually, spoonful by spoonful, until all the oil is incorporated into the emulsion. Depending on the quality of the cod and the gelatin content of its skin, it will take anywhere from 15 to 30 minutes to make the sauce.

Divide the cod evenly among individual plates and spoon the sauce over the top. Garnish with the reserved garlic and chile. Serve hot or warm.

BACALAO AJOARRIERO CHIVITE ▪▪
Navarran Braised Salt Cod ▪▪ (Navarra)

I owe this recipe to the Chivite family, proprietors of the acclaimed winery of the same name in Cintruénigo, the bustling Navarran town well known for its production of alabaster. Not only does the Chivite family make my favorite Navarran wine, but also, as is often the case with winemakers, they have a rich culinary heritage. I was fortunate that Mercedes Chivite, materfamilias, took the time to teach me this recipe. And I was equally fortunate to have a trio of family members, Mercedes Jr., Julián, and Fernando, at my former New York restaurant to do a "quality check" on the dish. They approved wholeheartedly!

Accompany the braised cod with slices of hot fried bread, if you like. You can also poach an egg for each diner in the *cazuela* during the last few minutes, allowing the whites to set and keeping the yolks soft. ▪▪ **Serves 6**

5 dried choricero or ancho chiles

1 pound salt cod, desalted (page 46) and divided into 4 pieces

1/2 cup olive oil

1 small boiling potato, peeled

1 small yellow onion, finely chopped

1 tomato, finely chopped

2 cloves garlic, peeled but left whole

1 heaping tablespoon chopped fresh flat-leaf parsley

2 hard-boiled eggs, peeled and yolks and whites separated

3 tablespoons whole milk

In a heatproof bowl, combine the dried chiles with boiling water to cover and let stand for 30 minutes, or until soft. Drain the chiles, reserving 1 cup of the liquid. Slit the chiles open and scrape off the flesh with the edge of a knife, discarding the seeds, skins, and stems. Set the flesh aside.

Pat the cod dry. In a *cazuela* (page 51), heat 1/4 cup of the olive oil over medium heat. When the oil is hot, add the cod and fry, turning once, for 2 minutes on each side, or until lightly golden. Using a slotted spoon, remove the cod and set aside on a plate to cool. Reserve the *cazuela* with the oil off the heat.

Cut the potato into irregular chunks the size of hazelnuts. Return the *cazuela* to high heat, and when the oil is hot, add the potato and fry, stirring often, for about 10 minutes, or until it begins to brown. Using the slotted spoon, transfer the potato to paper towels to drain. Reserve the *cazuela* with the oil off the heat.

Remove any errant bones and the skin from the cod, reserving about 1 tablespoon of the skin. Shred the reserved skin with your fingers. Then, with a fork or your fingers, flake the cod and return it to the *cazuela*. Add the shredded skin and the fried potatoes and mix well.

In a sauté pan, heat the remaining 1/4 cup olive oil over medium heat. Add the onion and cook, stirring often, for about 15 minutes, or until tender and translucent. Add the tomato and cook, stirring often, for 5 to 10 minutes longer, or until the tomato begins to break down. Using a slotted spoon, transfer the onion and tomato to the *cazuela*.

In a mortar, combine the garlic and parsley and pound with a pestle until a paste forms. Add the chile flesh and mash until the paste is smooth and uniform. Add the paste to the *cazuela* and mix well with the rest of the ingredients.

In a small bowl, using a fork, mash together the egg yolks and milk until smooth, and then gently stir into the contents of the *cazuela*. Very finely chop the egg whites and add them as well, mixing gently.

Place the *cazuela* over medium-low heat for about 10 minutes, or until all the ingredients are heated through and well blended. Do not stir the mixture as it cooks. Instead, rotate the *cazuela* in circular motions over the burner to help the cod skin release its gelatin and emulsify the sauce. Serve hot.

TIZNAO ◼ Salt Cod with Spring Onions ◼ (Castilla–La Mancha)

This is arguably the most singular dish of La Mancha, and it is quite different from other cod preparations in Spanish cooking. It is a little labor-intensive, too, but it is well worth the time. Here, the salt cod, in contrast to most recipes, is not desalted before it is used, but is instead held under running water to wash the salt from the surface. Miraculously, the dish is not salty. The cod simply yields its salt to the rest of the ingredients, lending the dish the perfect amount of seasoning. *Tiznao* means "dirty with ashes and slightly burnt" in Spanish, so it important that the vegetables in this recipe are grilled until they are slightly charred over a charcoal fire. Local cooks always make this dish a day in advance of serving to allow time for the flavors to settle. ◼ **Serves 4**

8 dried choricero or ancho chiles, halved lengthwise
   and seeded

8 cloves garlic, unpeeled

6 spring onions or 12 scallions, white part only

1 pound salt cod (page 46), cut into 4 pieces

1/2 teaspoon hot red pepper flakes

2 cups extra virgin olive oil

Boiling water as needed

1 hard-boiled egg, peeled and finely chopped

Prepare a hot fire in a charcoal grill. Arrange a fine-mesh screen on the grill rack.

Place the chiles directly over the fire and grill, turning frequently, until slightly blackened. At the same time, grill the garlic and spring onions directly over the fire until nicely browned and a little blackened. The timing depends on the intensity of the fire, but plan on about 10 minutes. Remove from the grill.

Briefly rinse the salt cod under cold running water and pat dry. Place on the grill rack directly over the fire and grill, turning the pieces several times, for 10 to 15 minutes, or until slightly blackened. Remove from the grill.

Peel the garlic, and finely chop the garlic, chiles, and onions. Remove the skin and any errant bones from the cod and shred into small pieces.

In a heatproof bowl, combine the cod, chopped vegetables, and red pepper flakes. Add the olive oil and mix well. Let stand for 1 hour, stirring the mixture with a wooden spoon several times. Add boiling water to cover by 1 inch and let stand for another 4 hours. Most of the water will be absorbed during this time.

Add 1 more cup boiling water, stir well, and let cool to room temperature. Cover and refrigerate overnight. The next day, bring to room temperature, garnish with the chopped egg, and serve.

BACALAO CON ALIOLI ▪▪
Salt Cod with Alioli ▪▪ *(Balearic Islands)*

In this simple room-temperature dish from the Balearics, a mixture of *bacalao* and potatoes is covered with creamy, rich *alioli*. You find this same dish in Catalonia, which has been closely linked, both in the kitchen and in history, to the archipelago since the time of the Moors. ▪▪

Serves 4

1 pound salt cod, desalted (page 46) and cut into
    4 pieces
1^1/$_2$ pounds boiling potatoes
1 cup Alioli (page 306)
2 hard boiled eggs, peeled and thinly sliced crosswise

In a saucepan, combine the cod with water to cover by 1 inch and bring to a boil over high heat. Decrease the heat to low and simmer the cod for about 5 minutes, or until it is tender. Using a slotted spoon, remove the cod from the pan and set aside to cool. Discard the water.

Meanwhile, in another saucepan, combine the potatoes with water to cover by 3 inches, bring to a boil over high heat, decrease the heat to medium, and cook, uncovered, for about 30 minutes, or until fork-tender.

When the salt cod is cool enough to handle, remove and discard the skin and any errant bones and cut the cod into small pieces.

When the potatoes have finished cooking, drain and let cool, then peel and cut crosswise into ^{1}/$_2$-inch-thick slices.

Arrange the potatoes on a serving plate and place the cod on top. Cover the cod with the *alioli* and garnish with the hard-boiled eggs. Serve at room temperature.

Cleaning fish outside a restaurant in the city of Corralejo, Fuerteventura (Canary Islands)

ATÚN ENCEBOLLADO ▪ Tuna with Caramelized Onion ▪ (Cantabria)

I have spent several summers with my friend Marga de La Viesca in the fishing village and beach resort of Liendo, just a stone's throw from Laredo. In the early mornings, we often go to the town's fish market, which always has a plentiful supply of bluefin (*atún*) and long-fin (*bonito*) tuna. Over the years, Marga and I have developed a wide range of recipes to keep us from growing tired of the fish. *Atún encebollado* is one of our favorites.
▪ **Serves 4**

1/2 cup plus 3 tablespoons olive oil

4 yellow onions, cut lengthwise into narrow strips

3 tablespoons brandy

Salt

Juice of 1/2 lemon

11/2 teaspoons coarse salt

4 (8- to 10-ounce) tuna steaks, about 1 inch thick

1/2 green bell pepper, seeded and cut lengthwise into narrow strips

In a large skillet, heat the 1/2 cup olive oil over high heat. When the oil is hot, add the onions and stir to coat well with the olive oil. Fry, stirring often, for 5 minutes, or until softened. Decrease the heat to medium and cook, stirring often, for about 30 minutes, or until golden brown. Add the brandy and season with salt and continue cooking for about 10 minutes longer, or until the brandy has evaporated and the onions are a rich brown. Remove from the heat and set aside.

In a shallow bowl, combine 1 tablespoon of the olive oil, the lemon juice, and the coarse salt and whisk until blended. Coat each tuna steak on both sides with the mixture.

Heat a stove-top grill pan or a skillet over high heat. Add 2 tuna steaks and sear on both sides, turning once, for 30 seconds on each side. The tuna should be undercooked. Transfer the steaks to a *cazuela* (page 51). Repeat with the remaining 2 steaks.

Add the reserved onions to the *cazuela* and distribute them evenly among the steaks, taking care not to break up the steaks. Place over low heat and simmer for 5 minutes.

Meanwhile, in a small skillet, heat the remaining 2 tablespoons olive oil over medium heat. Add the bell pepper and sauté for 5 minutes, or until soft. Season with salt.

If you like your tuna moist and medium to medium-rare, arrange the bell pepper strips over the tuna and serve immediately in the *cazuela*. If you prefer your tuna well done, let it simmer for 3 to 5 minutes longer, or until opaque at the center when tested with a knife tip, and then serve.

ATÚN EN ROLLITO ⁑
Asturian Tuna Roll ⁑ (*Asturias*)

Whenever I ask Asturians which recipe from their region must be included in a regional cookbook such as this one, the answer is nearly always the same: *atún en rollito*. It is originally from Cudillero, a fishing village close to Avilés, where it is prepared with the *bonito* that is abundant there during the summer months. The white-fleshed *bonito* is not easy to find in the United States, but the dish can be made with the pinker-fleshed bluefin tuna instead. ⁑ **Serves 4**

1 pound lean tuna fillet

$1/2$ teaspoon salt

$1/2$ teaspoon freshly ground black pepper

$1/2$ cup olive oil

1 small yellow onion, finely chopped

1 clove garlic, finely minced

1 tablespoon chopped fresh flat-leaf parsley

2 tablespoons chopped green olives

3 ounces jamón serrano or other dry-cured ham, finely chopped

2 tablespoons finely chopped preserved piquillo pepper or roasted red bell pepper

2 eggs, lightly beaten

1 tablespoon fine dried bread crumbs

2 tablespoons all-purpose flour

2 cups Carrot and Onion Sauce (page 311)

Using your fingers, shred the tuna into small pieces and place in a bowl. Season with the salt and pepper.

In a sauté pan, heat the olive oil over medium heat. Add the onion and cook, stirring often, for about 10 minutes, or until golden and tender. Using a slotted spoon, transfer the onion to the bowl holding the tuna. Reserve the oil in the pan.

Add the garlic, parsley, olives, *jamón serrano*, *piquillo* pepper, eggs, and bread crumbs to the tuna and mix well. Using your hands, shape the mixture into a log about 8 inches long and 3 inches wide.

Spread the flour in a shallow dish. Add the tuna roll and turn it in the flour to coat the surface evenly, then tap off any excess.

Return the sauté pan with the reserved oil to high heat. When the oil is hot, carefully place the tuna roll in the pan and fry, turning as needed, for about 5 minutes, or until browned on all sides.

Just before serving, transfer the tuna roll to a *cazuela* (page 51), cover it with the sauce, place over medium heat, and heat through. Remove the roll from the sauce, cut crosswise into eight 1-inch-thick slices, and place 2 slices on each plate. Spoon the sauce over the top and serve.

BONITO EN ACEITE ::
Home-Canned Tuna in Olive Oil

Home-canned *bonito* or tuna is almost better than fresh. I saw my mother make it so often, especially during the summer when the fish are at their best, that when I had a family of my own, I carried on the tradition. The procedure is so easy and the results so rewarding that I highly recommend dedicating a morning or afternoon to preparing this recipe.

The smaller, tastier *bonito* is hard to find in the United States, but good fresh tuna, which is widely available, is an excellent substitute. The most succulent and tender part of both fish is the *ventresca*, or "belly." It runs across the bottom of the fish close to the head, and has slightly fatty layers and a looser density than the muscular top of the fish.

Use only superior olive oil, preferably extra virgin of a mild varietal, such as Arbequina. :: **Makes about 10 half pints**

6 pounds tuna steaks, each 2 inches thick

About 3 pounds coarse salt

1 head garlic, unpeeled

Extra virgin olive oil for canning

Place the fish in a shallow bowl and cover completely on all sides with the salt. Let stand at room temperature for 1 hour.

Fill a large, wide saucepan or other pot with water and bring to a boil over high heat. Using a meat mallet or the bottom of a heavy skillet, pound the garlic head, without smashing it completely, and add it to the water. Remove as much of the salt from the fish as possible and place the pieces in the water, preferably side by side. (If the pan is not large enough, the tuna pieces can be stacked.) Decrease the heat to medium and, when the water begins to boil again, turn off the heat. Allow the tuna to cool in the water.

When the tuna has cooled, have ready 10 sterilized half-pint canning jars. Remove any skin or bones and cut away any dark spots. With a wet cloth, rub the surface to remove any traces of salt. Using your fingers, tear the tuna into pieces, following the natural grain of the flesh. Make the pieces as small or as large as you wish, bearing in mind that they have to fit into canning jars.

Place the tuna pieces in sterilized jars, leaving as little empty space as possible but without packing too tightly. Pour the olive oil into the jars to fill to within 1 inch of the rim. Let rest for 1 hour; the oil will settle slightly. Add more oil as needed to fill again to within 1 inch of the rim. Make sure the tuna is fully immersed.

Seal the jars with sterilized two-part canning lids (rubber-rimmed top and metal ring) and place in a single layer in 1 or more large pots. Add water to cover by 1 inch, and slip small kitchen towels between the jars to prevent them from clanging together when the water boils. Bring to a slow boil over medium-low heat, and boil for 1 hour, adding more hot water as needed to keep the jars covered at all times. Turn off the heat and let the jars cool completely in the pot(s).

Remove the jars from the pot(s), wipe dry, and check for a good seal (the tops should be slightly concave). Store jars with a good seal in a cool, dark place for up to 2 months. Store jars without a good seal, and jars once they have been opened, in the refrigerator for up to 1 week.

Grilled turbot at an asadores *in Getaria, Basque Country*

RAPE CON VINAGRETA PICANTE
▪ Seared Monkfish Medallions with Spicy Vinaigrette ▪ (Basque Country)

Topping grilled fish with a spicy vinaigrette is one of the preferred ways to prepare fish fillets in Spain. It is especially popular in the Basque Country, where establishments known as *asadores*, basically grill houses, specialize in fish *a la espalda*, or "on its back," a name derived from cooking the fillets skin side down on a grill. Here, I have used monkfish cut into medallions and pan searing instead of grilling and paired it with the same excellent vinaigrette. ▪ **Serves 4**

2 pounds monkfish fillet

Salt

3/4 cup olive oil

Juice of 1/2 lemon

2 cloves garlic, thinly sliced

1 teaspoon hot red pepper flakes

1 tablespoon sherry vinegar

2 tablespoons chopped fresh flat-leaf parsley

Cut the monkfish crosswise into 1/2-inch-thick medallions. Season the medallions on both sides with salt. In a small bowl, stir together 1/4 cup of the olive oil and the lemon juice. Brush the oil mixture on both sides of each medallion.

Heat a large sauté pan over high heat. Working in batches, if necessary, place the medallions in the hot pan and sear on the first side for 1 minute. Decrease the heat to medium and cook for 2 minutes longer. Increase the heat to high again, turn the medallions, and sear on the second side for 1 minute. Decrease the heat to medium and cook for 2 minutes longer. The medallions should be just opaque at the center. Transfer the medallions to a warmed serving platter.

In a small skillet, heat the remaining 1/2 cup olive oil over high heat. Add the garlic and red pepper flakes and fry, stirring constantly, for 1 to 2 minutes, or until the garlic starts to turn golden. Immediately but cautiously add the vinegar, stepping back slightly in case the oil flares up. Remove from the heat and stir with a long-handled wooden spoon for 20 to 30 seconds to mix the vinegar with the oil, creating a vinaigrette.

Pour the vinaigrette over the fish and garnish with the parsley. Serve immediately.

SALMÓN A LA RIBEREÑA ::
Wild Salmon with Cider :: (*Asturias*)

The Asturian rivers that descend from the Picos de Europa, the mountain range along the coast of northern Spain, to the Bay of Biscay were once plentiful with wild salmon. Although today the catch is much reduced, Asturian salmon is still considered the best in Spain.

Asturians cook salmon in many different ways, but salmon baked with cider, a staple of Asturian gastronomy, is arguably the most representative. Though the usual cut for this recipe is salmon steaks, I often prepare it with fillets instead. :: **Serves 4**

1/2 pound baby red potatoes, halved, roasted, and kept hot
4 (1 1/2-inch-thick) salmon fillets or steaks
Salt

1/4 cup olive oil
Unsalted butter, at room temperature, for rubbing on fish
1 cup cider or sparkling white wine
Chopped fresh flat-leaf parsley for garnish

Preheat the oven to 400°F. Select a roasting pan large enough to accommodate the salmon in a single layer.

Season the salmon on both sides with salt. In a large skillet, heat the olive oil over high heat. Add 2 salmon fillets and sear for 2 minutes on each side, or until golden. Transfer to a plate, rub both sides of each fillet with butter, and then place in the roasting pan. Repeat with the remaining fillets.

Pour the cider over the salmon and bake for 15 minutes, or until opaque throughout when tested with a knife tip. Sprinkle with the parsley and serve immediately with the potatoes.

:: Asturian Cider ::

Asturias is rich in apple orchards, and most rural families have their own apples trees, even if only a few. Much of the harvest is used for making *sidra*, or "cider," the region's signature drink. During the winter, the pressed apple juice, typically made from a selection of apple varieties in specific proportions, is fermented without additives in chestnut barrels and then shifted to dark green bottles in February. The alcohol content is low, usually about 5 percent, and before bottling, a traditional *espicha*, or "tasting," takes place, at which family members and friends gather to sample the season's production.

Natural cider is also produced on a large scale and sold at *chigres*, or "cider bars." The ritual of decanting and drinking cider cannot be altered: bartenders raise one arm above their head and pour the cider from the greatest height possible into a slightly inclined wide glass, so that the stream of cider hits the side and never the bottom. This action (illustrated on page 12), which causes the slightly carbonated beverage to form a head of froth, is believed to help further develop the flavor of the cider. Only a small quantity, about two ounces, is poured, and the same glass is refilled and passed from one person to the next after each quickly swallows the delicious cider in a single gulp. Chorizo sausage cooked in cider, cut into slices, and served with country bread is a classic in *chigres*, and you will also sometimes find Cabrales, the region's famous blue cheese, mixed with a little cider and spread on bread.

At large family gatherings and other celebrations, children are usually served a slightly carbonic, sweet, nearly alcohol-free cider produced by the prominent El Gaitero company. At the end of such events and in *chigres*, too, Asturians often sing "Asturias Patria Querida," a song that celebrates their homeland. This custom is so well known that when Spaniards anywhere in Spain leave a party a little tipsy, they often characterize the experience by recalling that everyone left singing "Asturias Patria Querida."

BOCARTES EN CAZUELA ::
Fresh Anchovies in Vinaigrette
:: (Basque Country)

If you come across fresh anchovies—especially when they are small—invite your friends over for dinner. This dish is one of my favorites, provided the anchovies are so fresh that they almost slip from your hands. I always buy extra because I also like to fry anchovies (page 67) and to marinate them in vinegar (page 66). :: **Serves 4**

  1 pound fresh anchovies

  1/3 cup olive oil

  1 clove garlic, minced

  Salt

  1 teaspoon hot red pepper flakes

  1 tablespoon red wine vinegar (optional)

Rinse the anchovies under cold running water. Working with 1 fish at a time, and using your thumb, break the neck and remove and discard the head. Slide your index finger into the belly opening, pull out the viscera and discard, and leave the central bone in place. Rinse the anchovy again and pat dry with paper towels. Repeat with the remaining fish.

In a *cazuela* (page 51), heat the olive oil over medium heat. Add the garlic and, before it begins to color, add the anchovies. Sprinkle them with salt and the red pepper flakes and cook, stirring them gently with a wooden spoon and being careful to keep them whole, for 5 minutes, or until opaque at the center when tested with the tip of a knife.

Sprinkle the vinegar over the fish and rotate the *cazuela* in circular motions over the burner a few times to mix the vinegar with the fish and oil. Serve immediately.

Fresh anchovies on display at the market in San Sebastián, Basque Country

MERLUZA Y ALMEJAS EN SALSA VERDE ▪ Hake Fillets with Clams in Salsa Verde ▪ (Basque Country)

This dish is one of the front-runners of traditional Basque cooking. *Salsa verde* appears in many dishes: with clams alone (page 71), with monkfish or fresh cod (page 222), or with a combination of clams and hake, as in this recipe. Hake, a noble and expensive fish when caught in Cantabria's local waters and in the Bay of Biscay, is also available in the United States at good fish markets, where it is sometimes imported from Chile. Basque hake is better if you can find it: the flesh is tighter and tastier, and the skin is darker and very shiny.

I recommend using white asparagus from Navarra (page 49), which, although canned, are exceptional. ▪
Serves 4

24 Manila or small littleneck clams

1 tablespoon coarse sea salt

4 cups water

1/3 cup olive oil

2 cloves garlic, finely minced

1/2 teaspoon hot red pepper flakes (optional)

1 tablespoon all-purpose flour

1 1/2 teaspoons salt

2 tablespoons chopped fresh flat-leaf parsley

1/2 cup dry white wine

2 pounds hake fillet, cut into 16 pieces

Salt

4 white asparagus, freshly cooked or canned, halved crosswise

2 hard-boiled eggs, peeled and quartered lengthwise, for garnish

Chopped fresh flat-leaf parsley for garnish

Scrub the clams under cold running water, discarding any that fail to close to the touch. In a large bowl, combine the clams, coarse salt, and water to cover and let stand for at least 30 minutes or up to 2 hours so that the clams release any sand trapped in their shells. Drain.

In a large saucepan, combine the clams with the 4 cups water and bring to a boil over medium-high heat. Cover and cook for about 5 minutes, or until they open. As the clams cook, uncover the pan occasionally and stir with a wooden spoon to encourage them all to open at about the same time. Drain the clams, reserving the cooking liquid. Discard any clams that have not opened.

In a large *cazuela* (page 51), heat the olive oil over high heat. Add the garlic and red pepper flakes, if using, and fry, stirring often, for 1 to 2 minutes, or until the garlic begins to turn golden. Sprinkle the flour over the garlic and stir with a wooden spoon until the mixture is well blended. Add 3 cups of the reserved cooking liquid and the salt, parsley, and wine. Decrease the heat to medium and boil, stirring occasionally, for 5 minutes, or until the sauce thickens slightly. Add more cooking liquid if you prefer a thinner sauce. Rotate the *cazuela* in circular motions over the burner to mix all the ingredients, and boil gently for 2 minutes, or until the sauce is blended and looks whitish green.

Sprinkle the hake pieces with salt and place in a single layer in the sauce. Cook, turning once, for 2 minutes on each side, or until opaque at the center when tested with a knife tip. Add the clams and asparagus, shake the pan gently to prevent sticking, and simmer for 2 more minutes to heat all the ingredients through.

Garnish with the egg wedges and sprinkle with the parsley. Serve immediately.

COCOCHAS EN SALSA VERDE ▪▪
Cocochas in Salsa Verde ▪▪ (Basque Country)

Cocochas, or *kokotxas* in Basque, are the small, gelatinous, meaty chunks on either side of the lower jaw of a hake or cod. They are sometimes mistakenly called cheeks, which are actually the tender, meaty morsels on each side of the head, behind the eyes. Not surprisingly, the tasty *cocochas* are highly coveted, not only in the Basque Country but throughout Spain, a fact reflected in their high price. Because they are so prized, fishermen have the prerogative of keeping them for themselves, whether for their own consumption or for selling privately at higher prices, and they skillfully and swiftly remove them from the fish before the ship even docks.

In the United States, it is easier to find cod *cocochas*. Ask your fishmonger to save cod heads for you, and use the heads for making fish stock after you have removed the *cocochas*. To free them, slide the tip of your finger underneath the front of the jaw on both sides. You won't miss them. Cut them out with sharp scissors, and leave the delicate skin on.

In this recipe, I have made a simple *salsa verde*, taking advantage of the gelatin in the skin of the fish. ▪▪ **Serves 2**

6 tablespoons olive oil

$1/2$ clove garlic, finely minced

$1/2$ pound cocochas (from about 12 cod or hake heads)

Salt

$1^1/_2$ teaspoons all-purpose flour

$1/4$ cup water

1 tablespoon chopped fresh flat-leaf parsley

In a small (about 8-inch) *cazuela* (page 51), heat the olive oil over medium heat. Add the garlic and fry, stirring often, for 2 to 3 minutes, or until it begins to turn golden. Add the *cocochas*, season with salt and sprinkle with the flour, and then stir them gently with a wooden spoon, mixing well. Cook for 1 minute, then add the water and parsley and rotate the *cazuela* in circular motions over the burner to help emulsify the oil and the gelatin from the fish skin. Continue cooking until the sauce begins to boil, then remove from the heat.

Continue shaking and swirling the *cazuela* for 5 more minutes off the heat (earthenware *cazuelas* retain heat long after they are off the stove). At this point, the *cocohas* should be opaque throughout and the sauce should have a nice consistency. Serve immediately.

DORADA A LA SAL ::
Gilt-Head Bream in a Salt Crust :: (*Murcia*)

Dorada, or gilt-head bream, is usually prepared by baking it in a salt crust. Most Spanish food scholars believe the method originated in Murcia, but it is now common practice in Andalusia as well. Don't be put off by the large amount of salt. It seals in the juices of the fish, resulting in a succulent dish that delivers pure fish flavor without a trace of saltiness.

Ask your fishmonger to clean the viscera from the fish without cutting the belly open, which can usually be done by pulling them through the gills. Also, make sure the fish is not scaled. During baking, the salt forms a hard crust that adheres to the scales, so that when you break the crust before serving the fish, the skin stays attached to the crust, peeling away easily to expose the juicy, succulent flesh underneath. The salt must be coarse, too—fine salt won't work. Some cooks like to sprinkle the salt with water. I skip this step because I have found that the water prevents the crust from getting nice and hard.

Other fish, such as snapper, sea bass, and turbot, can also be baked in salt with good results. Figure on 15 minutes per pound for baking. Serve the fish with boiled potatoes. :: **Serves 4**

4 pounds coarse salt

1 (4-pound) gilt-head bream, snapper, sea bass, or turbot

$^1/_2$ pound boiling potatoes, boiled and kept hot (optional)

1 cup Alioli (page 306)

Preheat the oven to 450°F.

Select a baking pan only slightly larger than the fish and cover the bottom of the pan with a layer of salt $1^1/_2$ inches deep. Place the fish on top of the salt and cover completely with the rest of the salt. With your fingers, press the salt against the fish to ensure that it is completely enclosed.

Bake the fish for 1 hour. Remove it from the oven and let rest for 5 minutes. With a chef's knife, crack the salt crust open lengthwise along the center of the fish. First lift off one-half of the crust in one piece, then the other; the skin should be attached to the crust. Gently remove any skin remaining on the fish. Using a spatula, lift the top fillet of the fish and divide it between 2 warmed plates. Remove the central bone and discard it. Carefully lift the bottom fillet and divide between 2 additional warmed plates.

Serve the fish immediately with the boiled potatoes, if desired, and the *alioli*.

A colorful selection of fish at a small fishmonger's stand, Catalonia

URTA A LA ROTEÑA :: Baked Urta with Vegetables and Sherry :: *(Andalusia)*

Urta, also spelled *hurta*, a reddish fish with delicate flesh, is caught in the coastal waters off Cádiz, and the town of Rota, which sits on the same bay and hosts an annual festival honoring the tasty fish, is well known for this recipe. Other white-fleshed fish, such as red snapper or sea bream, can be substituted. The addition of the fat of *jamón serrano* gives the dish an extra layer of flavor. As is always the case with fish that is baked whole, serving is a little more inconvenient, but the fish is moister and worth the trouble. :: **Serves 4**

1 (3- to 4-pound) urta, sea bream, or red snapper, cleaned

Salt

2 ounces fat from jamón serrano or other dry-cured ham or bacon, cut into strips

$1/2$ cup dry sherry

$1/3$ cup olive oil

4 tomatoes, peeled and finely chopped

2 green bell peppers, seeded and finely chopped

1 yellow onion, finely chopped

2 cloves garlic, minced

Preheat the oven to 350°F.

Season the fish inside and out with salt. Using a sharp knife, make 2 cuts, each $1/2$ inch long and 4 inches apart, crosswise on one side of the fish. Fill the slits with the fat strips.

Place the fish in a roasting pan just large enough to accommodate it and pour the sherry over the top. Bake the fish for 30 minutes, or until it is opaque when tested with a knife tip near the backbone.

Meanwhile, heat the olive oil in a skillet over medium heat. Add the tomatoes, bell peppers, onion, and garlic and cook, stirring often, for 10 to 15 minutes, or until all the vegetables are tender. Keep warm.

When the fish is ready, transfer to a warmed platter and spoon the vegetables alongside. Serve immediately.

TRUCHA A LA NAVARRA :: Baked Trout with Jamón Serrano :: (Navarra)

Pamplona, capital of Navarra, is so close to Bilbao that when my friends and I were younger, we often went there just to eat at a magnificent restaurant called Las Pocholas, where three single elderly ladies, probably sisters or cousins, cooked like angels in the heart of the city. (Las pocholas means "the cute ones.") The place was so highly regarded and popular that even during San Fermín week—the famous running of the bulls, when Pamplona is bustling with people from around the world—the ladies never opened on their closing day. In fact, the restaurant's fame was such that I am sure even Hemingway ate there. The ladies didn't have children and never shared a culinary secret; and unfortunately, the restaurant closed long ago. This recipe is my rendition of one of my favorite meals served by las pocholas.

:: Serves 4

4 (1/2-pound) trout, cleaned with heads intact
Salt
Juice of 1/2 lemon
1/4 cup olive oil
5 thin slices jamón serrano or other dry-cured ham
All-purpose flour for coating
2 cloves garlic, minced
2 tablespoons chopped fresh flat-leaf parsley

Preheat the oven to 500°F.

Season the trout with salt inside and out. Sprinkle the lemon juice inside the trout and set aside.

In a wide skillet, heat the olive oil over high heat. Place 4 ham slices in the pan and sear, turning once, for 1 to 2 minutes total, or until lightly browned on both sides. Using tongs, remove the ham from the pan and lay 1 slice inside each trout. Reserve the oil in the skillet.

Spread the flour in a shallow bowl. One at a time, roll the trout in the flour to coat on all sides, shaking off any excess.

Return the skillet with the oil to high heat. When the oil is hot, add the trout and fry, turning once, for 2 to 3 minutes on each side, or until the fish are golden on the outside but undercooked inside. Using a wide slotted spatula, transfer the trout to a roasting pan just large enough to accommodate them. Again, reserve the oil in the skillet.

Finely chop the remaining ham slice. Return the skillet with the oil to high heat and add the chopped ham. Sauté briefly, then add the garlic and sauté for 1 minute, or until it begins to turn golden. Remove from the heat and spoon the contents of the skillet evenly over the trout.

Bake the trout for 10 minutes, or until they are opaque when tested with a knife tip near the backbone. Remove from the oven and transfer to warmed plates, spooning any sauce from the pan over the top. Sprinkle with the parsley and serve immediately.

MERO A LA MALLORQUINA ::
Grouper with Vegetables :: *(Balearic Islands)*

When a fish is prepared *a la mallorquina*, you know that it will be cooked with a variety of vegetables piled on top. Ideally, the fish is whole and weighs at least five pounds. Grouper is a good choice, but so is red snapper, striped bass, John Dory, or any other lean, white-fleshed fish. The crown of colorful vegetables not only looks pretty but also infuses the fish with sensational flavor.

If you cannot find a whole large fish to cook, you can buy steaks or fillets, calculating $1/2$ pound per serving and cooking them for only about 20 minutes. :: **Serves 6**

$1^1/2$ lemons

2 artichokes

1 (5- to 6-pound) whole grouper, cleaned

Salt

$1/2$ teaspoon freshly ground black pepper

1 bunch fennel leaves, plus 1 tablespoon chopped

$1/2$ cup olive oil

3 boiling potatoes, about $1^1/2$ pounds total weight, peeled and cut into $1/2$-inch-thick slices

$1^1/2$ teaspoons sweet pimentón or paprika

$1/2$ cup dry white wine

4 scallions, white part only, finely chopped

1 leek, including tender green tops, cut into $1/4$-inch-thick slices

2 carrots, peeled and cut into $1/4$-inch-thick slices

1 bunch Swiss chard, stems removed (reserve for another use) and finely chopped

1 bunch spinach, finely chopped

2 tomatoes, thinly sliced

2 tablespoons chopped fresh flat-leaf parsley

$1/4$ cup pine nuts

$1/4$ cup raisins

2 tablespoons fine dried bread crumbs

1 cup Fish Stock (page 304)

Squeeze the juice from a lemon half into a bowl filled with water and set aside. Working with 1 artichoke at a time, peel off the tough, dark outer leaves. Cut off the stem flush with the bottom, cut off the top two-thirds of the leaves, and quarter the artichoke lengthwise. Using a small, sharp knife or a spoon, remove and discard the fuzzy choke, then cut the quarters into small pieces and slip them into the lemon water. Repeat with the second artichoke.

Season the fish inside and outside with salt and the pepper. Slice the remaining lemon crosswise into 4 slices, and insert the lemon slices and the fennel leaves into the cavity of the fish. Set aside.

Preheat the oven to 400°F.

In a skillet, heat the olive oil over high heat. Add the potatoes, and fry, turning them occasionally, for about 5 minutes, or until they are lightly browned on the outside but still undercooked inside. Remove from the heat and, using a slotted spoon, arrange the potatoes on the bottom of a large rimmed baking sheet. (Make sure the sides of the baking sheet are high enough to accommodate not only the fish and vegetables, but also the stock that is added later.) Lay the fish on top of the potatoes. Sprinkle the *pimentón* on top of the fish and drizzle with the wine.

Drain the artichokes and pat dry. In a bowl, combine the artichokes, scallions, leek, carrots, Swiss chard, spinach, and tomatoes and stir to mix well. Place the vegetables on top of the fish. Don't worry if some fall to sides of the fish. Sprinkle the parsley, the chopped fennel, pine nuts, and raisins on top and finally the bread crumbs.

Pour the fish stock evenly over the fish and vegetables. Bake for 2 hours, or until the fish is opaque near the backbone when tested with a knife tip and the vegetables are tender.

Remove from the oven and serve the fish and vegetables immediately directly from the pan. Even though this dish is a little messy to serve, it looks impressive and tastes delicious.

RODABALLO A LA GALLEGA ::
Galician Turbot :: (*Galicia*)

The Galicians are the great fishermen of Spain, and the turbot is the king of the catch. Even if it is farmed, as is increasingly the case today, turbot is a great fish. But when it is wild, the flesh is firmer and its characteristic flavor is more intense. No matter how you cook it—seared, fried, baked, roasted whole—turbot tastes exquisite.

In this Galician recipe, the fish is not filleted, but rather cut crosswise through the central bone. In my opinion, the head contains the best parts of the fish and, if you sit among family members or friends, don't be shy about nibbling on it. :: **Serves 6**

1 (4-pound) turbot with head and tail intact, cleaned
    and cut crosswise into 3 portions

Coarse salt

3 cups water

1 cup dry white wine

2 yellow onions, cut into quarters

2 carrots, peeled and cut in half crosswise

1 leek, including tender green tops, cut into
    1-inch-thick slices

3 boiling potatoes, about 1 1/2 pounds total weight,
    peeled and cut into quarters

3 flat-leaf parsley sprigs

5 black peppercorns

SAUCE

1 cup olive oil

3 cloves garlic, thinly sliced

1 yellow onion, cut into thin rings

1 bay leaf

1 1/2 teaspoons sweet pimentón or paprika

Juice of 1/2 lemon

Salt

Season the turbot with coarse salt and set aside.

In a saucepan, combine the water and wine and bring to a boil over high heat. Add the onions, carrots, leek, potatoes, parsley, and peppercorns, decrease the heat to medium-low, and cook, uncovered, for about 30 minutes, or until the potatoes are tender.

Pour the contents of the pan through a fine-mesh sieve held over a sauté pan large enough to accommodate the fish pieces. Remove the potatoes from the sieve, place in a covered heatproof vessel, and place in a low oven to keep warm. Discard the rest of the vegetables in the sieve or set aside for another use.

Place the turbot pieces in the sauté pan and bring slowly to a boil over medium-low heat. Decrease the heat to low and simmer, uncovered, for about 20 minutes, or until the fish is opaque throughout when tested with a knife tip.

Meanwhile, to make the sauce, in a medium sauté pan, heat the olive oil over high heat. Add the garlic, onion, and bay leaf and cook, stirring often, for 10 minutes, or until the onion is golden brown.

When the turbot is ready, cut each piece in half lengthwise and arrange on a warmed platter with the boiled potatoes; keep warm.

To finish the sauce, remove the sauté pan from the heat, add the *pimentón* and lemon juice, and mix well. Season with salt, stir again, and pour over the fish and potatoes. Serve immediately.

BURRIDA DE RAYA ▪ Skate in Fish Stock with Alioli ▪ *(Balearic Islands)*

Fish soups with names similar to this one are common in the Mediterranean, with the type of fish and the seasonings varying with the locale. For example, Provençal cooks make *bourride* and serve it with the rust-colored sauce known as *rouille*, while Ligurian cooks make *buridda* and accompany it with fried bread. The *burrida* of the Balearics calls for skate in an *alioli*-enriched stock and thin slices of country-style bread. ▪ **Serves 6**

2 pounds skate

Salt

Juice of 1 lemon

2 cups Fish Stock (page 304)

$^{1}/_{2}$ teaspoon saffron threads

1 cup Alioli (page 306), at room temperature

2 tablespoons chopped fresh flat-leaf parsley

6 thin slices country-style bread

Remove the central cartilage from the skate and cut the fish into 3-inch squares. Place in a shallow dish, sprinkle with salt, and drizzle evenly with the lemon juice. Let stand at room temperature for 1 hour. Rinse under cold running water and set aside.

In a large saucepan, combine the stock and the saffron and bring to a boil over high heat. Immerse the skate in the stock, decrease the heat to medium, and cook, uncovered, for 10 minutes, or until the fish is opaque at the center when tested with a knife tip. Using a slotted spoon, remove the skate from the pan, place on a platter, cover, and set aside. Increase the heat to high and boil the stock for 5 minutes longer.

Remove the stock from the heat and whisk in the *alioli* and parsley.

Place a slice of bread in each soup plate, place the skate on top, and cover with the stock. Serve immediately.

Fishing in Sanlúcar de Barrameda, Andalusia

CALDERETA DE LANGOSTA ▪
Lobster Stew ▪ (Balearic Islands)

On the Balearic Islands, the locals argue over who has the best *caldereta*. Minorcans claim that their blue spiny lobsters are unequaled in the dish, while the Majorcans claim their light red lobsters are better. In New York, I made a *caldereta* using American lobster and it tasted sublime. This recipe for *caldereta de langosta*, given to me by my nephew Gonzalo, is from the lovely Es Pla restaurant in the Minorcan port of Fornells. I imagine eating it there, surrounded by the intense blues of the Mediterranean and the sky, would be like dining in heaven.

There are two primary species of lobster: the American lobster (*Homarus americanus*) and the European lobster (*H. gammarus*). In Spain, the former, known as *bogavante*, is caught in the Bay of Biscay and is highly valued. But when the Spanish refer to the *langosta*, they are talking about the European lobster, which is pulled from the Mediterranean Sea, is quite spiny in appearance, and is known in English as spiny lobster or rock lobster. ▪ **Serves 4**

2 (2-pound) live lobsters

$1/3$ cup plus 2 tablespoons olive oil

2 pounds tomatoes, cored and cut into eighths

1 (8-ounce) can tomato paste

2 yellow onions, chopped

1 small green bell pepper, seeded and chopped

Salt

Pinch of sugar

3 cloves garlic, peeled but left whole

1 tablespoon chopped fresh flat-leaf parsley

4 thin slices whole-grain country-style bread, toasted (optional)

4 teaspoons Alioli (page 306, optional)

Place the live lobsters in ice water for 1 hour. The lobsters need to be alive to make the dish sublime, but they should not suffer when we kill them. Putting them in the ice water will help numb them.

In a skillet, heat the $1/3$ cup olive oil over high heat. Add the tomatoes, tomato paste, onions, and bell pepper and cook, stirring often, for about 10 minutes, or until the vegetables begin to soften. Decrease the heat to medium, season with salt and the sugar, and cook for about 20 minutes, or until the mixture has thickened. Pass the mixture through a food mill fitted with the medium plate held over a deep *caldero* or large saucepan. Place on the stove top over the lowest heat setting possible. Keep an eye on the sauce, as you don't want it to scorch.

While the vegetables are cooking, remove the lobsters from the ice water and place them, belly down, on a cutting board. Working with 1 lobster at a time, and using a sharp knife, separate the head from the tail and remove the legs. Pull out and discard the insides, but reserve the liver (the greenish mass inside the head) and the roe if any (the reddish mass, also called the coral, found in females). Place the liver and roe in the refrigerator. Crack the legs open a bit with a small hammer, so that they will release more flavor when they are broiled. If you are cooking American lobsters, reserve the claws, since they are very meaty, and cook them later with the tails.

In a small saucepan, combine the heads and legs with water to cover and bring to a boil over high heat. Decrease the heat to medium and simmer for about 30 minutes to create a flavorful stock. Strain the stock and set aside.

Cut each tail crosswise into 4 pieces and add them and the claws, if using American lobsters, to the simmering tomato sauce. With a wooden spoon or spatula, turn the lobster, mixing it well with the tomato sauce. Add the reserved stock, which should just cover the lobster. Season with salt, increase the heat to medium, and bring to a boil. Cover and cook for 20 minutes.

In a mortar, combine the garlic, parsley, the remaining 2 tablespoons olive oil, and the lobster liver and roe. Pound with a pestle until a uniform paste forms. Add the paste to the lobster and tomato sauce, mix well, and cook for 5 minutes longer to blend the flavors.

To serve, spread each bread slice with 1 teaspoon *alioli* and place in the bottom of a soup plate. Ladle the lobster pieces and plenty of liquid on top. Place an empty dish for the shells in the center of the table.

SUQUET DE PESCADOS ::
Seafood Stew :: *(Catalonia)*

Suquet is the diminutive form of *suc*, or "juice," in Catalan, which means that this wonderfully flavored dish is more correctly called juicy fish stew. The fish and shellfish used vary from cook to cook, and so does the amount of liquid—in fact, some people call this a stew, while others call it a soup—but saffron and almonds are typically part of the mix. In Barcelona, my favorite place for *suquet* is El Suquet de l'Almirant, located in the picturesque port area of Barcelonetta. :: **Serves 6**

12 Manila or small littleneck or cherrystone clams

1 tablespoon coarse salt

1/2 cup olive oil

2 cloves garlic, peeled but left whole

8 blanched almonds

1 tablespoon chopped fresh flat-leaf parsley

1 tablespoon water

1 yellow onion, finely chopped

1 tomato, halved crosswise, grated on the large holes of a handheld grater, and skin discarded

Pinch of saffron threads

6 cups Fish Stock (page 304)

2 pounds monkfish fillet, cut into small pieces

1 pound hake fillet, cut into small pieces

1 pound squid, cleaned and cut into thin rings (page 196)

6 large shrimp in the shell with heads intact

12 medium shrimp, peeled

1/2 pound mussels, scrubbed and debearded

1/2 cup cava or sparkling white wine

Scrub the clams under cold running water, discarding any that fail to close to the touch. In a large bowl, combine the clams, coarse salt, and water to cover and let stand for at least 30 minutes or up to 2 hours so that the clams release any sand trapped in their shells.

Meanwhile, in a deep *cazuela* (page 51), heat the olive oil over high heat. Add the garlic and fry, stirring often, for about 1 minute, or until golden. Using a slotted spoon, transfer the garlic to a mortar. Reserve the oil in the *cazuela* off the heat.

Add the almonds, parsley, and water to the mortar and pound with a pestle until a paste forms. Set aside.

Return the *cazuela* to medium heat, add the onion, and sauté for 5 minutes, or until soft. Add the tomato and saffron, mix well, and cook for 5 minutes longer to blend the flavors. Meanwhile, in a saucepan, bring the stock to a boil, then decrease the heat to maintain a gentle simmer.

Add the monkfish, hake, squid, and large and medium shrimp to the *cazuela* and mix well with the onion and tomato. Stir in 1 cup of the hot stock and cook for 30 minutes, adding the remaining stock 1 cup at a time at 5-minute intervals. At the end of this time, all the fish will be cooked and the flavors will be blended.

Season to taste with salt. Drain the clams and add them to the *cazuela* along with the mussels, discarding any that fail to close to the touch, and *cava*. Cook for 5 minutes longer, or until the clams and mussels open.

Discard any mussels or clams that failed to open. Serve immediately.

VIEIRAS EN SU CONCHA ::
Broiled Scallops :: (*Galicia*)

Scallops are common in Galicia and are typically sold in the shell. In the United States, scallops in the shell are far less common, but you can buy just the shells at many cookware shops. I have suggested the number of shells you will need in the recipe, but you may need more or less depending on what you find. If you can't find the shells, use your favorite small flameproof ramekins. ::

Serves 4

6 tablespoons olive oil

1 yellow onion, finely chopped

1 clove garlic, finely chopped

1 tablespoon sweet pimentón or paprika

1/2 cup dry white wine

2 tablespoons Tomato Sauce (page 311)

1/2 teaspoon salt

1/2 teaspoon freshly ground black pepper

1 pound sea scallops, cut into quarters, or whole bay scallops

2 tablespoons fine dried bread crumbs

1 tablespoon chopped fresh flat-leaf parsley

In a sauté pan, heat the olive oil over medium heat. Add the onion and garlic and sauté for 5 minutes, or until soft. Decrease the heat to low and add the *pimentón*, stirring to prevent it from burning. Add the wine and cook for about 10 minutes, or until it evaporates. Add the tomato sauce, salt, and pepper and mix well with the rest of the ingredients. Cook for 2 minutes, or until heated through. Taste and adjust the seasoning with salt and pepper.

Preheat the broiler. Have ready 8 sea scallop shells or at least 16 bay scallop shells.

Fill a saucepan two-thirds full with water and bring to a boil. Add the scallops, remove from the heat, and let the scallops sit in the hot water for 5 minutes, or until just opaque throughout. Drain well.

Arrange the shells in a rimmed baking sheet. Spoon an equal amount of the scallops into each shell. Spoon the tomato mixture evenly over the scallops. Sprinkle with the bread crumbs and then the parsley. Slip under the broiler and broil for 2 to 3 minutes, or until the tops are golden. Serve immediately.

:: Grilled Sardines ::

Laredo has one of the most spectacular beaches in Spain and is only an hour by car from Bilbao and from Santander, the capital of Cantabria. In July and August, the village is buzzing with visitors who spend their summers at the beach. But in September, my favorite month to visit northern Spain, this small fishing port is a beautiful place to be.

My sister Piedad and her family own an apartment on the beach promenade overlooking the Bay of Biscay, and they have been spending their summers in Laredo for as long I can remember. When I visit them, I love to stop at one of the humble bars with outdoor grilling at the nearby fishing docks, where wonderful sardines, *espetones de sardinas*, and *ensalada mixta* are all that are served.

Espetones, long metal skewers with wooden handles, are used for grilling the sardines. The perfectly fresh fish are slipped onto the rods and cooked over glowing hot embers until they are nicely branded with grill marks and are opaque but still succulent. The sardines are then treated to a shower of coarse salt and served piping hot.

ERIZOS DE MAR GRATINADOS ::
Broiled Sea Urchins :: *(Asturias)*

Sea urchins are abundant along the Asturian coastline, where the locals prize them for their delicate orange roe. I especially like to eat them raw with just a little lemon juice. It is difficult to describe the intense, seductive flavor of the roe, or coral, concealed inside the prickly urchins other than to say that it carries the essence of the sea. Have on hand a pair of sturdy kitchen scissors to break open the spiny creatures. :: **Serves 4**

24 sea urchins

1 tablespoon unsalted butter

3 scallions, white part only, finely chopped

$^{1}/_{2}$ cup cava or Champagne

$^{1}/_{2}$ cup heavy cream

Salt

Freshly ground black pepper

Using strong, sharp, narrow-bladed scissors, cut off the top half of each urchin shell and discard it, being careful not to break the bottom part of the shell. You want to remove the top and keep the bottom intact for serving. With a spoon, scoop out the orange roe from the shells and reserve. Rinse the bottom halves of the shells under running cold water, drain well, and set aside.

Preheat the broiler.

In a small sauté pan, heat the butter over medium heat. Add the scallions and sauté for 5 minutes, or until soft. Add the urchin roe and *cava*, mix well, and cook, stirring gently with a wooden spoon, for 2 minutes longer, or until the mixture is well blended. Add the heavy cream and season with salt and pepper. Decrease the heat to medium and cook, stirring occasionally, for about 5 minutes, or until a creamy texture is achieved. Remove from the heat.

Fill the reserved shells with the urchin mixture, dividing it evenly, and place on a rimmed baking sheet. Slip under the boiler for about 2 minutes, or until golden brown.

Place 6 urchin shells on each plate and serve.

:: Gooseneck Barnacles ::

Tube shaped, as thick as an index finger, and about three inches long, *percebes* (gooseneck barnacles) grow in clusters on rocks along the coasts of northern Spain and Portugal. They are expensive because of their scarcity and the difficulty and danger involved in gathering them. Harvesters must wait for low tide and then scale the sharp rocks where the barnacles are growing, always keeping an eye on the heavy surf that threatens to sweep them away.

On one end, the barnacle is attached to a rootlike cluster on the rock; the other end looks almost like a hoof with whitish nail-like pods. If I hadn't already developed a taste for them and instead saw them for the first time, I probably would raise my eyebrows at the sight of these prehistoric-looking specimens. But take my word for it, if you are in Spain and see *percebes*,

order some even if they are expensive. They are among the most delicious morsels the sea has to offer.

In America, these tasty creatures grow along the Pacific coast all the way from Alaska to Chile. The Chileans value them highly but, to my knowledge, they are not appreciated in the same way in the rest of the Americas.

If you happen to come across *percebes* in a market, they are easy to prepare. Just place them in salted water, bring them to a boil, cook for 10 minutes, turn off the heat, and allow them to cool in the water. Drain them and serve warm or at room temperature.

Eating them is just as easy. Pierce the outer skin near the "hoof," tear it off with your fingernails, and then bite off the entire pink stalklike flesh.

CHIPIRONES EN SU TINTA ▪ Baby Squid in Black Ink Sauce ▪ *(Basque Country)*

Chipirones, or *txipirones* in Basque, are small squid, 2¹/₂ to 4 inches long. In one of the Basque Country's most emblematic dishes, these prized shellfish are prepared in an onion, leek, and tomato sauce to which squid ink is added. The beautiful, velvety sauce is often made separately and used in other ways, such as in *arroz negro* (page 188), as an accompaniment to fried fish, or as a decorative element with stuffed *piquillo* peppers. Unlike the cooks of other regions, Basque cooks like to stuff their squid with nothing other than their tentacles. Serve the squid hot with White Rice (page 186) or wedges of fried bread. ▪ **Serves 4**

³/₄ cup olive oil

3 yellow onions, chopped

2 leeks, white part only, thinly sliced

1 clove garlic, minced

2 small tomatoes, peeled and chopped

1 flat-leaf parsley sprig

24 baby squid, cleaned and stuffed with their own tentacles (page 196)

Salt

2 tablespoons squid ink

In a large sauté pan, heat the olive oil over medium heat. Add the onions, leeks, garlic, tomatoes, and parsley and sauté, stirring frequently with a wooden spoon or spatula, for about 10 minutes, or until the vegetables are soft.

Add half of the squid, arranging them in a single layer. Season the squid with salt and cook, turning once, for about 5 minutes on each side, or until the squid turn opaque. Using tongs, gently lift the squid from the pan and transfer to a large sieve or colander, placing them with the opening downward to drain any remaining liquid. Reserve the vegetables in the pan. Cook the remaining squid in the same way and transfer to the sieve.

Add the squid ink to the vegetables, mix well, increase the heat to high, and boil, stirring constantly to blend the ink with the vegetables, for about 5 minutes, or until fully incorporated. Pass the contents of the pan through a food mill fitted with the medium blade, and then process in a blender or food processor until the sauce is smooth.

Arrange the drained squid in a *cazuela* (page 51) and cover them with the sauce. Place over medium-high heat and cook for 2 to 3 minutes, or until well blended. Serve immediately.

:: CHAPTER 10 ::

Poultry, Meats, and Game

SPANISH COOKS READILY draw on a broad palette of poultry, meats, and game for the everyday table, just as their ancestors have for centuries. Chickens and stewing hens (the latter older, larger birds known as *gallinas* that are becoming ever-more rare these days) are prepared all over Spain. Roasted chickens are regularly served in every corner of the country, but other dishes, such as the pepper-rich *pollo al chilindrón* of Navarra and the saffron-tinted *escabeche de pollo* of Extremadura, a Christmas tradition, have strong regional moorings. Rabbit is also popular, prepared either simply with a sauce, or as an ingredient in one of the many rice dishes of Levante.

Pork shows its grandeur in *cochinillo asado* (page 249), suckling pig traditionally seasoned with nothing more than salt and sometimes a little garlic and roasted in a wood-burning oven. No other pork roast can compete with its savor. Baby lamb (ideally the Churra breed) and baby goat are also roasted in old-fashioned vaulted ovens, and every village in northern and southern Castile boasts at least one place that specializes in roasting all of these exquisite meats.

A traveler in Spain will also discover pork simmered in milk in Murcia, combined with New World corn in the Canary Islands, and preserved in various ways, including the *lomo de orza* of Andalusia, in which pork is cooked with seasonings and then buried in lard in an earthenware crock. Other conserved meats are common as well, such as the *cecina* of León, thin strips of beef that are salted and smoked and then air dried, and the famed *lacón*, salted pork, of Galicia. In the past, Castilian herdsmen typically packed this preserved specialty for sustenance on long cattle drives.

Cattlemen in Castile and Galicia raise the best beef in Spain, and both regions claim a number of first-rate breeds grazing on local pasturelands. Spaniards everywhere are quick to order grilled beef steaks from these local producers, especially in Basque *asadores*, or steakhouses, where diners invariably find them cooked to perfection. Sometimes these quickly cooked cuts are dressed up with a sauce, such as in the Asturian *solomillo de buey con salsa de Cabrales*, filets mignons topped with a creamy blue cheese sauce.

Galicians and Castilians are great hunters as well, as reflected in such signature Castilian dishes as *galianos*, which combines rabbit, hare, partridge, and shards of unleavened bread. But so, too, are many Andalusians, who enjoy *carne de monte*, venison cooked in wine and vinegar, and Aragonese, who marry venison with pine nuts and raisins in a tasty ragout.

Spaniards are also universal in their appreciation of such variety meats as kidney, heart, liver, tongue, and trotters, although Madrid residents are arguably their greatest champions. Sometimes eschewed in the past by the rich but always on the tables of the poor, such meats are now eaten by everyone in Spain—further proof of the inclusive palette of the Spanish cook.

La Boqueria market, Barcelona

::
237

ABOVE, FROM LEFT TO RIGHT: *Chorizo; grazing sheep in the Deva valley, Cantabria; cured meat at the Boqueria market, Barcelona*

GALLINA EN PEPITORIA ::
Braised Hen in Almond Sauce :: (*Aragón*)

This dish has its origins in Aragón and in neighboring Navarra, though it is highly valued in other parts of the country as well. Most people serve it on festive occasions, but I don't wait for a special day, since it is both easy to make and delicious, especially with wedges of fried bread served alongside.

In Spain, we use a young stewing hen for this dish. But in the United States, young, relatively small stewing hens are not readily available, and the older birds that are sold tend to be tough and require considerably longer cooking than is usual for this recipe. I have found that a free-range chicken is an excellent substitute. :: **Serves 6**

1 (3-pound) young stewing hen or chicken,
    cut into small pieces

Salt

All-purpose flour for coating

$^1/_2$ cup olive oil

1 yellow onion, finely chopped

1 clove garlic, peeled but left whole

1 bay leaf

2 tablespoons pine nuts

Pinch of saffron threads

10 almonds, blanched

1 tablespoon chopped fresh flat-leaf parsley

$^1/_2$ cup dry white wine

2 cups Chicken Stock (page 304) or water

2 hard-boiled eggs, peeled

2 thin slices jamón serrano or other dry-cured ham,
    minced

Season the chicken pieces with salt. Spread a little flour in a shallow dish and coat the chicken pieces evenly on all sides, shaking off any excess.

In a large skillet, heat the olive oil over medium heat. Working in batches if necessary, fry the chicken pieces, turning often, for 5 minutes, or until lightly golden on all sides. Using a slotted spoon, transfer the chicken pieces to a large *cazeula* (page 51), arranging them evenly over the bottom, and set aside. Reserve the oil in the skillet.

Return the skillet to medium heat and add the onion, garlic, and bay leaf. Sauté, stirring often, for 15 minutes, or until the onion begins to brown. Add the pine nuts and saffron, stir several times to mix well with the onion mixture, and cook for 1 minute to blend the flavors. Using a slotted spoon, transfer the contents of the skillet to a mortar or blender. Reserve the oil in the skillet.

Add the almonds, parsley, and a little salt to the mortar or blender and pound or process until a paste forms. Set the paste aside.

Pour the oil from the skillet evenly over the top of the chicken in the *cazuela*. Then distribute the almond paste evenly over the chicken and add the wine and stock. Stir to mix the ingredients, so the flavors blend, and then place over high heat. Bring to a boil and cook for 5 minutes. Decrease the heat to low and cook slowly, uncovered, for $1^1/_4$ to $1^1/_2$ hours, or until the chicken is very tender and the flavors of the sauce are fully blended.

Remove the *cazuela* from the heat. Halve the hard-boiled eggs and separate the yolks from the whites. Mash the yolks with a fork, add to the *cazuela*, and stir to distribute evenly. Finely chop the whites, sprinkle on top, along with the *jamón serrano*, and serve immediately.

POLLO AL CHILINDRÓN ▪
Chicken Braised with Red Peppers ▪
(Aragón)

In Spain, La Ribera is the area between Navarra and Aragón where the Ebro River flows, creating fertile lowlands that are cultivated with some of the country's best vegetables. This productive region is where *chilindrones*, everyday preparations of chicken or lamb braised in a mixture of peppers, tomatoes, *jámon serrano*, onion, and garlic, are among the most popular dishes. ▪ **Serves 4**

1 chicken, about 3¹/2 pounds, cut into small pieces

Salt

6 tablespoons olive oil

2 (¹/4-inch-thick) slices jamón serrano or other dry-cured ham, about 6 ounces total weight, cut into ¹/4-inch dice

2 cloves garlic, finely chopped

1 yellow onion, finely chopped

3 red bell peppers, seeded and cut into narrow strips

3 tomatoes, halved crosswise, grated on the large holes of a handheld grater, and skins discarded

5 black peppercorns

¹/2 cup dry white wine (optional)

1 tablespoon chopped fresh flat-leaf parsley

Season the chicken pieces with salt. In a large skillet, heat the olive oil over high heat. Working in batches if necessary, add the chicken pieces and fry, turning as needed, for 5 to 10 minutes, or until golden on all sides. Add the *jamón serrano*, mix well, and sauté briefly. Using a slotted spoon, transfer the chicken and ham to a large *cazuela* (page 51). Reserve the oil in the skillet.

Return the skillet to medium heat. Add the garlic, onion, and bell peppers and sauté, stirring occasionally, for about 15 minutes, or until the onion and peppers have softened. Transfer to the *cazuela* holding the chicken.

Add the tomatoes, peppercorns, and wine to the *cazuela*, place over medium-low heat, and cook uncovered, stirring occasionally, for 20 to 30 minutes, or until the chicken is tender. Remove from the heat, sprinkle with the parsley, and serve immediately.

POLLO EN ESCABECHE ▪
Chicken Marinated in Vinegar ▪
(Castilla–La Mancha)

Cooking chicken this way is ideal for the summer, when you want to prepare a dish ahead of time. It is a simplified version of the traditional *escabeche* (page 73), and the process couldn't be easier. You can keep this dish refrigerated for a few days and then serve it cold or at room temperature. A green salad is a good accompaniment. ▪ **Serves 6**

¹/2 chicken, about 2 pounds, cut into 1- to 2-inch pieces

Salt

1 yellow onion, cut into thin rings

1 clove garlic, minced

2 bay leaves

10 black peppercorns

¹/4 cup red wine vinegar or sherry vinegar

³/4 cup olive oil

Season the chicken pieces with salt and place them in a bowl. Add the onion, garlic, bay leaves, and peppercorns and mix well. Add the vinegar and olive oil, stir until all the ingredients are evenly distributed, cover, and refrigerate for at least 2 hours or up to 24 hours.

Transfer the contents of the bowl to a deep skillet or a wide saucepan and bring to a boil over high heat. Decrease the heat to medium and simmer for 10 minutes, or until the chicken is tender.

Remove from the heat and let cool. Serve at room temperature, or cover and refrigerate in the sauce and serve cold.

ESCABECHE DE POLLO DE NAVIDAD ▪ Christmas Chicken ▪ (*Extremadura*)

This unusual *escabeche* recipe is prepared in Extremaduran households for Christmas Eve. Although several steps are involved, the recipe is not difficult, and its extraordinary flavor is worth the preparation time. Cilantro is rarely used in Spain except in the kitchens of the Canary Islands, but in this dish it is mandatory, according to my friend Antonio Linares, who shared his mother's recipe with me. ▪ **Serves 4**

1 (3-pound) chicken, cut into small pieces

Salt

5 cloves garlic, peeled but left whole

2 bay leaves

1/2 cup olive oil

1 slice day-old country-style bread

Pinch of saffron threads

1 egg yolk

2 blanched almonds

2 cilantro sprigs

All-purpose flour for coating

2 whole eggs

Grated zest of 1 orange

Season the chicken with salt and place in a large saucepan. Add 2 of the garlic cloves, 1 of the bay leaves, and water to cover and bring to a boil. As soon as the boil is reached, decrease the heat to medium-low and cook for 15 minutes. Using a slotted spoon, remove the chicken from the pan and set aside. Measure out 2 cups of the cooking liquid and set aside. Discard the remaining liquid.

In a skillet, heat 3 tablespoons of the olive oil over high heat. When the oil is hot, add the bread and fry for 1 minute or so on each side, or until lightly golden. Transfer the bread to a mortar. Add the remaining 3 garlic cloves to the same oil over high heat and fry, turning as need, for about 5 minutes, or until golden on all sides. Transfer to the mortar. Add the remaining bay leaf to the mortar and pound the mixture together with a pestle until a paste forms. Add the saffron, egg yolk, almonds, cilantro, and 1/2 cup of the reserved cooking liquid and pound and stir until uniformly blended. Set aside.

Spread a little flour in a shallow bowl. In a second shallow bowl, break the 2 eggs and beat lightly with a fork until blended. One piece at a time, roll the chicken pieces in the flour, coating evenly and shaking off any excess. Then roll the chicken pieces in the beaten egg, again coating evenly and allowing the excess to drip off.

In a large skillet, heat the remaining 5 tablespoons olive oil over high heat. Working in batches if necessary, add the chicken and fry, turning as needed, for about 5 minutes, or until golden brown on all sides. Transfer the chicken to a large *cazuela* (page 51).

Add the paste from the mortar to the *cazuela* and mix well. Pour in the remaining 1 1/2 cups cooking liquid and add half of the orange zest. Place over medium heat and bring slowly to a boil. Decrease the heat to medium-low and simmer, uncovered, for about 10 minutes, or until the chicken is tender. Remove from the heat, let the chicken cool to room temperature in the liquid, and then cover and refrigerate for several hours.

Remove from the refrigerator and bring to room temperature. Serve the chicken with the sauce, sprinkled with the remaining orange zest.

POLLO A LA ZAMORANA ::
Chicken with Peppers and Tomatoes ::
(Castilla y León)

In Zamora, known for its lovely Romanesque churches and its elegant *parador* that was once a fifteenth-century castle, this recipe is usually made with a young rooster, but I prefer to make it with a free-range chicken. To save time, ask your butcher to cut the chicken into small pieces. Serve with White Rice (page 186) or *patatas fritas* (Fiery Potatoes, page 64, prepared without the sauce). :: **Serves 4**

1 chicken, about 3 pounds, cut into small pieces

Salt

Freshly ground black pepper

2 tablespoons all-purpose flour

5 tablespoons olive oil

1 yellow onion, finely chopped

2 carrots, peeled and thinly sliced

1 red bell pepper, seeded and coarsely chopped

1 green bell pepper, seeded and coarsely chopped

2 tomatoes, finely chopped

6 blanched almonds

3 cloves garlic, peeled but left whole

1 thin slice day-old country-style bread

$1/2$ teaspoon saffron threads

1 bay leaf

$1/2$ cup white wine

Season the chicken pieces with salt and pepper. Spread the flour in a shallow dish. One at a time, roll the chicken pieces in the flour to coat lightly and evenly, shaking off any excess.

In a large skillet, heat 3 tablespoons of the olive oil over high heat. Working in batches if necessary, add the chicken pieces and fry, turning as needed, for 5 to 10 minutes, or until golden on all sides. Using a slotted spoon or tongs, transfer to a large *cazuela* (page 51).

Add 1 tablespoon of the olive oil to the oil remaining in the skillet and return to medium heat. Add the onion, carrots, bell peppers, and tomatoes and cook, stirring occasionally, for about 10 minutes, or until the vegetables have softened. Transfer the vegetables to the *cazuela* holding the chicken.

In a small skillet, heat the remaining 1 tablespoon olive oil over medium heat. Add the almonds, garlic, and bread slice and fry, stirring the almonds and garlic often and turning the bread as needed, for about 5 minutes, or until the bread and garlic are golden. Transfer the contents of the skillet to a mortar and add the saffron threads. With a pestle, pound the ingredients until a paste forms. Transfer the paste to the *cazuela* holding the chicken and vegetables.

Add the bay leaf and wine to the *cazuela*, mix all the ingredients well, and place over medium heat. Cook for 5 minutes, decrease the heat to low, cover, and cook slowly for about 1 hour, or until the chicken is tender.

Remove the *cazuela* from the heat. If you prefer a smoother-textured sauce, using the slotted spoon, transfer the chicken to a plate and keep warm, and then pass the contents of the *cazuela* through a food mill fitted with the medium plate. Return the sauce and chicken to the *cazuela* and heat through over medium heat if necessary. Serve hot.

PATO CON PERAS ::
Roasted Duck with Pears :: *(Catalonia)*

Cardona, a medieval town close to Barcelona, is home to an amazing ninth-century castle that sits on a hilltop, dominating the local landscape. Luckily, Spain's state-owned hotel chain, Paradores, has renovated and modified the large castle, transforming it into a comfortable hotel. A visit to this magnificent place, which with its mazelike corridors is more like a feudal home than a hotel, will take you back centuries. The hostelry's dining room serves this memorable duck with pears, a classic of Catalan cuisine. :: **Serves 4**

2 (3-pound) ducks

Salt

Freshly ground black pepper

1 tablespoon duck fat or lard, at room temperature

2 cups Chicken Stock (page 304)

3 pears, peeled, halved, and cored

10 cloves garlic, minced

2 yellow onions, chopped

2 carrots, peeled and sliced

1 leek, white part only, sliced

1 tablespoon chopped fresh flat-leaf parsley

1 thyme sprig

1 tablespoon all-purpose flour

2 tomatoes, halved crosswise, grated on the large holes of a handheld grater, and skins discarded

$^1/_2$ cup dry sherry

Preheat the oven to 450°F.

Rinse the ducks inside and out and pat dry with paper towels. Season the ducks with salt and pepper and then rub the outside of each bird with the duck fat. Place the ducks, breast side up, in a roasting pan and roast for about 1 hour, or until golden brown. Transfer the ducks to a cutting board. Reserve the juices in the pan.

Meanwhile, in a saucepan, bring the stock to a boil over high heat. Add the pears and parboil for 10 minutes. Remove from the heat and set the pears aside in the stock.

Measure out $^1/_4$ cup of the duck juices, add to a large *cazuela* (page 51), and place over medium heat. Discard the remaining duck juices. Add the garlic, onions, carrots, leek, parsley, and thyme and cook, stirring occasionally, for about 30 minutes, or until the vegetables have softened and turned golden. Add the flour and stir to incorporate. Add the tomatoes and sherry and cook for 5 minutes longer. Remove and discard the thyme sprig.

Quarter the ducks, add them to the *cazuela*, and stir with a wooden spoon to mix the ingredients well. Remove the pear halves from the stock, cut each half into 4 wedges, and add the wedges to the *cazuela* along with the stock. Place the *cazuela* over low heat and heat for about 10 minutes, or until all the ingredients are hot.

Using a slotted utensil or tongs, transfer the duck pieces and pears to a warmed serving platter. Pass the contents of the *cazuela* through a food mill fitted with the medium plate held over a bowl. Spoon the sauce over the duck and serve hot.

ESCALDUMS ▪ Turkey Stew ▪
(Balearic Islands)

Turkeys on the Balearic Islands, and on the mainland, are much smaller than their American cousins. This stew is also delicious prepared with a chicken. An optional but common practice is to add some *albóndigas* (page 80) and sautéed mushrooms during the last several minutes of cooking. This is an especially good idea if you are feeding a crowd. ▪ **Serves 6**

4 pounds turkey breast or leg, cut into small pieces

Salt

Freshly ground black pepper

$1/2$ cup olive oil

1 head garlic, left whole

2 yellow onions, finely chopped

2 tomatoes, peeled and diced

3 tablespoons brandy

1 bay leaf

1 thyme sprig or 1 teaspoon dried thyme

$1/2$ cup blanched almonds or pine nuts

Season the turkey pieces with salt and pepper. In a large *cazuela* (page 51), heat the olive oil over medium heat. Working in batches if necessary, add the turkey pieces and fry, turning as needed, for 5 to 10 minutes, or until golden brown on all sides. Using a slotted spoon or tongs, transfer the turkey pieces to a plate and set aside. Reserve the oil in the *cazuela*.

Return the *cazuela* to medium heat. Add the garlic, onions, and tomatoes, season with salt and pepper, and sauté for 15 minutes, or until the onions and tomatoes have softened. Add the brandy and cook for another 5 minutes, or until the brandy has evaporated and the vegetables are tender. Remove from the heat and remove and discard the garlic head. Pass the contents of the *cazuela* through a food mill fitted with the medium blade held over a bowl and set aside.

Return the turkey pieces to the *cazuela*, add water just to cover, and bring to a boil over high heat. Add the bay leaf, thyme, and the puréed sauce and decrease the heat to medium-low. Mix well and cook slowly, uncovered, for 1 to $1^{1}/_{2}$ hours, or until the turkey is tender.

In a mortar, crush the almonds with a pestle until finely ground. Add the nuts to the stew, mix well, and cook for 5 minutes to blend the flavors and thicken the sauce slightly. Serve hot.

La Boqueria market, Barcelona

CONEJO CON CASTAÑAS ::
Rabbit with Chestnuts :: (Aragón)

Aragón, known for its harsh climate of cold winters and hot summers, is also famous for its majestic mountain peaks and remote medieval villages. Both rabbits and chestnuts are abundant in this landscape, making this pairing a natural. Accompany the dish with wedges of fried country-style bread. :: **Serves 4**

1 pound chestnuts

1 (3- to 4-pound) rabbit, cut into small pieces

Salt

2 tablespoons all-purpose flour

1/4 cup olive oil

1 yellow onion, finely chopped

3 cloves garlic, finely chopped

1 tablespoon chopped fresh flat-leaf parsley

2 cups water

Using the tip of a sharp paring knife, score the flat side of each chestnut with an X, cutting through the hard outer shell. In a small saucepan, combine the chestnuts with water to cover, bring to a boil, and boil for 5 to 8 minutes, depending on the size of the nuts. Drain and, while still warm, peel away the hard, spiny outer shell and the softer inner light brown membrane of each nut. Set the nuts aside.

Season the rabbit pieces with salt. Spread the flour in a shallow dish. One at a time, roll the rabbit pieces in the flour to coat lightly and evenly, shaking off any excess.

In a large skillet, heat the olive oil over medium-high heat. Working in batches if necessary, add the rabbit pieces and fry, turning as needed, for 5 to 10 minutes, or until golden brown on all sides. Using a slotted spoon or tongs, transfer to a large *cazuela* (page 51). Reserve the oil in the skillet.

Return the skillet to medium heat. Add the onion, garlic, and parsley and sauté for 8 to 10 minutes, or until the onion begins to soften. Transfer the onion mixture to the *cazuela* holding the rabbit.

Add the water to the *cazuela*, place over high heat, and bring to a boil. Decrease the heat to medium and boil gently, uncovered, for 20 minutes, or until the rabbit is nearly tender. Add the chestnuts and continue cooking for 10 minutes longer, or until the chestnuts and rabbit are tender and the flavors are blended.

Serve hot directly from the *cazuela*.

CONEJO EN SALMOREJO ::
Rabbit in Spicy Vegetable Marinade ::
(Canary Islands)

This is a signature dish of the Canary Islands, and the marinade, or slight variations of it, is common in the local cooking. The word *salmorejo* can be confusing. Here, it refers to the marinade and has no relation to the delightful cold gazpacho from Córdoba also known as *salmorejo* (page 87), nor to the similarly spelled Aragonese *huevos en salmorrejo* (page 126), which brings together eggs, pork, and asparagus.

Start the recipe the day before you plan to serve it, as the rabbit needs to marinate for a full day. If you are not keen on rabbit, try this recipe with chicken, although it is exceptional with rabbit. Serve with Wrinkled Potatoes (page 121) and Spicy Red Mojo (page 309). :: **Serves 6**

6 cloves garlic, halved

2 yellow onions, each cut into 8 wedges

1 flat-leaf parsley sprig

1 cilantro sprig

1 thyme sprig

1 fresh hot red chile, cut crosswise into $1/2$-inch-wide slices, or 1 teaspoon hot red pepper flakes

1 cup red wine vinegar

1 cup plus 3 tablespoons olive oil

1 tablespoon sweet pimentón or paprika

3 bay leaves

1 teaspoon black peppercorns

2 small rabbits, about 2 pounds each, cut into small pieces

Salt

Freshly ground black pepper

Beef Stock (page 303), if needed

In a large bowl, combine the garlic, onions, parsley, cilantro, thyme, and chile and pour in the vinegar and 1 cup olive oil. Stir well, then add the *pimentón*, bay leaves, and peppercorns and stir again.

Season the rabbit pieces with salt and pepper and add to the marinade in the bowl. Mix well and add stock if needed to immerse the rabbit completely in liquid. Cover and refrigerate for 24 hours.

Lift the rabbit pieces from the marinade, reserving the marinade, and pat dry with paper towels. In a large sauté pan, heat the remaining 3 tablespoons olive oil over medium-high heat. Working in batches if necessary, add the rabbit pieces and fry, turning as needed, for 5 to 10 minutes, or until golden on all sides. Pour the marinade into the pan, mix well with the rabbit, decrease the heat to medium, and cook, uncovered, for about 20 minutes, or until the rabbit is tender.

Using a slotted spoon or tongs, transfer the rabbit pieces to a warmed serving platter. If you desire a smoother sauce, pass it through a food mill fitted with the medium plate held over a bowl. Spoon the sauce over the rabbit and serve at once.

COCHINILLO ASADO ▪
Roasted Suckling Pig ▪ *(Castilla y León)*

You'll find this dish served all over Spain, but it is typically Castilian. Segovia, famous for its Roman aqueduct, is also well known for its wonderful *cochinillos*, or "suckling pigs," which many local establishments specialize in roasting to perfection. Throughout Castile, most cities and even small villages also have restaurants that serve *cochinillos* to the delight of residents and tourists alike. One of my favorite places to go for this delicacy in Madrid is Restaurante Botín, whose owner is a true master of this roasting art.

In the United States, it can be difficult to find a pig the size of a typical *cochinillo*, which is only six to seven pounds. More readily available are pigs three to four times that size, destined for outdoor pig roasts. But a good butcher should be able to obtain a pig small enough to be roasted in the oven. The search is worth the trouble! The little pigs are easy to prepare and so tender that they practically fall apart when cooked, yielding succulent meat that can never be replicated with a larger pig. The tender, crispy skin, lined with a very thin layer of baby fat, is eaten like potato chips. I serve this dish with nothing more than a simple green salad. ▪

Serves 8

> 1 (6- to 7-pound) suckling pig
> Salt
> 2 cups water
> 1 clove garlic, thinly sliced
> 2 tablespoons lard or olive oil

Position 1 rack in the middle of the oven and a second rack in the upper third of the oven and preheat to 400°F.

Place the pig, back side up, on a cutting board. Using a heavy knife, cut it in half along the backbone, stopping just short of cutting all the way through, so that it will lie flat like an open book. Season the pig generously on both sides with salt. Place the pig, skin side down, in a large roasting pan and place on the middle rack in the oven. Roast the pig for 1 hour, adding 1/2 cup water to the pan every 15 minutes.

In a small bowl, mix together the garlic and the lard. After the pig has cooked for 1 hour, remove it from the oven and increase the oven heat to 450°F. Being careful not to burn yourself, turn the pig skin side up and rub it with the garlic and lard mixture. Return the pig to the top rack of the oven and roast for about 30 minutes longer, or until the skin is golden brown and crisp.

Remove the pig from the oven, then transfer the pig to a cutting board. Strain the pan juices through a fine-mesh sieve held over a small saucepan and heat gently on the stove top. Cut the pig into serving pieces and arrange on a warmed platter. Spoon the pan juices over the pig and serve immediately.

Baby suckling pigs at Madrid's Botín restaurant, founded in the 1720s

LOMO DE CERDO AL CARAMELO ▪▪
Pork Loin with Caramelized Milk ▪▪
(*Murcia*)

Spanish cooks regularly prepare simple fried pork cutlets or roast pork loin for supper. This dish, with its subtly sweet, velvety sauce, requires a little more effort, but you will be well rewarded. Serve with olive oil mashed potatoes. ▪▪ **Serves 8**

1 boneless pork loin, about 2 pounds, tied

$^1/_4$ cup olive oil, plus extra for rubbing on loin

Salt

Freshly ground black pepper

1 quart whole milk

1 cinnamon stick

Peel of 1 orange, removed in a single piece if possible

Peel of 1 lemon, removed in a single piece if possible

1 cup sugar

2 cups water

1 cup Syrup (page 316)

Trim the excess fat, if any, from the pork loin. Rub the loin with a little olive oil, coating it evenly, and season with salt and pepper. In a heavy saucepan large enough to accommodate the pork loin comfortably, heat the $^1/_4$ cup olive oil over high heat. Add the pork and fry, turning as needed, for 5 minutes, or until nicely browned on all sides. Decrease the heat to medium-low and add the milk, cinnamon stick, citrus peels, all but 2 tablespoons of the sugar, and the water. Cover and cook for about 1 hour, or until the pork is tender.

Meanwhile, in a small, heavy saucepan, bring the syrup to a boil over high heat. Add the remaining 2 tablespoons sugar and boil, without stirring, for 5 minutes, or until the syrup turns into a dark golden caramel sauce. Remove from the heat and set aside.

When the pork is ready, remove it from the pan and set aside on a plate. Using a slotted spoon, remove the citrus peels and cinnamon stick and discard.

Add the cooled caramel sauce to the liquid remaining in the saucepan, mix well, place over medium heat, and cook, stirring occasionally, for 20 minutes, or until it reduces and is pale brown. Remove from the heat and pass the sauce through a food mill fitted with the medium plate held over a small bowl.

Snip the strings, cut the pork into $^1/_2$-inch-thick slices, and arrange on a warmed platter. Spoon the sauce over the top and serve.

LOMO DE ORZA ::
Preserved Pork Loin :: (*Andalusia*)

An *orza* is a large earthenware, jarlike container with a round opening at the top. Traditionally, it has been used to preserve foods in lard, especially pork after the yearly *matanza*, or "slaughtering." The advent of refrigeration has made *orzas* nearly obsolete, but the wonderful flavor of this dish will make you want to return to the past. You can use an earthenware crock or similar container in the absence of a classic *orza*. And don't be concerned about the large amount of lard, as the bulk of it is used only to prevent spoilage. Ask your butcher for high-quality pork lard for the best result. :: **Serves 8**

2 pounds lard
1 boneless pork loin, about 2 pounds, cut into
   ¹/₂-inch-thick slices
Salt
Freshly ground black pepper
15 cloves garlic, peeled but left whole
2 thyme sprigs
4 bay leaves
1 tablespoon fresh or dried oregano leaves

In a large, deep skillet or sauté pan, heat 3 tablespoons of the lard over high heat. Lay the pork slices in the pan, season with salt and pepper, and fry, turning once or twice, for about 2 minutes total, or until browned on both sides. Add the remaining lard to the pan. When it melts, add the garlic, thyme, bay leaves, and oregano. The pork should be submerged in the lard. Decrease the heat to medium and cook the pork for 15 minutes, or until cooked through.

Remove the pan from the heat, let cool slightly, and transfer its contents to an earthenware crock. The meat must be fully covered by the lard, so arrange the slices as needed. Let stand until cool and the lard has solidified. Cover and store in a cool cellar or other cool area or in the refrigerator. The preserved pork will keep for up to several months.

To serve, remove as many pork slices as desired from the lard and heat them briefly, turning as needed, in a skillet over high heat. Serve hot.

FLAMENQUÍN :: Thin Pork Roll with
Jamón Serrano and Egg :: (*Andalusia*)

Flamenquines are typically served as a tapa, but I most often eat them as a light dinner main course at the home of friends in the Andalusian town of Andújar, which is surrounded by beautiful fields of sunflowers in full bloom in September. You can also make these rolls with beef instead of pork, and some people like to add slices of cheese. Whichever ingredients you choose, these rolls are unforgettable. :: **Serves 4**

8 (¹/₄-inch-thick) pork cutlets
Salt
8 thin slices jamón serrano or other dry-cured ham
1 cup fine dried bread bread crumbs
3 eggs
Olive oil for frying

One at a time, using a meat pounder, pound each pork cutlet until it is a rectangle measuring about 5 by 7 inches. Be careful not to let any holes form in the meat. Season lightly with salt (the *jamón serrano* is already salty, so don't add too much). Lay the pork rectangles flat on a work surface, and top each with 1 *jamón serrano* slice. Starting from a long side, roll up the ham-topped pork slices into cylinders about 1 inch in diameter. Pierce a toothpick along the seam of each roll to prevent it from unfolding during frying.

Spread the bread crumbs in a wide, shallow bowl. Break the eggs into a second wide, shallow bowl and beat lightly until blended. One at a time, coat the rolls evenly with the bread crumbs. Then dip each roll into the beaten eggs, again coating evenly. Finally, coat the rolls again with the bread crumbs.

Pour olive oil to a depth of 1 inch into a deep skillet or sauté pan and heat over high heat. When the oil is very hot but not yet smoking, add the rolls in batches and fry, turning often, for about 5 minutes, or until they are crisp and golden on all sides. Using tongs, transfer to paper towels to drain and keep warm in a low oven. Repeat with the remaining rolls.

Slice the rolls on the diagonal into ³/₄-inch-thick slices and arrange on a warmed platter. Serve immediately.

COCHINO CON MILLO ▪ Pork Roast with Corn ▪ (*Canary Islands*)

This recipe originated on the island of Lanzarote. It calls for *millo*, Canarian for "corn," evidence of the early influence of New World foods on this way station for the conquistadors. It also uses basil, which is unusual for Canarian cooking, despite the fact that it grows wild alongside the roads. Spareribs are delicious prepared this way, too; they need to cook for only about half the time. ▪ **Serves 8**

Pictured opposite

1 (2¹/₂-pound) bone-in pork loin or pork shoulder roast
Salt
Freshly ground black pepper
5 tablespoons olive oil
2 yellow onions, chopped
1¹/₂ cups water
4 ears corn
1 cup dry white wine
3 carrots, peeled and sliced
¹/₂ teaspoon black peppercorns
3 basil sprigs
Pinch of freshly grated nutmeg

Preheat the oven to 400°F. Season the pork with salt and pepper and brush with 2 tablespoons of the olive oil. In a skillet over high heat, brown the pork on all sides. Transfer the pork to a roasting pan large enough to accommodate the addition of the vegetables later. Roast for 45 minutes.

Meanwhile, in a skillet, heat the remaining olive oil over medium heat. Add the onions and sauté for about 10 minutes, or until lightly browned. Set aside.

In a wide saucepan, bring the water to a boil over high heat. Add the corn and boil for 10 minutes. Drain, reserving the cooking liquid. When the corn is cool enough to handle, cut crosswise into 2-inch-thick rounds. Set aside.

After the pork has been roasting for 45 minutes, pour the wine and the reserved corn cooking liquid over it. Add the sautéed onions, corn, carrots, peppercorns, and basil to the pan and season them lightly with nutmeg. Roast for 45 minutes longer, or until the pork and vegetables are tender.

Remove from the oven. Slice the roast and arrange on a warmed serving platter with the vegetables. Serve hot.

LACÓN CON GRELOS ▪ Boiled Ham with Greens ▪ (*Galicia*)

In Galicia, the meat used for this recipe is the lower portion of the front leg, or hock, and is salt cured. I prepare it with fresh hocks, and it is also delicious. *Grelos*, or turnip greens, are tender when young, usually during the winter, which is when this dish is normally eaten. Galician chorizo sausages, which are slightly hot, are a perfect partner to the ham and greens.

Start this recipe the day before you plan to serve it if you are using cured hocks, as they will need to soak for a day. ▪ **Serves 6**

3 pounds salt-cured or fresh ham hocks or fresh ham
    on the bone (in a single piece)
1 salt-cured or fresh pork ear (optional)
2 pounds turnip greens or kohlrabi greens, coarsely
    chopped
5 or 6 (3-ounce) chorizos
2 pounds boiling potatoes, peeled and cut into
    big chunks
1 tablespoon lard (optional)

If using cured hocks and cured pig ear, soak them in cold water to cover for 24 hours in the refrigerator, then drain. If using fresh hocks, fresh ham on the bone, or fresh pig ear, disregard this step.

In a stockpot, combine the hocks and the pork ear with water to cover and bring to a boil over high heat. Skim off any foam that forms on the surface, decrease the heat to medium-low, and cook for 2 hours, or until the meat begins to loosen from the bone. Add water if necessary to keep the meat covered with water at all times.

Lift the hocks and ear from the pot, reserving the liquid in the pot, and set the meat aside in a warm oven. Bring the liquid to a boil over high heat. Add the greens, decrease the heat to medium, and cook for 5 minutes. Add the chorizos, potatoes, and lard, if using, and cook for about 30 minutes, or until the potatoes are tender.

Drain the contents of the pot, discarding the liquid. Cut the meat from the hocks and the chorizos into small pieces and arrange them on a serving platter. Surround the meat and sausages with the potatoes and greens. Serve hot.

SOLOMILLO DE CERDO MUDÉJAR
▪ Pork Tenderloins with Dates and Walnuts ▪ (*Murcia*)

The term *mudéjar* is used for Muslims—and for their culture—who converted to Christendom during the Reconquista. The first *mudéjares* date back to the late eleventh century, when the Castilian king, Alfonso VI, expelled the Muslims from Toledo, allowing only converts to stay. Almost half a millennium later, in 1502, just ten years after the conclusion of the reconquest in Granada by the Catholic Kings, a royal decree ordered that every Muslim in the newly united country must convert or leave.

The use of pork in this dish illustrates the degree to which the *mudéjares* assimilated the culinary customs of their Christian neighbors. Accompany the tenderloins with mashed potatoes. ▪ **Serves 4**

2 pork tenderloins, about $3/4$ pound each

$1/4$ cup pitted dates

$1/4$ cup walnut halves

Salt

Freshly ground black pepper

6 tablespoons olive oil

2 tomatoes, diced

1 small carrot, peeled and cut into 1-inch-thick slices

$1/2$ celery stalk, diced

1 yellow onion, coarsely chopped

$1/2$ cup dry white wine

1 cup Beef Stock (page 303)

$1/2$ teaspoon dried thyme

$1/2$ teaspoon dried rosemary

1 teaspoon cornstarch dissolved in $1/4$ cup cold water (optional)

Preheat the oven to 350°F.

To butterfly each tenderloin, cut it in half horizontally, stopping just short of cutting all the way through. Open each tenderloin flat, cut side up, as if it were a book. Insert the dates, alternating with the walnuts, in the opening, forming a row. Close the "books" tightly, season with salt and pepper, and brush with the olive oil.

Place the stuffed tenderloins in a baking pan. Cover with the tomatoes, carrot, celery, onion, wine, and stock. Place in the oven and cook, carefully turning the tenderloins at the halfway point without allowing the stuffing to fall out, for about 20 minutes, or until tender. Using a wide spatula, lift the tenderloins from the pan and set aside on a plate; keep warm.

Transfer the contents of the baking pan to a saucepan and add the thyme and rosemary. If you like a thicker sauce, stir in the cornstarch mixture. Place over high heat and bring to a boil, stirring constantly. Boil for 5 minutes, remove from the heat, and then pass through a food mill fitted with the medium plate held over a bowl; keep warm.

Cut the tenderloins on the diagonal into $1^1/2$-inch-thick medallions and arrange on a warmed platter. Spoon the sauce over the tenderloin slices and serve immediately.

MENESTRA DE CORDERO ‣ Spring Lamb and Vegetable Stew ‣ (Navarra)

In Navarra in springtime, this colorful stew is a time-honored centerpiece of Sunday dinner. The vegetables are harvested from the rich soil along either side of the Ebro River, and though suckling lamb, also raised in the region, is the usual meat, the older, more widely available spring lamb is an excellent substitute. Serve with *patatas fritas* (Fiery Potatoes, page 64, prepared without the sauce). ‣ **Serves 6**

All-purpose flour as needed

3 pounds boneless spring lamb shoulder or leg, cut into 1-inch pieces

Salt

1 cup olive oil

2 yellow onions, finely chopped

1 cup water

3 tablespoons dry sherry

1/2 lemon

6 medium artichokes

6 Swiss chard stems

1 carrot, peeled and cut crosswise into 1-inch-thick slices

1/2 cup fresh or frozen shelled English peas

2 raw eggs

3 hard-boiled eggs, peeled and quartered

Spread a little flour in a shallow bowl. Season the lamb pieces with salt and then coat with the flour, shaking off any excess. In a large skillet, heat 1/2 cup of the olive oil over high heat. Working in batches, add the lamb and fry, turning often, for about 5 minutes, or until browned on all sides. Using a slotted spoon, transfer the lamb to a large *cazuela* (page 51). Reserve the oil in the skillet.

Return the skillet to high heat, add the onions, and sauté, stirring often, for about 5 minutes, or until lightly browned. Decrease the heat to medium, add 1 tablespoon flour, and stir until well mixed. Add the water and sherry, stir well, decrease the heat to medium-low, and cook uncovered, stirring occasionally, for about 20 minutes, or until the mixture thickens and turns brownish.

Pass the onion mixture through a food mill fitted with the medium plate held over a bowl, and then pour it over the lamb. Mix the lamb with the sauce, place over low heat, and cook uncovered, stirring frequently, for 1 hour, or until the lamb is tender.

Meanwhile, squeeze the juice from the lemon half into a bowl filled with water and set aside. Working with 1 artichoke at a time, and using a large, sharp knife, cut off the leaves of the artichoke where they meet the base and then cut off the stem flush with the bottom. Using a small, sharp-edged spoon, scoop out any fuzzy choke that remains, and then trim the bottom, cutting away the dark outer layer. Slip the artichoke bottom into the lemon water. Repeat with the remaining artichokes.

Bring a saucepan filled with salted water to a boil over high heat. Drain the artichoke bottoms, add to the water along with chard stems, and boil for about 30 minutes, or until the vegetables are tender. Meanwhile, bring another saucepan filled with salted water to a boil over high heat and add the carrot. After 5 to 7 minutes, add the peas and continue to boil for 8 to 10 minutes, or until the carrot and peas are tender. As each pan of vegetables is ready, drain the vegetables, pat dry, and set aside.

Spread more flour in another shallow dish. Break the raw eggs into yet another shallow dish and beat just until blended. One at a time, coat the artichoke bottoms and the Swiss chard stems with the flour on all sides, shaking off any excess, and then dip them into the beaten egg. As each one is ready, set aside on a plate or tray.

Rinse the skillet you used for browning the lamb, add the remaining 1/2 cup olive oil, and place over high heat. When the oil is hot, decrease the heat to medium and, working in batches if necessary, fry the artichoke bottoms, turning as needed, for about 2 minutes, or until evenly golden. Transfer to paper towels to drain. Add the Swiss chard stems to the same hot oil and fry, turning as needed, for about 2 minutes, or until evenly golden. Using the slotted spoon, transfer the chard stems to paper towels to drain.

When the lamb is ready, add the artichokes, chard stems, carrots, and peas to the *cazuela*, mix with the sauce, and cook for 2 minutes to heat through. Serve hot, garnished with the hard-boiled eggs.

PIERNA DE CORDERO ASADA CON MIEL Y NARANJA :: Roasted Leg of Lamb with Honey and Orange ::
(Balearic Islands)

Juan Torrens, chef and owner of the restaurant Es Baluard in Palma, on Majorca, is highly regarded and has represented the cuisine of the Balearic Islands in numerous gastronomic events in Spain and abroad. He roasted a leg of lamb, one of his favorite dishes, during my last visit to Majorca. I loved it, especially the final touch of an orange-and-honey glaze, which gives the roast a beautiful shiny finish and adds great flavor.

You will need to begin making the dish the night before you plan to serve it, as the lamb needs to sit overnight. Accompany it with roasted potatoes. ::
Serves 6

1 bone-in leg of lamb, about 4 pounds
Salt
Freshly ground black pepper
2 heaping tablespoons lard
1/3 cup olive oil
2 leeks, white part only, chopped
2 yellow onions, roughly chopped
1 tomato, roughly chopped
1/4 cup amontillado sherry
1/4 cup honey
1 cup Orange Syrup (page 316)

If necessary, trim any excess fat from the lamb leg. Rub the lamb generously with salt and pepper and with the lard. Cover and let rest overnight in the refrigerator.

Preheat the oven to 425°F.

Place a roasting pan large enough to hold the lamb leg over 2 burners on the stove top, turn the heat to high, and add the olive oil. Add the leeks, onions, and tomato and sauté, stirring often, for 10 minutes, or until browned. Push the vegetables to one side of the pan, add the lamb, and fry, turning as needed, for about 10 minutes, or until browned on all sides. Spread the vegetables over the bottom of the pan again, place the lamb on top, and pour the sherry over the lamb.

Place the roasting pan in the oven and roast for 30 minutes. Decrease the heat to 350°F and bake for 30 minutes longer, or until the lamb is tender.

Remove the roasting pan from the oven. Raise the oven temperature to 500°F. Lift the lamb from the pan and place it on a clean surface. Generously brush it with the honey and with the orange syrup. Return the lamb to the pan, return the pan to the oven, and cook for 10 minutes, or until the lamb is a shiny brown. Transfer the lamb to a platter and let rest for 10 minutes.

Meanwhile, pass the contents of the roasting pan through a food mill fitted with the medium plate held over a small saucepan and place over low heat to keep warm.

Carve the lamb, arrange on a warmed platter, and serve hot with the sauce.

FRITO MAJORQUÍN ■ Majorcan Lamb Liver with Vegetables ■ (Balearic Islands)

On Easter Sunday, this dish is on household menus all over Majorca. When it was still customary for families to slaughter a lamb for the Easter table, Majorcans would separate out the variety meats (mainly heart, kidneys, and liver) and fry them with vegetables. Nowadays, of course, these meats are most often purchased. I use only the liver because my children dislike the others. On a visit to Majorca, I had the opportunity to cook many local dishes with my friend Tina Read. As I helped her with the *frito*, I was surprised to see her using a cast-iron skillet with high, flared sides, similar to a wok but shallower and with a broader base. She explained that the pan and the *greixonera*, a clay casserole equivalent to the *cazuela* of other regions but much deeper, are indispensable tools in a Majorcan kitchen.

You can serve this dish as a *plato único*, that is, not preceded by a first course, or it can follow a first course.

■ Serves 6

1/2 lemon

4 small or 2 medium artichokes

1 cup olive oil

1 pound lamb liver, cut into 1/2-inch-wide strips

Salt

Freshly ground black pepper

3 cloves garlic, unpeeled

1 teaspoon hot red pepper flakes

3 tablespoons chopped fresh fennel leaves, plus 1 fennel sprig

3 bunches scallions, white part only, thinly sliced

2 cups fresh or frozen shelled English peas

1 red bell pepper, seeded and cut into pea-sized pieces

1 cup small cauliflower florets

1 cup shelled tender, young fava beans (optional)

2 bay leaves

6 small boiling potatoes, about 1 1/2 pounds total weight, peeled and diced

Squeeze the juice from the lemon half into a bowl filled with water and set aside. Working with 1 artichoke at a time, peel off the tough, dark outer leaves until you reach the pale green leaves. Cut off the stem flush with the bottom, trim off the top one-third or so of the leaves, and then halve the artichoke lengthwise. Using a small, sharp knife or a spoon, remove and discard the fuzzy choke, and then cut the artichoke into pea-sized pieces. Slip the pieces into the lemon water. Repeat with the remaining artichoke(s).

In a deep skillet, heat 1/2 cup of the olive oil over medium heat. Season the liver strips with salt and pepper, add to the hot oil along with the garlic and the red pepper flakes, and fry, stirring constantly to prevent scorching, for about 10 minutes, or until browned and just cooked through. Remove from the heat and, using a slotted spoon, transfer the liver to the bottom of a *greixonera* or other deep flameproof earthenware vessel or a deep skillet. (Or, use a baking dish if you will be reheating the assembled *frito* in the oven.) Remove and discard the garlic from the skillet but reserve the oil. Sprinkle the liver with 1 tablespoon of the chopped fennel leaves.

Drain the artichokes and pat dry. Return the skillet to medium heat and add the artichokes, scallions, peas, bell pepper, cauliflower, fava beans, if using, and bay leaves. Fry the vegetables, turning often and seasoning with salt and pepper, for 15 minutes, or until tender. Using the slotted spoon, transfer the vegetables to the *greixonera*, placing them on top of the liver. Sprinkle 1 tablespoon of the chopped fennel leaves over the vegetables.

Add the remaining 1/2 cup olive oil to the skillet and place over medium heat. Add the potatoes and fry, turning often, for 15 minutes, or until golden and tender. Using the slotted spoon, transfer the potatoes to the *greixonera*. Sprinkle with the remaining 1 tablespoon chopped fennel leaves.

Using the fennel sprig, mix the different layers together to blend the flavors. If necessary, reheat on the stove top over medium heat or in a 350°F oven until hot, and then serve.

SOLOMILLO DE BUEY CON SALSA DE CABRALES ▪ Filet Mignon with Cabrales Sauce ▪ (Asturias)

More than two dozen distinct types of cheese are made in Asturias, among them two deservedly celebrated blues, Cabrales and Valdeón. Either one can be used for this quick but elegant beef dish. These and many more extraordinary cheeses from Spain are available in the United States, where the opening of Artisanal, a cheese sanctuary on the west side of Manhattan, has given the concept of cheese tasting an entirely new meaning. It is an impressive resource, making nearly any imaginable cheese accessible to anyone through its online store (see Sources).

When preparing this dish, I break the golden rule of salting steaks only after frying or grilling because here I need the released meat juices for the sauce. Serve the filets mignons with mashed potatoes. ▪ **Serves 4**

4 (10-ounce) filets mignons

Salt

3 tablespoons olive oil

$^1/_4$ pound Cabrales, Valdeón, or other blue cheese, mashed with a fork

$^3/_4$ cup heavy cream

Season the filets mignons on both sides with salt. Have ready 4 warmed dinner plates.

In a large skillet, heat the olive oil over high heat. Add the filets mignons and cook for about 1 minute on each side for rare, or longer if you prefer. Transfer the steaks to the warmed plates and keep warm. Reserve the oil and juices in the skillet.

Return the skillet to medium heat, add the cheese, and stir for 2 minutes, or until the cheese begins to soften and blend with the juices. Add the heavy cream and whisk it into the cheese. Increase the heat to high and cook, stirring constantly, for 2 to 3 minutes, or until the sauce turns golden brown and thickens.

Spoon the pan sauce over the steaks and serve.

A meat stall in Zaragoza's mercado central *that specializes in* toro *meat*

PIMIENTOS DEL PIQUILLOS RELLENOS DE CARNE ▪ Piquillo Peppers Stuffed with Ground Meats ▪ (La Rioja)

Vegetables don't care about territorial borders, and even if *piquillo* peppers (page 47) are considered a Navarran specialty, neighbors next door in La Rioja claim some rights over the celebrated peppers. Here, they are stuffed in the manner of Logroño, the capital of the region and a good starting point for visiting a number of excellent nearby wine cellars. Begin the recipe the night before serving to allow the meat to marinate. ▪ Serves 4

3 cloves garlic, peeled but left whole

1 tablespoon chopped fresh flat-leaf parsley

2 tablespoons water

$1/2$ pound ground veal

$1/2$ pound lean ground pork

Salt

1 cup olive oil

1 yellow onion, grated

2 tablespoon finely chopped jamón serrano or other dry-cured ham

3 eggs

1 tablespoon fine dried bread crumbs

1 (10-ounce) jar preserved whole piquillo peppers (about 18 peppers)

1 cup all-purpose flour

2 tablespoons whole milk

In a mortar, pound together 2 of the garlic cloves, $1^1/2$ teaspoons of the parsley, and 1 tablespoon of the water until a paste forms. Place the veal and pork in a bowl, season well with salt, add the garlic paste, and mix well. Cover and refrigerate overnight.

In a skillet, heat $1/4$ cup of the olive oil over high heat. Add half of the grated onion and sauté for 5 minutes, or until shiny and tender. Add the veal and pork mixture, decrease the heat to medium, and cook, breaking up the meat with a wooden spoon and then stirring constantly, for 5 minutes, or until the meat starts to crumble a little.

Transfer to a bowl and let cool. Add the *jamón serrano*, 1 of the eggs, and the bread crumbs to the bowl. Mix well and reserve.

Drain the *piquillo* peppers in a sieve or colander placed over a bowl. Measure out $1/2$ cup of the brine and set aside.

In a small saucepan, heat $1/4$ cup of the olive oil over medium heat. Add the remaining grated onion and sauté for about 5 minutes, or until it starts to turn golden. Meanwhile, in a mortar, pound together the remaining garlic clove, $1^1/2$ teaspoons parsley, and 1 tablespoon water until a paste forms. Add the garlic paste to the onion in the saucepan and mix well. Add 1 teaspoon of the flour, stirring to incorporate with the onion. Add the pepper brine, increase the heat to high, and cook, stirring, for 5 minutes. Decrease the heat to low and cook the sauce for 10 minutes longer, or until thickened. Remove from the heat, let cool, and then pass through a food mill fitted with medium plate held over a large *cazuela* (page 51).

With a small spoon, carefully fill each pepper with the meat mixture, taking care not to tear the pepper by overfilling it. Close the opening of each pepper by gently folding the edges. Spread the remaining flour in a shallow bowl. In a bowl, combine the remaining 2 eggs and the milk and whisk them together lightly.

In a large skillet, heat the remaining $1/2$ cup olive oil over high heat. One a time, lay the peppers in the flour, coating them on both sides and shaking off any excess, and then dip into the beaten egg and set aside on a plate. When the oil is hot, add 5 or 6 peppers, decrease the heat to medium, and fry for 2 minutes on each side, or until browned. Using a slotted spoon, transfer the peppers to paper towels to drain. Fry the remaining peppers in the same way, always making sure the oil is hot again before adding the next batch.

Just before serving, place the peppers in the *cazuela* with the sauce, place over medium heat, and heat through. Serve hot.

RABO DE TORO MERIDIANA ⁂
Oxtails in Red Wine ⁂ (Andalusia)

La Meridiana is a spectacular restaurant in Marbella. Nestled in a tropical garden with beautiful flowers, a decorative Moorish-inspired pond with water lilies, and a forest of vegetation, it offers a spectacular backdrop for alfresco dining. The inside dining room is equally beautiful, and when I sit there with owner Paolo Ghirelli, a dear friend, I feel transported to the tales of *Thousand and One Nights*. Despite his Italian origin, Paolo presents Spanish cuisine of the highest quality—sophisticated and traditional dishes hand in hand. This oxtail dish is a classic of the kitchen. Serve with White Rice (page 186) for soaking up the wonderful sauce. ⁂ **Serves 4**

> **6 pounds oxtails, cut crosswise into 2- to 3-inch pieces**
> **Salt**
> **Freshly ground black pepper**
> **All-purpose flour for coating**
> **³/4 cup olive oil**
> **4 yellow onions, coarsely chopped**
> **1 leek, white part only, sliced crosswise**
> **2 cloves garlic, chopped**
> **3 carrots, peeled and sliced**
> **2 cups Beef Stock (page 303)**
> **3 cups dry red wine, preferably Rioja or Ribera del Duero**
> **1 tablespoon chopped fresh flat-leaf parsley**
> **2 tablespoons Tomato Sauce (page 311)**

Season the oxtail pieces with salt and pepper. Spread a little flour in a shallow bowl. One at a time, roll the oxtail pieces in the flour to coat on all sides, shaking off any excess. Set aside on a plate.

In a large, wide saucepan, heat the olive oil over high heat. Working in batches if necessary, add the oxtails and fry, turning as needed with tongs, for about 5 minutes, or until browned on all sides. If the oxtails have been fried in batches, return them all to the pan and add the onions, leek, garlic, and carrots and mix well. Cook over high heat, stirring occasionally, for 10 to 15 minutes, or until the onions begin to brown.

Decrease the heat to medium-low and add the stock, wine, parsley, and tomato sauce. Stir to mix all the ingredients, cover, and cook for about 2 hours, or until the oxtails are tender.

Using a slotted spoon or tongs, transfer the oxtails to a *cazuela* (page 51). Pass the contents of the saucepan through a food mill fitted with the medium plate held over a bowl, and spoon the sauce over the oxtails.

Place the *cazuela* over medium heat for 5 minutes to heat through and blend the flavors. Serve hot.

HÍGADO DE TERNERA ENCEBOLLADO ■ Calf Liver in Caramelized Onion ■ (Madrid)

Variety meats are a long-standing tradition of the Madrid table. Even now when they have gone out of fashion elsewhere and because a generally prosperous national economy has allowed most people to buy more expensive foods, there are still small taverns in old Madrid that specialize in these meats. This liver dish is particularly delicious because of the sweetness contributed by the onions and sherry. Serve it with crispy *patatas fritas* (Fiery Potatoes, page 64, prepared without the sauce). ■ **Serves 4**

1¹/2 pounds calf liver

Salt

¹/4 cup plus 3 tablespoons olive oil

3 yellow onions, thinly sliced crosswise

1 clove garlic, thinly sliced

¹/4 green bell pepper, seeded and thinly sliced

¹/4 cup sweet sherry

Chopped fresh flat-leaf parsley for garnish

Rinse the liver under cold running water and remove as much of the filmlike skin from the surface as you can. Pat dry with paper towels. Cut the liver into ¹/2-inch-wide strips, season with salt, and set aside.

In a large skillet, heat the ¹/4 cup olive oil over high heat. Add the onions, garlic, and bell pepper and sauté, stirring often, for about 5 minutes, or until the onions begin to brown. Decrease the heat to medium and cook, stirring often, for about 30 minutes, or until the onions brown and caramelize. Add the sherry, mix well, and cook for 5 minutes, or until the sherry nearly evaporates.

Just before the vegetables are ready, in another skillet, heat the remaining 3 tablespoons olive oil over high heat. When the oil is hot, add the liver strips and cook, gently stirring and turning them constantly, for 2 to 3 minutes, or until lightly browned and but still pale pink in the center.

Using a slotted spoon, transfer the liver to the skillet with the vegetables. Mix gently and cook for 1 minute over medium heat. Sprinkle with the parsley and serve hot.

PERDIZ ESCABECHADA ■ Partridge Marinated in Wine and Vinegar ■ (Castilla–La Mancha)

As you leave behind the famous plains in Spain and head south, you reach the Sierra Morena, which leads into neighboring Andalusia. This large, mountainous area is a haven for hunters, who come for the partridges, among other game. La Carolina, a town in the area, has a hotel and restaurant called La Perdiz, which is renowned for its partridge dishes, including the birds prepared *en escabeche* (page 73). This recipe echoes a dish served there. Some poultry dealers carry fresh partridges, or you can order them frozen by mail. ■ **Serves 6**

6 partridges, about ³/4 pound each

Salt

¹/2 cup olive oil

3 yellow onions, thinly sliced

2 carrots, peeled and thinly sliced

4 cloves garlic, halved

1 cup white wine vinegar

¹/2 cup dry white wine

¹/2 cup water

10 black peppercorns

1 teaspoon sweet pimentón or paprika

2 bay leaves

1 thyme sprig

Rinse the partridges inside and out and pat dry with paper towels. Season with salt and truss the birds, tying the legs to the bodies with kitchen string.

In a large *cazuela* (page 51), heat the olive oil over high heat. When the oil is hot, add the partridges and cook, turning as needed, for about 5 minutes, or until evenly browned on all sides. Add the onions, carrots, and garlic and fry with the birds for 5 minutes longer, or until the vegetables begin to soften. Add the vinegar, wine, water, peppercorns, *pimentón*, bay leaves, and thyme and bring to a boil. Decrease the heat to low and cook for 1 to 1¹/2 hours, or until the birds are tender.

Remove from the heat, let cool to room temperature, and serve. Or, cover and refrigerate and serve cold.

CARNE DE MONTE ▪▪
Venison Stew ▪▪ (*Andalusia*)

When I drive from Madrid to my house in Ronda, I always try to spend one night en route with Juan and Paqui Parras in Andújar. Nestled on the skirt of the sierra of the same name, this gorgeous village enamors every visitor. Juan and Paqui, who own the local radio station, Radio Andújar, always treat me with culinary surprises, such as this typical regional venison dish.

This area of Spain is famous for its *cotos de caza*, or areas reserved for hunting. *Carne de monte*, literally "meat from the mountain," is perfectly understood by the locals to mean venison will be on the table. Allow plenty of time to prepare this dish, as the venison needs to soak overnight. ▪▪ **Serves 8**

2 pounds venison loin or tenderloin, in one piece

Salt

3 small dried hot chiles, or 1 teaspoon hot
    red pepper flakes

Pinch of saffron threads

1$^1/_2$ tablespoons sweet pimentón or paprika

10 black peppercorns

4 cloves garlic, peeled but left whole

2 teaspoons dried oregano

$^1/_2$ cup red wine vinegar

$^1/_3$ cup olive oil

1 bay leaf

$^1/_3$ cup white wine

In a bowl, combine the venison with water to cover and refrigerate overnight. The next day, drain the meat, discarding the soaking water.

Season the venison generously with salt and place it in a saucepan. Fill the pan with water just to cover the venison and add the chiles, saffron, *pimentón*, and peppercorns.

In a mortar, pound the garlic with the oregano and a few drops of water until a paste forms. Add the garlic paste, vinegar, and olive oil to the saucepan. Bring to a boil over high heat. Decrease the heat to medium, cover, and cook for 1 hour, turning the venison every 10 minutes. After 1 hour, add the bay leaf and wine and continue to cook for 30 minutes longer, or until the meat is tender.

Lift the venison from the pan and transfer it to a cutting board. Cut the meat into 1-inch cubes and return them to the pan. Mix well with the sauce and cook over low heat for 10 minutes to blend the flavors. Serve hot.

GALIANOS ▪ Game and Bread Stew ▪
(Castilla–La Mancha)

Don Quixote and his sidekick, Sancho Panza, ate this dish centuries ago—at least that is what Cervantes tells us. *Galianos*, or *gazpachos manchegos*, as it is called in such neighboring regions as Albacete, Murcia, and "Castilian" Valencia, is a game stew to which an unleavened bread called *torta de pastor* is added at the end of cooking. (Despite the similarity, the use of the term *gazpachos* has nothing to do with gazpacho, the cold soup; rather, the plural form is unique to this game dish.) Although pita bread is not exactly the same as *torta*, it is similar enough for me to use it as an alternative. And if you cannot find hare and partridge, chicken and squab can be used instead. Local cooks, however, would never approve of anyone using lamb or beef. Make this dish when you are having a large group for dinner; it is both unusual and satisfying. ▪ **Serves 10**

1/2 **hare, about 2 pounds**

1 **rabbit, about 3 pounds**

1 **partridge, about** 3/4 **pound, quartered**

Salt

Freshly ground black pepper

3 **bay leaves**

2/3 **cup olive oil**

4 **cloves garlic, finely minced**

1/2 **green bell pepper or 1 green Italian sweet pepper, seeded and cut lengthwise into narrow strips**

1 **heaping tablespoon sweet pimentón or paprika**

2/3 **pound pita bread, about 6 rounds, or day-old soft lahvosh, lightly toasted**

1 **teaspoon dried oregano**

Cut the hare and rabbit into large pieces. Season the hare, rabbit, and partridge with salt and pepper. Put all the pieces in a large stockpot with water to cover by 2 inches, add the bay leaves, and bring to a boil over high heat, skimming off any foam that forms on the surface. Decrease the heat to medium-low and simmer gently uncovered, skimming as needed, for 2 hours, or until the meats are tender and start loosening from the bones. Add water if necessary to keep the meats covered with water at all times.

Using a wire skimmer, lift out the meats from the pot and set aside to cool. Pour the cooking liquid through a fine-mesh sieve into a clean pot and reserve. When the meats are cool, remove and discard the bones. Shred the meats into pieces about the size of prunes.

In a large *cazuela* (page 51), heat the olive oil over medium heat. Add the garlic and bell pepper and sauté for about 5 minutes, or until the pepper has softened. Add the *pimentón* and stir to mix well. Add 6 cups of the reserved cooking liquid and bring to a boil. Tear the bread into small pieces the size of postage stamps and add to the *cazuela*. Cook for 5 minutes over medium heat, or until much of the liquid has been absorbed, the bread has softened, and the mixture has thickened.

Add the reserved meats and the oregano and cook, stirring several times with a wooden spoon to mix the ingredients well, for 5 minutes longer to heat through and blend the flavors. When the dish is ready, it should be a little loose but not too soupy. Serve immediately in shallow soup plates.

View from Ronda, Andalusia

CHAPTER II

Desserts and Other Sweets
and Beverages

MANY OF SPAIN'S best-known desserts are smooth, creamy, rich custards—fashioned from the country's high-quality milk and eggs—such as flan, *crema catalana*, and *tocino de cielo*. The latter, along with crumbly, cookielike *polvorones*; various *yemas*, or egg-yolk confections; and other sweets, were once widely made by nuns, who sold their products to help maintain their convents. Many of the recipes relied heavily on egg yolks, which the nuns received free from winemakers who needed only the whites to clarify their sherries and red wines. Today, fewer religious orders sell these centuries-old delicacies, though some convents in cities and towns in Andalusia, Castilla y León, and elsewhere are keeping the tradition alive.

Of course, such classic tarts as the almond-flavored *técula mécula*, which dates to the early sixteenth century, and the mint-laced *flaó*, a specialty of Balearic cooks, rely on eggs and dairy as well, as do wonderfully rich ice creams and a variety of cheese desserts, including *greixonera de brossat* and *quesadas*—all of them satisfying finales to a meal. But this chapter also delivers a number of sweets that are not strictly desserts. The long, slender, crisp fritters known as churros are irresistible treats that never appear on a dessert menu, but are eaten for breakfast all over Spain. Majorcan *ensaimadas*, fluffy pastry coils

that are sometimes plain and sometimes filled with preserves or cream, are also enjoyed as the first meal of the day. Both the fritters and the pastries are eaten for *merienda*, the Spanish teatime, too, serving as perfect midafternoon pick-me-ups in anticipation of the long wait for Spain's legendary late dinner hour.

Andalusia is famous for its *mermelada de naranja acida*, yet another breakfast-table favorite. The marmalade, made from the region's bitter Seville oranges, is delicious spread on the day's first bread. In contrast, the popular, mildly floral-tasting preserve known as *carne de membrillo*, or quince paste, is typically served after dinner with cheese, with a slice of each placed together on a plate.

At the end of this chapter, you will discover a quartet of beverages, including the thick, rich hot chocolate into which Spaniards traditionally dunk their breakfast churros; two recipes for hot summer days, iced coffee and sangria; and the unusual *horchata de chufas*, made from a tuber cultivated primarily around Valencia. The latter, a creamy, ivory-hued drink, sometimes translated as "tiger nut milk," is reputedly good for you, promising extra energy, improved digestion, and high doses of potassium and iron—marrying good flavor and good health in a single tall, cool glass.

LEFT: *Galician Almond Cake (page 286)* PAGES 268–69, FROM LEFT TO RIGHT: *Ripe cherries at market; wedge of artisanal goat cheese, Cantabria; a strawberry growing in the black volcanic soil of Lanzarote (Canary Islands); the barrel room of La Gitana, producer of some of Spain's finest sherries*

FLAN ∷ Caramel Custard

This is the classic flan, which is as light and delicious as it is timeless. This basic recipe is also used to make flans of different flavors by substituting another liquid for part or all of the milk. For example, the best sweet oranges in Spain come from the Valencian Community and Murcia, and an orange flan, made from freshly squeezed juice, is popular there.

Because flan takes a while to cool, I usually prepare it early in the morning or on the previous evening. When making it for a large group, I find it practical to prepare a single large flan in a 5 by 9-inch mold and slice it for serving, rather than use individual cups. This recipe works well in the large mold and will bake in about the same amount of time. ∷ **Makes 12 servings**

1 recipe Caramelized Sugar Coating (page 316)

4 cups whole milk

2 strips lemon zest

1 cinnamon stick

5 whole eggs

2 egg yolks

1 cup granulated sugar

Preheat the oven to 300°F.

Prepare the caramelized sugar coating as directed and use it to coat the bottom and sides of 12 custard cups each $3^1/_2$ inches in diameter. Set aside.

In a saucepan, combine the milk, lemon zest, and cinnamon stick over high heat and bring to a boil. Immediately decrease the heat to low and simmer for 10 minutes to infuse the milk with the flavor of the seasonings. Remove from the heat and let cool.

In a bowl, combine the whole eggs, egg yolks, and granulated sugar and whisk until foamy. Pour the cooled milk through a fine-mesh sieve held over the egg mixture and whisk until well blended. Pour the mixture into the coated custard cups.

Arrange the custard cups, not touching, in a large, deep baking pan or roasting pan. Pull out the oven rack, put the baking pan on it, and pour boiling water to a depth of about 1 inch into the pan to create a water bath. Bake for about $1^1/_2$ hours, or until set when tested with a thin-bladed knife in the center. Carefully remove the water bath from the oven, and then carefully remove the custards from the water bath and set aside to cool completely.

You can cover and refrigerate the cooled custards and serve them cold, or you can serve them at room temperature. One at a time, run a knife around the inside of each cup to loosen the edges of the custard and then invert the custard onto a dessert plate.

A bakery in Zaragoza, Aragón

CREMA CATALANA ::
Catalonian Cream Custard :: *(Catalonia)*

Isidre, owner of the famous Ca L'Isidre restaurant in Barcelona, graciously toured me through La Boquería, the city's beautiful market hall. I couldn't have wished for a better guide; we had to stop at every single booth because Isidre is known and loved by everyone there. Among the large city markets in Spain, such as those in Madrid, Valencia, and San Sebastián, La Boquería is arguably the most striking. Just as impressive as the superior quality of the fresh produce, meats, dairy, fish, and shellfish—nearly everything you could want—is the careful, colorful way all the goods are displayed. Even if you are only looking and not buying, spending time in the market is always a wonderful experience.

After our tour, Isidre took me for a *cafelito* (what we affectionately call a little coffee) at El Turia, a nearby bar, where we were greeted by Nuria, the owner, who also joined us at a table. These two gave me the simplest recipe for *crema catalana* that I have ever come across. And it works perfectly. :: **Serves 6**

6 egg yolks

$^3/_4$ cup sugar, plus extra for topping

$2^1/_4$ cups whole milk

$1^1/_2$ teaspoons cornstarch

Zest of 1 lemon, cut into wide strips

1 cinnamon stick

In a bowl, using a whisk or handheld mixer, beat together the yolks and $^3/_4$ cup sugar until thoroughly mixed. Place a few spoonfuls of the milk in a small bowl or cup, add the cornstarch, and stir to dissolve. Add the diluted cornstarch and the remaining milk to the egg yolk mixture and mix until smooth.

Transfer the yolk-milk mixture to a saucepan, add the lemon zest and cinnamon stick, and bring just to a boil over medium heat, stirring constantly. Immediately remove the pan from the heat and stir the custard for 1 minute off the heat. Return the pan to medium heat and again bring the custard just to a boil while stirring constantly. Immediately remove the pan from the heat and stir for 1 minute off the heat. Repeat the same process a third and final time. If you dip the spoon into the custard at this point and then lift it out, the spoon should be nicely coated with the thick, smooth custard. Stir the custard a few more times and then distribute it evenly among 6 small, shallow ramekins. It will thicken further as it cools. Cover and refrigerate until chilled.

Sprinkle the tops of the chilled custards evenly with a coating of sugar and caramelize for 1 minute or so with a butane kitchen torch, or until the sugar is transformed into a thin, brittle golden brown topping. Serve immediately.

TOCINO DE CIELO ::
Rich Caramel Custard :: (*Andalusia*)

The literal translation of *tocino de cielo* is "fatback from heaven." I have asked myself and others about this unusual name and have come to the conclusion that the finished dish may indeed resemble a piece of fatback. When the custard is unmolded, the dark caramel that lined the dish becomes the top, reminding some people of the dark skin on fatback. This egg-yolk custard is very rich, so serve it in small portions. Accompany with ice cream and/or meringues, if desired. :: **Serves 6 to 8**

Caramelized Sugar Coating made with only
    6 tablespoons sugar (page 316)
$1/2$ cup granulated sugar
$1/2$ cup water
6 egg yolks

Prepare the caramelized sugar coating as directed, using only 6 tablespoons sugar, and use it to coat the bottom and sides of a 3 by 6-inch loaf pan with 2-inch sides. Set aside.

Preheat the oven to 400°F.

In a small, heavy saucepan, combine the granulated sugar and water, place over high heat, and bring to a boil, stirring to dissolve the sugar. Decrease the heat to medium-high and boil, stirring occasionally, for about 10 minutes, or until the syrup starts to thicken. Remove from the heat and let cool to lukewarm.

Put a teakettle of water on to boil. In a bowl, using a whisk or a handheld mixer, beat the egg yolks until well blended and pale yellow. Add the cooled syrup a little at a time, beating after each addition until fully incorporated. The mixture will be thick and shiny. Strain the mixture through a fine-mesh sieve held over the prepared loaf pan.

Cover the loaf pan with aluminum foil. To prepare a water bath, place the loaf pan in a baking pan or small roasting pan. Pour boiling water into the baking pan to reach halfway up the sides of the loaf pan. Carefully transfer to the oven and bake for 45 minutes, or until set when tested with a knife in the center. Turn the oven off and allow the custard to cool completely in the water bath with the oven door closed. This will take about 2 hours.

When cool, remove the loaf pan from the water bath and uncover the custard. Run a knife blade around the inside edge of the pan to loosen the sides of the custard. Invert a serving plate over the pan, invert the pan and plate together, and lift off the pan. Cut into small squares to serve.

TUPINAMBA ❚ Caramelized Meringue with Sweet Custard ❚ *(Cantabria)*

This funny-sounding dessert, found almost exclusively in the scenic village of Pedreña, in Cantabria, is Cuban in origin. It is part of the Spanish table because a significant wave of Cantabrians and neighboring Asturians migrated to Cuba in the early twentieth century. Many of them returned with riches along with the recipe for this dessert. Today it is common to see palm trees and other tropical vegetation in front of some houses in Cantabria, another echo of the Cuban connection. If you find yourself in the area and want to try an excellent example of this *tupinamba*, stop in at the restaurant attached to the Pedreña Golf Club, where you may also encounter famed Spanish golf guru Severiano Ballesteros, who lives nearby.

The luscious cold custard that is spooned into the center of the meringue is known as *natillas*. Creamy and soft, it also makes a good accompaniment to fruit desserts, tarts, and cakes, and the recipe is easily doubled. ❚

Serves 6

CUSTARD

2 cups heavy cream

1 cinnamon stick

1/2 vanilla bean, or 1/2 teaspoon vanilla extract

3 eggs

6 tablespoons sugar

1/4 teaspoon cornstarch

CARAMELIZED MERINGUE

Unsalted butter for preparing pan

6 egg whites, at room temperature

9 tablespoons sugar

To make the custard, in a heavy saucepan, combine the cream, cinnamon stick, and vanilla bean (if using vanilla extract, add later) and bring to a boil over medium-high heat, stirring constantly. Decrease the heat to low and cook, stirring occasionally, for 10 minutes to allow the flavors to blend. Set aside to cool, stirring occasionally to prevent a skin from forming.

In a bowl, combine the 3 eggs, 6 tablespoons sugar, and cornstarch and, using a whisk or a handheld mixer, beat until smooth. Add the cooled cream and mix well, being careful not to break the cinnamon stick.

Pour the cream mixture into a heatproof bowl that fits into the rim of a saucepan. Pour water to a depth of 2 to 3 inches into the saucepan and bring to a simmer. Rest the bowl in the pan rim (the water should not touch the bottom of the bowl) and cook the custard, stirring constantly with a wooden spoon, for about 30 minutes, or until it thickly coats the spoon. Remove from the heat and let cool; stir the custard occasionally as it cools, incorporating the vanilla extract, if using.

Pass the cooled custard through a fine-mesh sieve into a bowl, cover, and refrigerate for at least 2 hours, or until cold. You should have about 2 cups.

Preheat the oven to 400°F. Grease a tube pan about 10 inches in diameter with butter.

To make the caramelized meringue, in a bowl, using a whisk or a handheld mixer, beat the egg whites until foamy. Add 6 tablespoons of the sugar a little at a time, continuing to beat until all the sugar has been added and stiff peaks have formed.

Put a teakettle of water on to boil. Place the remaining 3 tablespoons sugar in a small saucepan, place over high heat, and heat without stirring. When the sugar dissolves and starts to turn golden, after about 3 minutes, immediately and carefully pour the caramelized sugar into the egg whites. Using a rubber spatula, fold the caramel into the egg whites until evenly mixed, being careful to deflate the whites as little as possible. Transfer the meringue to the prepared pan, spreading it evenly.

To prepare a water bath, place the tube pan in a baking pan or small roasting pan and add boiling water to a depth of 1 inch to the roasting pan. Bake for 7 minutes. The meringue will have set but will look essentially the same.

Carefully remove the tube pan from the water bath. Invert a large, round serving plate over the pan and, holding the pan and the plate, invert them together. Lift off the pan. Spoon the cold custard into the hole in the center of the meringue and serve immediately.

ARROZ CON LECHE ::
Creamy Rice Pudding :: (*Asturias*)

After a main course of *fabada asturiana* (page 168), it is almost mandatory to end the meal with *arroz con leche*, an equally typical Asturian dish. The milk in Asturias is known to be of the best in Spain, so it is no surprise that this rich milk dessert is a favorite there.

The best Spanish cooks take pride in the almost puréelike texture of their rice pudding, a result that is possible only if you have the patience to stir the slow-cooked mixture. I have seen Asturian friends sprinkle a thin coating of sugar over the surface of the finished creamy pudding and then caramelize it with a hot iron disk. If you wish to do as the Asturians do, I recommend using a more practical butane kitchen torch. Or skip this caramelizing step and simply stir in some heavy cream and add a sprinkle of cinnamon before serving. :: **Serves 10**

2¹/₂ quarts (10 cups) whole milk
2 cinnamon sticks
1 wide strip lemon zest
1 cup Spanish rice
³/₄ cup sugar, plus extra for topping
Ground cinnamon for dusting

In a large, heavy saucepan, combine the milk, cinnamon sticks, and lemon zest and bring to a boil over high heat. Add the rice, decrease the heat to medium-low, and cook, stirring gently and often with a wooden spoon, for 1¹/₂ hours, or until the rice kernels have swollen and are tender and the mixture is smooth.

Remove the cinnamon sticks and zest and discard. Sprinkle the sugar evenly over the rice and continue to cook over medium-low heat, stirring gently and constantly to prevent burning, for 30 minutes longer. This final 30 minutes of cooking and stirring will result in a very smooth and creamy pudding. Once you have added the sugar, the rice can burn easily, so you must stir constantly, always running the spoon over the bottom and into the corners of the pan. Remove from the heat.

My husband loves to snatch a serving of this creamy pudding when it is just off the stove, but I recommend serving it in small bowls at room temperature or cold. Sprinkle the tops of the rice pudding with sugar and caramelize for 30 seconds or so with a butane kitchen torch, or until the sugar is golden brown. Sprinkle with cinnamon before serving.

BIENMESABE CANARIO ::
Rich Almond Dessert :: (*Canary Islands*)

Bienmesabe is the name for two different desserts. This simple almond one is from the Canary Islands, while the other dessert is from Andalusia, where it is traditionally made by cloistered nuns in Antequera, in Malaga Province. It is a sponge cake to which custard, *cabello de ángel* (page 296), and ground almonds are added, and it is typically purchased from the nuns or from pastry shops, rather than homemade. To make the term even more confusing, *bienmesabe* is also the name of an Andalusian recipe for fried fish (page 68). :: **Serves 6**

2 cups finely ground almonds

1 cup water

3/4 cup sugar

4 egg yolks

2 tablespoons whole milk

2 tablespoons Malvasía wine or sweet sherry

Grated zest of 1 lemon

1 teaspoon ground cinnamon

In a dry skillet, toast the ground almonds over medium heat, stirring constantly, for about 5 minutes, or until golden. Transfer to a bowl and let cool.

In a small, heavy saucepan, combine the water and sugar and bring to a boil over high heat, stirring to dissolve the sugar. Decrease the heat to medium-low and simmer, without stirring, for about 20 minutes, or until a thick syrup forms. Decrease the heat to the lowest setting, add the ground almonds, and mix well. Cook for 1 minute and then remove from the heat.

In a bowl, combine the egg yolks and milk and beat with a fork or whisk until foamy. Slowly add the yolk mixture to the pan holding the almond mixture while stirring constantly. Then add the wine and lemon zest, stir well, and return the pan to medium heat. As soon as the mixture reaches a boil, stir well, and immediately remove from the heat.

Divide the mixture among bowls, or among martini glasses for a more elegant presentation, cover, and refrigerate until cold. Serve cold, dusted evenly with the cinnamon.

MOUSSE DE CHOCOLATE CON ACEITE DE OLIVA :: Chocolate Mousse with Olive Oil :: (*Madrid*)

My friend Gabriela Llamas is a cooking instructor and an editor at *Cocina Futuro* magazine. Years ago, she gave me this special recipe for a velvety, dairy-free, and delicious chocolate mousse. It is made with extra virgin oil, which blends beautifully with chocolate and intensifies its flavor. Orange segments, or fresh orange zest sprinkled on top, are perfect accompaniments. :: **Serves 10**

7 ounces semisweet chocolate

1/2 cup mild extra virgin olive oil, preferably Arbequina

4 eggs, separated

2/3 cup confectioners' sugar

1/3 cup brewed espresso, or 1 tablespoon instant coffee powder

2 tablespoons Cointreau

In a small, heavy saucepan, melt the chocolate over low heat, stirring occasionally. Remove from the heat and let cool to room temperature. Add the olive oil to the cooled chocolate and mix well.

In a bowl, combine the egg yolks and sugar and whisk until foamy. Add the espresso and Cointreau and whisk until well blended. Add the chocolate mixture and mix well with a rubber spatula.

In another bowl, using a whisk or a handheld mixer, beat the egg whites until they form stiff peaks. Scoop up about one-third of the egg whites and fold into the chocolate mixture with a rubber spatula. Repeat with half of the remaining egg whites, and then with the remaining egg whites just until no white streaks are visible. Transfer the mixture to a 10-inch round cake pan, cover, and place in the refrigerator for at least 8 hours, or until well chilled, or place in the freezer for at least 3 hours, or until frozen.

Remove the mousse from the refrigerator or freezer. If frozen, leave at room temperature until still quite cold but no longer hard. Serve the mousse cold, cut into wedges or shaped with 2 spoons into ovals that recall quenelles or croquettes.

LECHE FRITA ▪ Fried Milk

This is one of my favorite desserts. I grew up with it, but people who try it for the first time also love it. In Bilbao, we call it *tostadas de crema*; in the rest of Spain, it is known as *leche frita*. Although it calls for only a handful of basic ingredients, it takes time to make and can be a little tricky. First you must prepare a béchamel-like mixture, which is then cooled and cut into little squares that are coated with flour and egg and individually fried. If you don't have an 8 by 10-inch pan, a 9-inch square cake pan will work as well. ▪ **Makes 20 squares; serves 4**

Olive oil for preparing pan, plus $1/2$ cup

3 cups whole milk

$1/3$ cup all-purpose flour, plus extra for dusting

2 tablespoons cornstarch

2 cinnamon sticks

$2/3$ cup sugar, plus extra for sprinkling

2 eggs

Ground cinnamon for sprinkling

Brush an 8 by 10-inch pan with olive oil.

In a bowl, combine 1 cup of the milk, the $1/3$ cup flour, and the cornstarch. Using a whisk or a handheld mixer, beat until smooth. Set aside.

In a saucepan, combine the remaining 2 cups milk and the cinnamon sticks and bring to a boil over high heat. Immediately decrease the heat to low, add the $2/3$ cup sugar, and stir with a wooden spoon until the sugar is dissolved. Remove and discard the cinnamon sticks.

Add the milk-flour mixture to the saucepan holding the milk and cook over medium heat, stirring constantly, for about 20 minutes, or until creamy and smooth. Transfer the mixture to the prepared pan. It should fill the pan to a depth of about $1/2$ inch. Let the mixture stand for about 2 hours, or until cooled to room temperature, and then cover and refrigerate until cold.

Cut the custard into 2-inch squares. Spread a little flour in a shallow bowl. Break the eggs into a second shallow bowl and beat with a fork until blended.

In a large skillet, heat the $1/2$ cup olive oil over medium-high heat until almost smoking. While the oil heats, carefully coat each square on all sides with the flour, shaking off the excess, and then dip into the eggs. Working in batches, add the squares to the hot oil, immediately decrease the heat to medium, and fry, turning once, for 1 minute on each side, or until golden. Using a slotted spoon, transfer to paper towels to drain. Repeat with the remaining squares, always reheating the oil over medium-high heat between batches.

Serve the squares warm or at room temperature, sprinkled with the sugar and cinnamon.

CHURROS ▪ Breakfast Fritters

Sprinkled with sugar and dipped into thick hot chocolate, churros are what I dream about whenever I am flying over the Atlantic home to Spain. When the plane touches down in Madrid in the early morning, the first thing I often do is take a taxi to one of my favorite *churrerías* in the city, small shops devoted to making and serving churros and *porras*.

The dough is simple—only flour, water, and salt—but forming the churros is more complicated. The *churrera*, the device used to shape the dough, is similar to a cookie press or a rigid piping cylinder. It applies pressure to the dough, ensuring that the churros won't break apart when they are fried. The dough is extruded through an opening that measures about 3/4 inch in diameter, and as it falls into the hot oil, it is wound into a coil. In the absence of a *churrera*, you can use a cookie press with an opening of more or less the same size.

Porras, which are similar though larger and hollow, are practically impossible to make at home because the device used to shape them and the pan in which they are fried are too big and cumbersome for a home kitchen. Luckily, there are many *churrerías* all over Spain, and when there, I never miss a chance to visit one and have a freshly fried churro or *porra* with hot chocolate (page 299) or *café con leche*. But when I am away, this recipe is the next best thing. ▪ **Makes about 30 fritters**

3 cups water
1 teaspoon salt
2 tablespoons olive oil, plus extra for deep-frying
2 cups all-purpose flour
Sugar for sprinkling

In a saucepan, bring the water to a boil over high heat. Add the salt and the 2 tablespoons olive oil and mix well. Add the flour all at once and immediately remove the pan from the heat. Using a wooden spoon, promptly and vigorously mix the flour with the water until the dough is firm and free of all air bubbles. This will take about 5 minutes. Pack a *churrera* or cookie press with some of the dough.

Pour olive oil to a depth of 2 to 3 inches into a deep, heavy, wide pot and place over high heat. When the oil is almost smoking, begin to release the dough into the oil, moving in a circular motion to form it into a coil. Stop releasing the dough when you have completed several spirals. Do not fill the surface of the oil, or the temperature will drop and the dough will absorb the oil. Watch the dough closely; it will turn golden in just 1 minute. Using a wide skimmer or slotted spatula, transfer the coil to paper towels to drain. Proceed with the rest of the dough in the same manner, repacking the *churrera* as needed.

Using kitchen scissors, cut the coils into 6-inch-long segments. Sprinkle with the sugar and serve immediately.

PESTIÑOS ▪ Sweet Fritters ▪ (Andalusia)

No seas pestiño means "don't get on my nerves." But while making *pestiños* is not nerve-racking, you do need to pay attention when both mixing and frying. These crunchy fritters are popular in Andalusia, where cooks fry with passion.

Interestingly enough, the best *pestiños* I have ever eaten were in New York. My friend Chita, who had long lived in Argentina, prepared them for me on one of her visits to the city. She was originally from Granada, and she never forgot how to cook this delight. I always think of her when I make this recipe. ▪ **Makes 25 fritters**

³/₄ cup olive oil, plus extra for frying

Zest of 1 orange, cut into long, narrow strips

1 teaspoon sesame seeds, plus extra for sprinkling

¹/₂ teaspoon aniseeds

1 tablespoon unsalted butter

1 tablespoon lard

¹/₃ cup plus ¹/₄ cup water

6 tablespoons sweet white wine

¹/₂ teaspoon ground cinnamon

Pinch of salt

1 teaspoon grated lemon zest

2 cups all-purpose flour, plus extra for dusting

¹/₂ cup honey

To flavor the olive oil, in a skillet, heat the ³/₄ cup olive oil over high heat. Add the orange zest and fry for about 2 minutes, or until the zest begins to turn golden. Remove from the heat and let cool to room temperature. Strain the oil through a fine-mesh sieve placed over a heatproof bowl, discarding the zest. Stir in the 1 teaspoon sesame seeds and the aniseeds.

In a saucepan, combine the butter, lard, ¹/₃ cup water, and the wine and place over medium-low heat. When the fats have melted, add the cinnamon, salt, and lemon zest and stir well with a wooden spoon. Stir in the flour all at once and then the seasoned oil and immediately remove the pan from the heat. Using the wooden spoon, promptly and vigorously mix the flour with the liquid until the dough is firm and free of all air bubbles. This will take about 5 minutes.

Lightly dust a work surface, preferably marble, with flour, and transfer the dough to it. Knead briefly until soft and flexible, and then shape into a ball. Cover with a kitchen towel and let rest for about 1 hour.

Clean the work surface, dust again with flour, and roll out the dough into a very thin 20-inch square. Cut the dough into 4-inch squares. You will have 25 squares. Working from a corner of each square, roll up the square on the diagonal, creating a cylinder with a ¹/₂-inch hollow center. To prevent the fritters from unfolding when you fry them, dampen your finger and press the point of the seam to the layer beneath it, sealing it in place.

Pour olive oil to a depth of 1 inch into a large skillet and heat over medium-high heat until almost smoking. Working in batches, fry the fritters, turning as needed, for 2 to 3 minutes, or until golden on all sides. Using a slotted spoon, transfer to paper towels to drain. Repeat with the remaining fritters, always reheating the oil until almost smoking before adding the next batch.

Meanwhile, in a small, heavy saucepan, heat the honey with the remaining ¹/₄ cup water over high heat. Boil briefly, stirring constantly, until a thick, syrupy consistency forms. Remove from the heat and let cool slightly.

Arrange the warm fritters on a serving plate, and spoon the honey syrup over them. Let the fritters cool completely. Serve at room temperature.

EMPANADA DE MANZANA ::
Apple Empanada :: (*Galicia*)

Though empanadas are most often thought of as savory pies, they can also be made with fruits and served as a dessert or for *merienda* (teatime). For the best results, I recommend using tart, slightly acidic apples for this recipe. The dough for most savory empanadas (page 144) is made with wheat flour; for dessert empanadas, I find that corn flour works better. To simplify your shopping, I have used wheat flour here, but if you decide to try corn flour, use the same amount. :: **Makes 1 (10 by 15-inch or 11-inch round) empanada**

DOUGH

1 egg

1 teaspoon sugar

Pinch of salt

2 teaspoons active dry yeast

1/2 cup whole milk, heated to lukewarm (90° to 100°F)

2 tablespoons unsalted butter, at room temperature

2 1/2 cups all-purpose flour, plus extra for dusting

Olive oil for preparing the pan

5 tart apples, halved, peeled, cored, and cut lengthwise into 1-inch-thick slices

5 tablespoons sugar

3 tablespoons apricot jam (optional)

1 egg, lightly beaten

To make the dough, in a large bowl, whisk together the egg, sugar, and salt until blended. In a small bowl, dissolve the yeast in the warm milk and let stand for about 5 minutes, or until foamy. Add the yeast mixture and the butter to the bowl with the egg mixture and mix well. Add about half of the flour and mix with a rubber spatula or wooden spoon until completely incorporated. Add the rest of the flour a little at a time, continuing to mix with the spatula. When all the flour has been added and the dough becomes too difficult to mix, turn the dough out onto a lightly floured work surface and knead until well blended and elastic but not sticky, about 10 minutes.

Place the dough in a large bowl, cover with a damp kitchen towel, and let rise at room temperature for about 1 1/2 hours, or until about doubled in size.

Preheat the oven to 450°F. Brush a 10 by 15-inch baking sheet or an 11-inch pie pan with olive oil.

Lightly flour the work surface. Punch down the dough and divide into 2 pieces, one slightly larger than the other (the larger portion will form the bottom crust, and the smaller portion the top crust). Using a rolling pin, roll out the larger portion into a sheet about 1/4 inch thick and slightly larger than the baking sheet or pie pan. Transfer the dough to the prepared pan. Using your fingers, press the dough over the bottom and up the sides of the pan. Pierce the dough with fork tines in several places to prevent bubbles from forming.

Layer the apple slices neatly and evenly over the dough. Sprinkle the apples evenly with the sugar and then brush with the apricot jam, if desired. Roll out the second portion of dough into a thin sheet slightly smaller than the bottom crust. Carefully lay it over the filling. Trim any raggedy edges. Using your fingers, press the edges of the top and bottom crusts together, sealing them securely. Trim off any excess dough (see note). Pierce the top of the dough several times with the fork tines to allow steam to be released during baking. Brush the top with the beaten egg.

Place the empanada in the oven and bake for 30 minutes, or until nicely browned. Transfer to a wire rack and let cool in the pan. Serve warm or at room temperature, cut into squares or wedges.

NOTE: If you wish to decorate the empanada using the excess dough, see page 144.

ENSAIMADA ::
Fluffy Puff Pastry :: *(Balearic Islands)*

Most Majorcans and many Catalans eat *ensaimadas* almost daily. It is a pastry that is hard to categorize: you can serve it as a dessert, or just as well for breakfast, as a midday snack, or along with coffee or tea for *merienda*.

In Majorcan, *saim* means "lard," so lard is obviously the fat of choice here. I love plain *ensaimadas*, but they are also made with a filling of *cabello de ángel* (page 296), whipped cream, or even with the savory *sobrasada* (page 124). (For filled pastries, the fried coil is cut in half horizontally, filled as desired, and then the top half is replaced.) Serve these pastries with Almond Ice Cream (page 290) for an irresistible pairing. :: **Makes three 8-inch diameter coils**

4 1/2 teaspoons active dry yeast

2/3 cup whole milk, heated to lukewarm (90° to 100°F)

3 1/2 cups all-purpose flour, sifted, plus extra if needed and for dusting

1/2 teaspoon salt

3/4 cup sugar

2 eggs

6 tablespoons olive oil, plus extra for oiling rolling pin, work surface, and baking sheets

1/2 cup melted and cooled lard

1/2 cup confectioners' sugar

In a small bowl, dissolve the yeast in 1/3 cup of the warm milk and let stand for about 5 minutes, or until foamy. In a large bowl, stir together the flour, salt, and sugar. Make a well in the center of the flour mixture and add the remaining 1/3 cup milk, the eggs, the 6 tablespoons olive oil, and the yeast mixture to the well. Using a spoon, gradually pull the flour mixture into the well, stirring together the wet and dry ingredients as you do. When the mixtures are combined and a uniform dough has formed, turn it out onto a lightly floured work surface and knead for about 10 minutes, or until smooth, elastic, and no longer sticky. If the dough remains sticky, work in a little more flour. Gather the dough into a ball, cover it with a kitchen towel, and let rise at room temperature for about 1 hour, or until it has doubled in size.

Divide the dough into 3 equal portions. Oil a work surface, preferably marble, a rolling pin, and 1 or 2 baking sheets. Roll out 1 portion of the dough into a thin rectangle about 10 by 6 inches. Brush the surface of the rectangle with some of the melted lard and fold it in half lengthwise. Brush the surface with melted lard and fold it in half again, so that the surface is one-fourth of the original size. Roll out the dough again into a thin rectangle about 10 by 6 inches. Starting from a long side, roll up the rectangle into a tight cylinder. It should be 10 inches long. Shape it into a snail-like coil. Repeat with the remaining 2 dough portions.

Place the 3 coils on the prepared baking sheet(s) with enough space between them to allow them to rise. Cover with a kitchen towel and let rest in a warm spot overnight. The dough will at least double in size.

Preheat the oven to 350°F.

Though not necessary, I like to mist the dough coils with cold water just before putting them in the oven and then mist them again after they have been in the oven for 5 minutes. This helps to keep them moist. Bake the coils for about 30 minutes, or until they are airy and golden and they spring back when pressed with a fingertip.

Remove from the oven and let cool to room temperature on the pan(s) on wire rack(s). Dust with confectioners' sugar and cut into segments of desired size just before serving.

ROSCÓN DE REYES ::
Three Kings Cake

All Spanish children go to bed on the night of January 5 filled with excitement. They have been waiting for this day all year, and tonight their wishes, at least partly, might come true. *Los reyes magos*, or the three wise men (literally "the magic kings"), have come to town—in fact, to every town in Spain—and all the residents have seen them at the Cabalgata, the parade held on every Main Street. In some places, *los reyes* even come riding in on camels, and have donkeys loaded with precious gifts as part of their procession. Although my children have outgrown the wish making associated with this celebration, I still enjoy seeing other youngsters' innocent faces full of hope and anticipation.

In the morning, after every box has been opened, and the house is full of torn wrapping paper, the children and adults sit down at the breakfast table, where *el roscón* makes its regal appearance. You can eat the cake at breakfast on a holiday morning or in the evening with hot chocolate (page 299), coffee, or tea. :: **Makes 1 (15-inch) or 2 (8-inch) coils**

1/2 cup sugar, plus extra for sprinkling

Minced zest of 1/2 lemon

Minced zest of 1/2 orange

21/2 teaspoons (1 envelope) active dry yeast

2/3 cup milk, heated to lukewarm (90°F to 100°F)

1/2 cup unsalted butter, at room temperature

3 eggs

3 tablespoons orange-flower water

1/2 teaspoon salt

3 cups unbleached all-purpose flour, plus extra for dusting

Olive oil for preparing pan

1/2 cup candied fruits, finely chopped (optional)

In a food processor or blender, combine the 1/2 cup sugar and both citrus zests and process on high speed until you have a mixture of fine particles. Set aside.

In a large bowl, dissolve the yeast in the warm milk and let stand for about 5 minutes, or until foamy. Add the sugar-zest mixture, the butter, 2 of the eggs, the orange-flower water, and the salt and stir with a wooden spoon until all the ingredients are well mixed.

Add half the flour to the milk mixture and mix with your hands until well blended. Add the remaining flour and continue mixing until all the flour is incorporated. Then knead the dough in the bowl for a few minutes until it is smooth, flexible, and no longer sticky. Cover the bowl with a kitchen towel and let the dough rest in a warm spot for about 1 hour, or until it has roughly doubled in size.

Preheat the oven to its lowest setting and brush a rimmed baking sheet with olive oil.

Punch down the dough. On a floured work surface, using your palms, roll the dough back and forth until it forms a log about 30 inches long and 21/2 inches in diameter. Place it on the prepared baking sheet and bring the ends together to form a circle with a hole in the center 4 to 5 inches in diameter, forming a "crown." Alternatively, divide the dough in half and form 2 logs each 15 inches long and 21/2 inches in diameter. Form the logs into 2 crowns on the baking sheet.

Fill an ovenproof bowl with water and place it at the rear of the oven. Place the baking sheet with the dough crown in the oven. Let the dough rise for about 1 hour, or until nearly doubled in size.

Remove the pan from the oven and increase the oven temperature to 400°F. Break the remaining egg into a small bowl, beat until blended, and then brush it onto the crown(s). Scatter the candied fruits evenly over the top(s), if desired, and sprinkle evenly with the sugar.

Bake the cake(s) for 25 to 30 minutes, or until golden. Transfer to a wire rack and let cool on the pan. Transfer to a serving plate and serve at room temperature.

GATÓ D'AMETLLA :: Majorcan Almond Cake :: (Balearic Islands)

This Majorcan cake is believed to have originated in Valldemossa, the island town made famous by Chopin and George Sand, who spent a winter together there in an abandoned Carthusian monastery that today draws many visitors. This version, a recipe from my friend Maria Vicens, is the best that I have ever tasted. :: **Serves 8**

Unsalted butter and all-purpose flour for preparing pan

8 eggs, separated

1 1/2 cups sugar

1 teaspoon grated lemon zest

1 teaspoon ground cinnamon

1/2 teaspoon vanilla extract (optional)

2 cups coarsely ground blanched almonds

1 recipe Almond Ice Cream (page 290) for serving (optional)

Preheat the oven to 400°F. Butter an 11-inch round cake pan with 2-inch sides and then dust it with flour, shaking out any excess.

In a large bowl, combine the egg yolks and sugar and whisk together until smooth and foamy. Add the lemon zest, cinnamon, and vanilla, if using, and mix well. Add the ground almonds a little at a time, mixing well after each addition to incorporate fully.

Using a whisk or a handheld mixer, beat the egg whites until they form soft peaks. Scoop about one-third of the whites onto the egg yolk mixture and, using a rubber spatula, fold them in to lighten the mixture. Then add the remaining whites and fold them in gently but thoroughly, deflating the batter as little as possible.

Transfer the batter to the prepared pan. Bake the cake for about 30 minutes, or until a knife inserted into the center comes out clean. Remove from the oven and, holding the cake pan 6 inches above a countertop, drop the pan onto the counter. This simple dropping action "shocks" the cake, making it easier to remove from the pan.

Transfer the cake to a wire rack and let cool in the pan until warm. Run a knife around the inside of the pan to loosen the cake sides and then invert the cake onto the rack and lift off the pan. Place the cake upright on a serving plate. Serve warm or at room temperature with the ice cream, if desired.

TÉCULA MÉCULA ▪ Imperial Almond and Egg Tart ▪ (*Extremadura*)

This tart is known as the imperial dessert because it was said to be a favorite of Emperor Charles V, who retired to Extremadura. In his court, the tart was prepared with rendered fatback, and today it is still made that way in the pastry shops of Olivenza in Extremadura, where it is a specialty of local bakers. I prefer a mixture of butter and lard, however, which I have used here. Served with Pedro Ximénez sherry, and perhaps a scoop of ice cream or a dollop of whipped cream, this dessert is truly regal.

▪ **Serves 10**

CRUST

5 tablespoons unsalted butter, at room temperature

5 tablespoons lard, at room temperature

6 tablespoons water

1/3 cup sugar

1 1/2 cups all-purpose flour, plus extra for dusting

Pinch of salt

FILLING

1 1/2 cups sugar

1 1/2 cups water

Grated zest of 1 lemon

1 pound slivered blanched almonds

1/2 cup (1/4 pound) unsalted butter, at room temperature

8 egg yolks

1 cup all-purpose flour

To make the crust, combine the butter, lard, water, sugar, flour, and salt in a bowl and stir with a wooden spoon until the ingredients combine together in a rough dough. Turn out the dough onto a lightly floured work surface and knead for about 10 minutes, or until soft and no longer sticky. Gather the dough into a ball, flatten into a disk, wrap in plastic wrap, and refrigerate for 2 hours.

On a lightly floured work surface, roll out the dough into a thin round at least 14 inches in diameter. Carefully transfer the dough round to a 10-inch springform pan with at least 2 1/2-inch sides, pressing it into the bottom and sides. Trim away the excess dough even with the pan rim. Place in the refrigerator until needed.

To make the filling, in a small, heavy saucepan, combine the sugar, water, and lemon zest and bring to a boil over high heat, stirring to dissolve the sugar. Decrease the heat to medium and simmer for about 20 minutes, or until a thick syrup forms. Remove from the heat and let cool to room temperature.

Preheat the oven to 400°F.

In a bowl, combine the almonds and butter and beat with a handheld mixer until the butter is creamy. In a large bowl, whisk the egg yolks until foamy. Add the flour to the egg yolks a little at a time, mixing well after each addition. When the flour is fully incorporated and the mixture is smooth, add the almond-butter mixture and mix with a rubber spatula until thoroughly blended and smooth. Add the cooled syrup and again mix well until thoroughly blended.

Transfer the filling to the crust. Bake the tart for 30 minutes, or until a toothpick inserted into the center comes out clean. Transfer to a wire rack and let cool in the pan.

Remove the pan sides and slide the cooled tart onto a serving plate. Serve at room temperature.

TARTA DE SANTIAGO ▪️
Galician Almond Cake ▪️ (*Galicia*)

This moist, shallow cake from Santiago de Compostela is probably the best-known almond cake in Spain. Bakers, both in pastry shops and in homes, traditionally use a stencil and confectioners' sugar to decorate the center with a scallop shell, the symbol of the city (page 33). If you cannot find a scallop-shell stencil at a cake-decorating shop, use stiff paper to cut out your own. ▪️ **Serves 8**

Unsalted butter and all-purpose flour for
    preparing pan

4 eggs

1/2 tablespoon grated lemon zest

1/2 teaspoon ground cinnamon

3/4 cup granulated sugar

3 cups (scant 1 pound) blanched almonds, finely ground

1/3 cup all-purpose flour

Confectioners' sugar for dusting

Preheat the oven to 400°F. Butter a 9-inch round cake pan with 2-inch sides and then dust it with flour, shaking out any excess.

In a large bowl, combine the eggs, lemon zest, cinnamon, and granulated sugar and whisk together until smooth and foamy. Add the almonds and mix well. Add the flour a little at a time, mixing well after each addition. Continue to mix until all the ingredients are fully incorporated and the batter is smooth.

Transfer the batter to the prepared pan. Bake the cake for about 30 minutes, or until a knife inserted into the center comes out clean. Remove from the oven and, holding the cake pan 6 inches above a countertop, drop the pan onto the counter. This simple dropping action "shocks" the cake, making it easier to remove from the pan.

Transfer the cake to a wire rack and let cool in the pan to room temperature. Run a knife around the inside of the pan to loosen the cake sides and then invert the cake onto the rack and lift off the pan. Place the cake upright on a serving plate. To serve, dust the top with confectioners' sugar, with or without a scallop-shell stencil.

BIZCOCHOS BORRACHOS ::
Drunken Sponge Cakes ::
(Castilla–La Mancha)

I make *bizcochos borrachos* in small squares, but I have seen them as rectangles, too. Feel free to substitute another wine or liqueur for the sweet sherry . . . just make sure the cake gets "tipsy." :: **Serves 6**

Corn or other neutral vegetable oil and all-purpose
    flour for preparing pan

6 eggs

3 cups granulated sugar

1²/₃ cups all-purpose flour

1¹/₂ cups water

1 cup firmly packed brown sugar

¹/₂ cup sweet sherry

2 tablespoons ground cinnamon

Preheat the oven to 350°F. Brush an 8-inch square cake pan with oil and dust it with flour, shaking out any excess.

In a large bowl, combine the eggs and 1¹/₂ cups of the granulated sugar and whisk until foamy. Add the flour a little at a time, whisking after each addition until well incorporated.

Transfer the batter to the prepared pan. Bake the cake for about 1 hour, or until set when tested with a knife in the center. Transfer to a wire rack and let cool in the pan.

While the cake cools, in a saucepan, combine the water, the remaining 1¹/₂ cups granulated sugar, and the brown sugar. Mix well and bring to a boil over high heat, stirring to dissolve the sugar. Decrease the heat to medium and cook, stirring occasionally, for about 30 minutes, or until a thick, sticky, brownish syrup forms. Remove from the heat and let cool completely. Stir in the sherry, mixing well.

Run a knife around the inside edge of the pan to loosen the cake sides. Invert the cake onto a cutting board and lift off the pan. Turn the cake right side up and cut into 16 (2-inch) squares. Arrange the squares on a platter. Pour the sherry syrup slowly and evenly over the top and let stand for about 1 hour. The squares will absorb the syrup. Sprinkle the cinnamon on top and serve.

QUESADAS ::
Lemon Cheese Cake :: (*Cantabria*)

This dessert is typical of La Vega del Rio, a rural village in the Santander Province of Cantabria where the milk, cheese, and butter are exceptional. There is a saying that sums up the popularity of this dessert: *si te vas a Santander y no pruebas las quesadas, tú te dejas lo mejor y viajaste para nada.* (If you go to Santander and don't try *quesadas*, you are missing the best and have traveled in vain.)

Although this cake is made with fresh cow's milk cheese, it doesn't resemble the ubiquitous American cheesecake, which has a much denser, heavier texture and is usually made with a crumb crust. I have used typical Spanish pans here for baking the two cakes, but you can use similarly sized pans, such as 7-inch square pans, keeping in mind that the cakes are not very high. :: **Makes 2 (6 by 8¹/₂-inch) cakes; serves 10**

1³/₄ pounds farmer cheese

4 eggs, beaten

1¹/₂ cups sugar

7 tablespoons unsalted butter, at room temperature

²/₃ cup all-purpose flour

1 tablespoon grated lemon zest

1 teaspoon ground cinnamon

Preheat the oven to 400°F.

In a medium bowl, lightly mash the cheese with a fork until evenly crumbled. In a large bowl, combine the eggs, sugar, and butter and mix with a rubber spatula until well blended. Gradually add the flour, stirring after each addition until fully incorporated before adding more. Add the crumbled cheese, lemon zest, and cinnamon and fold them in gently just until combined.

Transfer the batter to 2 pans each 6 by 8¹/₂ inches and 1 inch deep. Bake for 20 minutes, or until a toothpick inserted into the center comes out clean. Transfer to wire racks and let cool in the pans.

To serve, cut the cooled cakes into squares or rectangles and serve directly from the pans.

FLAÓ ∷ Cream Cheese Mint Tart ∷
(Balearic Islands)

Flaó is similar to American cheesecake, but the use of mint leaves and aniseeds sets it apart and makes it particularly refreshing. It calls for *requesón*, a fresh milk cheese, also known as Quark, and though you can easily make your own, I have also obtained spectacular results using the more readily available cream cheese.

You can order *flaó* at nearly any restaurant in Ibiza. This recipe, however, comes from my friend Carlos Posadas, currently the chef at the magnificent Madrid restaurant El Amparo. ∷ **Serves 6**

CRUST

3 tablespoons olive oil

3 tablespoons lard, at room temperature

6 tablespoons water

2 tablespoons anisette liqueur (optional)

1 tablespoon aniseeds

1 cup all-purpose flour, plus extra for dusting

1 tablespoon granulated sugar

Pinch of salt

FILLING

3 fresh mint leaves

1 tablespoon minced lemon zest

1/3 cup granulated sugar

1 cup (1/2 pound) Quark (page 317) or cream cheese, at room temperature

2 eggs

Juice of 1/2 lemon

6 fresh mint leaves for garnish

2 tablespoons confectioners' sugar

Preheat the oven to 400°F.

To make the crust, in a bowl, combine the olive oil, lard, water, liqueur, if using, aniseeds, flour, granulated sugar, and salt and stir with a wooden spoon until the ingredients combine together in a rough dough. Turn out the dough onto a lightly floured work surface and knead for about 10 minutes, or until soft and no longer sticky.

Clean the work surface, dust again with flour, and roll out the dough into a thin round at least 13 inches in diameter. Carefully transfer the dough round to a 10-inch springform pan with 2-inch sides, pressing it into the bottom and sides. Trim away the excess dough even with the pan rim.

To make the filling, combine the mint leaves, lemon zest, and granulated sugar in a blender or food processor and process on high speed until you have a mixture of fine particles. Add the cheese, eggs, and lemon juice and process until smooth. Pour the mixture into the crust.

Bake the tart for 30 minutes, or until set when tested with a knife in the center. Transfer to a wire rack and let cool in the pan. Remove the pan sides and slide the tart onto a flat serving plate. Garnish with the mint leaves and dust with the confectioners' sugar. Serve at room temperature.

GREIXONERA DE BROSSAT ▪
Baked Cheese with Lemon and Cinnamon
▪ (Balearic Islands)

Brossat is the Marjorcan name for a fresh milk cheese called *requesón* in Spanish and known as Quark in English. During a springtime vacation in Majorca, I learned to make this typical Easter dessert from my friends and hosts Tina Read and Miguel Sard. The recipe is astonishingly simple. I have included a recipe for making the cheese, but if you don't have time to make it, you can use commercial Quark or even cream cheese (at room temperature). If you like, accompany each serving with a scoop of almond ice cream (right). ▪ **Serves 10**

    Lard, olive oil, or butter for preparing pan
    4 cups (2 pounds) Quark (page 317)
    12 eggs
    3¹/₂ cups sugar
    1 tablespoon ground cinnamon
    Grated zest of 2 lemons

Preheat the oven to 400°F. Grease a 12-inch *cazuela* (page 51) or other 12-inch ovenproof dish with 2-inch sides with lard.

In a bowl, stir the cheese with a fork until smooth. In another bowl, whisk the eggs until well blended. Add the eggs to the cheese and whisk until smooth. Add the sugar, cinnamon, and lemon zest and whisk until evenly distributed.

Transfer the mixture to the prepared *cazuela*. Bake for 45 minutes, or until pale gold and set when tested in the center with a knife.

Remove from the oven and let cool completely. Spoon into small dishes to serve.

HELADO DE ALMENDRA ▪
Almond Ice Cream ▪ (Balearic Islands)

Whether served with *ensaimadas* (page 282) or alone, this ice cream makes a perfect dessert. ▪ **Makes about 1¹/₂ pints**

    1 pound (3 rounded cups) blanched almonds
    8 cups water
    2¹/₂ cups sugar
    2 tablespoons grated lemon zest
    1 cinnamon stick

In a blender or food processor, very finely grind the almonds. Use the pulse function and watch carefully. You do not want the nuts to release too much oil, which will turn them into nut butter.

In a heavy saucepan, combine the water, sugar, lemon zest, cinnamon stick, and half of the almonds. Place over high heat and bring to a boil, stirring constantly. Decrease the heat to medium and add the rest of the almonds, continuing to stir. As soon as the mixture boils again, remove from the heat and let cool completely.

Transfer the cooled mixture to an ice-cream maker and freeze according to the manufacturer's instructions. If you do not have an ice-cream maker, transfer the mixture to a 4-cup container (a glass, stainless-steel, or plastic bowl will do) and place in the freezer for about 1 hour, or until half frozen. During this hour, remove the ice cream from the freezer every 5 to 10 minutes and beat with a whisk to prevent ice crystals from forming. After the first hour, return the ice cream to the freezer and leave it there for at least 2 hours, or until fully frozen. When made by either method, transfer the finished ice cream to an airtight container and store in the freezer. It will keep for up to 1 week.

When ready to serve, remove the ice cream from the freezer about 20 minutes in advance to allow it to soften slightly. Spoon into small dishes to serve.

HELADO DE LECHE CONDENSADA :: Sweetened Condensed Milk Ice Cream

This ice cream brings back memories of my childhood, when my brothers and I would fight over the last spoonful. Its flavor is similar to the *dulce de leche* ice cream available in many stores today, and it is a good accompaniment to a simple cake or can be served alone. You will need to begin this recipe the day before you plan to serve it. Though you can make the ice cream by hand using a whisk, a mixer renders the task much easier because the cooked condensed milk is quite dense. :: **Serves 10**

1 (10-ounce) can sweetened condensed milk, unopened

$1/2$ cup heavy cream

1 cup whole milk

Place the can of milk in a small stockpot and add water to cover by a few inches. Bring to a boil over high heat, decrease the heat to medium to medium-low, and maintain a gentle boil for 3 hours. Add more water if necessary to keep the can covered at all times. Remove the pan from the stove and allow the can to cool completely in the water. (The can will hold heat for a long time.)

In a large bowl, using a whisk or a handheld mixer, whip the cream until soft peaks form. Open the can of condensed milk and spoon the contents, now the color of toffee, into the whipped cream. Add the milk and mix by hand or with a mixer until the mixture is well blended. Transfer to an airtight container and place in the freezer for 24 hours.

When ready to serve, remove the ice cream from the freezer about 20 minutes in advance to allow it to soften slightly. Spoon into small dishes to serve.

MELOCOTONES EN VINO BLANCO :: Peaches In White Wine :: (*Aragón*)

In Aragón, Calanda is famous for its vegetable gardens and orchards, and its aromatic and juicy peaches are arguably the finest fruits of the area. Their extraordinary flavor is showcased in this simple recipe. While the Aragonese peaches are ideal, I find that even a less-flavorful peach improves when prepared this way. You will need to start the recipe the day before you plan to serve it, as the peaches must marinate overnight. :: **Serves 4**

1 cup dry white wine

$1/2$ cup sugar

1 cinnamon stick

5 peaches, peeled, pitted, and cut into large chunks

In a bowl, combine the wine and sugar and stir with a wooden spoon until the sugar dissolves. Add the cinnamon stick and the peaches and stir several times to mix well. Cover and refrigerate for 24 hours.

Spoon the peaches and their liquid into small bowls and serve cold.

ROBIOLS Y CRESPELLS ❖
Turnovers and Cookies ❖ *(Balearic Islands)*

These pastries and cookies always go together: *robiols* are filled turnovers, while *crespells* are cookies that are cut out of the leftover turnover dough, which is supplemented with some sugar. Majorcans enjoy making *crespells* with their children, and nearly every house has a set of cookie cutters in a variety of shapes just for this purpose.

The cheese filling can be used for any cake or other dessert that calls for a fresh cheese or cream cheese filling. You can also forgo the cheese filling and instead fill the *robiols* with 2 cups Pumpkin Preserve (page 296) or your favorite jam. ❖ **Makes about 20 turnovers and 30 cookies**

CHEESE FILLING

2 cups (1 pound) Quark (page 317) or cream cheese, at room temperature

2 egg yolks

$1/4$ cup granulated sugar

Grated zest of 1 orange

Grated zest of 1 lemon

$2/3$ cup milk

$2/3$ cup olive oil, plus extra for brushing

$2/3$ cup freshly squeezed or store-bought orange juice

$1^1/2$ cups plus 2 tablespoons granulated sugar

3 egg yolks

$1^1/4$ cups (10 ounces) lard, at room temperature

6 cups all-purpose flour, plus extra for dusting

Confectioners' sugar for dusting

To make the cheese filling, in a bowl, combine the cheese, egg yolks, granulated sugar, and both zests and mix well with a wooden spoon until light and smooth. Cover and refrigerate until needed.

In a large bowl, combine the milk, the $2/3$ cup olive oil, the orange juice, the $1^1/2$ cups granulated sugar, the egg yolks, and the lard. Using your fingers, mix together until all the ingredients are evenly distributed. Add the 6 cups flour in 4 equal batches, mixing well with a wooden spoon after each addition until fully incorporated. Turn the dough out onto a lightly floured work surface and knead for about 10 minutes, or until a smooth, elastic, firm dough forms.

Position 2 oven racks in the center of the oven and preheat to 350°F. Have ready 2 rimmed baking sheets.

Divide the dough into 3 equal portions. Set 1 portion aside, covered with a kitchen towel, for making the *crespells* later. Clean the work surface and then lightly dust again with flour.

To make the *robiols*, roll out 1 dough portion as thinly as possible. Using a round cookie cutter or the rim of a glass 4 to 5 inches in diameter, cut out as many circles as possible from the dough and set them aside on a clean work surface. Gather up the dough scraps, add them to the second dough portion, and repeat the rolling and cutting. Gather the scraps a final time, roll, and cut as before.

Brush each dough circle with a little olive oil. Spread a little filling on one-half of each circle and then fold the other half over to enclose the filling. Pinch the edges of the semicircles together with your fingertips or use the tines of a fork to seal securely. Arrange the turnovers on a baking sheet, spacing them about 1 inch apart.

Clean the work surface and dust it again with flour. To make the *crespells*, add the 2 tablespoons granulated sugar to the reserved dough portion, distributing the sugar evenly. Then roll out the dough about $3/4$ inch thick. Using whichever cookie cutter or cutters you like (they should yield roughly 2-inch cookies), cut out as many cookies as possible and arrange on the second baking sheet, spacing them about 1 inch apart. Gather together the dough scraps and repeat the rolling and cutting.

Bake the *crespells* and *robiols* for 1 hour, switching the baking sheets between the racks and rotating them 180 degrees after about 30 minutes to ensure even baking. When they are done, they will have a cookie consistency and should be quite pale. Transfer to wire racks and let cool on the pans.

Dust the cooled turnovers and cookies with confectioners' sugar. Arrange them in 1 or more airtight containers between sheets of waxed paper or parchment paper. They will keep at room temperature for up to 1 week.

POLVORONES ◼
Almond "Cookies" ◼ *(Andalusia)*

I have yet to come up with a good translation for *polvorones*. Even though a *polvorón* looks like a cookie and is somewhat like shortbread, the taste and texture are completely different. *Polvo* means "powder," and indeed, the texture is powdery, so that eating one of these round sweets requires a bit of skill if you don't want it to crumble away after the first bite. When you shape the *polvorones*, you will need to press them lightly between your palms to firm their otherwise loose texture. And then you must wrap them individually in small pieces of thin, white, nearly translucent silk paper (look for it in shops selling fancy wrapping papers).

During the holiday season, *polvorones* are readily available in supermarkets and pastry shops around Spain in many different styles: with and without spirits, with and without almonds, with and without chocolate. They are sold by weight, with about a dozen to a pound, and I always take advantage of this seasonal bounty.

This recipe was given to me many years ago by a friend from Estepa in Andalusia, where *polvorones* are said to have originated. It is my favorite, and it is fairly simple to make. Don't hesitate to use lard; I find it works much better than butter for making these treats. ◼
Makes about 30 "cookies"

2/3 pound (about 2 cups) blanched almonds

3 cups all-purpose flour, plus more if needed

2 cups firmly packed confectioners' sugar, plus extra for dusting

1 tablespoon ground cinnamon

1 pound lard, melted and cooled to room temperature

Preheat the oven to 300°F.

Spread the almonds on a rimmed baking sheet and toast in the oven for about 10 minutes, or until fragrant and lightly golden. Stir the nuts occasionally so they color evenly. Remove from the oven, pour onto a large plate, and let cool completely. Leave the oven set at 300°F.

Spread the 3 cups flour in another rimmed baking sheet in as shallow a layer as possible. Toast in the oven for about 5 minutes, or until very pale; be careful not to let it color very much. Remove from the oven, pour into a bowl, and let cool completely.

In a blender or food processor, combine the almonds and about 2 tablespoons of the confectioners' sugar and very finely grind the almonds. Use the pulse function and watch carefully. You do not want the nuts to release too much oil, which will turn them into nut butter. (The sugar helps prevent this.) They must also be fully cooled, too, or you will end up with a sticky consistency.

Transfer the almonds to a large bowl and stir in the remaining confectioners' sugar. Sift the flour into the mixture and add the cinnamon. Add the lard to the bowl a little at a time, while stirring the mixture with a spatula. Once the lard is completely incorporated, the mixture should be moist but not wet. If the mixture feels very sticky, add a little more flour. Cover and refrigerate for at least 2 hours or up to overnight. The *polvorones* are much easier to shape if the mixture is cold.

Position 2 oven racks in the center of the oven and preheat to 250°F. Line 2 rimmed baking sheets with parchment paper. Using your hands, form the almond mixture into round lentil-like shapes about 2 inches in diameter and about 1/2 inch thick and arrange them on the prepared baking sheets.

Place the baking sheets on the oven racks and bake for 45 minutes, switching the baking sheets between the racks and rotating them 180 degrees after about 25 minutes to ensure even baking. The rounds will set up but should not color at all. Transfer to wire racks and let cool on the pans.

Dust the cooled cookies with confectioners' sugar. Wrap them individually in 6 by 8-inch sheets of white silk paper and twist both ends, like wrapping candy, to make tiny packages. Store them in an airtight container at room temperature for up to 2 weeks.

GUIRLACHE DE ZARAGOZA ::
Almond Crunch :: (Aragón)

Guirlache is to Aragón what *turrón* is to Alicante—a hallmark of regional cuisine. The sweet almond candy gained international recognition during the Spanish-French Zaragoza Fair of 1908, when it was sold in metal boxes decorated with the flags of both countries. Traditionally this treat, which was introduced by the Moors, is made with almonds, although versions made with peanuts, pine nuts, or hazelnuts are also common. ::
Makes 20 bars

> 1 pound (3 rounded cups) blanched almonds
>
> Almond oil or vegetable oil for preparing work surfaces
>
> 1 pound sugar
>
> 2 tablespoons freshly squeezed lemon juice
>
> 1 tablespoon aniseeds (optional)

Preheat the oven to 300°F. Spread the almonds on a rimmed baking sheet and toast in the oven for about 10 minutes, or until fragrant and lightly golden. Stir the nuts occasionally so they color evenly. Remove from the oven and pour onto a large plate to cool.

Brush a work surface (preferably marble) and a rolling pin with almond oil. Crush the almonds a little in a mortar and then place them in a heavy saucepan. Add the sugar and lemon juice, place over high heat, and stir until the sugar starts to caramelize, turning light brown and coating the almonds. Be careful not to burn the sugar, or the candy will have a bitter taste.

Immediately pour the caramelized almonds onto the prepared work surface and spread with a heatproof spatula into a rectangle roughly 6 by 10 inches. Sprinkle the aniseeds evenly on top, if desired. Roll the oiled rolling pin over the rectangle to smooth and level the surface, and then, using a long-bladed knife, press the edges toward the center to form a neat 6 by 10-inch rectangle. When the rectangle is lukewarm, cut it into small bars about 3 inches long by $1/2$ inch wide, or to a size of your liking.

When the bars are completely cool, arrange them between sheets of waxed paper or parchment paper in an airtight container. They will keep at room temperature for a week or so.

:: Turrón ::

People from other countries often describe Spaniards as free spirits—inveterate nonconformists who are always going their own way. But that is only partially true. On New Year's Eve, every Spaniard, young and old, rich and poor, does the same thing. When the clock begins ringing the arrival of midnight, every citizen quickly gulps down one grape after each *campanada*, or strike of the bell. Indeed, it is inconceivable to start the New Year any other way. When the bells have stopped ringing and the last grape is eaten, everyone drinks a toast for good wishes in the coming year and then eats plenty of *turrón*, the popular Christmas-season nougat made with almonds and honey.

There are two basic types of *turrón*: *turrón blando*, or soft, known as Jijona *turrón*, and *turrón duro*, or hard, known as Alicante *turrón*. The Valencian town of Jijona, in the province of Alicante, is the oldest and most important center of Spanish *turrón* production. The Moors, who brought a version of the nougat to Spain, worked closely with Jewish communities around Jijona to produce the candy, which was exported to Japan as early as the sixteenth century. Today, the *maestros turroneros*, the masters of the art, continue to keep the secrets of their trade within the family.

Nowadays, shops are stocked with many different kinds of *turrón*, including versions flavored with egg yolks, chocolate, coconut, candied fruits, or toffee. But the traditional *turrones*, made from roasted almonds, honey, sugar, and egg white, remain the most popular. *Turrón duro* has coarsely chopped almonds and is topped with a paper-thin wafer, while *turrón blando* has finely ground almonds.

YEMAS DE SANTA TERESA ▪
Candied Egg Yolks ▪ (Castilla y León)

These sweet egg yolks are found all over Spain, but they are usually associated with Castile, and especially Ávila, the birthplace of Saint Teresa. I had always regarded these candied yolks as too sweet and heavy, until I tried the ones produced by the Yemas Santa Teresa in Ávila. The same company also produces the best quince paste in Spain (page 297).

Start the *yemas* a day in advance of serving, as they need to rest for 24 hours in the refrigerator. ▪ **Makes about 18 small balls**

10 egg yolks

$^1/_2$ cup granulated sugar, plus extra for shaping the balls

$^1/_2$ cup water

Confectioners' sugar for dusting

Pass the yolks through a fine-mesh sieve placed over a heavy saucepan. Set aside.

In a small, heavy saucepan, combine the $^1/_2$ cup granulated sugar and the water, place over high heat, and bring to a boil, stirring to dissolve the sugar. Decrease the heat to medium-high and boil, stirring occasionally, for about 10 minutes, or until the syrup starts to thicken. Remove from the heat and let cool completely.

Add the cooled syrup to the egg yolks, place over high heat, and bring to a boil. Boil, stirring constantly, for 7 minutes, or until the yolks look crystallized. Remove from the heat and stir for 5 minutes longer. Pour the mixture into a $4^1/_2$ by $8^1/_2$ by $2^1/_2$-inch loaf pan. Cover and refrigerate for 24 hours.

The next day, you will notice that the surface of the yolk mixture has crystallized slightly. This is fine. Spread some confectioners' sugar in a small, shallow bowl, and sprinkle a little granulated sugar on your palm. (The sugar keeps the yolk mixture from sticking to your hands.) Then, using a small spoon, scoop out a little of the yolk mixture and roll it between your palms to form a ball about $1^1/_2$ inches in diameter. Roll the ball in the confectioners' sugar, shake off any excess, and set the ball aside on a platter. Repeat until you have shaped all of the mixture into balls and dusted them with confectioners' sugar.

Serve the *yemas* at room temperature, or cover and refrigerate and serve cold. To store, pack into an airtight container and store in the refrigerator for up to a few months.

CABELLO DE ÁNGEL ⠿
Pumpkin Preserve

The long, yellow fibers inside a pumpkin likely account for the name of this preserve, *cabello de ángel*, or "angel's hair." Whatever the origin of the name, this wonderful preserve is popular all over Spain. It is mainly used as a filling for turnovers like *robiols* (page 292), pastries like *ensaimadas* (page 282), cakes, and other sweets. This recipe is a simplified version of the more time-consuming original formula, but it works well.

You can use any flavorful winter squash in place of the pumpkin. Just make sure that it has the bright yellow-orange flesh. Start preparing the preserve the day before you need it, as the pumpkin should rest overnight. ⠿

Makes about 2 pints

    1 or 2 pumpkins or winter squashes, about 4 pounds
        total weight
    1¹/₂ cups water
    2 pounds sugar
    Grated zest of 1 lemon
    Grated zest of 1 orange

Halve the pumpkin and remove and discard the seeds. Carefully remove the fibers from the center of the pumpkin and reserve. Peel the pumpkin and cut it into small chunks.

In a saucepan, combine the pumpkin chunks and 1 cup of the water, bring to a boil over high heat, boil for 1 minute, and remove from the heat. Drain the pumpkin well, place in a bowl, and add the reserved fibers, the sugar, and the citrus zests. Mix well, cover, and let rest at room temperature overnight.

Transfer the pumpkin mixture to a nonreactive saucepan and add the remaining ¹/₂ cup water. Place over medium heat and bring to a boil. Decrease the heat to low and cook, stirring constantly with a wooden spoon, for about 30 minutes, or until the pumpkin chunks have broken down and the fibers are no longer stringy and are fully incorporated.

Remove from the heat. Let cool, transfer to jars with tight-fitting lids, and store in the refrigerator for up to 1 week.

CARNE DE MEMBRILLO SANTA TERESA :: Quince Paste

I owe the inclusion of this recipe to Silvia Girón and Julián Gil, owners of the highly acclaimed Yemas Santa Teresa, based in Ávila, which wins every competition it enters for the best *yemas* (page 295), *mahonesa*, and quince paste. When I began writing this book, I knew this recipe had to be in it. The reason is simple: I was having dinner with Silvia and Julián at the very moment that the publisher contacted me to tell me that my proposed book had been accepted.

Beyond starting with ripe quince of excellent quality, the most important thing to remember when making this paste is to keep the proportions at 60 percent fruit and 40 percent sugar. The quince lose considerable weight once they are cored and peeled, which means the final paste will be only a fraction of the original weight of the combined ingredients. The amounts I have given here follow this formula. If you have more or less quince, you can still make the paste by simply adjusting the amount of sugar.

Serve the paste with a fresh or cured cheese. Queso Manchego and Queso Idiazábal (the smoked type), both aged sheep's milk cheeses, and fresh cow's milk Queso de Burgos are good choices. :: **Makes about 3¹/₂ pounds**

    5 pounds ripe quince
    3¹/₄ pounds sugar

In a large stockpot, combine the whole quince with water to cover by 2 inches and bring to a boil over high heat. Decrease the heat to medium and boil the fruits, stirring often, for 45 minutes, or until they are soft when pierced with a knife. Using a slotted spoon, lift the quince from the pot and set aside to cool slightly.

As soon as you can touch the fruits, halve them through the stem end, remove the core, and trim away the stem and blossom end. Do not peel the quince, however. The fiber present in the skin is important not only for a good culinary result, but also for your health. Pass the quince through a food mill fitted with the coarse plate held over a saucepan.

Add the sugar to the quince, stir well, and place over high heat. Bring to a boil and cook, stirring constantly with a wooden spoon, for about 40 minutes. At it cooks, it will turn golden and then brownish and then it will thicken until it is very sticky and difficult to stir. At this point, remove it from the heat.

Transfer the mixture to an 8-inch square cake pan or to smaller individual cups or containers. Let cool, cover, and store at room temperature or in the refrigerator. Though it will keep for quite a long time, it will disappear quickly because it is so delicious. Serve at room temperature, cut into slices, squares, or other shapes.

Squash stand at a neighborhood market, Barcelona

MERMELADA DE NARANJA ACIDA
⠿ Orange Marmalade ⠿ (Andalusia)

England has long been recognized as the source of some of the world's best orange marmalade. Until recently, the bitter oranges the English used were grown in the public parks and streets of Sevilla. Picking oranges from the city's orange trees was strictly forbidden, and fines were handed out to those who dared take the precious fruits. The entire harvest was shipped to England by virtue of a contract between the municipality of Sevilla and major English marmalade producers. Occasionally, an officer could be bribed to look the other way while five or six oranges were picked, which is just the amount needed to make this recipe. It is from my friend Regina Cassinello; it was her very Sevillian mother's, who was actually English.

You will need bitter oranges, often labeled Seville oranges, for this recipe. Allow plenty of time to prepare the marmalade, as the fruit must soak overnight. ⠿

Makes about 12 pints

    6 bitter oranges
    1 sweet orange
    1 lemon
    2 cups hot water
    3 quarts cold water
    6 pounds sugar

Peel all the oranges and the lemon and cut the peels into fine julienne. Halve the fruits and remove the seeds. Place the seeds in a small bowl, cover with the hot water, and let stand for 24 hours. Cut each citrus half into quarters, place them in a large bowl, add the cold water, and let stand for 24 hours.

Drain the seeds, reserving the water. Place the seeds on a square of cheesecloth, bring the corners together, and tie securely with kitchen string to form a pouch. Transfer the fruits and their soaking water to a large nonreactive pot, add the reserved soaking water from the seeds and the pouch of seeds, and place over high heat. Bring to a boil, decrease the heat to medium-low, and boil gently, stirring frequently, for about 3 hours, or until the fruit is very soft and the mixture looks like a purée.

Remove and discard the seed pouch. Add the sugar a little at a time, stirring well after each addition. Continue to cook over medium-low heat, stirring frequently, for about 30 minutes, or until the mixture is very thick. At the same time, sterilize canning jars and two-part canning lids.

To check whether the liquid is thick enough, drop a small spoonful of it onto a saucer, slip the saucer into the freezer for a few minutes, and then remove the saucer from the freezer and turn it upside down. If the liquid has set up and doesn't fall from the saucer, the marmalade is ready. If it does fall, cook for a little longer and test again.

Ladle the marmalade into the hot sterilized jars, leaving $1/4$-inch headspace. Using a damp cloth, wipe any spills from the jar rims and then attach the lids. To process in a hot-water bath, set the jars, not touching, on a rack in a large, wide kettle, add water to cover by 2 inches, bring the water to a boil, and boil for 15 minutes. (You may need to do this in batches.) Remove the jars with tongs and let cool to room temperature.

Check the jars for a good seal; the lids should be slightly concave in the center. Store in a cool, dry, dark cupboard for up to year. If the seal is not good, or once the marmalade is opened, store in the refrigerator for up to several months.

Oranges growing along the village streets of Zahara de la Sierra, Andalusia

CHOCOLATE HECHO A LA ESPAÑOLA ▪ Hot Chocolate

Spaniards like their hot chocolate thick, so they let it simmer on the stove, stirring it all the while, until it has reduced to the correct density. They also believe that it tastes best when they are enjoying it with family or friends at one of the many places that serves hot chocolate and churros (page 279) for breakfast. ▪ **Serves 4**

Illustrated on page 278

   4¹/₂ **cups whole milk**
   1 **pound semisweet chocolate, coarsely chopped**
   1 **tablespoon cornstarch**
   ¹/₄ **cup sugar**
   ¹/₂ **cup whipped cream (optional)**

In a large saucepan, bring 4 cups of the milk to a boil over high heat. As soon as it boils, remove the pan from the heat. Add the chocolate to the milk and let it melt, stirring it several times as it does.

While the chocolate is melting, combine the remaining ¹/₂ cup milk and the cornstarch in a small bowl and stir until the cornstarch dissolves.

Return the saucepan to medium heat, bring the chocolate milk just to shy of a boil, and cook, whisking constantly, for about 30 minutes, or until the mixture has thickened and reduced slightly. Add the cornstarch mixture and sugar, decrease the heat to low, and cook, whisking constantly, for 10 minutes longer, or until the chocolate has thickened to a good consistency. To test the chocolate, dip a spoon into it and then lift it out; the spoon should be thickly coated with the chocolate.

Remove from the heat and immediately divide evenly among 4 cups. Top each cup with a spoonful of whipped cream, if desired, and serve right away. Once the chocolate cools, it becomes too thick to serve. If this happens, add a little milk and reheat over low heat while stirring constantly.

CAFÉ CON HIELO Y LIMÓN ▪ Iced Black Coffee with Lemon Peel

This is the perfect drink for a hot summer day, which has made it popular all along the coast of Spain. You can make the coffee as strong as you like—from espresso to American—but keep in mind that the ice cubes will dilute it as they begin to melt, so stronger is usually better. The lemon peel gives the coffee a distinctive taste and aroma. ▪ **Serves 6**

   1 **lemon**
   4 **cups brewed coffee, at room temperature or chilled**
   2 **tablespoons sugar (optional)**
   2 **cups ice cubes**

Using a vegetable peeler, remove the peel from the lemon in 6 long strips. Set the strips aside. Reserve the lemon for another use.

In a pitcher, combine the coffee and sugar, if using, and stir until the sugar dissolves. Distribute the ice cubes among 6 glasses, and then pour the coffee into the glasses. Rub each glass rim with the white side of a lemon peel strip, twist the strip over the coffee, and then drop the strip into the glass. Serve immediately.

HORCHATA DE CHUFAS ▪ Iced Tiger Nut Drink ▪ (*Valencian Community*)

Ice-cold *horchata* is a delight on a hot summer day. It is originally from Valencia and the surrounding area, but it is also popular in Madrid and the Canary Islands. Commercial *horchata* is available, but it cannot compete with the freshly made *horchata* served in ice-cream stores and in bars. The drink is made from tiger nuts, which are homely tubers with a peculiar, almost coconut-like taste. Because they are difficult to find in the United States, I have suggested blanched almonds as an alternative. ▪
Makes about 2 quarts

1/2 **pound tiger nuts or blanched almonds**
1 **cup sugar**
1 **cup ice water**
3 **trays ice cubes**
Ground cinnamon for sprinkling

In a food processor, combine the nuts, sugar, ice water, and ice cubes and process until blended and smooth; tiny slivers of ice will remain. Pour into chilled glasses, sprinkle with cinnamon, and serve.

SANGRÍA

Sangría, Spain's national beverage, has become popular around the world. It is a great drink to serve whenever you are entertaining guests, as it can be made ahead of time and refrigerated. Then, just before serving, all you need to do is add ice cubes.

I like to use a dark, intensely flavored, full-bodied red wine from Rioja, Ribera del Duero, or even from Priorat. Whichever wine you choose, make sure you follow a simple rule: the better the wine you use, the better the sangría will turn out. When peaches are in season, they are a good addition along with the oranges.

You can make sangría for anywhere from 10 to 100 people using these proportions: 8 parts wine, 4 parts orange juice, 1 part brandy, 1 part Cointreau or Triple Sec, and 2 parts lemon-lime–flavored soda. And then garnish the mix with fresh fruits as you like. You can also use dry white wine in place of the red, keeping all the other ingredients the same. ▪ **Makes 1 quart**

1/2 **orange, cut into small dice (optional)**
1/2 **lemon, cut into small dice (optional)**
1 **peach, peeled, pitted, and cut into small pieces (optional)**
1 **cup freshly squeezed orange juice**
1/4 **cup brandy**
1/4 **cup Cointreau or Triple Sec**
1/2 **cup lemon-lime–flavored soda**
2 **cups good-quality dry red wine**
1 **tray ice cubes**

In a large punch bowl or in a pitcher, combine the orange, lemon, and peach (if using), orange juice, brandy, Cointreau, soda, and wine and stir to mix well. Add the ice and serve.

Sloe berries and a bottle of pacharán (patxarán *in Basque), the anise liqueur that is made from them, San Sebastián, Basque Country*

:: CHAPTER 12 ::

Basic Recipes

STOCKS

CALDO DE CARNE :: Beef Stock

I like mild stocks because I prefer to preserve the flavors of the foods that will be cooked with or in the stock as much as possible. For a more intense flavor and a darker color, you can roast the bones, meat, and vegetables in a 400°F oven for 30 to 45 minutes, or until they are browned, before you simmer them in the water with the seasonings. Ask your butcher for meaty bones to ensure a richly flavored stock. :: **Makes about 2 quarts**

1 pound beef shank, round, or chunk

2 pounds meaty beef bones

2 leeks, green tops only, coarsely chopped

1 turnip, coarsely chopped

1 yellow onion, halved

2 carrots, coarsely chopped

1 bunch flat-leaf parsley

4 quarts water

Salt

In a stockpot, combine the beef shanks, beef bones, leeks, turnip, onion, carrots, parsley, and water and bring just to a boil over high heat, using a slotted spoon to skim off any foam that forms on the surface. Decrease the heat to medium-low, cover partially, and simmer gently, skimming as needed, for 2 to 2$^1/_2$ hours, or until the liquid is reduced by half and the meat is falling off the bones.

Strain the stock through a fine-mesh sieve into a clean vessel. If using immediately, skim off as much fat as possible from the surface with a large spoon. Season the stock to taste with salt. If storing for later use, prepare an ice bath in your sink, pour the stock into a tall container, and place it in the ice water to cool quickly. Stir the stock periodically to help reduce the cooling time, minimizing the opportunity for bacteria to grow.

When the stock is at room temperature, cover and place in the refrigerator until well chilled. Remove from the refrigerator and lift off and discard the layer of fat that has solidified on top. Re-cover and refrigerate for up to 3 days or freeze for up to 6 months.

Olive oil from Andalusia

CALDO DE POLLO ▪ Chicken Stock

Using homemade chicken stock will always improve your dishes, but when you are short of time, a low-sodium canned stock can be used. Making your own chicken stock is easy, however, when you have both the time and a whole chicken for another use. For the stock, I typically use only the carcass of the chicken and a single additional breast. I have also used the carcass of a roasted chicken with good results. ▪ **Makes about 2 quarts**

Carcass of 1 uncooked chicken

1 chicken breast

2 carrots, coarsely chopped

2 leeks, green tops only, coarsely chopped

1 turnip, coarsely chopped

1 bunch flat-leaf parsley

Salt

Place the chicken carcass and chicken breast in a large stockpot and add water to cover by about 2 inches. Bring to a gentle boil over high heat, using a slotted spoon to skim off any foam that forms on the surface. Add the carrots, leeks, turnip, and parsley, decrease the heat to medium-low, cover partially, and simmer gently, skimming as needed, for about 2^1/$_2$ hours, or until the liquid is reduced by almost half.

Strain the stock through a fine-mesh sieve into a clean vessel. If using immediately, skim off as much fat as possible from the surface with a large spoon. Season the stock to taste with salt. If storing for later use, prepare an ice bath in your sink, pour the stock into a tall container, and place it in the ice water to cool quickly. Stir the stock periodically to help reduce the cooling time, minimizing the opportunity for bacteria to grow.

When the stock is at room temperature, cover and place in the refrigerator until well chilled. Remove from the refrigerator and lift off and discard the layer of fat that has solidified on top. Re-cover and refrigerate for up to 3 days or freeze for up to 6 months.

CALDO DE PESCADO ▪ Fish Stock

The heads and central bones, or fish frames, of white fish, such as snapper, cod, hake, or bass, make a mild but tasty stock. Avoid what the Spanish call *pescado azul*, or "blue fish," such as tuna, sardines, and salmon, among others, which are fatty fish and yield a strongly flavored stock that can overwhelm other foods. Mussels are a good addition, as they impart a subtle flavor, and you can use the cooked mussels in another recipe, such as Mussels in Vinegar and Wine (page 73). Never simmer the stock too long, or it will become too strongly flavored and bitter. A half hour will suffice. ▪ **Makes about 2 quarts**

2 pounds fish frames and heads (gills removed) from white fish (see recipe introduction)

1 cup shrimp shells

1 pound mussels, scrubbed and debearded

2 leeks, green tops only, coarsely chopped

1 yellow onion, halved

2 carrots, coarsely chopped

1 bunch flat-leaf parsley

2 quarts water

Salt

In a stockpot, combine the fish frames and heads, shrimp shells, mussels, leeks, onion, carrots, parsley, and water and bring to a gentle boil over high heat, using a slotted spoon to skim off any foam that forms on the surface. Decrease the heat to medium-low, cover partially, and simmer gently, skimming as needed, for 30 minutes.

Strain the stock through a fine-mesh sieve into a clean vessel. Retrieve the mussels from the sieve, discard their shells, and reserve the meats for another use. Season the stock to taste with salt. If storing for later use, prepare an ice bath in your sink, pour the stock into a tall container, and place it in the ice water to cool quickly. Stir the stock periodically to help reduce the cooling time, minimizing the opportunity for bacteria to grow.

When the stock is at room temperature, cover and refrigerate for up to 3 days or freeze for up to 6 months.

CALDO DE VERDURAS ▪ Vegetable Stock

I like this subtle and mild vegetable stock because it enhances every dish to which I add it. The romano beans, flat green beans sometimes called Italian beans, add a delicious flavor, and if you don't mind eating vegetables cooked quite soft, retrieve the beans from the finished stock and serve them cold with a little Mayonnaise (page 306). ▪ **Makes about 7 cups**

2 pounds romano (flat) beans or regular green beans, ends trimmed

3 leeks, green tops only, coarsely chopped

2 yellow onions, peeled and halved

2 carrots, coarsely chopped

1 bunch flat-leaf parsley

2 quarts water

Salt

In a stockpot, combine the beans, leeks, onions, carrots, parsley, and water and bring to a gentle boil over high heat, using a slotted spoon to skim off any foam that forms on the surface. (Far less foam and impurities collect on the surface of vegetable-based stocks than meat stocks.) Decrease the heat to medium-low, cover partially, and simmer gently, skimming as needed, for 45 minutes. It will reduce slightly.

Strain the stock through a fine-mesh sieve into a clean vessel. Season the stock to taste with salt and use immediately. If storing for later use, prepare an ice bath in your sink, pour the stock into a tall container, and place it in the ice water to cool quickly. Stir the stock periodically to help reduce the cooling time, minimizing the opportunity for bacteria to grow.

When the stock is at room temperature, cover and refrigerate for up to 3 days or freeze for up to 6 months.

Sevilla, Andalusia

SAUCES

SALSA MAHONESA ▪ Mayonnaise

Although many think of mayonnaise as a French creation, Spaniards place its invention on the island of Minorca, where it was named after the capital city of Mahón. Not surprisingly, the French and the Minorcans have a different view of who first beat together eggs and oil, even on the island. According to the French, it was the chef employed by Duke Richelieu who came up with the sauce for a celebratory meal honoring the siege of Mahón in 1756. Spaniards, in contrast, believe that the duke's chef picked up the secrets to the now-famous sauce by watching a humble Minorcan cook.

Many other sauces can be made from this basic recipe by simply adding herbs, anchovies, mustard, capers, or garlic. Homemade mayonnaise tastes much better than its commercial counterpart, and because it is easy to make and keeps well, it is worth whipping up a batch. For the best results, have all of your ingredients at room temperature. If you are concerned about using raw eggs, feel free to substitute a commercial product in recipes that call for mayonnaise. ▪ **Makes about 1 cup**

1 egg, at room temperature

1 teaspoon salt

1 tablespoon sherry vinegar, at room temperature

1 cup extra virgin olive oil, at room temperature

Freshly squeezed orange juice (optional)

In a blender, combine the egg, salt, and vinegar and blend at the lowest speed just until combined. With the motor running at low speed, add the olive oil in a slow, thin, steady stream, continuing to process until the oil is completely incorporated and the sauce has emulsified. You can adjust the consistency of the sauce once the oil has been added. If you prefer a thinner mayonnaise, with the motor still running, add a little hot water or orange juice. If you prefer a thicker consistency, increase the blender speed to the maximum and blend for about 10 seconds.

Transfer to a bowl and use immediately, or cover and refrigerate for up to 1 week.

AJO ALMENDRA ▪ Garlic and Almond Mayonnaise

In the village of Vélez Blanco in Almería, the easternmost province of Andalusia, my friends Ludmila and Chencho Arias serve this sauce with grilled lamb chops and rice dishes. Green almonds are nuts that are picked early, usually in May in the United States, before the shell and the kernel have had a chance to harden. They are lime green on the outside and covered with a downy fuzz. This hull is easily cut with a knife and peeled away to reveal the still-soft, ivory nut. Green almonds can be difficult to find, unless you or a friend has an almond tree, although sometimes they are available at farmers' markets or online directly from orchards. ▪ **Makes about 2 cups**

1 clove garlic, coarsely chopped

20 green almonds, peeled

1 egg

1 teaspoon salt

1 cup extra virgin olive oil

Juice of 1/2 lemon

In a blender or food processor, combine the garlic, almonds, egg, and salt and process until smooth. With the motor running, add the olive oil in a slow, thin, steady stream, continuing to process until the oil is completely incorporated and the sauce has emulsified. Add the lemon juice and process to mix.

Transfer the sauce to a bowl. Use immediately, or cover and store in the refrigerator for up to 1 week.

ALIOLI ▪

The name of this sauce is derived from the Catalan *all i oli*, which means "garlic and oil," and it is basically just that. Many people outside of Spain have the mistaken notion that the sauce contains eggs, but an authentic *alioli*, which is best described as a white and shiny sauce with a strong garlic flavor, does not. If you are not fond of garlic, you can use a smaller amount than the recipe calls for, or you can replace the recipe with Mayonnaise (left) to which you add a little garlic. I have found that mixing equal parts olive oil and another subtler vegetable oil, such as corn oil, makes a better emulsion than using solely olive oil, and adding a little water helps keep the emulsion from breaking, especially if you are using a blender, instead of making the sauce by hand as most Catalans do. (You can even use all corn oil, if you like.) If you decide to make the sauce in a mortar, make sure all the ingredients are at room temperature, omit the water, and proceed in the same sequence, being sure always to stir the mixture in the same direction to prevent the emulsion from breaking. ▪ **Makes about 1 cup**

6 cloves garlic, coarsely chopped

3 tablespoons water

1 teaspoon salt

1/2 cup olive oil

1/2 cup corn oil

In a blender or food processor, combine the garlic, water, and salt and process until a smooth paste forms. Combine the olive and corn oils in a measuring cup with a spout. With the motor running, add the oils in a slow, thin, steady stream, continuing to process until the oils are completely incorporated and the sauce has emulsified.

Transfer the sauce to a bowl. Use immediately, or cover and store in the refrigerator for up to 1 week.

▪▪ BASIC RECIPES

307

:: Mojos ::

Canarian *mojos* are versatile sauces that usually accompany meat or fish dishes, and, of course, *papas arrugadas* (page 121), the wrinkled potatoes that are the official side dish of the local cuisine. All *mojos* are made with raw ingredients, and all include garlic, olive oil, vinegar, salt, and cumin. You can also add day-old bread, either dry or soaked in water, as a thickener to any *mojo*.

The two basic classes are red *mojos*, including *mojo picón* and *mojo colorado*, and green *mojos*, including *mojo verde* and *mojo de cilantro*. There is also a cheese *mojo* known as *almogrote Gomero* (page 317), but it is more of a spread than a sauce. *Mojo picón* is the best-known *mojo* in all of Spain. It is similar to *mojo colorado* except that it is made with hot chile and a larger amount of garlic and cumin. The only difference between *mojo verde* and *mojo de cilantro* is the choice of herb, parsley in one and cilantro in the other. Adding a ripe avocado to either lends a smoothness to the sauce, and though it is a modern innovation that most old-fashioned Canarians dismiss, the young islanders love it.

Traditionally, *mojos* are made in a mortar with a pestle. Great results are possible with a blender, too, so I include instructions for both methods in my recipes. You can give your blender-made *mojos* a handmade quality—and a good bite—by omitting the ground cumin in the recipes and folding a scattering of whole cumin seeds into the finished sauce with a spatula.

Red *mojos* are good keepers and can be stored in tightly covered jars in the refrigerator for several weeks. If you discover one that you really like, double or triple the amounts indicated in the recipe and have it always at the ready. Adapt the amount of spiciness to your own taste.

MOJO VERDE Y MOJO DE CILANTRO ▪ Green Mojos

▪ **Makes 1 cup**

6 cloves garlic, peeled but left whole

1/2 teaspoon hot red pepper flakes

1 ripe avocado, halved, pitted, and peeled (optional)

Pinch of ground cumin

1 teaspoon salt

2 cups loosely packed fresh flat-leaf parsley or
   cilantro leaves

3/4 cup Sherry Vinaigrette (page 314)

In a blender or mortar, combine the garlic, red pepper flakes, avocado, cumin, and salt. Blend or pound until a paste forms. If using a blender, add the parsley or cilantro all at once and, with the motor running, add the vinaigrette by the tablespoonful, blending until all the vinaigrette has been added and the sauce is smooth. This will take about 2 minutes. If using a mortar and pestle, add the parsley or cilantro all at once to the mortar and then add the vinaigrette by the tablespoonful, working the ingredients together with the pestle until the sauce is smooth. This will take a bit longer than 2 minutes.

Transfer the sauce to a jar, cover tightly, and store in the refrigerator for up to 1 week.

MOJO PICÓN ▪ Spicy Red Mojo

▪ **Makes about 1 cup**

6 dried Canarian sweet peppers or ancho chiles

6 cloves garlic, peeled but left whole

1 1/2 teaspoons sweet pimentón or paprika

1 1/2 teaspoons hot red pepper flakes

2 teaspoons ground cumin

1/2 teaspoon salt

3/4 cup Sherry Vinaigrette (page 314)

In a heatproof bowl, combine the dried peppers with boiling water to cover and let stand for 30 minutes, or until soft. Drain the peppers, slit them open, and scrape off the flesh with the edge of a knife, discarding the seeds, skins, and stems. Set the flesh aside.

In a blender or mortar, combine the garlic, *pimentón*, red pepper flakes, cumin, and salt. Blend or pound until a smooth paste forms. If using a blender, add the flesh from the peppers. Then, with the motor running, add the vinaigrette by the tablespoonful, blending until all the vinaigrette has been added and the sauce is smooth. This will take about 2 minutes. If using a mortar and pestle, add the flesh from the peppers to the mortar and then add the vinaigrette by the tablespoonful, working the ingredients together with the pestle until the sauce is smooth. This will take a bit longer than 2 minutes.

Transfer the sauce to a jar, cover tightly, and store in the refrigerator for up to several weeks.

MOJO COLORADO ▪ Red Mojo

▪ **Makes about 1 cup**

6 dried Canarian sweet peppers or ancho chiles

6 cloves garlic, peeled but left whole

1 1/2 teaspoons sweet pimentón or paprika

1/2 teaspoon ground cumin

1/2 teaspoon salt

3/4 cup Sherry Vinaigrette (page 314)

In a heatproof bowl, combine the dried peppers with boiling water to cover and let stand for 30 minutes, or until soft. Drain the peppers, slit them open, and scrape off the flesh with the edge of a knife, discarding the seeds, skins, and stems. Set the flesh aside.

In a blender or mortar, combine the garlic, *pimentón*, cumin, and salt. Blend or pound until a smooth paste forms. If using a blender, add the flesh from the peppers. Then, with the motor running, add the vinaigrette by the tablespoonful, blending until all the vinaigrette has been added and the sauce is smooth. This will take about 2 minutes. If using a mortar and pestle, add the flesh from the peppers to the mortar and then add the vinaigrette by the tablespoonful, working the ingredients together with the pestle until the sauce is smooth. This will take a bit longer than 2 minutes.

Transfer the sauce to a jar, cover tightly, and store in the refrigerator for up to several weeks.

SALSA BÉCHAMEL ⠸ Béchamel Sauce

Salsa béchamel is mainly used for topping pasta dishes, but it is also the base for preparations like *croquetas* and is often used to bind the ingredients in stuffing. You can make a thicker sauce by increasing the amounts of butter and flour or a thinner one by decreasing the amounts, always keeping them in equal parts. ⠸ **Makes a scant 2 cups**

> 2 tablespoons unsalted butter
>
> 2 tablespoons all-purpose flour
>
> 2 cups milk, heated to lukewarm
>
> Salt
>
> Pinch of freshly grated nutmeg (optional)

In a saucepan, melt the butter over medium heat. Add the flour, mixing well with a wooden spoon for 1 to 2 minutes, or until the butter is completely absorbed and the mixture is smooth. Do not let it color. Add the milk a little at a time, stirring constantly to prevent lumps from forming. When all of the milk has been added, season with salt, add the nutmeg, if using, and cook, stirring constantly, for about 10 minutes, or until the sauce is smooth and creamy and coats the back of the spoon.

Remove from the heat. If not using immediately, let cool, cover, and store in the refrigerator for up to 3 days.

SALSA ROMESCO ⠸ Romesco Sauce

Romesco sauce originated in Tarragona, one of the coastal provinces of Catalonia. The term is also used in the names of dishes that include fish or shellfish simply cooked—grilled, baked, simmered—in the sauce or with the sauce served on the side, such as Tarragona's well-known *romesco de peix*, an elaborate mix of fish and shellfish prepared in the sauce. The sauce's main ingredients are dried red peppers, olive oil, almonds and/or hazelnuts, white wine, and sometimes a little chile. ⠸ **Makes about 3 cups**

> 6 dried ñora, choricero, or ancho chiles
>
> 3/4 cup olive oil
>
> 2 slices 2-day-old country-style bread
>
> 3 cloves garlic, peeled but left whole
>
> 12 blanched almonds
>
> 2 blanched hazelnuts
>
> 1 1/2 teaspoons salt
>
> 1 yellow onion, chopped
>
> 1 tomato, chopped
>
> 1 teaspoon salt
>
> 1/2 cup dry white wine
>
> 1 tablespoon red wine vinegar (optional)
>
> 1/2 teaspoon hot red pepper flakes (optional)
>
> 2 cups water or Fish Stock (page 304), if using the sauce with fish

In a heatproof bowl, combine the dried chiles with boiling water to cover and let stand for 30 minutes, or until soft. Drain the chiles, slit them open, and scrape off the flesh with the edge of a knife, discarding the seeds, skins, and stems. Set the flesh aside.

In a large skillet, heat 6 tablespoons of the olive oil over medium-high heat. Add the bread and fry, turning once, for 2 or 3 minutes on each side, or until golden. Remove from the pan, let cool slightly, and break into several pieces. Set the skillet aside.

In a mortar, blender, or food processor, combine the fried bread, garlic, almonds, hazelnuts, and salt. Pound or process until a paste forms. Add the flesh from the peppers and pound or process until fully incorporated. The paste should be slightly coarse. Set aside.

Add the remaining 6 tablespoons olive oil to the skillet and place over medium-high heat. Add the onion and sauté, stirring often, for 3 to 4 minutes, or until lightly golden. Add the tomato and salt, mix well, decrease the heat to medium, and cook, stirring occasionally, for 5 minutes, or until the ingredients are well blended.

Add the pepper paste; wine; vinegar, if using; red pepper flakes, if using; and water, mix well, and bring to a simmer. Decrease the heat to medium-low and cook for about 15 minutes, or until all the vegetables are soft and the flavors are blended. If you prefer a smoother texture, pass the sauce through a food mill fitted with the medium plate held over a bowl.

The sauce can be served hot or cold. If not using immediately, cover and store in the refrigerator for up to 1 week.

SALSA ESPAÑOLA ▪ Onion and Carrot Sauce

Spanish cooks use this sauce mainly for meat dishes, for making stuffed peppers, and for vegetable dishes in general. For example, it is an essential element of the old-fashioned *patatas a la importancia* (page 122). ▪ **Makes 2 cups**

2/3 cup olive oil

1 1/2 large yellow onions (about 1 pound), coarsely chopped

2 small carrots, peeled and sliced

2 heaping tablespoons all-purpose flour

2 cups water

1/2 cup dry sherry or dry white wine

1 1/2 teaspoons salt

In a wide saucepan, heat the olive oil over high heat. Add the onions and cook, stirring constantly, for about 10 minutes, or until golden brown. Add the carrots and flour, mix well, and cook, stirring often, for 10 minutes. Add the water, sherry, and salt, mix well, and cook, stirring occasionally, for about 10 minutes longer, or until the sauce thickens slightly.

Remove from the heat and let cool until tepid. Transfer the contents of the pan to a blender or food processor and process until smooth. If not using immediately, cover and store in the refrigerator for up to 1 week.

SALSA DE TOMATE ▪ Tomato Sauce

My life would not be the same without a large container of *salsa de tomate* always in the refrigerator. With it on hand, I can put together a dish in no time. For example, I combine it with mussels or pasta or serve it with fried eggs. I am not embarrassed to admit that there is no better tomato sauce than the one that Fina, our family's guardian angel, has been perfecting over the years she has lived with us. I taught her to cook all our favorite dishes and, of course, my *salsa de tomate*. She has been slowly diverging from the original recipe ever since. I recently asked her how she now makes it, and here is her wonderful formula. ▪ **Makes 3 cups**

1 cup olive oil

1 1/2 large yellow onions (about 1 pound), finely chopped

1 (28-ounce) can whole tomatoes, with juice

1 1/4 cups water

1 1/2 teaspoons salt, plus more if needed

1 1/2 tablespoons sugar

In a large sauté pan, heat the olive oil over medium heat. Add the onions and sauté, stirring often, for about 15 minutes, or until golden. Add the tomatoes with their juice, water, salt, and sugar and bring to a boil. Decrease the heat to low and simmer uncovered, stirring occasionally, for about 1 1/2 hours, or until very soft and almost puréelike.

Remove the sauce from the heat and let cool slightly. Pass the sauce through a food mill fitted with the medium plate held over a bowl. Taste and adjust the seasoning with salt.

If not using immediately, let cool, cover, and store in the refrigerator for up to 1 week.

SALSA DE TOMATE MALLORQUINA ::
Majorcan Tomato Sauce

Nearly every tomato sauce tastes better when made with fresh tomatoes picked at the height of the season, even my *salsa de tomate* (page 311). But because wonderful tomatoes are in the market for such a short time, and I need a good basic tomato sauce year-round, I rely on high-quality canned tomatoes most of the time. Here, in a recipe from Majorca, I have used fresh tomatoes, however, because of the extraordinary *tomates de ramellet* that are cultivated there. I was fascinated to discover that Majorcans harvest these tomatoes at the end of summer, braid them into long bunches, and hang them from their balconies. The tomatoes are used over the winter, and mysteriously they never appear to dry. On a visit to Majorca one year in March, I tasted some of the tomatoes and couldn't believe how juicy they still were after months in the open air.

As with my everyday tomato sauce, you can use this sauce for pasta, for egg dishes, for mixing with seafood, or just about any time you need a classic tomato sauce. :: **Makes 3 cups**

1/2 cup olive oil

4 cloves garlic, unpeeled

2 pounds ripe tomatoes, cored and cut into eighths

1 1/2 teaspoons salt, plus more if needed

1 teaspoon sugar

In a deep saucepan, heat the olive oil over medium heat. Add the garlic cloves and fry briefly to release their fragrance. Add the tomatoes, salt, and sugar and bring the mixture to a boil. Decrease the heat to low and cook uncovered, stirring occasionally, for about 1 hour, or until the tomatoes have broken down and thickened.

Remove from the heat and let cool slightly. Remove and discard the garlic. Pass the sauce through a food mill fitted with the medium plate held over a bowl. Taste and adjust the seasoning with salt. If not using immediately, let cool, cover, and store in the refrigerator for up to 1 week.

SALSA DE TINTA DE CHIPIRÓN ::
Black Ink Sauce

This intensely black sauce is as delicious as it is striking. Although it includes three onions, they do not overwhelm the distinctive flavor of the squid ink. The sauce is used in my recipe for Black Rice (page 188)—and a similar sauce appears in Baby Squid in Black Ink Sauce (page 235)—and it can combined with olive oil and vinegar for an unusual and delicious vinaigrette (page 315).

Commercially fished squid are caught in large nets, which causes them to lose most or all of their ink. But squid ink, usually frozen in small plastic jars or bags, is available in many North American fish stores and specialty-foods markets. After adding the ink to the sauce, be sure to cook the sauce for at least 5 minutes to remove the ink's slight toxicity. The cut-up squid is used only to flavor the sauce. When you remove it, reserve it for adding to the finished dish, if making Black Rice, or to another dish, such as a seafood salad. :: **Makes 3 cups**

1/2 cup olive oil

3 yellow onions, chopped

1 leek, white part only, thinly sliced

2 small tomatoes, peeled and chopped

1 clove garlic, minced

1 large squid, about 3 ounces, cleaned and with body cut into rings and tentacles halved (page 196)

1 1/2 teaspoons salt

2 tablespoons squid ink

In a sauté pan, heat the olive oil over medium heat. Add the onions, leek, tomatoes, and garlic and cook, stirring often, for about 10 minutes, or until the vegetables are soft.

Add the squid pieces and the salt and cook, stirring often, for about 5 minutes, or until the squid is opaque. Using a slotted spoon, remove the squid pieces and reserve for another use. Add the squid ink to the pan, increase the heat to high, and boil, stirring constantly, for at least 5 minutes. At this point, the ink should be thoroughly blended with the other ingredients.

Remove from the heat and let cool slightly. Pass the sauce through a food mill fitted with the medium blade, and then process in a blender or food processor to achieve a smoother texture. If not using immediately, cover and store in the refrigerator for up to 3 days.

SALSA VIZCAÍNA ▪▪ Biscayne Sauce

This is one of the most prominent sauces of the Basque Country, where it is served with salt cod, snails, or tripe, among other foods. It is often the subject of heated discussions among Basque gastronomes: some say that a true *salsa vizcaína* never uses tomato sauce; others argue that chopped *jamón serrano* should always be included; still others contend that one or two *galletas Maria*, plain cookies sold all over Spain, should be added. For many years now, I have been preparing this sauce the way my mother taught me, which is the recipe I've included here. ▪▪ **Makes about 3 cups**

10 dried choricero or ancho chiles

^{1}/$_2$ cup olive oil

2 yellow onions, chopped

1 red onion, chopped

1 clove garlic, sliced

1 teaspoon salt, plus more if needed

Pinch of sugar

^{1}/$_2$ cup Tomato Sauce (page 311)

In a heatproof bowl, combine the dried chiles with boiling water to cover and let stand for 30 minutes, or until soft. Drain the chiles, reserving 1 cup of the water. Slit the chiles open and scrape off the flesh with the edge of a knife, discarding the seeds, skins, and stems. Set the flesh aside.

In a sauté pan, heat the olive oil over medium heat. Add both onions and the garlic and sauté, stirring often, for 10 minutes, or until soft. Add the flesh of the peppers and cook, stirring often, for 5 minutes, or until the pepper flesh begins to soften. Decrease the heat to low and add the reserved 1 cup water, salt, and sugar. Cook uncovered, stirring often, for 20 to 30 minutes, or until the pepper flesh is very soft and the cooking liquid has reduced slightly. Add the tomato sauce and cook, stirring occasionally, for 5 minutes longer to blend the flavors.

Remove from the heat and let cool slightly. Pass the sauce through a food mill fitted with the medium plate held over a bowl. Taste and adjust the seasoning with salt. If not using immediately, let cool, cover, and store in the refrigerator for up to 3 days.

Morning stroll on a farm outside Ronda, Andalusia

VINAIGRETTES AND AROMATIC OILS

Vinaigrettes and aromatic oils are great inventions: not only do they add flavor, enhancing the taste of the ingredients in everything from simple salads to elaborate appetizers, but they also give dishes an appealing touch of color. They keep well in the refrigerator and are easy to make. I usually prepare them in quantities of about 1 cup and store them in small plastic bottles. I have included recipes for ten vinaigrettes and oils that I regularly use. Once you try making these, you will want to experiment with your own creations using other ingredients.

VINAGRETA DE ACEITE DE OLIVA EXTRA VIRGEN Y VINAGRE DE JEREZ ::
Sherry Vinaigrette

:: **Makes 1 cup**

1/4 cup sherry vinegar
3/4 cup extra virgin olive oil
1 1/2 teaspoons salt
Pinch of sugar

Pour the vinegar into a small bowl. Slowly add the oil, whisking constantly until the oil and vinegar are emulsified. Add the salt and sugar and whisk to incorporate. Transfer to a covered container and store in the refrigerator for up to a few weeks. Mix well before using.

VINAGRETA DE ACEITUNAS NEGRAS ::
Black Olive Vinaigrette

:: **Makes about 1 1/2 cups**

20 black olives, pitted
1 cup Sherry Vinaigrette (above)

In a blender or food processor, combine the olives and vinaigrette and process until the olives are almost reduced to a paste. Transfer to a covered container and store in the refrigerator for up to 1 week. Mix well before using.

VINAGRETA DE ACEITUNAS VERDES ::
Green Olive Vinaigrette

:: **Makes about 1 1/2 cups**

20 green olives, pitted
1 cup Sherry Vinaigrette (left)

In a blender or food processor, combine the olives and vinaigrette and process until the olives are almost reduced to a paste. Transfer to a covered container and store in the refrigerator for up to 1 week. Mix well before using.

VINAGRETA DE ZANAHORIAS ::
Carrot Vinaigrette

:: **Makes about 1 1/3 cups**

1/2 cup tightly packed chopped boiled carrots
1/2 cup Sherry Vinaigrette (left)

In a blender or food processor, combine the carrots and vinaigrette and process until a beautiful orange sauce forms. Transfer to a covered container and store in the refrigerator for up to 1 week. Mix well before using.

VINAGRETA DE REMOLACHA ::
Red Beet Vinaigrette

:: **Makes about 1 1/3 cups**

1/2 cup tightly packed chopped boiled red beets
1/2 cup Sherry Vinaigrette (left)

In a blender or food processor, combine the beets and vinaigrette and process until a beautiful burgundy sauce forms. Transfer to a covered container and store in the refrigerator for up to 1 week. Mix well before using.

VINAGRETA DE PIMIENTO ROJO Y COMINOS ⠿
Red Pepper and Cumin Vinaigrette

⠿ **Makes about 1 cup**

1 red bell pepper, roasted, peeled, and seeded
1/2 cup Sherry Vinaigrette (page 314)
1 1/2 teaspoons cumin seeds

In a blender or food processor, combine the bell pepper and vinaigrette and process until a bright reddish orange sauce forms. Add the cumin seeds and process to incorporate. Transfer to a covered container and store in the refrigerator for up to 1 week. Mix well before using.

VINAGRETA DE SALMOREJO ⠿
Salmorejo Vinaigrette

⠿ **Makes 2 1/2 cups**

2 cups Thick Cordoban Gazpacho (page 87)
1/2 cup Sherry Vinaigrette (page 314)

In a bowl, combine the gazpacho and vinaigrette and whisk to combine. Transfer to a covered container and store in the refrigerator for up to 1 week. Mix well before using.

VINAGRETA DE SALSA DE CHIPIRÓN ⠿
Black Ink Sauce Vinaigrette

⠿ **Makes 1 cup**

1/2 cup Black Ink Sauce (page 312)
1/2 cup Sherry Vinaigrette (page 314)

In a bowl, combine the sauce and vinaigrette and whisk to combine. Transfer to a covered container and store in the refrigerator for up to 1 week. Mix well before using.

ACEITE DE PIMENTÓN ⠿
Pimentón Oil

⠿ **Makes 1/2 cup**

1/2 cup extra virgin olive oil
1 tablespoon sweet pimentón or paprika

In a small saucepan, heat the olive oil over medium heat until lukewarm, then remove from the heat. Add the *pimentón* and mix well. Let cool, transfer to a covered container, and store in the refrigerator for up to 1 week. Mix well before using.

ACEITE DE PEREJIL ⠿ Parsley Oil

⠿ **Makes 1/2 cup**

1/2 cup extra virgin olive oil
1 tablespoon finely chopped fresh flat-leaf parsley

In a small bowl, whisk together the olive oil and parsley. Transfer to a covered container and store in the refrigerator. The parsley loses its flavor and aroma relatively quickly, so keep for no more than 3 days. Mix well before using.

SYRUPS AND CARAMELIZED SUGAR COATING

ALMÍBAR ▪ Syrup

This simple syrup is easy to make and keeps well in the refrigerator. Syrups can vary in sweetness, but I have found that this ratio of water to sugar is ideal for most of my recipes. ▪ **Makes 1¹/₂ cups**

> 1¹/₂ cups water
> 1 cup sugar

In a small, heavy saucepan, combine the water and sugar and bring to a boil over high heat, stirring to dissolve the sugar. Decrease the heat to medium or medium-low and simmer, stirring occasionally, for about 20 minutes, or until a thick syrup forms.

Remove from the heat, let cool to room temperature, transfer to a jar with a tight-fitting lid, and refrigerate until needed. It will keep indefinitely.

ALMÍBAR DE NARANJA ▪ Orange Syrup

You can use this syrup to add flavor and color to both savory and sweet dishes. ▪ **Makes 2 cups**

> 2 oranges
> 2 cups sugar
> ¹/₃ cup water

Using a vegetable peeler or a paring knife, remove the zest from both oranges and cut it into fine julienne. Then halve the oranges and squeeze the juice. You should have about ²/₃ cup juice. Set aside.

In a heavy saucepan, combine the sugar and water and bring to a boil over high heat without stirring. Watch the mixture closely, and as soon as it turns a caramel color—this can happen quickly—decrease the heat to medium, add the orange juice and orange zest, and simmer for about 20 minutes, or until the orange and the caramel flavors blend fully.

Transfer to a heatproof bowl, let cool to room temperature, and then transfer to a jar with a tight-fitting lid and refrigerate for up to several weeks.

CARAMELO ▪ Caramelized Sugar Coating

Mastering this coating is indispensable if you want to make flan or similar desserts. If you are a beginner, the process can be tricky, but once you have made the caramel a few times, it becomes easy. I recommend that you start by preparing it in "slow motion" over low heat, and then when you get a feel for it, you can reduce the cooking time by increasing the heat. The amount of sugar used here will be enough for the recipes in this book, but you can use more or less, depending on your needs. If you have an unlined copper saucepan, use it here: copper conducts heat better than other metals. ▪ **Makes enough to coat 1 (5 by 9-inch) mold or 8 to 12 custard cups**

> ¹/₂ cup sugar

Spread the sugar evenly in the bottom of a heavy saucepan and place over medium-low heat. It may take several minutes before the sugar begins to melt. Without stirring, watch the sugar closely as it begins to liquefy at the edges. All of it will slowly turn first into a yellowish and then a golden syrup and finally into a brown caramel sauce. When the liquefied sugar is turning from golden to brown, immediately remove the saucepan from the heat. (If you miss this point, the sugar will quickly turn too dark and taste bitter and you will need to discard it and begin again.) Working swiftly, pour the liquid caramel into the mold (or molds) and tilt to cover the bottom and sides evenly. It is important to do this transfer quickly, as the change in temperature causes the caramel to solidify rapidly.

Any bits of caramel stuck to the saucepan can be removed easily. Add water and bring to a boil; the caramel will liquefy, allowing you to pour it out and then wash the pan.

CHEESES

REQUESÓN ⠿ Quark

I use *requesón*, known as Quark in English (which translates as "curds" in the original German), in some dessert recipes, and because it is very easy to make, I have included the recipe here. You can easily increase the volume of milk to make whatever amount of cheese you want. You can also add some salt, freshly ground black pepper, and finely chopped chives to the finished cheese for a delicious spread for toast or bagels. ⠿ **Makes about 2¹/₄ cups (just over 1 pound)**

  6 quarts whole milk, preferably raw

Pour the milk into a large pitcher or other vessel, preferably with a spout, cover with a kitchen towel, and let it stand at room temperature for 48 hours. It will sour and solidify somewhat, forming soft curds.

Line a colander with cheesecloth and place over a large bowl. Pour the partially solidified milk into the colander. The whey will immediately begin to separate from the curds. Gather the ends of the cloth up and tie them in a knot to make a pouch. Hang the pouch from your kitchen sink faucet, or somewhere else less trafficked, and leave it to drain for 30 hours. When the pouch has stopped dripping completely, you will have fresh cheese with the consistency of thick sour cream.

Untie the pouch and scrape the cheese from the cloth into a bowl, cover, and refrigerate. It will keep for up to several days.

ALMOGROTE GOMERO ⠿
Cheese Pâté

The people of Gomera, in the Canary Islands, eat this cheese spread with white country-style bread and a glass of wine. They make it with an aged goat cheese, but I have made it with aged Manchego, which is readily available in the United States, with great success. ⠿
Makes about 2 cups

  3 cloves garlic, coarsely chopped
  ¹/₂ cup olive oil
  1 teaspoon hot red pepper flakes
  2 tomatoes, halved crosswise, grated on the large holes of a handheld grater, and skins discarded
  ¹/₂ pound Manchego cheese, grated
  ¹/₂ teaspoon salt

In a blender, combine the garlic, 1 tablespoon of the olive oil, and the red pepper flakes and process until a smooth paste forms. Add the tomatoes and cheese and process until well combined. With the motor running, add the remaining 7 tablespoons olive oil 1 tablespoon at a time, processing until all the oil is fully incorporated. This should take about 2 minutes. The finished mixture should have a smooth, spreadable consistency. Alternatively, combine the garlic, 1 tablespoon of the olive oil, and the red pepper flakes in a mortar and pound with a pestle to form a smooth paste. Add the tomatoes, cheese, and salt and continue pounding and mixing until well combined. Add the remaining 7 tablespoons olive oil 1 tablespoon at a time, mixing with the pestle after each addition to incorporate the oil fully.

Transfer the spread to a bowl. If not using immediately, cover and store in the refrigerator for up to 3 weeks.

:: SOURCES ::

These sources carry many more foods and other items than I have listed here, so call them or check online for any ingredient, prepared food, or piece of cookware you need.

Artisanal Cheese Center
Tel: (877) 797-1200
www.artisanalcheese.com
Carries a large selection of Spanish cheeses.

Browne Trading Company
Tel: (800) 944-7848
www.browne-trading.com
Will ship a variety of fresh fish and shellfish overnight, including turbot, monkfish, and diver-harvested scallops and occasionally fresh baby eels from Maine, gooseneck barnacles, and spider crabs.

D'Artagnan, Inc.
Tel: (800) 327-8246
www.dartagnan.com
Carries duck, rabbit, venison, suckling pig, chorizo, and *morcilla*, among other fresh and cured meats.

Despaña Brand Foods
Tel: (718) 779-4971
Fax: (718)779-7438
www.despanabrandfoods.com
Carries house-made chorizo and *morcilla*, excellent frozen baby eels, olive oils, vinegars, rice, cheeses, saffron, *piquillo* peppers, and asparagus from Navarra, among many other foods, plus paella pans and *cazuelas*.

An assortment of artisanal goat cheeses in the Peña Remoña quesería in the Picos de Europa, Cantabria

La Tienda
Tel: (888) 472-1022
www.tienda.com
Importers of many Spanish foods, wines, and other goods; carries chorizo and other cured meats, baby squid and squid ink, and tuna preserved in olive oil; various dried legumes, including beans for *fabada asturiana* and lentils; olive oils and sherry vinegars; natural, roasted, and blanched Marcona almonds, and *polvorones*.

Olé Olé Foods
Tel: (800) 986-8279
www.oleolefoods.com
Importers of a wide variety of Spanish foods, including olive oils, vinegars, rice and pasta, cheeses, *jamón serrano*, *lomo embuchado*, saffron, *piquillo* peppers, preserved tuna, *turrón*, and many other products.

Spain Wine Collection
16 Route 9W
Congers, New York 10920
Tel: (845) 268-2622
Importer and distributor (for New York, New Jersey, and Connecticut) of fine wines from Spain; gladly provides information on distributors in your area.

The Spanish Table
Tel: Santa Fe (505) 986-0243; Seattle (206) 682-2827; Berkeley (510) 548-1383
www.spanishtable.com
Well-stocked source for cookware (*cazuelas*, paella pans), wines, and foods, from *pimentón*, *sobrasada*, and *jamón serrano* to Bomba rice and varietal olive oils. Stores in Seattle, Washington; Berkeley, California; and Santa Fe, New Mexico.

:: BIBLIOGRAPHY ::

Academia Castellano Manchega de Gastronomía. *La gastronomía de Castilla–La Mancha*. Madrid: Agedime S.L., 1996.

Academia Española de Gastronomía. *Mis restaurantes favoritos en Madrid*. Madrid: Lunwerg Editores, 1998.

Adrià, Ferran, and Juli Soler. *El Bulli, El sabor del Mediterráneo*. Barcelona: Editorial Empúries, 1993.

Álvarez, Cristino. *Rancho a bordo*. Madrid: Ministerio de Agricultura, Pesca y Alimentación, n.d.

Andrews, Colman. *Catalan Cuisine*. Boston: Harvard Common Press, 1999.

Anonymous. *Ranchos a bordo*. Madrid: Secretaría General de Pesca Marítima, 1991.

Arenillas, Angeles, José Carlos Capel, and Clara María Gonzalez de Amezúa. *From Spain with Olive Oil*. Madrid: Asoliva and ICEX, 1988.

Arguiñano, Karlos. *El menú de cada día*. Barcelona: Publicaciones de RTVE y Ediciones del Serbal, 1992.

Aris, Pepita. *La cuisine de la campagne espagnole*. Paris: privately printed, 1991.

Arzak, Juan Mari. *Las recetas de Arzak*. Madrid: El Pais Aguilar, 1997.

Asúa, Roberto, and José Luis Iturrieta. *La cocina vasca en Bizkaia*. San Sebastián: R&B Ediciones, 1997.

Azcaray y Eguileor, Ursula, Sira Azcaray y Eguileor, and Vicenta Azcaray y Eguileor. *El amparo. Sus platos clásicos*. 2nd ed. Bilbao: Escuelas Gráficas de la Santa Casa de la Misericordia, 1930.

Barrenechea, Teresa. *The Basque Table*. Boston: Harvard Common Press, 1998.

Batterberry, Michael. "Andalusia: Gardens of Paradise, Fat of Heaven." *Food Arts* 14, no. 4 (May 2001): 187–205.

Berasategui, Martín, David de Jorge, and Andoni Luis Aduriz. *La joven cocina vasca*. San Sebastián: R&B Ediciones, 1996.

Burns, Tom. *Hispanomanía*. Barcelona: Plaza y Janés, 2000.

Capel, José Carlos. *Manual del pescado*. Madrid: Penthalon, 1982.

Casas, Penélope. *¡Delicioso!: The Regional Cooking of Spain*. New York: Alfred A. Knopf, 1996.

Davidson, Alan. *The Tio Pepe Guide to the Seafood of Spain and Portugal*. Malaga: Ediciones Santana, 2002.

Dawes, Gerry. "Alta Expresión Vino." *The Wine News* 18, no. 2 (April–May 2001): 28–37.

——. "Spanish Rosado. A Rosé for all Seasons." *Wines from Spain News* 19, no.1: 13–14.

Díaz Rivas, Jerónimo. "Olive Growing: The Spanish Varieties (I)." *Gourmetour*, no. 44 (January–April 1998): 27–35.

——. "Olive Growing: The Spanish Varieties (II)." *Gourmetour*, no. 45 (May–August 1998): 31–39.

Díaz Yubero, Ismael. *Sabores de España*. Madrid: Ediciones Pirámide, 1998.

Domecq, Marina, and Toño Pérez. *Gusto y gustos de Extremadura*. Cáceres: Iberdrola y la Caja de Extremadura, 1999.

Doménech, Ignacio. *Marichu, la mejor cocinera española o todos los platos del día*. 5th ed. Barcelona: Editores Quintanilla, Cardona y Cia., 1944.

Domingo, Xabier. *El sabor de España*. Barcelona: Tusquet Editores, 1975.

Equipo Editorial Ediciones Añil. *El libro de oro de las tapas*. Madrid: Ediciones Añil, 1999.

Equipo Editorial Libsa. *Cocina tradicional española*. Madrid: Editorial Libsa, 2002.

Gallardo Rodríguez, Fernando. *Hoteles con encanto*. Madrid: Santillana Ediciones, 2001.

García, María Luisa. *Platos típicos de Asturias*. Gijón: privately printed, 1971.

García Santos, Rafael. *Lo mejor de la gastronomía*. Barcelona: Ediciones Destino, 2002.

García Vicente, Fernando, Antonio Beltrán, and José Luis Acín Fanlo. *La arquitectura y la cocina popular aragonesa*. Madrid: Telefónica y Lunwerg Editores, 2001.

González Soto, Emilio. *El bacalao: biología y gastronomía*. Bilbao: privately printed, 1996.

Herbst, Sharon Tyler. *Food Lover's Companion*. Hapappauge, NY: Barron's Educational Series, 1995.

Inchausti de Prellezo, Florentina. *Libro de cocina*. Bilbao: J.A. Lerchundi, 1925.

Kurlansky, Mark. *Cod: A Biography of the Fish That Changed the World*. New York: Walker, 1997.

Letamendía, Ana de, Lourdes Plana, and Gonzalo Sol. *El buen gusto de España*. Madrid: Ministerio de Agricultura, Pesca y Alimentación, 1999.

Llamas, Gabriela. "Perdices para ser felices." *Cocina Futuro*, no. 35 (May 2003): 56–57.

Llano Gorostiza, Manuel. *Clásicos de la cocina vasca*. Bilbao: Banco de Vizcaya, 1986.

Llona Larrauri, Jesús, and Garbiñe Badiola. *Cocina vasca*. Léon: Everest, S.A., 1999.

Maestre, Isabel. *Repostería y panadería*. Madrid: Espasa-Calpe, 1991.

——. *Repostería y pastelería*. Madrid: Espasa-Calpe, 1991.

Marrugat, Antonia. *La cocina de Antonia Marrugat*. Barcelona: Ediciones Irusa S.L., n.d.

Martinez-Cubells, Ivan. *Pequeños hoteles con estilo*. Madrid: Taller de Editores, 2000.

Mendel, Janet. *My Kitchen in Spain*. New York: Harper Collins, 2003.

Meyaster de Echagüe, María. *Confitería y repostería*. Madrid: Espasa-Calpe, 1992.

Mitchell, Angus. *Spain*. London: George Weidenfeld & Nicholson Ltd., 1990.

Ortega, Simone. *1080 recetas de cocina*. Madrid: Alianza Editorial, 1972.

Ortega, Sonia. "El Bierzo, Hidden Treasures." *Gourmetour*, no. 37 (September–December 1995): 42–53.

Puente, Zacarías. *La cocina de Cantabria, de la mar a Peñas Arriba*. Hondarribia, Spain: privately printed, 1997.

Rios, Alicia, and Lourdes March. *The Heritage of Spanish Cooking*. Sydney: Weldon Russel Pty. Ltd, 1993.

Saloña, Antonio. *Arte nuevo de la cocina española*. Bilbao: privately printed, 1965.

Sanz Pech, Mariano. "Sheep Chic, a Taste of Biodiversity." *Gourmetour*, no. 48 (May–August 1999): 45–52.

Simón Palmer, María del Carmen. *La cocina de palacio*. Madrid: Editorial Castalia, 1997.

Subirós, Jaime. *Las recetas del Hotel Ampurdán*. Barcelona: Ediciones de la Magrana, 1993.

Torres, Marimar. *The Catalan Country Kitchen: Food and Wine from the Pyrenees to the Mediterranean Seacoast of Barcelona*. London: Boxtree, 1994.

Vega, Luis Antonio de. *Viaje por la cocina española*. Madrid: Salvat Editores, 1967.

Veiga López, Manuel. *Plasencia y el Valle del Jerte*. Cáceres: Patronato de Turismo y Artesanía, 1994.

Vera, Felisa, Remedios Sosa, Ana Leal, and Yurena Díaz. *Lo major de la cocina canaria*. Santa Cruz de Tenerife: Centro de la Cultura Popular Canaria, 1987.

Weinzweig, Ari. "The Denomination of Origin: What is it? What does it do for you?" *Foods from Spain News*, Summer 2001, 9–10.

Wells, Gully. "Spain at the Extreme." *Condé Nast Traveler*, March 1998, 132–139, 174–180.

Wolke, Robert. *What Einstein Told His Cook*. New York: W.W. Norton & Company, 2002.

Zarzalejos, María. *Secretos de familia*. Madrid: Planeta, 1997.

:: INDEX ::

*A bottle of cider at a sidrería in Villaviciosa, Asturias (between
glasses, the cork is always balanced on top of the cider bottle)*

Wild plums, Catalonia

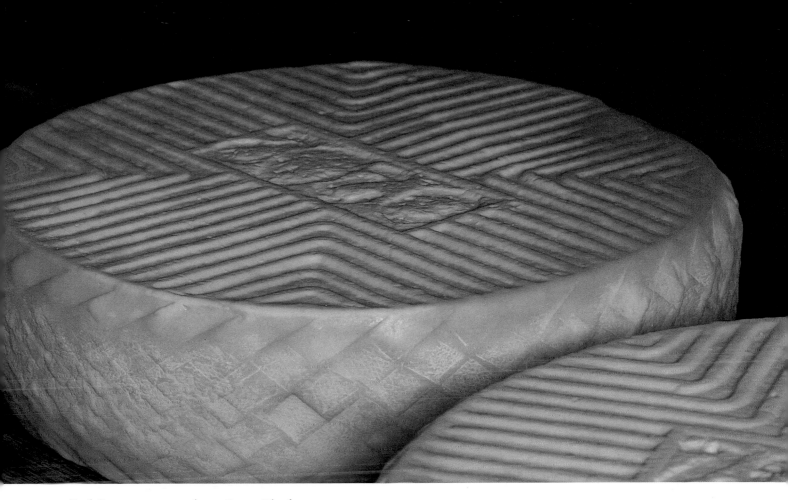

Fresh Fuerteventura goat cheese, Canary Islands

INDEX

337

PAGE 338: *A goat—the symbol of Fuerteventura (Canary Islands)—roaming on the northern coast*